THE INHERITED BOUNDARIES

The Inherited Boundaries

Younger Poets of
the Republic of Ireland

THOMAS McCARTHY

AIDAN CARL MATHEWS

HARRY CLIFTON

DERMOT BOLGER

MICHAEL O'LOUGHLIN

MATTHEW SWEENEY

SEBASTIAN BARRY

Edited with an Introduction by
Sebastian Barry

THE DOLMEN PRESS

The Inherited Boundaries
is designed by Liam Miller,
set in Galliard type by Koinonia Limited
and printed by

for the publishers,

The Dolmen Press
Mountrath, Portlaoise, Ireland

The Dolmen Press receives financial assistance from
The Arts Council (An Comhairle Ealaíon), Ireland.

First published 1986

British Library Cataloguing in Publication Data:
The Inherited boundaries : younger poets of the
    Republic of Ireland.
    1. English poetry—Irish authors
    2. English poetry—20th century
    I. McCarthy, Thomas, *1954–*   II. Barry, Sebastian
    821'.914'0809415   PR8858

ISBN 0 85105 439 0
© 1986, The Dolmen Press Limited

Printed and bound in Great Britain
by Billing & Sons Limited, Worcester.

for Liam Miller

'It is only in the exceptions, in the few minds
where the flame has burnt, as it were, pure,
that one can see the permanent character of
a race.'

W. B. Yeats

Contents

Aidan Carl Mathews

Harry Clifton

Contents

Dermot Bolger

Michael O'Loughlin

Matthew Sweeney

Contents

Sebastian Barry

The Inherited Boundaries

Introduction

THE HISTORY AND TOPOGRAPHY
OF NOWHERE

In 1962 The Dolmen Press published a miscellany of Irish writing, called handily *The Dolmen*, meant as the initial issue of a magazine, and in the upshot the first and last of it. But it still managed, under the editorships of John Montague and Thomas Kinsella, to be a remarkable gauge to that generation. As well as prose writers, it presented seven poets: Pearse Hutchinson, Valentin Iremonger, Thomas Kinsella. James Liddy, John Montague, Richard Murphy, and Richard Weber, and claimed them as a proper group, bar the second poet, who was older. Apart from the exclusion of, say, Desmond O'Grady, it stands as a percipient choice.

All of the poets were connected one way or another with The Dolmen Press, which was single-mindedly and single-handedly creating the means to a literature of the Republic, at least in poetry. The generator of this condition was Liam Miller, running on unusual belief and an extraordinary relationship with the stuff and apparel of books.

This present volume then is the first anthology of younger poets from The Dolmen Press in twenty-three years. The poets here could be children of young marriages of the writers above. By accident there also happens to be seven of them, and less accidentally they are a generation of a particular sort: all born in the Republic of Ireland in the nineteen fifties, when the contributors to *The Dolmen* were just beginning to make their reputations.

The point of an anthology often shifts rapidly, but initially, in this case, it is this: to clear up a misunderstanding. No one in Ireland, or England for that matter, imagines that there is only one political sensibility on this island. And yet a unified poetic sensibility is presumed, easily, to exist, and it is not so. It can not be the same to grow up within the inherited bound-aries of the Republic, as to manage a like feat inside the markers of the Northern province, and this is clearly reflected in the two poetries. Paul Muldoon, Tom Paulin, Gerald Dawe, Medbh McGuckian, and their confrères and consoeurs, do not share a

sensibility with these poets of the South, unhappily or
otherwise.

This is a poetical condition, not a political one, but in the
politics of poetry it has had a bad effect: the work of the younger
Northern poets has received a (due) prominence, partly because
of its excellence, partly because of the Troubles, and partly
because of Faber and Faber; and they have come to seem, in
England and probably elsewhere, the full story, or most of it.
They are a fine part of the story of an island, but they are no
part of the story of the Republic. This anthology is the latest
report on an increasingly neglected progress – the poetic of a
separate, little-understood place. None of the poets here had
anything to do with the setting of topographical or impolite
boundaries – indeed, all cross borders with relish – and yet, first
and last, whether they like it or not, they come from *here*.

One of the quickest Welsh-Normans into Ireland, Gerald
Cambrensis, who was a Barry, wrote a book about the new wild
place, called in its English translation *The History and Topography
of Ireland* (Dolmen Press and Penguin Classics), and *Topographia
Hiberniae* in its first Latin. Yet another well-dressed tongue and
body had come to possess the oily scales of a shocking country.

Gerald of Wales was not bowled over by the native Irish:
'They know only of the barbarous habits in which they were
born and brought up, and embrace them as another nature.'
Perhaps he is not to be relied on for his facts, but his attitude
is plain – the Irish of the twelfth century were to him other and
lazy and barbarous. Yet his family remained and increased and
eventually was absorbed into the accepting blotting-paper, and
dried there, till only a faint mark remained to show its point of
entry. The new foreigner become the new native in time, and
if his metamorphosed face registered shock, it was the merest
shock – and so Ireland embraces her critics, if they linger on.
And so we are all foreigners gone to native, whether we belong
to this invasion or that, since Ireland is the sum of her intruders.

It is sometimes more simplifying to feel a foreigner in the
Republic than a native. But, though the notion of being outsider
hangs on after everything else, the condition disappears. You
are native, native with a vengeance. The only way to wrestle
with it is, to try and make sure you are never foreign to yourself,
and this can reasonably be done by proceeding like Gerald

Introduction

Cambrensis, and mapping and talking about the visible and invisible country, crudely or faithfully, whatever is your temperament. The protection is argument, whether in Latin, Irish, Hiberno-English, and this argument with ourselves, in order to make ourselves in summation a country, has been going on for more than a thousand years, in a number of languages, and at a number of stages of those languages.

Nothing is so native as a toppled opinion. The worried place needs it and lives by it. On an island where everyone is an exile from some previous, however remote, culture or wildness of Europe or the East, argument, as a means of definition, must preoccupy each bewildered head, a radio for survival and description.

The true Ireland, the real Ireland, some professional traditionalists say, is that of the seventeenth century, before the final triumph of the seventeenth-century English, and when, for instance, the Gaelic order was in good kick, and chieftains and princes and earls and tribesmen were mainly untouched, and for that matter, poets were an aristocratic hereditary caste all to themselves, and the forests were still standing, and basically, things were Irish and words were Irish.

It would be more truthful to say that the real Ireland is that treed-over island with a few peaceful communities of proto-fishermen and shell-fish eaters that would appear to have been the first inhabitants, and yet not indigenous at that. These were the first, the only group of arrivers who did not have to choke and murder and even mate with an earlier people. God knows what language they spoke those eight or nine thousand years ago (how recent the Celts are, with their swollen millenium of possessive history), and God knows what god they curried favour with. It was the true Ireland though, all the same, as far as human arrivals go. Everyone else, from the Tuatha de Danainn to the German and Dutch in West Cork today, is an unwanted intruder, not Irish and with no claim to the environs except by force of sword or latterly and better, money. Irish then, is everyone or no one, and obviously the choice should have been made years ago, or could conveniently be made soon.

Each invader, after a proper interval, has imagined he is the real Ireland, because the years pass and the new gate-crashers turn up, and he does not like their strength, much less their attitude to him. Sometimes, very early on, the people that some

15

new race got rid of became the mythology for the new race – an old history and character and resource of tall-story given respectability by way of turning into a religion. A genocide with one hand and a celebration with the other.

There can also be complex variations on this: the men of nineteen sixteen, who were disapproved of by the middle-classes of their time, and who lost their lives while finding their country, have become the icons of the present middle-classes, thus preventing any worthwhile description of Ireland – an integral view of a place can not really appear on such a hypocritical canvas. Some of the nation's most fervently-held views of politics are thus mythologised propagandas.

A country without definition is nowhere at all. That is where this poetry collected here comes from – not from the wishful coloured toy that some Americans brood about, nor from the wild, rebellious colony that some English people still complain about. Neither of these conceptions arguably exists. And an educated man in Switzerland once expressed the view that Ireland must be an unhandy place to visit, because a civilised person could not bring himself to live in a cabin made of mud, even for a holiday – so perhaps it is better not to stray for worse opinions into the rest of the world.

Gerald Cambrensis found one element in Ireland worthy of praise – the music and musicians in it. That was in the twelfth century, and presumably he missed any number of other qualities which he was too civilised or haughty to penetrate, or too blind with his fold of foreignness. In the twentieth century, after a royal paradox of a revolution, and decades of censorship and fright, Ireland, whether she likes it or not, and very often she does not, has begun to find a few more reliable histories and topographies. The ancient practise of denigrating the invader, which survived even into the fifties in our history books, has been put aside in the absence of a fresh target. The Republic of Ireland does not seem likely to be taken over by anyone for a while, at least not in the old aggressive, murderous, celebratory manner, unless one counts the invasion of disembodied cultures, such as the surface totems of America.

Therefore we are given a breathing space at last, and whoever is here, and has a bureaucracy to give him a piece of paper to say he was born locally, and is a citizen, should he need it, is probably, tentatively, Irish, or, as some strainedly say, Southern

Introduction

Irish. It is these people that the poetry of this anthology belongs to.

When the Anglo-Irish tradition ended politically with Yeats, and the Gaelic tradition to all large-scale purposes, or national purposes, with the seventeenth-century poets (though there is an important neo-Gaelic matter to be discussed a little later), the Hiberno-English tradition, having been an element alongside the other two traditions, found itself abruptly and horrifyingly on its own. The Protestants were out, the Gaelic were smothered, and it, difficult to define too, and extremely nervous of definitions, was in – or at least *there*, the astonished survivor. The adjectives Anglo-Irish (which the universities rather mindlessly persist with still, as a description of material written in the mother-tongue of Ireland), native, Gaelic, Ascendancy, fell away as indicators, just as the adjectives Norman, Norse, Fir-Bolgian and so on, had to in the past. It was the very first chance to call everyone here Irish, the spoken language Hiberno-English (which has a history of at least seven hundred years in the country, a respectable length of time, no matter how much it smacks of empire to speak it. After all, the French speak a sort of Franco-Latin, and they feel little shame about it at this distance to Rome. Is Hiberno-English what we will someday call more simply Irish?), and the country the Republic of Ireland.

There are some who still think Ireland must step back before it can step forward and be itself. This is a fine notion, but if it were to be done honestly, and rigorously, then many would have to relearn their ancestral Norman-French, and a salad of other languages. The poets assembled here, the first uncluttered generation, free from justified anger about England, free from justified enthusiasm for revolutions, free from residual hang-ups about these matters after their solving, seem to disagree with the philosophy of the cultural back-track. They examine themselves and their country, grateful to find reason in some things, sever with the meannesses. They are not colonial, provincial, or even what Patrick Kavanagh praised, parochial. They are Irish, the first Irish poets ever in a way, because that adjective has meant so many things in the past that it meant nothing. If poetry is honest and integral as it strives to be, and if this is poetry (and this anthology demands judgement), then this is a first if fragmentary map to a new country. Everything has been dismissed except what each poet sees around him. Nothing is trusted till it is tried by hook and crook, with all the parsimony and affection and courage of ragged military scouts. And if some poems deal with Europe, even with Africa and elsewhere, it is because a sensibility must travel for comparison and self-creation. Even a country surrounded by water is eventually surrounded by other land and other foreigners.

So, to be born in the fifties in the Republic of Ireland was to be born, with no great ceremony, nowhere. It was a country without definition, because it was a new place. But all the acceptance of foreign rule, the dominion of priests, the isolated desire for revolution – islands inside an island – had metamorphosed quaintly into dullness, dismay, and inaction. Everything was done by way of freedom, nothing by way of peace.

The great feeling growing up then, through the sixties and seventies, was that the Republic was run by jobbers and gombeenmen, who could not be taken seriously, and much less admired. It was impossible to look up to government, unless you were a minister – then the claptrap sounded. Within the country aspirations were low, and if not low, defeated and frustrated – some parents went to England with their ambitions, and carried off their children with them. There, a thoroughly foreign race – that an Irish school, out of sheer intellectual idleness it seems now, taught one to abhor – was miraculously ordinary and efficient. It was much more accepting of individual difference than the guffawing, nasty desire for sameness that Ireland housed. To be other than Catholic, third-class – a very bready form of an excellent religion, characterised by a Sunday morning piety and a Sunday evening vulgarity – and small-minded to boot, was traitorous to the strange new emblems of one untroubled country.

The only simple colour in the place was the cheerfulness of the Dublin parks in summer, and the Walt Disney cinema in Grafton Street. It is an exaggeration, but not a greater one than the exaggerated lowliness of what your fellow countrymen wanted for themselves. There was to be nothing only mediocrity – superiority was English, possibly.

Under all this watery cover, the wily were moving like deepsea sharks on all possible prey – land, position, rights to this and

Introduction

that. In the great chattering monotony of this unusual land, people were rising up like gray dough, explaining wordlessly the difference between them and former colleagues – in other words, the new classes were clumsily forming. The English had been intolerable as a crust (and they were, doubtless) – now an intolerable cupidity was to take their place.

To be aware of that at the back of your head was to be sick in your heart. You moved carefully. You found some members of your family to revere – it was a good category of accident that brought Aidan Carl Mathews to revere Cearbhall Ó Dálaigh, as that statesman was his godfather – and for the rest, you ignored it or gave it the conspiratorial smile that it demanded. Smile, a chara, or leave.

Born into this bloodless flat catastrophe, being 'Irish' without being welcome, undefined, the wrong sort of Catholic, the wrong sort of Protestant (one that hadn't left), the wrong sort of agnostic (any agnostic), it is a wonder in a way that anything has been achieved at all. And yet, for poetry, it seems to me a special generation had its glimmer in that decade, and represents a crazy justification for it. Any generation that throws up my six confrères can not be called wholly mean.

And I think that between these six men there is a particular bond, unusual among worried Irish poets. If they did not know each other personally, they were aware of each other's work. Here was a form of excellence that was allowed, if only because it was almost completely ignored. Poetry! No one in Ireland reads poetry – most of the inhabitants think it is something to do with school-children. Poetry is not for children. Sooner give poteen to children than poetry. It can not be a wholly benign thing in a country that is always finding new ways of poisoning itself. There must be something dangerous in it to stand against all mean dangers. In other words, it must have honesty, a fighting, critical, uncompromised, paradoxical honesty, half-good and half-evil. If it must talk of death, it must talk of your death first. The new poetry of this country is the poetry of everyone – few want it. Perhaps the abstainers do not want to risk any explication of themselves.

Nevertheless, the poets here have gone on writing, increasing in their purpose as surely as their audience remains the same. The earliest poems in this anthology were published in book form in 1977, the latest are due for that sort of publication in

1986. So this anthology represents somewhat less than a decade of endeavour. It seems to me a good-hearted decade in Irish poetry, to say the least, and it is time the poets here found their audience, even if their audience proves to be the 'enemy' English or the 'funny' Americans. Then perhaps an Irish audience might follow. An Irish poet *prefers* his own people, despite their indifference.

The grave question of the official national language, Gaeilge, was unanswerable by most Hiberno-English poets, even into the generation under the light of this anthology. Irish schools for the most part are famous for their extraordinary work in the toxification of an ancient, clear alphabet. English-language poetry rarely survives its school-time reading. With no direct reason to embrace it, many Irish poets have ignored or run from Irish as clean-heeledly as anyone else.

But just in the last few years a powerful reinstatement of the attractions of the language has felt its beginnings in the charismatic courage of Michael Hartnett — the language as a friend to poets, I mean. This is something fresh and is not reflected here. Of all the collections that have been cannibalised for this book, none contained any significant translation from the Irish. Micheal O'Loughlin's poem *Babel* expresses something of the difficulty of such attempts. Aidan Mathews' *The Death of Irish* says:

> The tide gone out for good,
> Thirty-one words for seaweed
> Whiten on the foreshore.

The real translation would appear to be from European and otherwise writers. Allegiance had to shift there, or remain there, because most good European poets are translated into English, and this entices a kinship and alternative glosses. A language is desired in proportion to the susurrus of its writers. But it is easier to penetrate the sign-posted wilderness of Vallejo than the new roads of Hartnett. This is unprettily odd.

When The Dolmen Press published *An Duanaire*, they rinsed this long-standing obfuscation of a betrayed language, and Thomas Kinsella's passionate retrieval of the *Tain* some years earlier arranged the mind for *An Duanaire*'s wider adventure, as did Desmond O'Grady's *Gododdin* in a Welsh/Celtic context.

Introduction

These over-the-shoulder rescues, voyages back into the interior of a ruined patrimony, have done something to the sensibility of younger poets. Irish has beaten off the direful fainne-sporters – Onans obsessed by omega – and its summer-school vulgarisation. The essential nobility of the pursuit of poetry in that tongue has come as a shaking, even preferable quality. There is nothing in English like it since a remote, guiltless Chaucerian innocence and confidence. So it is we who are the real dispossessed, and part of the future belongs to Hartnett and anyone who has this new faith in an eager, back-from-the-dead arsenal of expression, and the gift to tax that faith. That these two expeditions, the Hiberno-English and the neo-Gaelic, might join thoroughly, at least through translation – and not just Gaeilge into Hiberno-English, but the darker language back into the white too – is a wish more wished now, I would say, than at any stage since the brilliant killing of Irish in the nineteenth century. Michael O'Loughlin, for instance, in Irish, would be one holiday of a metamorphosis.

When Penguin published their *Contemporary British Poetry* recently, the editors were at pains to establish the influence of Seamus Heaney on their anthology, and yet it would be tricky to detect his influence on the younger poets of the South, at least in this pattern of them. It is not all that surprising, given that the Northern Irish sensibility forms within different boundaries, and is preoccupied with a struggle in quite another manner than the way Southern poets only hear of and rarely see that struggle. The main influences in the Republic have been those older poets who have talked about the swathe of extraordinary land that is contained by an old political decision: Thomas Kinsella and Richard Murphy, for instance, and more distantly now, Yeats. An exception to divisions has been the cross-border work of John Montague, who has powered the beginnings of many young poets in the South. He is less known in England than Seamus Heaney partly because of this: he belongs somehow to the Republic, or is an aspect of it, and has therefore not always been blessed by British fashion. This is not to say that the achievement of Seamus Heaney is due to vogue – far from it, but the excellence of the Northern work has certainly occluded the equal quality of the Republic. Strange that a poet of Northern origins should see this fate, but the situation will improve and has improved. If a similar figure were to be placed as older confrères to this anthology, as Seamus Heaney was to *Contemporary British Poetry*, then it would have to be Montague, arguably, and fruitfully.

Of course, taken individually, there are other poets both Northern and Southern who have been valuable to writers here – Derek Mahon, Anthony Cronin, Desmond O'Grady, and Paul Durcan, for example. The point is, if there has been rebellion, it has been against the tawdriness of the country, not its older poets, and on the whole a necessary, allied relationship exists between the generations, at least on the common, deserted ground of paper.

W. B. Yeats, speaking into the arrogantly-guessed familiarity of the future, ordered or perhaps asked, in his avuncular way, Irish poets to 'learn their trade'. He gave fair warning that if they did not skip the mere voguish, and preserve his two classes of Ireland, the peasant and the horseman, things would not go too well with their posterior immortality.

But the peasants decided to leap up on the careering nags of the dispossessed Anglo-Irish – an answering paradox – Yeats' preferred group in all of king-ridden Europe, and so his warning and his advice fell into redundancy and irony respectively. Not that there were many kings left when he stamped his phrase – but the empty thrones were kings enough to him.

These younger poets of the Republic banded here, born in the strange male hiatus of the fifties, *are* men of their trade, the trade of alphabets and private metres, whether it results in the idiomatic cliché-made-new forms of Harry Clifton, or the slightly-crazed necessary new blocks of Dermot Bolger. But somehow I think they are not all quite what Yeats had in mind.

Yeats is an important palimpsest for Thomas McCarthy, and by a sort of coloured implication, Aidan Carl Mathews, but their work has skewed away from the real moonish paths over deep water, that Yeats wanted as the highway across the new Ireland. McCarthy and Mathews have looked for heroes in a very chroniclar Irish manner (though Mathews has done so less obviously in his poetry than in his editing), but their heroes are not the heroes of change and revolutionary bravado, but men of a static recent past who had no fight except with the unhistoric present of a rather nasty, lowly modern era: De Valera for McCarthy and Cearbhall Ó Dálaigh, briefly in the published canon, for Mathews. Yeats once wrote: 'There is scarcely a man who has led the Irish people at any time, who may not give some day to a great writer precisely that symbol he may require for the expression of himself.' (First Principles, 1904). This reads now as half-caveat and half-commendation.

Thomas McCarthy follows paternal themes not for revelation so much as position and survival, discrete map-making in potentially hostile country. He has won a number of prestigious prizes, which, as in the case of Mathews, supposes an acceptance among the older generation (who usually judge these matters), and not without good reason. For his work is adroitly surfaced and generally 'made', and succeeds in being both redolent and resonant. He and Mathews represent whatever is best in the middle-class, but an emergent middle-class, rather than one which might have shared in the minimal, treacherous excesses of that group, in Ireland or indeed in other places with a longer history of 'freedom'. He searches out the heroes not, as I said, of revolution so much as stasis: the makers rather than the mould-breakers:

> (the soft glow
> of De Valera's land, and her bog neutrality).

> *A Neutral State,* 1944

McCarthy is an extremely affectionate poet, and celebrates unashamedly a number of figures: Francis Stuart, Bashevis Singer, AE, MacLiammoir (the Dublin actor), Parnell. He can even boost a Countess of Desmond without a trace of animosity, because he is a poet of post-revolutionary Ireland, whose middle-class is busy constructing, at its best, not a mythology, but a reference-book for a sufficient contemporaneity: new heroes, more liberal gods, that neither shun the matters of history nor take sides in them. McCarthy tends to side, if he sides at all, with men who were victims of convention, and yet were truly the protectors of it: the prophets of the persecutors. Ireland has for a long period tended towards a private self-protective onslaught on its own best qualities, a kind of madness that perhaps went with the sanity of real organised dominion, such as England perfected in an island it always considered pure trouble, but never wanted actually to drop, as it might have

23

done, from time to paper time.

Though McCarthy will make love poems, and what can be called semi-private, semi-public poems about a father, Aidan Mathews' work is, I think, primarily preserved land. His poem *History Notes*, for instance, turns out to describe the poet watching his wife at work on notes for a lecture. History for him, of the sort that exists as thesis and antithesis, the stuff of general time, is left to its improper recorders; but still it is plain that he considers a personal familial poetry to be the real history:

> But choose
> The charity of rooms that are small, shut out
> A clockface flinching on the mantel piece,
> Or ask a second time. I tell you, love,
> We found the place long since and never left,
> Staying absolutely still, still travelling.

His 'second time', an alternative further time, expert, latinate, is seconded by the marginal precision of his line, and his confident pattern.

Aidan Mathews has himself remarked on the charge brought against him now and then, that his work is not political enough, or rather, *too* domestic. This seems an amateurish attitude in the face of what he has achieved. If the close-hearted paleography and neography of a marriage or a family can not be seen as an enterprise at the very basement of all trouble, whether violant or political, then I would guess at some limiting fault in a reader's vision. Such a claim against him ignores the essential metaphorical and metamorphic anatomies of poetry anyway. To talk of people turning towards and away from each other, is, as far as map-making is concerned, to talk of that in all arenas.

Far from being too domestic in his themes, it would be easier to concoct an argument that he is too political and engagé. His passion towards his world is so gifted and unavoiding that his poetry becomes that world – things as they are are changed upon his blue guitar, and he has something of Wallace Stevens' metaphorical philosophy. Aidan Mathews is a brilliant and gentle personality, and this is also true of his poetry – it is brilliant and gentle, political and domestic, truly poised work. Readers who look for obvious this-or-that in him will always be disappointed. He is not a pop singer. The subtlety of his poetry does not survive simple enthusiasm for right over wrong.

Introduction

He is not any brand of youthful politician, the sort of personage who is rarely political, and becomes less so. He is only and even a poet, giving the world as an unexpected gift to itself.

So these two tradesmen trade over the counter of the oldest establishment in Irish literature, stemming from the Irish language itself, and the later slightly-incongruous borrowing and additions of Yeats. The latter, in the strange estuary of his Anglo-Celtic mouth, preached the synthesis of a new Ireland that never materialised, as he perhaps suspected in the paradoxical bleakness of his public poems. Now McCarthy and Mathews give a poetry that says 'Yes, but. . .' to much of Yeats, and discovers a very fruitful (Mathews' first collection is titled *Windfalls*) strength in this friendly apostasy. They are proffering a valuable, committed answer to Yeats' tradition, and through that inheritance (about which Mathews in a short poem records dismay), to the divided tail of Irish poetry, which, in a heartening way, they almost succeed in joining.

Outside this dangerous apprenticeship of setting old, if brilliant, misconceptions in a second expurgated edition, is a small number of poets who owe little to the National Bank of Irish Poetry, but who, in spite of revolutions and supposed hatred, and while still being 'Irish' and not slavish, work best inside the British tradition, and whose work is closer to the contemporary British poets, than any other colour.

Representative of these, and one of the best of them, is Matthew Sweeney, who comes from an ambiguous district of Ireland that is neither North nor South, or rather South politically and North geographically, the county of Donegal. Situated so, he could choose any tradition he or his temperament preferred. He appears naturally to have assimilated the British, not of course for any political reason, excepting the unbloody, sanguine politics of the heart, but for the normal inscrutable reasons that bring a poet to his pass.

He is the trader of a rather distant, fighting personality. His world is at first mark familiar, but threatened, and so newly described that it becomes strange, and truly recognisable, as in *The Dancehall*. Armageddon seems never that far over the hills of his boundaries, but he adequately stares in the face of these popular (in both senses) fears, and ploughs them back into a fertile, unique and often funny (of a choke-back-the-laughter type) performance. He is the sort of poet who is difficult to pursue critically – like Robert Herrick, in a very different track – because he is self-contained, and almost warlike in his fenced integrity. But his stance and tone are magnificent: belling, acute, and challenging.

Sweeney and Harry Clifton have both spent time out of Ireland, the former longer than the latter. But while Sweeney's residence in England may have something to do with his englished verse, which I suppose in the end talks out of an undefined country that is only Ireland by possibility, Clifton's time in Africa and elsewhere gives some of his work a very attractive subject matter peculiar, of necessity, to himself. Far from travelogue, he has found charts for himself in these half-imaginary destinations, perhaps some that would have remained uninked had he remained more ordinarily at home.

By profession he is a civil servant, like some Irish writers before him, notably in this respect Thomas Kinsella. By sensibility he is astute, rather self-accepting, with aristocracy on his mind (he uses the word himself in an odd context in one of his poems, *Droit de Seigneur*), and adventurous: there are not many Irish poems about prostitutes, especially in Clifton's precise, solitary vein:

> and her beside me
> Like Second Nature, until I can put an end
> To this rendezvous, become lonely again
> Within the law of the land.

A wry, allowed loneliness is a special tone with him, for example the simple, meshed poem called *Loneliness in the Tropics*.

His poetry shifts its reader, and when the reader catches up with himself he finds a new, well-lighted place. Clifton has made such a pact with the marginal, and such a non-profit business of it, with such virtuosity, that his edged Ireland has curiously inched towards the centre: his apartness is probably more Irish than the Irish habit of unavailability itself. To imagine Clifton compromising this tagged self of his can not get beyond the faintest speculation: and his ledgers include the debunking of himself here and there. He has Austin Clarke's interest in prosody, but an additional and more important human gesture of tone and communion.

Introduction

Dermot Bolger is a new phenomenon in the literature of the Republic. In an early book he shows a confraternal affection for Francis Ledwidge, which is an indication of a sort. But Bolger has chosen not to cross over from the rained-on concrete of his place, but, as Aidan Mathews writes in another context, to 'rest his faith in that quotidian'. Neither obviously British or Irish in his affiliations, he is an often frightening barer of an Ireland without historical resonance, the part that is at the same time most local (the crippled housing-estates of North Dublin) and most European (his poems are probably signals from all such places: the scattered kingdom of the newest lost tribe) and even International. That is not to say his work is thematically universal, it is not, but it offers its sense of place universally and without prejudice. Let they who wish for survival read here. Even sign here. Because his collections, especially his second, *Finglas Lilies*, are a petition not against injustice or ugliness or poverty, but from right inside these things, saying, here where all bearable form has been scraped off and unconsidered, is attraction. Attraction though is not really in his vocabulary: it is the firm poems that have form in themselves, in a violent, gentle way, like war sculpture:

> her hair in sprays of seaweed
> salty and drenched to touch –
> like a song of clubbed seals

> a girl lying in the grass
> screaming at the houses
> rain answering her back

Much of his work has this hypnotic, courageous power, and needs to be read in bulk. His books are presented as thematically whole, as an antidote to the anarchic horror and happiness in them. He puts the older group of Mathews and Sweeney and so on at some distance to his estate.

Michael O'Loughlin has a crusading quality, and he grew up in the same absence as Dermot Bolger. He is a highly-confident swordsman, with a forceful convinced music that is in cahoots with poets such as Neruda and Vallejo more than previous Irish or English writers, as if he had made a South America, with its European umbilicals, of the drifting bear of Ireland. His gesture would be adolescent and amateurish if it was not so sincere.

Like a good revolutionary he brings principle to his threat, even the same principle that his opposing mass cherishes, and he adds a morning intelligence to that. He abhors the easy histories and banana mythologies of Ireland. He does not simply attack and destroy, but attempts to put animals in place of what he tracks, such as a more honest relationship with the totems of his emerging country (the poem *Cuchulainn* is an example).

There is a brand of freedom in his expression that other poets seem to shy away from, as being indulgent and posturing: he manages to make virtues of these attitudes, because he has European writing behind him, and is worthy of his inheritance by dint of a superior talent and a bladed honesty. He has refused the traditional jackets of Irish poetry: reserve, moderation, colloquial easiness, even in monstrous themes – Irish poetry of the last few decades, that is, which is usually the first few fields that a poet strolls around in. As far as he is concerned, Finglas is a capital of Europe, or anyway the place that Dublin and Ireland kept mean and small, because Dublin, also in its richer districts, is mean and small itself. He does not live in Ireland anymore, which is hardly surprising. He has put his inheritance in his pocket and carried it back to what it came from: the difference of Europe.

This anthology aims to be representative rather than comprehensive. The poets here, with their bonds and differences, are not the full catalogue of Younger Irish Poets – a contentious question at best. To be born in the Republic of Ireland in the 1950s was the criterion for inclusion. To have published at least two books was important too, in consideration of the desired length of each selection. Each poet was offered a large say in the choice from his work, and all took it.

Because this anthology is the first for younger poets of the Republic, and is in some way an answer to the brilliant Northerners, and in others an answer to the Republic itself, it was important it kept to its first premises. A few poets of the same generation were born in the fifties, but in London or Germany or whatever, not a bad thing in itself, but enough to keep them out here. Sean Dunne and Aidan Murphy have not published quite enough to glean thirty or so pages from, and it would have unbalanced the book to include shorter selections from them – anyway, they deserve an equal representation, and I trust

Introduction

they will get it in some future anthology. Peter Sirr was born in 1960, though he has affinities with some writers here.

A number of poets I personally could not come to terms with, as regards their work. So this is inescapably at base a personal choice, and the best answer to it would be, I should think, a further book by someone else. That there will be challenging anthologies, that they will contain poets excluded here, and that they will show the first harvest between writers in Irish and Hiberno-English, is my firm wish. And what parsimony of blood was it that the fifties could produce no discernible (to me) Hiberno-English poet who also happens to be a woman? I do not know.

But these selected poets are arguably worth the expedition of reading, are convinced and special, and will not lose their necessity either today or quite tomorrow, despite the nervous provisions of Yeats. They are talking about a new country that is often hard to make out at all in the thick rain of its history and the sullen, dangerous roll of the land – but they are talking about it with the courage of an inherited, doubted freedom.

Acknowledgements

For permission to publish or reproduce the material in this anthology, acknowledgement is made to the following copyright holders:

For THOMAS MCCARTHY: poems from *The First Convention,* to The Dolmen Press; from *The Sorrow Garden,* to Anvil Press; from *The Non-Aligned Storyteller,* to Anvil Press; new poems, to the author.

For AIDAN CARL MATHEWS: poems from *Windfalls,* to The Dolmen Press; from *Minding Ruth,* to The Gallery Press; new poems, to the author.

For HARRY CLIFTON: poems from *The Walls of Carthage,* to The Gallery Press; from *Office of the Salt Merchant,* to The Gallery Press; from *Comparative Lives,* to The Gallery Press.

For DERMOT BOLGER: poems from *The Habit of Flesh,* to Raven Arts Press; from *Finglas Lilies,* to Raven Arts Press; from *No Waiting America,* to Raven Arts Press; from *Internal Exiles,* to the author.

For MICHAEL O'LOUGHLIN: poems from *Stalingrad: The Street Dictionary,* to Raven Arts Press; from *Atlantic Blues,* to Raven Arts Press; from *The Diary of a Silence,* to Raven Arts Press.

For MATTHEW SWEENEY: poems from *A Dream of Maps,* to Raven Arts Press; from *A Round House,* to Raven Arts Press and Allison and Busby; from *The Lame Waltzer,* to Raven Arts Press and Allison and Busby.

For SEBASTIAN BARRY: poems from *The Water-colourist,* to The Dolmen Press; from *The Rhetorical Town,* to The Dolmen Press; new poems, to the author.

Thomas McCarthy

STRANGER, HUSBAND

Strange he seemed to her dark
eyes; strange, his lack of interest,

his incessant breaking of wood.
His every swing seemed blessed

in its fruitfulness: a broad
spray of chippings covered the

ground like a net, catching split
wood, cupping it within his range.

What would happen, she thought, what
would the dark-haired working-man
do if I dared the first approach?

There was the sound of an axe finding
rest in wood, touching equilibrium
when she entered his place of work.

STATE FUNERAL

'Parnell will never come again, he said. He's there,
all that was mortal of him. Peace to his ashes.'
                                        James Joyce, *Ulysses*

That August afternoon the family
Gathered. There was a native *deja-vu*
Of Funeral when we settled against the couch
On our sunburnt knees. We gripped mugs of tea
Tightly and soaked the TV spectacle;
The boxed ritual in our living-room.

My father recited prayers of memory,
Of monster meetings, blazing tar-barrels
Planted outside Free-State homes, the Broy-
Harriers pushing through a crowd, Blueshirts;
And, after the war, De Valera's words
Making Churchill's imperial palette blur.

What I remember is one decade of darkness,
A mind-stifling boredom; long summers
For blackberry picking and churning cream,
Winters for saving timber or setting lines
And snares: none of the joys of here and now
With its instant jam, instant heat and cream:

It was a landscape for old men. Today
They lowered the tallest one, tidied him
Away while his people watched quietly.
In the end he had retreated to the first dream,
Caning truth. I think of his austere grandeur;
Taut sadness, like old heroes he had imagined.

LAST DAYS IN THE PARTY

You let the razor-wound bleed in the warm
Wet silence. In the stains on your bright
Shirt I could gauge developing sorrows:
Earlier, you had forgotten the discussion
Papers, abandoned them in the locked car
As if they were blood-hardened criminals.

You planned to leave with dignity: after
Years of election committees and country
Meetings you had hoped for an after-glow
Of respect, a friendly exchange of roles:
Instead, you discovered a packed meeting,
Delegates like matadors waiting for blood.

Ten years ago you brought me to the first
Conference. Then you handled words calmly,
Juggled with complaints from the platform,

Tied hostilities neatly on a long string
Of language. Trapped in that jungle of old
Men, I made a beacon of your word-play.

Tonight, father, master of tough language,
It's you I find trapped on a tightening
Syntax; pulled out of depth. The young man
In the trendy suit laughs when he takes
Your place. His broad smile is your dead
Old cheer; a flourish without permanence.

DAEDALUS, THE MAKER
(for Seán Lucy)

Dactylos was silent and impersonal;
hidden behind false names, he achieved
a powerful *persona*. There was only
his work; a chipping of rock into form
and the rhythmic riveting of bronze,
diminishing his need for company.

Learning to keep silent is a difficult
task. To place Art anonymously at
the Earth's altar, then to scurry away
like a wounded animal, is the most cruel
test-piece. A proud maker, I have waited at
the temple doors for praise and argument.

Often I have abandoned an emerging form
to argue with priests and poets –
only to learn the wisdom of Dactylos:
that words make the strangest labyrinth,
with circular passages and minotaurs
lurking in the most innocent lines.

I will banish argument to work again
with bronze. Words, I have found, are
captured, not made: opinion alone is
a kind of retreat: I shall become like
Dactylos, a quiet maker; moving between
poet and priest, keeping my pride secret.

THE RAREST THYME

For you I would have built a herb-garden,
Not a pathetic patch for mint and chives

But a real olitory, with old-
Fashioned southernwood and rarest thyme.

I might have built a wooden seat between
Two plants of rosemary, their astringent

Scent seeping through your workshirt to the clean
Flesh of your back. I would have grown a plant

Of basil for you to stroke into form;
And, certainly, a row of lavender

To infuse carefully over a warm
Stove, for you to sip at whenever

The world became darkened with sick headaches,
Or a loss of blood whitened your small hands.

GREATRAKES, THE HEALER

'He himself tells us that an inward inspiration
informed him he had the gift. . . which per-
suasion grew so strong that he touched
several persons and fully cured them.'
Smith's *Waterford*, 1745

His was a landscape of wounds and disease;
the women crying at his gate-lodge had
collapsed into skin and bone; bone itself
might have hosted some terminal disease;
their children playing together had seen
the scab of death break frequently and bleed.

On summer days he had to flee the riot
of sufferers gathering at his windows,
screaming through the iron bars, their
eyes blown into bulbs of expectation:
then he would run to the stable and mount
the fastest hunter to flee from his gift.

On days when the gift took control he would
be pulled into its tight ritual of healing;
he would chant Ease and Health into sick
bodies, reinstating balance with his touch –
But later his calls to cure became less
frequent; spasms of doubt had sapped the will

Of the suffering peasantry. Dying will-
power caused a collective lethargy.
Unwilling to be cured, they died quietly
in smoke-filled cottages. From the roadway
he saw them. Too many wounds, making Faith-
Healing seem a neutral, pathetic act.

DE VALERA, LINDBERG
AND MR COOPER'S BOOK OF POEMS
for Jane Cooper

Mr Lindberg wore his aeroplane like a tight suit, his eyes pierced
the mist, wings dipped to the sea. Mr Cooper stretched from
the dripping cockpit to watch islets and water, the intricate
basketry of landforms in the ocean. What he tried to imagine,
as the air-frame shivered, was a book of sentimental poems like
a quiet daughter on his mother's knee.

> De Valera worked in his subdued room,
> squinting echoes on the wooden floor shivered
> when his pencil rose and fell. Somewhere in
> the blind country farther West the dripping
> biplane traced an arc. Dev dreamed a map of
> the future, of the astonished country threaded
> by planes; cargoes landing on tarmac like the
> last consoling phrases in a civil-war poem.

After they had landed they met him in his tall room. His hands
stretched out to shake the air, his eyes never adjusting to the
lack of light. Thus he met the new Americans, the tough and
technical. O *tough* they seemed, and *technical,* until Mr Cooper
saw the poems that his mother would have loved. Poems broke

the strangeness, there and then, as they roamed through the verses of a resolved civil war. Although Mr Lindberg wore his knowledge like a tight suit; his eyes piercing the mist, wings dipping to the sea.

THE SORROW GARDEN

I   HOLE, SNOW

It is an image of irreversible loss,
This hole in my father's grave that needs
Continuous filling. Monthly now, my
Uncle comes to shovel a heap of earth
From the spare mound. Tear-filled, he
Compensates the collapse of his brother's
Frame. I arrive on my motor-bike to help
But he will not share the weight of grief.

It is six months since my father's death
And he has had to endure a deep snow;
All night it came down, silently like time,
Smoothing everything into sameness. I
Visited the winter-cold grave, expecting
A set of his footprints, a snow-miracle.

II   SMALL BIRDS, VOICES

These are the neatly twisted sounds of death,
Those small brown birds singing, small winter
Birds clinging to an overhanging bough.
Never in life did I know him to stare
So silence-stricken for one brief moment.

These birds recall the voices of his life:
A low cold note is the voice of torment
From childhood poverty and the brief, light
Notes are the tones of Love and Marriage.

'There's the beginning of *your* life's troubles,'
A neighbour said at his grave. I arranged

The Inherited Boundaries

The wilting wreath-flowers, feigning numbness.
Something, perhaps his voice, told me even then
How much of Love, Sorrow, Love one life contains.

III   MISTING-OVER

These bright evenings I ride
through the young plantation
by the river; at times I can
see the young trees clearly
through the collapsing mist.

Sometimes in the misted river
at dusk his face at my left
shoulder has become distinctly
settled and lined with peace.

But now in the clouded pools
I drive through on the avenue,
he no longer calls out as if
injured by my rear wheel, but
is happy as clay, roads, memory.

IV   LOST WORDS, SORROWS

It's difficult to believe that it could
go on; this wanting to participate
in a rigid plan of water and wood,
words and wood and other inanimate
worlds that cannot explain sorrow.

Around me I find the forms that know
his lack of living. The wooden sculpture
on a shelf points to its lack of finish,
calls for a finishing touch, for his sure
and solid polish. I pray for its wish.

As if water could explain my crying,
I visited the salmon-weir after
a snow-fall. The fish were manoeuvring

through the spray, determined to get over
protective obstacles of wood and stone.

Like salmon through water, like virgin wood
disturbed into its form in art, his death
obfuscates words irrecoverably. Death plays
its own tune of vision and shadow. It has
attached itself as a vocabulary of change.

A NEUTRAL STATE, 1944

I   THE LIGHTS OF DUNLEARY

On the night journey there would be talk
of future pleasures, a subalterns' chorus
in relaxed voice about Irish chocolate cake,
real eggs and bacon and the Curragh races.

There would be the neutral yawning of the sea
above immediate memory; troubles in the black
city of war would move across their night eye
like the wash of a periscope causing an ache

of fear. But they would look across the bow
beyond the wash of sorrow, over the war-sea
to the naked lights of Ireland: (the soft glow
of De Valera's land, and her bog neutrality).

II   MACLIAMMOIR AT CAPPOQUIN

On tour he motored into the enchanted place
where dogs and cattle slept on the road, where
geese chased the actresses like jealous players
disturbed within their protected circular tour.

Between acts they floated on the tidal river,
Renaissance colours diffusing in the iridescent
pools; Coralie in her cinnamon Jewish garment
priming the water with her long, playful fingers.

That July their war-figures became broadly slow,
making Raymond say (in his eau-de-nil tights
and softened by the neutral summers of the South),
'If only the folks at the wars could see us now.'

THE PHENOMENOLOGY OF STONES
for Catherine

These summer days I carry images of stone,
Small pebbles from a photographer's shelf
Made smooth by a million years of sea and salt.
Sunlight shines roundly into their small room,
Twisting black grains into crystals and gems:
Lights call like young birds from their surfaces,
Sparrows of light flying from graves, from places
Where the dead had grown; the sorrow-gardens.

But the silence of stone quietens the mind
and calms the eye. Like their girl-collector –
In her deep solitude the stones are moved.
She is their dream-collector, pouring her kind-
ness into their sleeping form. They gather
Fables about themselves to entertain such love.

CLAUD COCKBURN

A flourish of sunlight in the room where
You live now, cigarette smoke in the air.
Your clothes move as if to meet your body
When you bend to watch sunlight on the sea.
Fishermen haul their lobster-pots below
Us, one or two signal to your window.
To be king of inlets and fuchsia bushes
After years of bitterness, an excessive
Dialectic of dreams and writing, is
One sweet reward for having fought alone –

Though words are never left alone. Unlike
Brickwork or well-vaulted art, words are
Dislodged from their makers. Think of the soldiers
Who bedded down with Hölderlin's irenic
Poems, or the way Fascism disfigured Goethe.
You Claud, *dear raconteur,* your toughest words
Came down on those who murdered print, absurd
Kings and magnates who kept Fascism afloat:
The wisdom of your life exposes both,
As well as war, which comes a deadly third.

Whose submarine lingers in our harbour then,
Its metal eyes bobbing in the water,
October sunshine bouncing from its nose?
The racing Ardmore tide tries to expose
Its menace. The brown heather lies asleep
While war and neutrality play hide and seek
Among the ruins of the harbour castle;
A breeze shaking its brass and ivied bell –
That breeze the most enlightened of us all;
Our politics as brainless as birdcall

And as colourful. What good is colour
If the navigators are blind? You Claud,
Only you have kept the millennial cause
While others settled for a luxury acre.
Now you weep for others barely employed
In the second Great Depression of our time.
Worry is training your neighbour and his kind
For war. You know how greatly they enjoyed
Our last Emergency, with high prices and
Good money from the most barren of land.

Go tell them about the latest nuclear device
And how the world is hanging from a precipice
That only journalists like you can cure.
Teach us what good politics may be for –
Social jobs and social good, clean rivers,
Guns into ploughshares, etc. An end to fear.
No doubt, dear author, you'd teach if you could
Simple politics for our common good.

Your ageing throat deserves some rest, and yet
You warn others to check for trouble in their nets.

SHOPKEEPERS AT THE PARTY MEETING

Listen! Listen to shopkeepers talking
about the problems of land,
the breaking up of an estate
or a new acquisition.
Their conversation is
proprietorial. To talk
about a landlord's problem,
to articulate his burden,
is their act of possession.
They are owning the landscape,
briefly, with the magical
deeds of speech.

The Minister on the other hand
has no such words.
Whatever he has is secret,
even his desires. Especially his desires.
Shopkeepers move around the room,
excited, in debt,
spilling their dreams like salt.

PARTY SHRINE

> *Come back,*
> *poor Twenty-Sixer. Live on lack.*
> AUSTIN CLARKE

My father is clearing the first Party shrine:
it is the summer of Sixty-Six.
He hates physical work and everything
that keeps him from the protection racket
of crosswords and history books.
But the rest of the Committee
has been drunk since the Jubilee
and can't break the spell of itself.

Weeds know nothing about the Party
or how it emerged, genie-like,
out of an abandoned shell case.
The weeds and their friends the shitting
pigeons want to bury this shrine
in a single summer.
I am holding the shovel for my father
while he reads inscriptions on brass:
sixteen golden names of the Party,
the twenty-six grammatical flaws.

THE CHAIRMAN'S WIDOW

The Secretary moves around the room, checking.
Whose membership cards are out of date, whose cousins
have just arrived to pack the Party meeting;
who hasn't made a change of district known?
To cheat is a common enough ambition,
as natural in the countryside as sexual sin.

As the only woman here I should know
what menfolk leave behind: their feelings of love
and fair play wave goodbye at every window.
Even caution weakens when they drive away,
making every vote inevitable and hard;
as learned by rote as numbers on a Party card.

Who now remembers the timid gait of my husband,
his damaged leg? Every polling day of his life,
the way he checked and schooled the most stupid.
How pain gave him a precise and concrete mind?
The way he found strength was a joy
to the Party. His integrity was a godsend.

God send them something new, better than all of this;
this double-checking male world of myth
that coagulates into a steel and vengeful thought
to cripple love. Teach them more than Party life,
or else politics will be an endless, wordy game;
whole futures dying in its bleak, marcescent frame.

Thomas McCarthy

THE PRESIDENT'S MEN

There's dust on Mr Dinneen's boots! Where has
he been canvassing, I wonder? What house
has unlatched a half-day of harvest work
to listen to his talk? My father knows
the Party poll, the roll-call of promise;
the roads we shall take when I am older
in search of power. We'll find it like cress
on farms of green and vegetal water.

The sound of bagpipe music! Just listen!
From my father's shoulder I can see above
the crowd, Mr Dineen's careful parade,
men struggling to keep the roadway open,
sunlight in my father's hair, the glitter of
pipers' braids; the President's cavalcade.

QUESTION TIME

Question time at the end of another Election Year;
Senators and their wives dancing on the ballroom floor;
children in corners dropping crisps and cream,
their fathers ordering them home, their mothers in crinoline
having to put them outside to sulk in the Christmas dark.
Enmities dissolving now in a sea of drink and smoke and talk.

Who was Robert Emmet's mistress? Who was Kitty O'Shea?
Which I.R.A. man was shot on his own wedding-day?
How many death-warrants did Kevin O'Higgins sign?
So much to answer between the buffet meal and wine—
But the prize is a week in Brussels, money for two,
and kisses from two Euro-M.P.s just passing through.

WINDOWS

The windows of our flat: their shutters
disperse the worst fogs of the winter
so that I can see the quays falling
into the tidal mouth of the river –
since I moved as high as these windows
I've overheard the nightlife of ghosts:
British officers taking their boots off,
Cork whores dropping hints and slips,
their accents putting on airs. Also,
servents in the evening (the year 1901,
maybe) when all their chores were done
tip-toeing to their bedrooms. The horses
on Wellington Road are made of glass,
their liveried coachmen are throwing
wet oats at the windows of our flat.

WINTER

Learning to keep you warm is a fair fight:
Which is more than I can say for the night
Outside, that bitter night at our window.
After three cold weeks I'd like you to know
How much I enjoy you when you are cold
But longing to travel on the linen veldt
With me. Though you like to be your own guide
On those lovely and critical campaigns,
With a gallant blue hot-water bottle
Like a cicisbeo at your cottoned side.

PARTICULARS

Tonight I think about your flat in Sundays Well;
the window where you worked at stories,
the high window where rainstorms whistled.
I wonder if that house was really haunted
by a ghost that wandered from the dripping hall?
Your little room was a store house of virtue,

simple blessings peeled from its walls.
I could see them peeling when you were happy,
humming the brown tunes of Randy Newman
or spreading pineapples on a grilled gammon.

I wish I could remake that most particular time –
the delayed action of toilet soap
when you breezed past after an evening shower,
your body wrapped in a black Malayan robe;
or your critical eyes in front of a picture,
knowing it had missed what you were after.
How can I recall all that new love had noted:
the shape of boxes, the roundness of shells, the firm
and lovely amber of your breasts. The rains
that touched your glass intrude now on my writing-desk.

HOURS AGO, 1973
for D. H. F.

It's two hours since you went to the river
In the green anglia with uncle Walter's satchel.
You forgot the box of flies on the dresser
Wrapped in a sheet of greaseproof paper.
The flies you took will serve you just as well,
You hunt for things with such exquisite care.

There's been dust at the cross-roads for weeks
With the heat, brilliant sunlight on the trees,
Every day of your annual leave. Pheasants leap
Into the tall grasses, wild animals hiss
And turn at play. So far from Ebury Street,
You've been hunting and saving their brightness

For a London winter. The warmed-up house
Is waiting for you with its brand new face.
Thirsty birds peck at the window, a vase
Of fresh foliage has been set in place.
Your soup has been left to simmer
For over two hours now. For nearly ten years.

MR NABOKOV'S MEMORY

For my first poem there are specific images
herded like schoolchildren into a neat row.
There is an ear and human finger hanging
from the linden tree in the Park north of
Maria Square and, between there and Morskaya
Street, other images of defeat. Such
as a black article in a Fascist newspaper
blowing along the footpath, or an old soldier
throwing insults at lovers out walking.
Even the *schveitsar* in our hallway
sharpens pencils for my father's meeting
as if sharpening the guillotine of the future.
There is only Tamara, who arrives with the poem
as something good; her wayward hair tied back
with a bow of black silk. Her neck,
in the long light of summer, is covered
with soft down like the bloom on almonds.
When winter comes I'll miss school to listen
to her minor, uvular poems, her jokes,
her snorting laughter in St Petersburg museums.
I have all this; this luxury of love; until
she says: 'a flaw has appeared in us,
it's the strain of winters in St Petersburg'–
and like a heroine from a second-rate
matinée in Nevski Street she steps into the womb
of the Metro to become a part of me forever.

So many things must happen at once in this,
this single chrysalis of memory, this poem.
While my son weeps by my side at a border
checkpoint, a caterpillar ascends
the stalk of a campanula, a butterfly comes to rest
on the leaf of a tree with an unforgettable
name; an old man sighs in an orchard
in the Crimea, an even older housekeeper
loses her mind and the keys of our kitchen.
A young servant is sharpening the blade
of the future, while my father leaps
into the path of an assassin's bullet

at a brief August lecture in Berlin.
All these things must happen at once
before the rainstorm clears, leaving one
drop of water pinned down by its own weight.
When it falls from the linden leaf I shall
run to my mother, forever waiting forever
waiting, with maternal Russian tears,
to listen to her son's one and only poem.

THE CANADIAN DIPLOMAT, 1942

Flowers have come out in our garden
While my London chorus-girl has gone insane.
Yesterday, I had an Hungarian family
Pleading for papers, wanting to get away.
This is too much for a Second Secretary:
All of Europe flees the lens of war.

Last night I walked down St James Street
To listen to the orchestra of guns. I had
Three brandies in my head, Byron's memoirs
In my arms to fill the void of flatlet
Chelsea. Bombs fell like the dregs
Of Cannes society pleading at my feet.

They have cut the railings from our park,
Now flowers are picked or trampled on. A quiet
Night is like a gift of potted cyclamen.
There are dead leaves in the Ritz vestibule
And whole streets with exposed beams –
Dead houses sizzling like spills of paper.

Today there was an Irishwomen in the shelter.
She said that the *Luftwaffe* would teach us
A thing or two. So vengeful. Why so vengeful?
Perhaps she has some intuition of decay –
More than a diplomat can have between *pate
fois* and talk: some natural glimpse of hell.

SEVEN ORANGE TULIPS

Such love had been around for years
like an unread book, a gold binding.
The poem has followed you everywhere
since you said hello. It has returned
to me frequently, carrying your echo;
like a daughter running before us
with an armful of gifts; such excitement.
Love has its own memory then, like
the best Muse or the most ordinary life.
It remembers the ugly smock
you used to wear, a blue chrysalis,
and the way your fingers were chipped
from work. The way we waited,
waited, at the top of the stairs.
Love's phone-call eventually came
after an aeon of turns and delays.
The poem has seen how you emerged;
how you brightened like a shell
revealed by the ocean, a new coral.
Yet our lives were shaped by what
had formed already, a certain tone
in feeling. Even the house was changed
into something it had contained –

its floors a familiar, resined beach;
lampshades and chairs were like daughters.
The windows before us were alive
with what you brought: an earthenware
jar like a veritable garden, double
narcissi, a wax camellia, viburnum and spikes
of forsythia. Outside, the first plants
that were strong enough to grow alone;
seven orange tulips with their own glow.

Thomas McCarthy

THE DYING SYNAGOGUE
AT SOUTH TERRACE

Chocolate-coloured paint and the July sun
like a blow-torch peeling off
the last efforts of love.
More than time has abandoned this,
God's abandonment, God's synagogue,
that rose out of the ocean
one hundred years from here.
The peeling paint is an emmigrant's
guide to America – lost on the shore
at Cobh, to be torn and scored
by a city of *luftmenshn;*
Catholics, equally poor, equally driven.

To have been through everything,
to have suffered everything and left
a peeling door. *Yahweh* is everywhere,
wherever abandonment is needed –
a crow rising after an accident,
wearing the grey uniform
of a bird of carrion, a badger
waiting for the bones of life
to crack before letting go:
wishing the tenth cantor to die,
the Synagogue to become a damp wall,
the wailing mouths to fester.
Too small. To be a small people
aligned to nothing is to suffer blame
like a thief in the night. An activist
threw a petrol-bomb for Palestine:

the sky opened and rained hail
like snow-drops. Flowers for memory,
petrol for the far-away.
To name one's land is to be a cuckoo
pushing others, bird-like, into a pit:
until, at the end, every sacred gesture
becomes vain, soiling the Synagogue
door like the charcoal corpses

at Mauthausen Station, 1944. A few
survived in the green valley of know-
nothing: spent themselves putting boots
on the Catholic poor, counting the brown
pennies, the corncrakes on their
trade routes, and the guerilla raids.

To sit here now, in the rancid sunshine
of low tide, is to contemplate
all of the unnoticed work of love –
exquisite children fall like jewels
from an exhausted colporteur's bag:
a mid-century daughter practises piano,
an *etude* to forget terror; a brother
dreams of the artistic life, another
shall practise law and become, in time,
the Catholic's tall Lord Mayor.
Where these jewels fall beside the peeling
door, let us place the six lilies of memory;
the six wounds of David's peeling star.

THE GATHERING OF WAVES
(for Catherine)

The waves gather differently off the shore of Crete:
they are less demented by the inland sea
though kicked by wind from the Turkish coasts,
the sea is grey there; Ottoman, moody.
At Agio Roumeli in the deep South
the shore is red-hot, the sea aquamarine,
plankton-less, like a melting mirror –
and the waves more generous, rhythmic, natal,
like a mould made specially for naked breasts.

You are always heading for the ocean,
unhappy until you can eavesdrop on water
and the wave's conversations. The sea
must be an adequate listener
or an expansive avuncular teller of tales.

Thomas McCarthy

Happy with your feet in water, sea-bride,
you are always calling me from the shore,
telling me what the sea is; what a man
is missing, what the ocean tells you.

Not to understand this is to be a mariner
beached or a convict on an island
watching the waves gather, listening;
waiting for the one chance to be gathered in –
Until there is a confusion of elements,
love, womanhood, the mind of the sea
with its own way of saying, its pedigree.
I see you most clearly by the ocean
in Crete or Kerry: you filling towards me,
tidal, telling me of the sea's love life.

Aidan Carl Mathews

CAVE PAINTER

A rope of rushlight wavers
On a damp ledge of sandstone.
His knuckle shapes an antler,
Tusks like a quarter moon.
Tomorrow's prey is promised
In the quarry of his art.

I was a boy-scout when
Stale air in his studio
Rushed on a probing torch.
A doctor in a caravan
Named with a number
A pestle stained with pigment.

Now, in a locked bedroom,
On the edge of utterance,
I ask strength of the dead;
Fearing a cave-in, nearing
A warm odour of wolfskin,
Glistening bone, faeces.

PROCESS
for Marilyn

Eight years of age and time enough to dream
Of larger worlds that lay beyond our parish,
A future empire crayoned on an atlas.
But the long walk home on huge evenings
Frightened us more than the catechism.

At twenty-one,
A faded rucksack rotting in the attic,
We clear the eaves of every swallow's nest.
We tend tall hedges till they hide our garden.

TO A CHILD

Through the window I see you running
In a loose blouse to the next field.
God only knows how many hundred times
It's ravelled on the brambles you explore,
Scouting for gnome and chipmunks.

You are kneeling now, an impulsive
Celebrant of things that adults can
Recognise but do not revel in,
Among an explosion of cowslips.
When you bottled wasps I felt no

Sadness such as now amazes me
Into wishing I had not spied you
Fumbling for butterflies that skip
Beyond your fingers' reach. Do not
Ask me to explain my anguish.

When you were sick no robins came
As in the Donald Duck cartoon
To decorate your sill and the gulls
Counted the crumbs in the bird bath.
All of which puzzled you to sobs.

Through the window I see you pitching
Carnivals I cannot share: but once
You told me the sun is a tangerine,
Tossed by a circus juggler, once
You smiled without a reason. Now

The Inherited Boundaries

I am left alone with my nonchalance
Who could not bring himself to adore,
Throttled tentative prayer. Is there
Time for the two of us to go
Gathering fruit while the rain holds off?

PERSPECTIVES

Ultimately, only the moment counts,
The composure of the immediate.
I cannot say why this awareness ought
Excite the sense of a discovery
But must record it lest I lose it
And so I lose myself in a poem,
Planting a flag on a claimed shore.

Minuets ended and the minstrels kept
Intensely silent when a voyager
Reported the exotic unfamiliar,
Spectacle the ocean's acreage hid.
In council chambers of Granada, kings
Leaned on their elbows over catalogues
Of panther, puma, khaki men.

Then there were those who, given to brooding,
Found shelter where the elements angered.
Off Kerry's coast, a settlement spread,
Sudden as seabirds, on perspiring rock.
Pools, random with porpoise, fed them.
Supple as grass, the high tides heaved.
Psalters stiffened in the salt air.

For me to locate that fascination,
That meticulous faith in one impulse,
Took nothing more than this: sitting alone
By a French window, smoking a cigarette,
I left aside the novel I had read
And saw a suntrap in an asphalt yard.
I rest my faith in that quotidian.

Aidan Carl Mathews

CHRONICLE

The demesne lord died in the gradual morning:
Oil on his forehead dribbled along his jawbone,
Hands that absolved closed firmly over coin.
The grinning serfs nailed daffodils over doorways.

Obsequies and incense followed. Tonsured friars
Sang psalms in aisles of cowl and candle grease.
Swordlings shuffled in the pews, remembered
Elbowing hounds, tables of boiled venison.

Barons remembered hooves plunged in the furrow,
Apple orchards, rumours of false titles.
They rifled chamber cupboards and his widow
Remembered them bareheaded round the altar.

RETURNING TO KILCOOLE

Hubcaps, horsedroppings rubble the sand.
Although I had managed to remember
The fabulous frenzy of alarmed snipe,
Hedges brown as a smoker's fingers,
The railway track was foremost in my mind.

Often in my eagerness, I anklesprained
Among those rails, was always terrified
Of trains running me over, had nightmares
Full of broken skulls, revolving wheels.
I used go there with my godfather
Who had a blackthorn and noticed everything.

I grew up to his hip, elbow, shoulder:
Then it was time to begin remembering
Important things. The heron we both saw
through his binoculars when I was twelve
And informed him it was a flamingo;
Or the time we were there around midnight

The Inherited Boundaries

To hear the ocean perspiring and blacker
Than tar. I suppose I was about fourteen
And needed to be alone and so we put
Two hundred yards between the two of us.
I think we were closer then than ever before.

A LANDING

At the boat-yard's dry-dock,
Crushed waters leak
Iodine like a hospital
From sponge and sea-urchin.

You wade through sail-bags,
Bales of soft cumulus,
Or stroke the bleached hulls
Hauled onto stocks. Your mouth

Is drawing their names
Out of cursives and capitals –
Stormpetrel, Gale Warning –
Forms looming like weather.

What do they almost disclose?
What language has chosen you
For itself and no other?
Once I'd have changed

Blue mounds of tarpaulin
To walrus basking, puffins
From a pumice sanctuary
Where you preside, keeper

Of trade-winds, of birds cast
Miles off course
In those cobalt skies.
Now I would relinquish

Aidan Carl Mathews

All but your image.
You stoop at a Sunball,
Its halyards like radar
Are humming with cloudbursts! ·

Listen. I resonate
A tart rapping of hammers,
The stiff sails folded
With a noise like brushfire.

There, your bright anorak
Appears and disappears
Between the tall *Sea Mist*
and the *Beacon Light*.

AT THE WAILING WALL
i.m. my brother John, 1945-1978

I make free with old albums,
Photographs that show
Your good side in profile.
From them all, I would choose
Shots of the Wailing Wall
Weeks after the truce
And the fall of Jerusalem.
Because I too stand
At the blank wall of a death
Not granted or forgiven –
Her pavilion sacked by louts,
her scriptures shat upon –
I recall you by picturing
A skull-cap and prayer-shawl,
Arms bare to the wrist
And lifted in hosanna,
Like that print of the Baptist
Wading through Jordan.

The Inherited Boundaries

Your head is bent forward
Towards a future unheard-of,
A four-year illness;
And the lightly downed neck
That I clung to on rides,
Burnt only by sunlight:
Neither hairless nor sutured.

SPECTRUM

Everything we stand up in,
Worn long enough, makes one load:
Our warm, discoloured underwear,
The shirts off our backs,
Or the rose-bordered bedsheets
We have made and must lie upon.
On washdays, we entrust it all,
This fabric of our lives together,
To the darkened floodwaters
Of a cycle marked *delicates*.
I think often how you sat up
The first night that we got it,
New to the heavy, heart-like churning
Of its cold wash and its warm wash;
And I think of the silence after:
A turning, a total immersion.
In the reddish glow of the pilot,
Your white hands at the dials.

Tonight the clotheshorse fills
Like the makeshift sails on liferafts
In those B-movies that show
Two stowaways waking
Bone-dry and uninjured
Among cockatoos and banana-crops.
I am trying to say that our lives
Are running into each other
Like the dyes from separates.
You see it in the wash:

My vests the pink of nappy rash
From a royal blue blouse,
And your whitest pair of trousers
Ruined for good, with stains
The colour of flesh and blood
From something I slipped in
Among our sustaining garments,
Watermarks water won't budge.

THE RIVER'S ELEGY
i.m. Cearbhall Ó Dálaigh

Not even the sherpas have heard
My first words among lichen,

Miles above the tree-line
In a land with no animal dirt,

A kingdom of minus temperatures
Where I was lonely.

Downriver, the oats
Fattened; the fields were all ears.

So I sang to them.
And the trees leaned over me

Like women drinking,
Holding their hair with one hand.

Fugitives sank in me
With their bamboo snorkels

While mastiffs waded
Yelping through the bulrushes;

And delicate children
Who had covered their genitals

The Inherited Boundaries

Strode singing from me
In towels of water.

Shallows dismembered me.
Limb from limb I was pulled apart,

Yet forgave them. I made of me
A ford for all travellers,

A sheepskin that the footsore
Might cross in dry clothes.

I am paid with an acrid
Odour of tides, a stink of chlorine.

For now there is a blinding
Light where people walk barefoot;

Now there is a pining
Of shorebirds and seabirds,

An oystercatcher poised
Over my white pouring.

This is reward for my toils,
For my haycocks and cattle,

Who had come down in the world
To no delta at sea-level.

MINDING RUTH
for Seamus Deane

She wreaks such havoc in my library,
It will take ages to set it right –
A Visigoth in a pinafore

Who, weakening, plonks herself
On the works of Friedrich Nietzsche,
And pines for her mother.

Aidan Carl Mathews

She's been at it all morning,
Duck-arsed in my History section
Like a refugee among rubble,

Or, fled to the toilet, calling
In a panic that the seat is cold.
But now she relents under biscuits

To extemporise grace notes,
And sketch with a blue crayon
Arrow after arrow leading nowhere.

My small surprise of language,
I cherish you like an injury
And would swear by you at this moment

For your brisk chatter brings me
Chapter and verse, you restore
The city itself, novel and humming,

Which I enter as a civilian
Who plants his landscape with place-names.
They stand an instant, and fade.

Her hands sip at my cuff. She cranes,
Perturbedly, with a book held open
At plates from Warsaw in the last war.

Why is the man with the long beard
Eating his booboos? and I stare
At the old rabbi squatting in turds

Among happy soldiers who die laughing,
The young one clapping: you can see
A wedding band flash on his finger.

ELEGY FOR A FIVE YEAR OLD

Bewildered tonight, how often
I lose and catch you as if
We two were at hide-and-seek
Round the house before lights-out.
Your mother is trying to speak.
Her mouth means it is I

Who must find you in bed,
Not moving, holding your breath.
You'll get your death of cold.
How can you know the trouble
You've caused, a hue and cry,
Vigil of 'phone-calls, candles?

And who am I to explain
You have slipped off without warning
To be by yourself, or to say
There is no point in our waking
All night at the least noise
Of footsteps over the gravel?

LETTER FOLLOWING

We promise letters and send postcards,
My father and I. The whole of Europe
Has passed between us without comment

Down through the years, but mostly sailboats,
Waterfronts, and the polaroid heavens
Reflecting the sea or being reflected.

Only this morning, he sent me
The *Victory* in dry-dock and 3-D,
Second time round. There's the usual

Men's talk about storms and maintenance:
When it worsened, then I worried would she
Drag her moorings, but she rode it well,

Her hatches battened. Is he talking
Marriages or jobs? Or a cabin cruiser
Idling at anchor, five sons and no crew?

Who can tell? Mid-afternoon,
I write him at his hospital
A card addressed to the Ancient Mariner,

Of an island ferry from six months back,
Its lifeboat circled and arrowed:
The best place to be in a headwind.

And I post it off from this dusty place,
Thirty miles inland, north of Salonica,
Among chickens and children. Word of thanks,

Word of greeting. This is our way.
We cover our multitudes, he and I,
Our silences carrying over the water.

KEEPING PACIFIC TIME

The last class over,
You are walking to your car now;

And your day winds down,
A penny spun on a table.

Gravel and crushed grass sigh
Where the night wind crosses them,

From the warm rubbish of picnics,
Toddlers held among bushes;

And the park, policed at nightfall,
Privately dreams of children

While the statues throw their arms
To a sky refusing pigeons:

The Inherited Boundaries

Many white faces,
Longhaired in the moonlight.

On the other side of the world
Where I live, missing you,

It is early morning. Light
Collects like rain in the awnings.

Dew on the closed newsstands,
And the first bread cooling.

Soon the crows will come,
Just as they do at home

To the trellis sloped like Pisa,
For the crumbs on my window:

A scone broken in bits,
And softened under the cold tap.

TWO MONTHS MARRIED

We can tell already
The history of chips in the skirting,
Hammer-marks at the towel-rail,

Or why the asparagus fern
Is housed in the cooking pot
With the hairline crack.

Today, I was cleaning
With the wrong cloth as you hid
Photographs behind photographs.

On the kitchen window there,
Natural Crystal Salt
Flared in a gust of sun;

Aidan Carl Mathews

The marked-down Sage and Mint
From the Nile's source
Unstoppered their genies.

In a room facing south,
A tree-house with the ladder drawn up,
We're home even as we set out.

Foodstore and software,
A clearing and a hideaway in which
We two may be together and alone

With a radio left on
Always, talking of envoys
Going back to a bombed city.

PASSAGES

Traipsing from school, I used mouth them –
Eleusinian, Rubicon–
Big and elaborate and lapidary,

Dominions of sound. Tonight I need
A second language like the silent reading
Of place-names for a homecoming,

A meal eaten under one red candle
Which you clear away, humming and swaying
To a quick clatter of stacked plates.

Listening, I would learn by heart
Those dialects of touch and gesture
That utter you like forms of greeting,

And would give them force of law
By right of seizure on old words,
The blue, possible vowels I starve for.

But you draw down your face to become
Other and hidden, a known country
I can cross to only in silences,

Through plain water. So I say nothing,
Hunkering over the fire-guard
To tend a small coal with the brass tongs.

DESCARTES AT DAYBREAK

The light stands over me,
And my red, expensive candle
Stops short as the curtains change colour.

Crossings, crossings-out,
a slantwise second thought cancelled,
Those unruled margins! Up all night,

My body against me, my life
In my own hand. Death of cold. Twice
She begged me to bed. Twice I refused.

To be greeted now, for my pains,
By catcalls of the sun happening
Everywhere but in my head!

If you would only listen, she said,
You would doubtless hear
The good noises of life being about to:

A newspaper slithering
Under the door, or the puppyfat
Milkgirls misting the spyhole;

And the sprinklers chattering,
Going *lovely, lovely,*
On the lawn below the window.

Something to believe on,
To start from, rise to; drops
For the sty late reading brought on. . .

I exist. I breakfast.
She brings me toast, my wife does,
With one of her hairs in the butter.

World of the precious little,
Of things taken in vain yet sworn by,
Dawn on me.

INTERIORS

I found myself alone, and I went there,
Like Admiral Perry dropping anchor
In fantastic silence, off my own Japan.

I was most at sea on that dry land.
In charity with the thought of margins,
My land-legs buckled beneath me.

There, packed tight as a pharmacy,
the ground gave freely or not at all
Of its green tonnage, its flowers beyond Latin.

Yet much like Admiral Perry,
Dolorous for the pumpkins
Of a different feast, and hearing

Over the weird string instruments,
A porchfront floorboard creaking,
I too tired of this place

I had dragged from hiding into history.
The truth is I knew no-one.
So, when the wind freshened, I let it.

The Inherited Boundaries

Now, come wind or high water,
I will stay put among my proper interiors,
Rooms two or more persons can share

In the grace of reliance,
The self gone west to escape its absence.
There's the noise of a vacuum

Making a clean sweep of the living space
(A metal detector
At beachheads where the dead throng like walrus)

Or stopping, in that best hush,
Its brushes clogged
Wth loose threads and stairwell housedust.

HOW WORDS MEET TO MAKE A POEM

There is a green ruin where they gather
In small groups. Some of them
Have been gone for years, some are strangers.
They caress without speaking. A handful,
With one foot in front of the other,
Measure the ground like tightrope artists.

The night before the work is to start
They grow silent. Fires are let die,
Or they talk in undertones.
The small hours gloss their sleeping bags
Like site machinery under moonlight,
But where they lie the frost does no harm.

Aidan Carl Mathews

HANDBOOK FOR REVOLUTIONARIES

In my second life,
I would like to be brought back
as the corner of Grafton Street;

If that were impossible,
As the monosyllable 'yes'
on the tip of everyone's tongue.

Best of all, though beyond me,
I would revive as two
Parts hydrogen, one oxygen.

Towns would start up round me,
Lawyers test my waters,
The kids wade through with no togs on,

And an old one waiting a bus
Spit at herself in my surface
For no good reason in the world.

Such cloudshapes I would put on,
Army convoys would stop in their trucks,
The nuncio cable Rome,

And amateur painters,
Agog at my swirlings,
Forget the numbers for grey and azure:

I would be black and blue for them
Yet the sin would pierce me through,
A picture of innocence.

On the benevolent I would fall as snow,
On the evil, even on Mozart's murderer,
I would settle as drizzle.

Men in the middle of cities,
Their foreheads blacker than miners,
Would angle their cheeks like children

For many swift kisses. Then
In my passing, the world's
Slate would be wiped clean as a window.

Meantime, I am happy to be
A puddle at the zebra,
Too muddy to look up anyone's skirt,

Or even a tupperware saucer
Of water left at a heater
To dampen down the atmosphere,

And shiver at the sound
Of a girl in a bed-sit dropping
First one shoe, then the other.

LAWRENCE O'TOOLE
Priest and prelate, patron saint of the city of Dublin

When I chose your name for mine
From a perfumed bishop at age twelve,
It was for men unknown to you
And my explaining parents.

It was for Lawrence of Arabia,
His stare searching me out
In the deep parterre, his hands
Beckoning through mosquitoes

To the water-hole on the far
Side of the intermission;
And the first Saint Lawrence
Whose sangfroid at boiling point

(Turfed onto a gridiron,
Toasting his captors with
'I am done enough on that side',
The ironist at his rarest)

Aidan Carl Mathews

Was how I would show them all
When grown-up overseas,
My whole family listening in tears
To an update on Father Aidan

At the hands of the Red Chinese,
Shanghai'd in a dungeon.
I am older now, my true patron.
Beyond wanderlust or witness

Your wry, monotonous taste
For the Word in the word-perfect
Ordnance of memoranda
Suits me down to the ground –

'Where were those gutters bought
For the sacristy in Poitiers?
And what of this new way
Of preserving parchment better?' –

Like your choice of a job of work,
Raising up Nazareth
In the bustle and dust-clouds
Of a junction of hovels.

For the truth is, El Auruns
Counted the stars like sheep
Yet when sleep came, it was English
Meadowsweet that he smelled;

And the fat part of a leg of lamb
That spattered my arm on Tuesday
Brought it home to me.
Men are not witty on the toasting fork.

So, in your low-keyed gaiety,
Preferring the punctilio
Of a well-kept parish register,
You speak to me. Moonlight,

You say, will make a hencoop even
Gleam like a helmet,
Sunlight a cart-shaft
Arrow-sharp at matins,

Aiming at heaven. And this, you say,
Is wierder, more newfangled
Than camels in the dry stretches,
A saint's holocaust,

Or the glass that filled to half-way
Only, obediently on the first
Sundays of Advent
With the colourless tears of Mary Magdalen.

CAEDMON

Because I could sing to High Heaven
The Abbot made me. Marched to the altar
Shotgun style by a scalping party,
My head felt eery, an oval shaved off
As if for delicate neuro-surgery.
What were they thinking beyond in the buttery,
My mates from the shepherds' dormitory
As I bent my neck, as I bent my knee?
'Sing me Creation' says the Master of Students,
The making of matter, a seven day wonder,
The universe forming from misty gases
Like a disprin dropped in a glass of water;
'Sing me the Exodus out of Egypt',
The sulphur springs of the Promised Land.
And I try with my mouthful of cavities
Among all the statues that throw their eyes
Blindly toward Heaven. I am gargling Latin
Like salt sea water for runny ulcers.
Still, in a month of Sundays, a full church calendar,
I'll never be home here.

74

Aidan Carl Mathews

What I want instead
Is the benediction of words like cabbage
Out in the back where the plot is thickening;
And the lipservice I languish for
Beyond any Latin is the parted mouth
Of my wife with the dental anaesthetic
Turning the other cheek as I kiss her.
Because this is it: when the accurate image
Cools and clears in the sacred mysteries
Like an egg whitening in the pan,
It is her curved spaces in the bed beside me
The sun, the moon and the stars shine out of,
This that I take to my heart and husband
Wholly, wholly, wholly.

ADAM'S COMMENTARY
AFTER THE FALL

Granted it came as something of a shock
To be shown the door in a stony silence,
We were not put out. We had made provision.

True, for a time we could only stare,
Moving slowly as if through water
And whistling to keep our bodies up.

Yet it ended well when the cattle waded
Welcoming, smelly toward the encampment
To be milked clean, to be manhandled.

In a maiden brainstorm I then invented
Firelighters, fish-hooks, funeral games
And a rudimentary method of blaming

Somebody else for my own misconduct,
While a trial five-year plan includes
Facsimiles in a brood of children

The Inherited Boundaries

Plus any amount of adjectives
To ensure that the view from my picture window
Will never leave me lost for words:

What I once called yokes I now call names.
You may quote me on this. I am thrilled silly
To have finished at last with the other fellow,

My godfather of gardening fame,
And I wash my hands of his shitty, seignorial
'Never mind me, I'm one of you' nonsense.

Though I have it on highest authority
That he misses us, there is no going back.
I draw the line at every horizon.

The world I want is what lies about me,
What crops up where you least expect it
In a surplus bigger than barns can harvest,

And slap bang in the middle there's me,
A master of ceremonies, an onion rooting
In thin air, in a fistful of sunlight.

And what of the angel looking daggers
At Eden's doorway? Of his brandished sword's
Acetylene tip going back and forth?

It moved off and away as if jealous
To circle me at a distance, and still does
Daylong till its blaze of glory.

Noblesse oblige. I take it lying down
On the flat of my back and watch it work
Wonders, tugging the barley by its ears,

Making the apples chubby, the cabbage
Sprawl as if it had a right to be there.
It touches even me when I let it. My forehead

Darkens beneath it to a brown study
While my shadow goes to enormous lengths
To take in as much ground as it can.

So I can state categorically and for us both
That I am happy, that I am about
To imagine a new god for myself. Already

I am kicking several ideas around.
I think I shall give him my own hands
And the wife's face, with or without tears.

Harry Clifton

THE WALLS OF CARTHAGE

Augustine, ended the priest,
Put it all too well.
Here am I, a priest
In my late forties, still

In the desert, still
Relativity's fool.
Wherever it is the will
Of lycée, college, school,

As here, God to conclude
From premisses, I am sent
For lectures, journées d'études.
Oases of discontent,

Paris, Maynooth, Louvain,
Define my forty-year desert,
My home from home, terrain
Of groundless visions, assert

The same topography
As he, Augustine, mapped.
Godless in Carthage city,
A dialectician, trapped

In a waste of comparisons,
His speech is my speech, speech
Of failure, of a man
Old enough now to preach

Of a God he may never know
Under the sun – a mirage.
So, with Augustine I tell you,
Alexandria, Carthage,

Harry Clifton

We, in inferior reason,
Travel until we fall,
To compare, in a desert season,
The beauty of their walls.

BLUE

One day, you wake,
Conscious of blue space
In which a pure sun has been blazing
For hours, while innocent trees
Perfect themselves invisibly
Just outside.
                Ethereal,
Neither near nor far,
The city is a grey rumour.

Summer crowds
Dream at the intersections, register
The blue boundlessness
Of morning with a look
Of vague pleasure.
                    A good day
For the painter of white lines
On cracked ground.

Your mind is plunged
In the wrong kind of work
Too deeply, when Mary disturbs you,
Brushing gently against you
With her body, courting recognition –
I am a woman.
                Later,
You feign indifference
To lost opportunity.

The Inherited Boundaries

Work dissolves
In legitimate failure. Returning
Across this morning's field, you notice,
Where something metal has happened,
A smell of mowing.
                        Afternoon
Blue glimpsed in a ditch,
Forgotten again.

Far at sea, the white regatta
In which your lost friend is a sailor
Catches breeze. You watch it,
Sprawled among warm rocks of the shoreline,
Calm as the bay at evening,
Listening in to yourself.
                        Time lulling
The innermost shore of perception,
Inlet of blue immensity.

Voices of children,
Tainted with obscenity,
Reach you; a man who is drunk
Attempts reconciliation
With a patient woman; the elderly
Proceed on crumbling terraces
Of summer.
                Night falls,
Lengthily, streaked with the blue
Of many mitigations.

MORNING

First light steals
Across the metal roofs
In silence, reveals
You sleeping, me standing aloof

At the open door,
Anonymous as when I gave
What you sheltered me for
Last night, assuring myself I have

Everything, while you keep
Night's language in a dark place,
In a rhythmic sleep
Suffusing your mystery face

From the inside.
Nor will I break
That sleep in you, confide
Who I was in the act of taking

Leave of you, but drop
Down five vertiginous floors
From the high silence
Of your room, to where the clanging doors

Give onto sun and courtyard
And the photographic eye
Of a caretaker, introducing himself
With goodbye.

IN WHOM WE TRUST

Where black gusts disarranged
Your fine golden hair
On a street crude with voltage,
You quickened in my trust,
Pale stimulus, disengaged

From a more irreplaceable
Source than charged
This precinct of old walls
And staggering gentlemen
With purpose. I was to call

You, spirit you away
From the troublesome algebra
Of people, failure, duty,
Combing the bright complexities
Out of your eyes, for
Innocence, girlhood, beauty.

PICARO

Between adventures, the picaro must lie down
On all-night streets where the warped and friendless are,
An indefinable character the master author leaves
Half-inchoate, while framing his social story.

Another night; unmapped dark between day-chapters
Of his ebullient wanderings in and out of character
Enough to queer the fiction – that's his anarchic way;
The carriers of vapid roadlamps leave him cold.

Action and life distracts itself indoors;
The picaro sags on a love-scarred bench like a puppet
With nexus-wires removed, nervelessly discomposed,
Eyeing the fictions ablaze in rooming-house windows.

He's in need of a room away from alarum and clangour,
To create himself anew, in these nights of no situation,
From all he has seen and been; take time out
From round-the-clock traffic emblazoned into his brain.

He's in need of a room who has nowhere to withdraw
From intentions not his own, picaresque contingencies
He must jump naked into, society's bedlamite,
Dying young, peradventure, or penned into sad institutions.

Between adventures, his author asleep or in ruins,
The picaro lies down out of social mind a while,
Nursing his self-sufficiency, numbed as it is,
Blinking in crazy perspective on stories he's out of.

Harry Clifton

STRANGE FILTH

After dark, I came in,
Having scoured
The adamant, fruitless streets
While light was failing.

One lucky hag I saw
Scurry off into the half-light
With her string bag full
Of assorted vegetables.

Before I could reach her,
She was gone. Everywhere
Was a closed shop. I returned
Clean as a whistle,

Except that my feet
Brought in strange filth,
And left it in the hall,
On the stairs, everywhere.

UPSTAIRS CHILD

Nights when there is talking downstairs,
I am to be found hovering
At the edges of the adult conversations.

It is mostly the working of faces
In hubbub, but sentences let fall
I seize upon.
            Later, I go away
Upstairs to my own room. Lights out,
I have all the time in the world
To compose myself, and quite self-consciously

To mince and mimic late into the night.

THE NIGER FERRY

Detachment, suspended animation
Between two shores. . . The Niger ferry,
Its shallow draught supporting
Heatstruck dreamers, halfway across

Green shallows. . . Lovesick and free,
Myself at the handrail
Of an upper deck, looking down
On unhistorical

Tradesfolk, brute soldiers
Dozing in military vehicles,
Mammywagons being floated from nowhere
To nowhere. . .
                          Is it still not time

To take control again, to resume
Wheels and levers? The dandy crewmen
Talk beauty, and I go on
Considering my love life,

Travels in search of a Rubicon,
Dividing, like this peaceful river,
Past from future.
                          It still approaches
(Thousands of miles away

In Northern Europe), that jungle shore
Inertia floats me towards. . . the future,
Organising itself
Into taxis, there by the slipway,

In the increasingly human
Faces of taximen. . . Beggars and salesmen
Of bogus watches I'll ignore,
Taximen never be in time for.

Harry Clifton

PLAGUE AND HOSPICE

Constantly ajar, as if created
For the acts of mercy
God is said to work through
Every day, this is the service door
The sisters use, crossing a yard
From mission to hospital,
Flooding stone steps with light
Since half past six, when the African darkness
Wakens. . .
                    Around the steps
Fat lepers, bloated with indulgence,
Mope for hours, the ugly question-marks
In the conscience
Of Sister Philomena. 'What if these
Were phenomena of Christ?'
Her heart whispers. A night-light burns
Along porches, where the people,
Black out-patients, sleep
Beside samples of themselves
In evil jars, dreaming of admittance
To the dripfeed
Of an understaffed heaven. . .

All quiet. An empty moment. . .
Sister Phelim watches
In the yard, where trainee nurses
Splash inflammable blue
Into tillylamps, lights for a Bible play.
Illumined, the animal beauty
Of their bodies. . . trimming wild flames
In the darkness, fixing the glass
To votive intensity.
                         Half past seven. . .
Everything normal today.
Rehearsals for the play –
The Devil said 'Hmm!' in an amusing way.
Two priests came through
From the interior, spreading rumours
Of an epidemic, preached about

Beautiful deaths. Insomnia and cassettes
For afternoon rest, while the cock in the garden
Crowed, crowed, crowed. . .
A stretcher passed down the road
To a desolate burial, one child following after –
Two thousand years since Christ
Was first betrayed. . . In his hands
A labourer's pick and shovel.
Prayers, goodnights. . .

GOVERNMENT QUARTERS

Reading the Greeks, negro statesmen divided
Between Athens and Sparta, as the draft constitution
Riddled with typing errors, clauses elided
For the public executions,

Goes to print. . . I look up their sources
Along the malarial shelves
Of our house in the tropics – basic texts of courses
J. and I are teaching, children ourselves.

The government electricity
Our memory units work by, switches itself on
At nightfall, and we play
Defunct McCartney and Lennon

Circa 1967. *'Nothing is real. . .'*
Floats from J's bedroom, where Chinese philosophy,
Local Indian hemp, form an ethereal
Adolescent, hired for his Greekish sophistry

In an adolescent nation. . .
Innocent and sensual, blackskinned boys
Who ran away from home, for a white education,
Keep house for us, bartering joy

For rational knowledge. Every day
Their unselfconsciousness
Wakens, sweeping the topheavy shards away,
Clickbeetles dead on the floor. We are needed less. . .

Harry Clifton

LATITUDE 5°N

A forest of background noises,
African classroom. . . Voices emerge from it,
Angry voices of children, whose names
I cannot decipher, demanding
Euclidean instruments, Oxford dictionaries,
Chairs of native wood
For their growing fundaments. Answering,
Drowned in the din of a construction gang
Levelling ground outside, I repeat myself,
Beseeching silence.

Or again, the night
Of the open forum. . . A forest of background noises
Planting itself in the crowd
Of black contemporaries, filibustering
The maiden speeches of girls
With shouts from the assembley. The M.C. drops
His faulty megaphone, imploring
Silence, but a man with a powerful voice,
Denouncing Western culture
Has the floor.

The catholic father, drunk
And disillusioned. . . 'Give us religious war
All over again – the privilege of suffering,
Comradeship and martyrdom. . .
Oppress us, like the church in Eastern Europe,
Where you can't postpone religion
The way we do,
Just to go on a weekend spree. Above all,
Keep us here in Africa. Never send us home
Where we have no meaning.'

Sitting in the jungle, engine ticking over,
Thinking all this. . . No forest of background noises
To distract me, no radio drummers
Nationalising the airwaves
For a blood revival. . . Nothing but silence
Five degrees from the equator –

Silence of growth, before growth
Proliferates into desires; and the agelessness
Of the man with no birth certificate,
Innocent of history.

TRIAL MARRIAGE

Listening, woman and man,
To a solitary drunk in the passage, his key out of place,
Or the rhythm of an old fan
In the darkness, chasing itself through space

Above our heads. . . is the government paying
For them too? It's casual as a universe
To keep cold in, this living with charges reversed
And our credit weakens, as the hotel moves into day.

When the nets are lifted
We slept under, and we're posted separate ways –
After months of arrogance, among beauty parlour facelifts,
Sad divorcees – I'll be scouring for days

A memory of pure flesh
From idle fingers. Nobody's shame or disgrace. . .
Am I free to exploit you afresh
In a marriage of words? The meaning behind your face,

Your hands' competence, anyway these prevail
Elsewhere than in words. From the first of our pleasure
You said of your long fingernails,
Too long for mending and tearing, 'Too much leisure. . .'

After the trial marriage, trial separations –
I hate them, the working selves we're paid to assume,
Transferred to indifferent stations, our working conditions
Never look back, simply resume.

Harry Clifton

LONELINESS IN THE TROPICS

No one coming home
From North, South, East or West
To the unlit aerodrome
Tonight. . . So they can rest,

The black nightwatchmen,
Behind deserted transit shacks
And talk. They wave again
As I reach the end of the airfield. . . I walk back,

My mind full of empty spaces,
Billowing like a windsock
On a pole. Already this restlessness,
An hour old by the clock,

Is wearing off. . . I can sleep it off
After German beer
At the village whorehouse, if they have enough –
I have been here a year.

DEATH OF THOMAS MERTON

Losing altitude, you can see below you the flames
Of the Tet Offensive, giving the lie to your visions
Of eastern mystics, like uncensored newsreel
In which the slaves of history are spreading the blame –
And so your mind records it, a sin of omission
In a mystic journal. Meanwhile the wheels
Descend for Bangkok, with one of the Catholic great,
In late October, Nineteen Sixty Eight.

A clean declaration. One a.m. and you're through
The bulletproof glass of security, like a conscience
Filtered through judgement, leaving behind
Temptations you were dead to, years ago –
Hippies frisked for heroin, women and incense

The Inherited Boundaries

For the American soldiers. Only the life of the mind
You hide on your person – all the rest you can shed
Like a stale narcotic. Shortly, you'll be dead.

So wake before daylight, breakfast alone,
Remembering what you came for. Below you a river
Seeps out of Buddhist heartlands, not in meditation
But in commerce, irrigating zones
Of military fleshpots, where the barges deliver
Rice and Thai girls, and a drifting vegetation
Drags at the chains of destroyers, moored in Bangkok –
And you wait to be chauffeured, at nine o'clock,

To the other side of the city. . . .
                                        Spiritual masters
Shrunken to skin and bone, await you in silence
On a neutral ground of Buddhas, golden and hollow,
Smiling from inner space, beyond disaster
To an old complacency. Starving for nonviolence
In saffron robes, their shavenheaded followers
Beg on the streets. From an airconditioned car
You can see them in passing, as cut off as you are –

Cut off from each other, disconnected by history
In Paris and Calcutta, linked alone by the airspace
Of a temporal pilgrimage. Diplomatic immunity,
This is your saving grace – to restore mystery
To a common weal, and resurrect from disgrace
The nonpolitical, kneeling in the unity
Of a moment's prayer, with the Dalai Lama and wife –
For the flash-photographers of *Time* and *Life*.

Judas has other betrayals. At your last supper
In a Hungarian restaurant, among friends in Bangkok,
It's left to the Chinese waiter to overprice you –
So unworldly. You can switch from corruption
Suddenly into wisdom, through an electric shock
Turning your hair white, resolving your crisis
Into anticlimax. But it leaves you dead,
With a powerline shortcircuited through your head. . . .

Harry Clifton

A small embarrassment, for the United States –
Your motherhouse at Gethsemani awaits
Its anti-hero. A gaggle of monks are released
To New Haven for the day, to identify and separate
Among the Vietnam dead, the maimed in crates
From an Air Force plane, this body of a priest
And holy fool – from beyond the international
Dateline, and the jungle war with the irrational.

MONSOON GIRL

In the airconditioned drone
Of a room we rent by the hour,
You go to the telephone
Lovely and naked, to put through a call
For drinks, or hire a car
To take us home.

Your nudity dapples the walls
With shadows, and splashes the mirrors
Like a vision, in the blue light
That bathes you, a pleasure-girl
On a lost planet, sincere
But only at night.

Outside, it will rain
For weeks, months on end. . . .
We'll come here again
As we did before, where Chinese women,
Blank and inscrutable, attend
Nightly to our linen.

We'll come again
In drunkenness, for the child's play
Of lovemaking, or to part the rain
Like curtains of jet beads,
And dream the rainy months away
On pampered beds

The Inherited Boundaries

Where forgetfulness lies down
With executive power
After hours, in a tangle of legs
And juices, a world turned upside down,
And I feed on the lotus-flower
Of your delicate sex.

At three, we'll be driven back
Though depths of Bangkok
Already tomorrow. There will be roads
Closed, and a dope squad
Flashing its query through windowglass,
Lettus us pass. . .

There will be lights
In Chinatown, sampans on the river –
The poor starting early. Elsewhere the night
Will separate us, having seeded within you
Miscarriage of justice forever,
And the rain will continue.

THE SEAMSTRESS

I have a seamstress, making a shirt for me
In sultry weather, in the months we are together.

She measures my shoulders with tape, I feel on my back
The cool of her wooden yardstick, and submit

To a temporary contract, binding me
To the new and the strange. Together we lose ourselves

Among shades of blue, the melancholy feast
A culture of silkworms creates, as Chinese tailors

Stand and wait. For me it's the stuff of dreams,
For her a labour of love. . . In her house on stilts

Where women are still slaves, she sews the collarless
Garment of pure freedom I have asked for

When I leave, keeping only for herself
Dry tailor's chalk, and the diagram of a body.

APROPOS OF THE FALLING SLEET

It is Winter, and the clerk
In this Dostoyevskian tale
Has eaten, replaced on his shelf
Philosophies to prepare himself
When he disappears into the dark
Of a howling gale,
Emerges again on Mount Street
Greatcoated, seeking contrition
From fallen angels he greets
In the words of a politician
Or a priest.
          Since September,
This is the way he consumes
The righteousness trapped in a room –
I can still remember.

Like an only child
Of solitude, the gas meter
Gapes its hungry mouth
To be fed all day on shillings.
Dreaming of the south,
Shivering, strangely exiled
From his own welfare state,
He shares this ancient house
With little men, wifebeaters –
What he is fulfilling
He cannot know, or anticipate
With a soul borrowed from literature
And the company of a mouse,
The total picture.

The Inherited Boundaries

Out in the snow, Jean Darling
Is feeding Winter starlings
The lonely, despotic bread
Of an actress gone in the head.
From upstairs, Satchmo jazz
Blurts into life, and wakes
Con Higgins in his bed
Slowly, cursing, to consume
The night's first bottle of perfume.
It's evening – or it was
Before the spell would break
Over the living dead
In Number Sixty Four,
When nobody worked anymore.

Quiet house, environment
Of early retirement –
I remember it. . . coming and going,
Aspiring to regular hours
With the government, in corridors
Of anonymous power,
Even a clerk must outgrow
His antihistorical gloom
Or quit, and live off the wages
Of someone who works from a room
Like Sonya.
                    Petersburg hovels
Housing Dublin's rages –
I turn them back like the pages
Of a Russian novel. . .

It's Winter, and the clerk
In this Dostoyevskian tale
Has lost himself in the dark
Of his own imagination,
Where bitterness prevails
Like sleet, through the centuries
Of misanthropic streets
Going nowhere. Troubled in soul,
Approaching his destination
Timelessly, placelessly,

Where can he turn, to meet
Someone as lonely as me
To complete himself, and be whole
In magnanimity?

IRELAND

Offshore, islanded
On a sleepless night
At summer's end, this girl and I
Look across at Ireland
As we lie. . .

The law ends,
And the sense of time
Over there. . . it's a sheltered lee,
Our unsuperintended
Eternity.

Wild seed,
Warrens of breeding
Everywhere. . . on the Atlantic side
Graveyards of joyrides,
Used cars.

A ferry
Left some hours ago
For the mainland. . .nothing to carry us
Back into history, now,
Until tomorrow.

Moonless
Tides black out the piles
Of the landing-stage. . . phosphorescent
Plash of smiles
In darkness

Plays
Between us, in silence
Of fondling, young points growing
Tenderer in violence,
Responding,

But no breakthrough
Into adulthood, no release –
Only merchantmen, destroyers
Riding the breeze
At anchor,

And lights
Across the strait
Winking, calling our adolescence
Into question, as overnight
Ireland waits.

SKETCHES FROM BERLIN

I
Greying, becoming equal
To the street, dying without sequel
In Kreuzburg tenements, in the huge shadows
Ruin casts, the war widows

Stand gossiping. . . everywhere
NATO crewcuts, young men from McNair
Barracks, representing peace,
And the German police

Inquiring, should
New neighbours appear in the neighbourhood,
For names. . . poor arrivistes
Might be terrorists,

Humanities
Students, whom elderly landladies
Shelter, might be, as everyone seems to sense,
Marriages of convenience.

Harry Clifton

2

Memories, questions of blood and genes,
Dominate evenings together
With Angelika, resurrecting scenes
His posthumous papers reveal, of her unknown father.

Angelika. . . twenty-eight
And still a student, able to laugh
At backwardness now, a guilty child reinstated
By analysis. We spread the photographs

According to generation
On the floor, and a man emerges
Less than whole, surviving his own desertion
From the Wermacht, SS purges –

Stepchild, left without
A background, where thoroughness
Doctored the reproductions, couldn't black out
The essential jewishness

Surviving. . .
            to marry and separate.
To rear through alimonies
Only a stranger – dying in Seventy Eight,
Obese, amoral, a middle fifties

Berlin banker, leaving a daughter
Hand-me-downs and a Volks, and no explanation
Of old unhappiness, Buchenwald slaughter,
Grandad's annihilation.

3

Still with us, at Friedrichstrasse
Station, as the electric train
Slides under East Berlin, a woman sits
Looking inward, by the window
Reflecting tunnels, reflecting intervals

Of darkness and light, her own face
Of private feelings, efforts
At self-control. . .
                    And now the checkpoint.
The electric train decelerates,
Stops. Politics extraverts
The soul of neutrality
In everyone, passionless under
Scrutiny by a blond Commmunist guard
In uniform. People in transit
Study the slogans, Brecht's writings
On both sides of the Wall, interpretations
Enemies told to die for –
The same poem.
                    No way back
Through the door with only one handle
History put there. . . old people
Pass through, wave goodbye
To Western relations, to fourteen days
Compassionate leave, disappear
In their own city, anonymous
Among streetcars and tramlines, scarcities
And huge queues, resuming
Inner life, priorities of love.

4
Where these two met, the streetcorner
Entered history. . . a shopfront
Collapses there, smashed in the Russian advance
On East Berlin, a plaque

On the brickwork
Gleams brazenly.
                    Under unthreatening skies
In the heat of August, Nineteen Seventy Eight,
I pass construction workers

Drilling, making sense
Of the rubble of World War Two, with the Wall
A few streets west, at this meeting-place
Of Marx and Engles, theory and consequence.

5

Ruins of 1945. . . and where
Something classic survived –
A flight of marble stairs –
Grey buildings are revived

Around it, grey streets
Lonely with immigrant workers
Approach it, entreating
Casual sex from the barkers

In the doorway. . . Upstairs
On professional floors
Analysts thrive, repairing
Traumas of two World Wars

Behind closed doors.
All peacetime, footsteps echo
On the marble stairs –
Prices are mentioned, check-ins

Check out, the landings
Hear phrases, concerning rooms,
From student lovers.
                              Understanding,
The janitor with his broom

Eavesdrops on excesses,
Wishes them in hell
From the black recesses
Of history, marble stairwells.

DROIT DE SEIGNEUR

I feel like the ghost of myself
In this day and age. . . a darkening of the mind
On summer evenings, turns me loose
In a blue car, as old as the Seventies are,

The Inherited Boundaries

To seek abandonment, in the Ward
Of Lord Fitzwilliam, haunted by women
Who emerge, from their own shadows,
To greet me.
              Here comes aristocracy
They flutter among themselves, the ladies of the night
Like apparitions. . . this is our meeting-ground,
This, and featureless rooms
Defeating memory, schizophrenic houses
Where the conscious life of Ireland
Is asleep, divided by next to nothing
From its own ghosts – the hushed incarnations
Of womanhood, spectres of impotence
In the dark, inhabiting the dreams
Of student and clerk. . .
                      The blue revolving lights
Of the Vice Squad, blazoning night
Into zones of patrol, create artificial day
In the dark through which I drive
With a hunted look, and her beside me
Like second nature, until I can put an end
To this rendezvous, become lonely again
Within the law of the land.

Dermot Bolger

THE WOMAN'S DAUGHTER

I
take down your dress and rock in my arms
the night's opening up I've come back
schoolgirls in dried up light push prams
for grandmothers to mind up the cul-de-sac

don't hide in a heap under the window
where the shutters flutter back and forth
like hands wanking your father in a seat
down the Casino's fleapits for a coort

eyes blink in the screen's spliced light
like a frozen dragon he breathes on my neck
he squeezes my body like I'm squeezing you
projector whirling as he shuddered and we left

an ambulance washed the street in blue and white
as we walked from the cinema through Ballygall
would my father know I was not in a friend's house
locked up here daughter you're safe from it all

II
between the bowls of light along the street
shadows of branches fork out like a tongue
under a hedge he pulled down my tights
and covered my mouth when the nettles stung

that's how we were sneezed into life
in a mixture of blood and of brambles
the feel of him shoveling up me
like a window caved in by vandals

the splinters jabbing into my flesh
when he helped me up from the ground
his hands skimming over his property
the jets of nails slowly touching down

I stop screaming and lie on the bedroom floor
someone lowers the radio again for my mother
my father puts his belt up and locks the door
the key blinks like one man winking to another

III
are you asleep daughter are you dead
the slight pause between each breath
stabs at me it's how I'll find you soon
a skeleton laid out in a habit of flesh

a starched corpse in the morning
with a clot of blood in an artery
crying through stiff lips for an explanation
beyond the official autopsy

a wreath of sunlight marking the raw skin
where I stretched you like a drum over my knee
beating the quiet fury out of my limbs
'I'll make a man out of you or a man out of me'

you'll lie the way I lay the night you were conceived
when my father took his belt down and the buckle sang
you'll lie the way I lay under the belly of the trees
impaled upon a branch in the shape of a man

IV
moonlight is like the sun through a filter
and locking your door on my way to work
as if looking at a negative choices are clearer
I think of the paths our lives could have took

to leave you alone and walk through the factory
machines spitting out rods and swallowing steel
and wonder how you spend your hours asleep while
the conveyor belt rolls like a giant orange peel

Dermot Bolger

to find you one morning with your skull caved in
and your body gummed to the mattress with blood
and hurry through streets in terror of footsteps
or in the starkness of morning realise we could

walk where seabirds rise up like an explosion before us
and light is sucked in along with the tide
grains of sand blown like sugar on your lips as we touch
like schoolgirls taking a boy's hand and swallowing their pride

CAPTAIN OF A SPACE SHIP

I pace upon the battlements and stare Yeats

I: morning

below concrete clouds
on a level with my eyes
the seagulls cry with
white electric noise

I'm watching from the balcony
of a high rise block
roads quiet as veins
when blood has stopped

it's freezing at this hour
as I huddle in my coat
Captain of a space ship
that never got afloat

when the first bus moves
from its terminus
sweet lord of morning
remember us

who watch from windows
the cars arm in arm
squinted out into lanes
from this fertility farm

or the kids skipping school
climbing into a field
beyone the estate
for a kiss and a feel

I send them the love
of these fifty years
but it's my experience
that needs to be shared

at this table all night
I've tried to find words
for the wounds of Liverpool
to somehow be cured

or the doss houses in Scotland
or drying out in the smoke
I fed them my life story
but the words never spoke

my poems are a bulb
in a subway at night
for those walking to work
they are swallowed by the light

only those in their boredom
who smash at the bulb
know the splinters of glass
have the outline of blood

II: afternoon

at half two this afternoon
a child climbed on a ledge
her face like a slapped arse
red with cold as she fell

a space capsule trailing
a parachute of skirt
explodes as it re-enters
the tarmacadam earth

Dermot Bolger

the red tape of traffic
collared on the roundabout
like a cobra eating itself
untouched by the fall-out

her mother late from work
climbing the beanstalk
reaches the 15th floor
exhausted from her walk

I'm watching from this window
my throat and palms are dry
but my eyes are bloodshot
and look towards the sky

III: night

later alone in my bedroom
when I turned out the light
ribs of coathangers shivered
like teeth through the night

noise of the flat downstairs
drifted round me as I lay
like a plug that had fused
like the word becoming clay

at such times I must imagine
how it will be when it comes
like rain's tapping to the deaf
or sudden language to the dumb

or some blind person waking
in a drenched green morning
watching from my crow's nest
for the land that is calling

through a gap in the blinds
I see my space ship dock
in clusters of green lights
it hovers by the tower block

every night from this window
I step on board verse-craft
the words igniting my mind
steer me safely in the dark

THE COUNTRY GIRL

1: September 1980

Sandra sleepless in a strange bedroom
slides her nightdress down her thighs
a cool fridge opening on a hot afternoon

moonlight like glistening butter spreads
ripening her flesh in pimples of fear
moist tremblings unbalance her legs

kneeling over a chair she hangs the cane
from the bundled folds of the nightdress
a changing world's only constant is pain

she's frozen there imagining the swish
breaking the static of the blocked-up night
surrendering awkwardly to a childish wish

Body: let this steel dam never burst
keep panic jammed in circuits of blood
may this first night in Dublin be enough
rooted here in terror like a two-prong plug

II: December 1980

to him she's polished as a carved doll
he smiles at the creeper of hair on her lip
like a mouse quivering warm and beautiful

yet no matter how close they are in the pub
he's suddenly a stranger when the light's out
and she feels him in the bed pushing at her

Dermot Bolger

a forked branch in some farmer's hands
sensing liquid and plunging downwards
towards legs spread like a boomerang

returning always to this forest of flats
above the city she will never call home
she hears a radio somewhere in the dark

'treat me right, treat me good,
treat me like you always should
for I'm not made of wood
and I don't have a wooden heart'

III: March 1981

when the white anger of a bulb dies
above the bed where they are sleeping
and the dark is straining for noise

in the moist forest of her pubic hair
minute insects drag a split end
across the mattress to their lair

she is no less beautiful by this erosion
of skin fragments to feed thousands
her breath is endless damp explosions

across the starched white globe
like an autumn wind bringing rain
to those living inside her pillow

love's actuality like a rubber sheath
comes between those who cannot feel it
as the loose sands form into concrete

we see the falsity in trying to pretend
cutting like a blade along the tongue
next morning he's like any lover or friend

The Inherited Boundaries

IV: June 1981· holidays, Spain

tired of waiting for him to shave
she pushes through the older crowd
lying in swimsuits near the cafes

all this week his eyes would shift
along the beach of topless girls
in the sea she reached for his grip

as naked bodies burnt to bronze
suddenly a wave cut between them
out of his depth his support had gone

an insect tearing itself from the bark
her wooden face blushes into a smile
as she reveals white borders under straps

Sandra shy on a Spanish afternoon
slides her briefs down her thighs
wiggles casually from her cocoon

as she kneels sun strikes her flesh
like moonlight through slitted blinds
opening like fingers over a scared face

words fade on the ancient headstone
of a postcard trampled into the sand
– lovely weather – long way from home –

FINGLAS LILIES

1: the party, June 1970

a girl lying in the grass
screaming at the houses
rain soaking her back

Dermot Bolger

flocks of leaves swarming
above us like water lilies
spread over a sunken garden

light in a streak of stubble
an unshaven morning surfaces
jaded and looking for trouble

her hair in sprays of seaweed
salty and drenched to touch —
like a song of clubbed seals

a girl lying in the grass
screaming at the houses
rain answering her back

II: December 1980

a tiny flat in West London
we live on frozen food
make friends across the landing

at night she often cries
we make love softly for
fear of waking the child

developing like a negative
in the pit of her stomach
we finally call her relatives

on the night crossing Dublin rose
a thick black curtain over a light
with thousands of bullet holes

like a famine child full of emptiness
she is so swollen by our honeymoon
she consummates marriage with her lips

III: February 1981

steel winds at dawn sting like a wasp
in this factory where men are cursing
and rust grows like hair on a corpse

she's off to work as I finish night-shift
today is our child's first birthday
I'll put his name on the housing list

taking a chair I sit in the garden
smoking Moroccan dope and tripping
the housing estate is disappearing

I feel I'm at the bottom of a pond
floating below rows of water lilies
with new names like Finglas & Ballymun

THE SINGER

III: Jan 1981

he woke next morning in the park
like a cloth frozen on a line
his vision slowly going dark

he welcomed the icy solidness
as rows of railings emerged
like ribs sliding from decayed flesh

a bulldozer lifting a skirt of glass
& cupping a firm breast of earth
plunged indifferently as he passed

through soil corrugated like a moonscape
he climbed stiffly through waves of air
from the crater to the planet's surface

later I would dream about that park
my dead child in a nightdress runs on grass
music comes from each house in the dark

streets stood like seats in a concert hall
every window was open every note beautiful
this symphony of anger was common to all

MY HEAD BURIED in the shelter of your hair I see
you walk under softblown trees in a blond morning
through glass doors into the disinfected hospital

behind drawn screens all night she has watched
the pulse draining from her blue flex of veins
strapped to frayed wrists beating for attention

she stares at the morning as if it might vanish
with naked feet stuck through the cot railings
dying within the terrible shadow of that promise

you did not turn from thin arms drawing you down
to the dried lips of a spinster in a child's form
your kiss rinsed away the loneliness of her vigil

I raise my head until your slow hair rustles back
shaking I hold you and those lips part under mine
your eyes show me that old women succumb to death

as she saw life in them crumble into a blind trust
death's burden carried from her in a moist seed
blossoming into life when our tongues slowly touch

STARDUST SEQUENCE

I

SHADOWS WHISPER A new language of possibilities
from hidden couplets telling us we are not alone
in searching for excitement and that indefinable
solidarity encountered by creating our own world
through steel shutters clasped across windows
the music invents a vocabulary that becomes ours

Strobelights on the walls beat up the air until
the brain keeps pace with the body's discovery

of roles in this disjointed black & white movie
Fridays you would laugh and dance away the hours
in gathering tempo until the cold shower of light
evicted you from a place that was never fully yours

Dropped into the silence you'd doss or go home
among couples & groups of girls singing of love
Tomorrow you will wander these incubator estates
and stare disbelieving at the brutality of dawn
at a people numbed into this silent testimony
with only cold anger left to begin a new existence

II

LAST NIGHT IN swirling colour we danced again
and as strobelights stunned in black and white
I reached in this agony of slow motion for you
but you danced on as if cold light still shone
merging into the crowd as my path was blocked
by snarling bouncers & the dead eyed club owner

When I screamed across the music nobody heard
I flailed under spotlights like a disco danger
and they formed a circle clapping to the beat
as I shuddered round the club in a violent fit
hurling through a dream without trembling awake
I revolved through space until I hit the ground

Lying among their feet tramping out the tunes
I grasped you inside my mind for this moment
your white dress bobbing in a cool candleflame
illuminating the darkness spinning towards me
a teenage dancing queen proud of her footwork
sparks rising like stardust all over the floor

III

WE ARE HERE along the edge of people's memories
a reference point in the calendar of their lives
our absence linked with acceptances or refusals
on summer evenings when love seemed attainable

and moist lips opened after dances in the parks
we are the unavoidable stillbirth of your past

That golden girl you loved pregnant at seventeen
your friends growing sour paralysed by the dole
your senile boss already rotting inside his skin
returns the look of hatred that's burning you up
drawing new breath from every young life wrecked
all those smooth men who would quietly forget us

who turn you on a spit over cold flames of dissent
are guilty of murder as if they chained the exits
when we stamped through their illusion of order
we have buried in your skull these ashes of doubt
and you believe nothing but one slow fuse of anger
since the night your thin candle of youth ran out

EPILOGUE

CHILD SAINT IN her boxed black vacuum   mercuried blood
weighing closed veins   single eye stupidly open   stagnant
skin incorrupt   inhuman

these wasted years while a century folded here nothing
happened   now let earth creak through   noise of clay   blind
inquisitiveness of worms   till in this wooden container under
a crust of earth meat bubbles through slow motion into blisters
of decay

let rib and skull emerge like this sleeping girl's flesh   gleaming
through dark into dawn   where I learn to touch the scar where
surgery kept a breast   the seam of stitches she tried to hide

do not shiver as if my fingers were ice   open your eyes loosely
into the risk of day   without mourning this miracle of
survival   pity those souls crippled through fear of the knife's
continuing life   the uncompromising worms' teeth promising
eternity

THE MAN WHO STEPPED OUT OF FEELING

I

folded hands darkening under the descent of the lid
the widow burying me under her body in the black room
    my child's eyes indifferent to the hammering nails
drawn out by skilled lips sucking youth from my hunger
    the brain shrinks back uncomprehending into fantasy
as her dried flesh spread across my summer in a cloud
    until that first betrayal of neglecting her memory
breaking her labia's grip with the strength she endowed

II

at night when I scream I wake and the sheets are torn
her hurt face leans over my dreams aged and abandoned
pursuing me as I fell through years real as nightmares
the dry insatiable flame on my throat mistaken for life
freezing under the heat of a tough man's leather jacket
running halfborn through the most helpless of nights

III

under neon clusters of leaves shone like stars exploding
streets echoed a mass of dead footsteps as I'd come down
so drunk and rigid with terror I would only be connected
by a silvergreen flex of urine earthing me to the ground

AMSTERDAM

he woke up at once and there was nothing he could feel
he switched on the light to make sure the girl had gone
the night air was humming like a shot had just torn it
he washed in icecold water and put his business suit on

the cocaine was strapped in bandages across his ribcage
the false handle of the briefcase opened just to his touch
he took a taxi from the hotel and the driver was singing
the airport officals saluted as he strode through the crush

if he could feel anything he would have remembered dreaming
of the taxi ride that was always supposed to bring him home
but turned instead in silence down an anonymous walled road
and stopped amid ranks of tombstones in a grey lifting dawn

This is as far as you take me. This is it. He spoke finally.
You catch on faster than most. The waiting driver replied.
But already he has forgotten as wings slice through air
he stares through shades at the earth rolling to one side.

THE GHOSTS IN THE ARK

Just before we slept your tongue crept into my mouth
I dreamt inside its aftertaste of a tide sifting out
And when I woke I was terrified you were taken from me
I pressed myself against your body waking you with my urgency
The room above your head was filled with the arms of men
From a foreign city in your dream holding you down again
Your body shuddered feeling mine lost between two worlds
And you gazed up at me fearfully not knowing who I was

Through your pupils I could see myself exhausted and anxious
But occluded from those memories that set adrift your brain
The future balanced while I tried to still your restlessness
And in my failure the post came crashing against our tiny ark
Now each time you open yourself to love the old pain rushes in
and ghosts hover like circling birds waiting to claim you back

SCARECROW

Another night alone when the price of sleep is too high
a scarecrow in the bare window of your one roomed flat
watching for the wren ensnared in her invisible cage
whose wings once flew above this soaring eagle's back:
now they have been smothered under a blue hospital gown
you are more naked than when you nested here in my arms.

Another night when a nurse's footsteps torture your mind
the whimpering girl and the old woman drugged into sleep
a saviour's arms nailed to the straightjacket of a cross
above the bed where thoughts are limbs straining to link:
we wait for day break to count the steps down the corridor
leaning to walk again from your ward to the locked window.

Grey moths of light press themselves against the glass
erasing the dark pain that bound your memories of love
come to me with skin shredded by the scalpel of drugs
I will be a skeleton drowning in the plankton of light
when we try to kiss our teeth scrape in a numb embrace
we will long to feel pain, suffering, anything of life.

FRANKENSTEIN IN THE MARKETS

the flickknife's steel wings unfurl in the man's palm
as he slices the slab of hash on the swaying tabletop
a nation of outcasts sown together by blazing eyelids
in this market flat where a burning altospy never stops
below in the street refrigerated lorries hum all night
ambulances spurt blue flames down shrunken passageways
where whores on stilts are picked up in the headlights

I reach the quays where the tide has been dredged out
and find on the webbed riverbed a monster's footprint
crippled with loneliness he tilts through the streets
confused by a dozen dismembered lives which he links:
Speak to me somebody! his limbs keep trying to gesture
blind child touch me with the lightening of your fingers
let coffined eyes come to life in the electrified air.

Dermot Bolger

BLUEBELLS FOR GRAINNE

Through the shuttered light of the blinking trees we race
then the van mounts the corner into the sleeping hamlet
where we climb down lightheaded after a night's drinking
for a final siesta before we part on our ultimate journeys.
The old driver arranges flowers in the folds of your dress
as we laze against the sunlit church indulgent in this day
that hangs like a kite we must finger lightly to keep alfoat
and soaring up under our weight of intimate memories and
    hopes.

Often the nights fell so dark we felt destined to collide
but we clung on at every hairbend to sit here now singing
the subversive song of friendship that flowers underneath
the schedules commanding us to vanish in a swirl of dust:
when it settles remember me grinning idiotically up at you
in a spring dress with bluebells spilling from your breast.

1966

> 'The bells of the midday angelus, ringing over Dublin and
> the country on this Easter Sunday, will carry, as well as a
> call to prayer, a special note of triumph and joy befitting
> the occasion of the Golden Jubilee of the Rising of 1916,
> that is being marked with pageantry and spectacle. Gun
> salutes, the rousing strains of marshal music and the sweep
> of jets from the Irish Corps will swoop out of the centre
> of the city.' *10th April, 1966*

> '*Drugs in City Beat Clubs:* It is well known to Gardai that
> boys and girls in their early teens are paying from 2s/6d
> to 5s for single "reefers" (cigarettes tipped with certain
> drugs) and 5s a cup for shot coffee.' *9th October 1966.*

An ordered ocean of flags swaying at dawn
We shall march forth to meet with destiny

Gold banners between houses in every town
We shall march forth to meet with destiny

The Inherited Boundaries

Their medals glinting in the ageing ranks
The survivors marched past the monuments
Faces proud and stiff in each camera lens
We shall march forth to meet with destiny

An ordered sea of feet among littered bread
We shall march forth to meet with destiny

Gulls shriek as teachers drill us into step
We shall march forth to meet with destiny

We paraded in line towards the wooden desks
Past a framed proclamation and a cruxifix
And begged God that our turn would be next
We shall march forth to meet with destinty

A tide of rhetoric flooding the platforms
We shall march forth to meet with destiny

Engraining a sense of duty into our bones
We shall march forth to meet with destiny

Images of snared men racing through flame
Left the incomplete ache of a phantom pain
But through our blood they would be freed
When we marched forth to meet with destiny

We would march forth to meet with destiny

DUBLIN GIRL, MOUNTJOY, 1984
do Nuala

I dreamt it all, from end to end, the carriageway,
The rivulet behind the dairy streaked with crystal,
A steel moon glinting in a guttered stream of rain,
and the steep hill that I would crest to find her.
My child asleep in my old bedroom beside my sister.

Dermot Bolger

I dreamt it all, and when I woke, furtive girls
Were clambering onto the bars of the windows,
White shapes waving against the sky's uniform
Praying for hands to reply from the men's cells
Before screws broke up the vigil of handkerchiefs.

I dreamt it all, the times I swore, never again
To walk that carriageway, a rivulet of gear glowing
In my veins until I shivered within its aftertaste
And hid with my child in the closed-down factory
Where my brain snapped like a brittle fingernail.

I dreamt it all, the longing to touch, the seance
In the cell when we screamed at the picture falling,
The warmth of circled hands after the numbing glass
Between my child and me, a warder following her words
To be rationed out and lived off for days afterwards.

I dreamt of you, who means all to me, my daughter,
How we might run to that carriageway by the rivulet,
And when I woke a blue pupil was patrolling my sleep,
Jailing my dreams into the vacant orbit of its world
Narrowed down to a spyhole, a globed eyelid closing.

SNUFF MOVIES

The wind shuffles through the cracked glass and the floorboards
    rot.
It has been eight days since I stepped outside this filthy flat
where I've sat watching and four times my vigil has been
    rewarded:
four times I have hung within the limbo of the static from the
    tube,
longing for release and yet not daring to believe it could happen,
and four times the picture hasn't jerked back on to
    advertisements –
my throat has dried up and my body trembled as I watched
the figure thrown naked into the room and the beating begin.

The Inherited Boundaries

Whole days wither stagnantly in this flat and nothing happens,
days when I'm stuck like an insect on fly paper unable to move,
trapped within the metallic hiss of that ocean of static,
and I wait and pray that the advertisements will not continue
as over and over the slogans repeat without commentary or pity,
hammering out messages at those remaining sealed in their
    rooms.
Once we walked down streets and worked in throbbing
    factories,
I remember oil on my overalls and the smell of sweat without
    fear,
but then the coalitions collapsed and regrouped and were
    submerged
by the corporations who had learnt how to survive without us.
Just four times the knife has flashed like an old matador's
and the youngsters raised their heads although blinded by the
    hood.
There is no way of knowing how many of my workmates are left,
caged up before crackling boxes terrified to miss the murders.
Last month I saw a man run with a plastic bag through the litter,
apart from him all streets to the superstore were deserted.
I breathe safely – I am too old for anybody's attention,
they will never come and shove me hooded into that studio,
I will never strain my head forward in expectation of the blow.
From this final refuge I can spy and be involved in their agony,
the flesh wincing and that final anonymous moan of pain;
and afterwards I breathe again in my renewed triumph of living.
Nobody knows any longer when the curfew begins or ends
but one evening I heard them come for somebody on the street.
I never knew which hooded neighbour I might have once passed
kept the whole of Ireland contained for a day with their death.
I know they are killing me too in this war of nerves I survive in,
It's been years since I've not slept sitting upright in this chair
dreaming of blood and waking fretfully to advertisements,
and yet I still cling on, speaking to nobody in the superstore,
running home frantic that I will miss a final glimpse of life.
Long ago I believed in God – now I believe what I am told:
there is no heaven except that instant when the screen comes
    alive,
no purgatory except the ceaseless static bombarding the screen,
hell could only be if they came for the television or for me.

Michael O'Loughlin

THE CITY
(after Cavafy)

You say you will leave this place
And take yourself off to God-knows-where
A Galway cottage, a village in Greece,
– Anywhere but here:
Paris, Alexandria, Finglas
The grey eroding suburb
Where you squandered the coin of your youth.
You wander down to the carriageway
And watch the lorries speeding by.
Swooning in their slipstreams
You raise your eyes in a tropical dream
To the aeroplanes overhead.

But too late you realize
that you shall never leave here!
This, or next, or any other year.
You shall pass your life, grow old
In the same suburban lounge bars
Draining the dregs of local beers
Fingering a coin in your otherwise empty pockets.
And no matter how you toss it
It always turns up the same:
The plastic sun of Finglas
Squatting on every horizon.
The squandered coin of your youth!
The slot machines you fed have rung up blanks
Not just here, but everywhere.

The Inherited Boundaries

COPENHAGEN DREAMING OF LENINGRAD

Warszava, the plaintive flute of the East,
Its ancient wooden melody bent
To the cello and drums of Moscow.

Over the drunken green Baltic
A black wind full of snow
Carries the straining orchestra.

Like the sand shifting beneath the waves,
Like the slash of flesh on bone!
Warszava, Warszava, I am drunk with your name

Till the glass-green Baltic floods
Like the mind of a mad composer
With the wind's unplayable melody

And the mountains scale the ground
To a symphony's frozen climax!
The note is held and then begins

The slow bass beat of Stadt and Grad
– A shimmer, the water is frozen:
Seductive and brutal as massed violins
The choral cathedral of Lenin!

CUCHULAINN

If I lived in this place for a thousand years
I could never construe you, Cuchulainn.
Your name is a fossil, a petrified tree
Your name means less than nothing.
Less than Librium, or Burton's Biscuits
Or Phoenix Audio-Visual Systems –
I have never heard it whispered
By the wind in the telegraph wires
Or seen it scrawled on the wall
At the back of the children's playground.

Michael O'Loughlin

Your name means less than nothing
To the housewife adrift in the Shopping Centre
At eleven-fifteen on a Tuesday morning
With the wind blowing fragments of concrete
Into eyes already battered and bruised
By four tightening walls
In a flat in a tower-block
Named after an Irish Patriot
Who died with your name on his lips.
But watching TV the other night
I began to construe you, Cuchulainn;
You came on like some corny revenant
In a black-and-white made for TV
American Sci-Fi serial.
An obvious Martian in human disguise
You stomped about in big boots
With a face perpetually puzzled and strained
And your deep voice booms full of capital letters:
What Is This Thing You Earthlings Speak Of

BABEL

She is a language I will never speak
– great is my sorrow this night.
I will never whiten a wall for her
nor make the grass grow greener.
Her skin was the colour of honey
stored by the bees in the damp river bank
– where the sun himself had not kissed her
it was cream in a cool stone kitchen
in the stillness of a summer's day.

In the purple dusk by the walled-in river
she glowed as she stood in the street
I had never seen such a sight before
and even the traffic parted that she might pass.
Great was the sorrow I could not speak
in the room where we sat that night
– as a man who stands upon a hill
in a place of ancient renown

and hears a phrase of a song
float up from the valley below
like a wisp of white smoke
from a sacred fire
that burns in the sun at noon
– and he knows not what it speaks of
nor learning nor lonesome quest
through dusty book and library
shall be of any use to him.
Blessed is he who is her song!
Blessed with her skin of honey and cream
her perfect instep of soft kid's leather
and thigh like a pillar wrought
by some miraculous Greek.

Blessed is he, and cursed am I
with nothing to keep me from madness and death
but this dull unlovely translation!

YELLOW

I stamped through the pastures
booting the heads off buttercups
I stormed in out of the wheatfield
into a country kitchen
and let out my gurrier roar:
'Yellah! Yellah! Yellah!'
But she took me on her knee
and said: no, it's yellow.
I glowed, I echoed yellow
but that was a colour
I had never seen
till I saw her stretched on a hospital bed
the yellow of cancer and nicotine

Michael O'Loughlin

THE IRISH LESSON

I thank the goodness and the grace
That on my birth have smiled,
And made me in these Christian times
A happy English child.

All I cared about was words
but I wouldn't learn their language;
they forced it down my five-year-old throat
I spat it back in their faces

I don't want to learn their language
It wasn't mine

When I got too old to fear them
they appealed to a baser emotion;
I was cutting myself off
from a part of the nation's heritage

but I didn't want to know their nation's heritage
it wasn't mine

'But Mr. O'Loughlin, you're not being fair
to yourself, you know you can do better
than this. And don't forget
you'll need it for the Civil Service'

but I didn't want to join the Civil Service

I still don't

THE FUGITIVE

In the hour before the Metro opens
I remember you, Richard Kimble
With my hands dug deep in my jacket pockets
Walking the streets of a foreign city.

The Inherited Boundaries

Tonight I suddenly remember it all –
the damp winter nights in Dublin
The living room with the curtain undrawn
And the streetlight spilling in

And myself, silent, hypnotised
Stretched out on the orange lino
Lost in the numinous images
Of the TV's black and white glow

And scarred by smoke and city dawns,
The muffled snarl of American accents
Coming in loud and razor sharp
Over the local interference.

I can't remember the stories now
But in the end it's only the ikons that matter,
The silent, anonymous, American city
With the rain running down the gutter

And the snatched glimpse of the one-armed man
Sinking back into the shadows,
The real victim, the truly guilty,
the man you're destined to follow.

This life, this city fits me
Like an old leather jacket
Picked up for nothing
In a second-hand market

And I light up a cigarette
Relaxing in the casual rhyme
That floats through the city
Binding other lives to mine

And like so many times before
I turn up my collar against the wind
And walk off down the dark side of the street
Dreaming already of another town

Remembering you, Richard Kimble
And the way you taught me to live;
Ending another forgotten episode
Still myself, still the Fugitive.

A LETTER FROM BARCELONA, 1937

I realised today we were going to lose the war.
It came over me suddenly while I was reading the paper
That I'd bought at a kiosk at the top of the Ramblas.
We were going to lose the war.
I flipped back frantically through the flimsy pages
Trying to find the word, the sentence
The fact that had swayed me;
But there was nothing.
Everywhere we were triumphant,
Victories in Aragon, the heroic defence of Madrid.
But I knew we were going to lose
And I suddenly saw how few we had grown
How the bootblacks were back on the street
With plenty of customers
And the restaurants were brightly lit
And full of well-dressed people.
I walked all day through the back streets of Gracia
And saw the hunted look on the anarchists' faces.
We're going to lose.
I cannot imagine what's going to come after.
Darkness falls on Montjuic.
Barcelona sleeps.
I got your letter three days ago.
Why? How? Who is he?

TWO WOMEN

Nadezhda Mandelstam

In the damp brown evening of early winter
I see him stumbling along through the frozen mud
Across the bridge at the edge of town
With nothing but the broken harp of himself
On the forced march of days
Towards a battle he'd rather avoid
With his life, his hope,
Trudging a long way behind him
His music held tight in her aching fingers.

Lotte Lenya

Give her a tune and she'll break it they said
And she did, just like the world that she lived in.
The boys in the leather jackets
Were hardly surprised to find her
The goddess with the nightclub sneer
And a voice like the ruins of Berlin
Because no matter what they played on the radio
Day followed day like notes
In harsh, unheard-of harmonies
Where the tune can only survive
On the black bread of love.

DECLASSE MEMORY

The smell of sawdust, the zing and muffled
Scream of the saw rattling into wood
Came out through an open doorway
As I passed by to work today
And there in the streets of Gracia
I was suddenly convulsed with nostalgia
For a world I never knew I'd left
and I stood there transfixed, bereft
Unable to imagine that that world was gone

Michael O'Loughlin

And I was on the outside looking in
Through the multi-coloured haze
Of petrol fumes in the choking summer days
When I travelled with my uncles
Around the Dublin sawmills
And various wholesale suppliers
Of Fine Quality Imitation Leathers.
The commercial travellers, especially, I loved
So casual and neat and stylishly dressed
Driving around in fairly new cars
Distributing largess of pin-up calendars;
Silver Ronsons and packets of Twenty Carrolls
In hand, they discussed the latest models
For hours on end, filling in time with stories
And gossip picked up in the factories
Who was doing well, who had pulled a dirty one
Like a postman gossiping with old parish women.
Smoothly as the music on the background radio
The afternoon flowed on towards a world I didn't know
Of drinks with the lads, and poker and darts
And serious talk about football and cars
Or else to the solemn amusements
Of a man and his commitments
Almost-new wives and brand-new houses
Mortgages, extensions, and higher purchase.
I stood there, silent, listening to it all
Surrounded by the smells of creosote and petrol
And breathing in that powerful fragrance
I caught my first glimpse of a man's inheritance.
Everything seemed so solid, immutable
Upper working class rising into lower middle
You did your job and you earned your pay
Maybe start up on your own someday
And politicians all a bunch of crooks
Or else they wouldn't be in politics
But say what you like, Johnny's one of our own
Just tip him the wink and consider it done
And every sunday, joking and half-embarrassed
Standing at the back of Twelve O'Clock Mass —
But the feeling of loss and the lump in my throat
Defy all attempts to deflate it.

The Inherited Boundaries

I did lose something, something of worth
And for what? For Ingmar Bergman and Jean-Paul Sartre
For Education, Culture, a place in the Vanguard
For standing around like a lord's bastard
Remembering smells and things from my childhood
Punched in the throat by a lost world.
But I rejected my patrimony and now it's too late
I've got another call to make
And I move off through the mediterranean evening
Sweating in my heavy Irish clothing
To give a class in English conversation
To a fat, racist, Catalan businessman.

VENUS IN CONCRETE

I'm standing at the bus stop at the shopping centre
Facing the camera, slightly right of,
The background is the concrete wall
That runs down to the Bank of Ireland
Behind me the Venus de Milo
Grows out of the bricks at a crazy angle
The passers-by don't even notice
And then I realise it's not on camera
It's a portrait I've painted of myself
And then I know it's a dream
But I've never awoken out of this dream
Merely embellished, allowed it to seep
Through my life, smoothing it out like acrylic
And the dream flowed into words
Lifting them off the page
Like people stepping out of a TV screen
And Heaven, what was Heaven, for example?
It was a cool gallery, modern and white
With powerful lighting and a glossy catalogue
And a girl attendant who was something I can't remember
And I can't remember, barely able
To distinguish the fantasy from the dream
The dream from mutating reality
And it's like the evening in Finglas
When everything's quiet

ncomprehensible mountains
Visible over Finglas South
And the concrete strains against the dusk
and it's like reading a bad translation
Of a poem by a great Czechoslovakian poet. . .
Like ice in the river, that's what we're like
That's what I tell myself day after day
Standing in the Metro on my way to work
Walking from bar to bar –
Like ice in the river, that's what I say
What does it matter, the drip
Of the sailor's tears in the ocean?
And I think of the image and what it's worth
And realise that even here
Obscurity is sometimes acceptable
Like Natasha and Sonia in *War and Peace*
Who never mentioned Prince Andrei
Because his memory was too sacred
And one day found they'd forgotten him
I no longer know which is the truth
And which is the dream
Except what I need
And I need to believe that this is me
Walking the streets
Pacing the walls of the English language
Looking for the chink in the concrete
That will let in my own light. . .

THE SHARDS

I. THE BUNKERS

Along the great coast south of Bordeaux
The bunkers still stare out to sea
High-water marks of the black wave
That swept up out of the sump of Europe.
Untouched, they stand, undying monuments,
Easter Island heads in cold concrete.

On the side of one I found
Some Gothic lettering, black paint
That hadn't faded in the years of sun and wind.
But the blonde naked daughters
Sleep rough in them during the summer nights
And in the morning run laughing
Into the ocean their fathers had scanned.

II. FRANK RYAN DEAD IN DRESDEN

The idea armed, like Ernie O'Malley
Another emerald-green incorruptible
Of course there was no place for the likes of you!
When you came bounding out of the prison camps
To join the shuffling battalions
Into the civil service offices
They gave you a job writing tourist brochures.
'Killarney is famous the wide world over
for the magnificent splendour
of its mountains and lakes. . .'
And after, marched off into the night
To practise the illegal alchemy
Of slogans and heavy printer's ink.
Now it speeds up. A handsome head, in uniform.
Then defeat. The tale grows complex.
Europe dividing under your feet.
Conspiracies, betrayals, and all the rest.
In that last passport photo taken in Berlin
You look like Rembrandt in his last self-portrait.
There is much there I don't know, nor want to.
You followed your river into the sea,
And drowned while your funeral pyre
Lit up the skies for a hundred miles around.

III. FROM A DIARY

I seem to have travelled this landscape for years.
Brown hulks of deserted factories, the dark wounds
Of their shattered windows, fragments of glass
Defying the wind. The yellow blocks of flats
And behind them the endless ordered fields

Michael O'Loughlin

Flecked with rusted iron.
The train slowed down near a flat broad river
And I saw fields full of green machines
Stretching out into the distance,
Tensing on black rubber. A lone sentry
Stood out against the skyline, looking in no
Particular direction. Behind him a filthy grey sky
Floundered into the night.

IV. HEINRICH BÖLL IN IRELAND

We slept through it. A stray bomber,
A black sheep strayed from the pack
Came crackling in out of the watching darkness.
Later, some stumbled across our shores
In search of green poultice
For wounds we couldn't have understood.
There, at last, a small destiny, ours.
This also; the skyways criss-crossed
By peaceful jets, their passengers reading
In magazines about the
Most profitable
Industrial
Location
In Europe.

V. CONCERT-GOING IN VIENNA

Our houses are open tombs that will survive us.
And so are our lives. No one survives a war like that.
That is obvious; also ridiculous.
Our eyes blink in the sullen gleam of the knife
But do not see the submerged balancing weight
Beneath the cutting edge. Tonight, I feel it
The solid drag, the tug and undertow
Of centuries of prosperity, watching
These faces and manners planed by music,
I had not thought death had missed so many.
This woman here in front of me, for instance
In pearls and grey hair in a stately bun
Nodding her head in time to Bruckner's Fourth.

She is not dead, nor am I. The sublime
And gracious she samples as familiar delicacies
And it is churlish of me to criticise this.
But still, I know, from the ranks of satisfied diners
A hungry ghost slips off into the forest
Trying on coats of clay for size.

VI. THE BOYS OF '69

'I don't know we didn't go –
we talked about nothing else.'
But they didn't go, didn't die
On the barricades of '69,
They survived to cushy jobs
In Luxembourg and Brussels.
Cushy but hopeless!
'Sure we hadn't a chance boy!
What do you think!
The French and the Dutch
were already dug in.'
He peels the silver wrapping
Off another bottle of beer.
I watch the alien sun sink red
Behind the blocks of flats.
'Poor Sean! They found his body
out there on the beach. Nothing
ever proved, of course. Never
saw him depressed. A boy
to drink though! He was barred
from the British Embassy
after that night,
I remember it well. . .'
I suddenly see him, poor Sean,
With his Aran sweater
And second-class degree in History
A pale-faced corpse
Drifting like a dead fish
Through a sea of foreign newsprint
Red-bearded idol of a scattered army
Of terylene shirts and expense accounts
In half the capital cities of Europe. . .

VII. THE SHARDS

For months, coming home late at night
We would stop at a traffic light
In the middle of nowhere
And sit there, the engine restless
For the empty motorway
While I looked out at the half-built flyover
That stood in the moonlight
Like a ruined Greek temple
And I suddenly felt surrounded
By the shattered and potent monuments
Of a civilisation we have not yet discovered
The ghost of something stalking us
The future imagined past perhaps
Or else the millions of dead
Rising and falling
Into the mud and carved stone
The ghost of the beast
Whose carapace we inhabit
Not knowing if we stand at the centre
Or circumference
Sensing that shards are our only wholeness
Carefully carving their shattered edges.

AN IRISH REQUIEM

Born in another country, under a different flag
She did not die before her time
Her god never ceased to speak to her.
And so she did not die. The only death that is real
Is when words change their meaning
And that is a death she never knew
Born in another country, under a different flag
When the soldiers and armoured cars
Spilled out of the ballads and onto the screen
Filling the tiny streets, she cried
And wiped her eyes on her apron, mumbling something
About 'the Troubles'. That was a word
I had learned in my history book.

What did I care for the wails of the balding Orpheus
As he watched Eurydice burn in hell?
I was eleven years old,
And my Taoiseach wrote to me,
Born in another country, under a different flag.
She did not die before her time
But went without fuss, into the grave
She had bought and tended herself, with
The priest to say rites at her entry
And the whole family gathered,
Black suits and whiskey, a cortège
Of Ford Avengers inching up the cemetery hill.
Death came as an expected visitor,
A policeman, a rate collector, or the tinker
Who called every spring for fresh eggs,
Announced by the season, or knocks on walls,
Bats flying in and out of rooms, to signify
She did not die before her time
Her god never ceased to speak to her.
Till the last, he murmured in her kitchen
As she knelt at the chair beside the range
Or moved to the damp, unused, parlour,
For the priest's annual visit.
Poète de sept ans, I sat on the polished wood,
Bored by the priest's vernacular harangue
As she knelt beside me on the stone church floor,
And overheard her passionate whisper,
Oblivious, telling her beads, and I knew
That I would remember this, that
Her god never ceased to speak to her.
And so she did not die. The only death that is real
Is when words change their meaning
And that is a death she never knew.
As governments rose and fell, she never doubted
The name of the land she stood on. Nothing
But work and weather darkened the spring days
When she herded her fattened cattle
Onto the waiting cars. It is not she who haunts
But I, milking her life for historical ironies,
Knowing that more than time divides us.

But still her life burns on, like the light
From a distant, extinguished star, and
O let me die before that light goes out
Born in another country, under a different flag!

THE DIARY OF A SILENCE

In Parnell Square it's always raining
On the junk heap of history where I was born
One wet night, in the Rotunda Hospital
While the crowds surged down O'Connell Street
And the shades did cluster round
My state-assisted birth, in this elephant's
Graveyard under grey skies!

The damp, disintegrating houses
Shuffle shoulder to shoulder through time
Stuffed with religious statues and creaking
Rooms, empty, forgotten, memorial halls
Marked by cracked plaques and faded signs
Of chipped gilt over fanlights
Everything living its posthumous existence
Hungering in me for an image
That is not mere archaeology
The casual coupling of history and self.

I probed the city's cracked grey ribs,
Noted the casual irony
Of the tottering Georgian tenements!
But one day they were gone
Thesis devoured by antithesis
Oratory swallowed by irony
Cancelling each other out
Leaving not even an aftertaste
Just silence tensing towards the word
That will define it,
In a language that doesn't yet exist.

The Inherited Boundaries

Where the buildings once had stood
The sky rushed into their virgin spaces
The mad light of Dublin battering my face
The great expressionist winter sky
Where light and dark wrestle like primitive gods
Like complex chemical formulae
Something struggling to become itself.

It has always been like this. What can be said
Is not worth saying, will not still the itch
That has always possessed me, gripped
And held fast from the start
And would not release, or burst into flower
Except suddenly, laboriously,
Like turning the corner into Parnell Square
To see the yellow buses throbbing in the rain
Pristine, orphic; obmutescent.

POSTHUMOUS

Something is pushing against my blood.
From the bus I watch the children
Set fire to sheets of paper
And scatter them, screaming, into the wind.
They burn down to nothing,
A black smudge on the concrete
Bleeding its greyness into the sky.
I think of Siberia, how clean it is.
I move around the city, denounced
To the secret police of popular songs.
A name flares in the darkness.
Moon-sister, twin.
Who are you? I don't know.
My mouth tastes of splintered bone.
I thought I'd left this place a long time ago.

Michael O'Loughlin

SUMMER IN MONAGHAN

my mouth is daubed with black and green!
gulping mouthfuls of dark air
black flags hang from the telegraph poles
I cannot breathe
love lies like a plague on the land
love? the greyness of summer?
(who are these faces, bright
and I think, familiar,
names, old loves, stirring
like nails in their rusty sockets)

a black sea rocks us to sleep

in the morning the darkness lightens
between murderous drumlins
the roads are smeared
with small furred corpses
sometimes a sweet rain washes the air
water colours a faint illusion
(in the dead hiss of a summer's evening
a lake has drifted from Persia)

ON HEARING MICHAEL HARTNETT READ
HIS POETRY IN IRISH

First, the irretrievable arrow of the military road
Drawing a line across all that has gone before
Its language a handful of brutal monosyllables.

By the side of the road the buildings eased up;
The sturdy syntax of castle and barracks,
The rococo flourish of a stately home:

The formal perfection and grace
Of the temples of neoclassical government
The avenues describing an elegant period. Then,

The Inherited Boundaries

The red-brick constructions of a common coin
To be minted in local stone, and beyond them
The fluent sprawl of the demotic suburbs

Tanged with the ice of its bitter nights
Where I dreamt in the shambles of imperial iambs,
Like rows of shattered Georgian houses.

I hear our history on my tongue,
The music of what has happened!
The shanties that huddled around the manor

The kips that cursed under Christchurch Cathedral
Rising like a madrigal into the Dublin sky
– But tonight, for the first time,

I heard the sound
Of the snow falling through moonlight
Onto the empty fields.

THE REAL THING

I shuffled the musty floorboards
Of your emporium, stuffed with baubles
And useless knick-knacks, melancholy
Mechanical toys from Hong Kong, that soon
Fell asunder, scattering pieces of coloured tin
And stone-age plastic all over the house,
Like indecipherable relics.

Where did you come from? I like
To think of you, a grey-bearded shuffler
Peddling your goods all round the Baltic
From Lübeck and Lublin to Dublin
Where the pale children from the nameless
Suburbs gawked at your gaudy mortal balloons
Their fingers and eyes hungry for gewgaws.

Michael O'Loughlin

After the war, you imported thousands
Of plywood fiddles and flogged them
At half-a-crown apiece, to some old fiddler;
Who would take them and bury them in shallow
Graves, in the uncertain soil of Dublin gardens
For six months or more, to resurrect them
Like Viking bones, grown moldy and seasoned
Their ears clogged with gritty earth;
To sell them all summer long
At feises and fleadhs all over the country;
And no one could tell them from the real thing.

IN THE SUBURBS

Closing my eyes I sink down into a darkness
Where your absence is the only presence.
Open again to a shout of light
Two lip-sticked girls, a glass of beer
Push you back into fragile limits.
I leave the bar and move out
Into the raw streets of this half-built suburb
Stepping over virgin pavements
And violated earth
Through a mesh of lives just beginning
And I'm the only prisoner
Of this heavy spring evening, this dull suburb
Unable to mortgage my life to the future.

LATIN AS A FOREIGN LANGUAGE

I suppose I should feel somehow vindicated
  To see our declensions bite deeper
      Than our legionaries' swords—
          But somehow I don't.
      We're a mixed lot here, devils
    To drink; old senatorial types and
Discarded favourites, poets without patrons, etc.

When asked why they're here they might answer
   About duty to the empire, missionary zeal
      Or simply the spirit of adventure–
         All rot, of course.
      No one leaves Rome unless
   He has to, or not exactly because he has to
Like a vulgar soldier in a press-ganged legion

But things somehow conspire to force him out.
   Not all poets find patrons, not all
      Fit smoothly into public life–
         You know how it is.
      One wrong word in the wrong ear,
   One fateful opportunity fluffed, and
You may as well forget it. Who understands these things?

Some say they lie in the lap of the gods but either way
   We end up here in the backwater of the empire
      Drumming our illustrious tongue
         Into barbarian skulls,
      And polishing up the phrases
   Of the oafs who govern in Rome's name.
Like I said, a mixed lot, refugees all from obscure failures.

Some marry local girls, and sprout blonde beards
   And curls overnight. Poor bastards!
      How can they take seriously
         Those bovine bodies
      And gaudy faces lisping bad breath.
   Who could write poetry for such as these?
I think about these things a lot, but come to no conclusion.

During the freezing winter nights sitting round the wine
   And olives, telling tales of sunnier days
      Sucking ancient bits of gossip
         Down to the dry pit
      Cato elaborates his pet theory;
   How Rome will someday crumble to dust
Beneath the barbarian heel, and only our precious language

Michael O'Loughlin

Will survive, a frail silken line flung across the years.
But I don't know. Who among these barbarians
Would give a fart in his bearskin
For Horace or Virgil
Or any of us? All they want is enough
To haggle with a Sicilian merchant, or cheat
The Roman tax collector out of his rightful due.

But late at night, when I stumble out into
The sleet and cold I was not born to
And feel the threatening hug
Of those massive forests
Stuffed with nameless beasts
And the great godless northern sky
Threatening me with its emptiness and indifference

To me and all that are like me – then, sometimes
I think he may be right; that
We are the galley slaves
Sweating below
Bearing the beautiful
Princess who sits in the prow
Across the ocean to her unknown lover.

Matthew Sweeney

A WINTER STORY

In a white room
a woman is stretching
& someone at a mirror
plots a straight parting.
The curtains open
to scarecrow trees.
She rises. He goes out.
The smell is coffee brewing.

A dull story. Let us pass outside.
Breath is ghostly there.
Let's flit through streets
fine as dancers
on a delft plate.
Admire the monuments,
the stone decor.
Note the stain of traffic.

And the theatres half-empty.
Their queues regaled
by a tap-dancing tramp.
The limousines
& the grim graffiti.
This is no background either.
Here is a bar,
the ale is good.

Now let us try again.
An active sector,
banks & plans.
See that window –
the lights stay on all day.

Matthew Sweeney

An old man is whistling
as his drawings gel.
They are long awaited.

And the radios stay on –
a recent development.
There is news expected.
Jobs are available
at the passport office.
and if it's games you need
look above you –
the planes play in squadrons.

No use either! Let's go abroad.
But *is* this abroad?
A shooting-range
in the suburbs of Zurich?
Resort manoeuvres? –
A shower of men
on the Alpine sheet.
And they have no skis.

That room, where was it?
That promising winter story?
Good, we are back there.
The woman is dressed
in a Chinese robe.
She dries her face.
Coffee is ready.
They breakfast; hardly speak.

A DREAM OF MAPS
(for Thomas McCarthy)

What would you say
if I took my dream,
spread it flat
on a table, and asked you
to scour it, pluck out
meanings, & stop my head
throbbing with gusts
of questions?

My dream was a map:
this planet, flat
as pre-Colombus,
all the lands
intact, each one
painted black or white –
after the bomb terrain.

Yes, I saw it
clear as history, white
was the place to be
yet here I am
housed in black.
What would you say
to that, friend?

THE PERMANENT CITY

We call it the permanent city.
We point our grin at shadows,
    drive the days on.

Yet the clocks are all set
to stop in unison. The
    sky is a drum.

146

Matthew Sweeney

And with each daily edition
the columns merge; sport
    hangs on.

Two hundred balls of fire
know our whereabouts: this
    distracts us.

And when sores spill out like Etna,
when the streets pile up with meat,
    who will hear

someone's pain croak out: Remember
the days of happy dying, the taxi
    to that clay.

Disease a friend of the hungry.
The silent queues. The frozen
    rushhour graves.

And those with tongues will whisper:
Where are the gods? They never could
    keep command.

The old will shake their eyes.
Did they read once of wars
    with fist & stone?

Let them start that climb again.
Which way was the sling? As for
    those others –

the poets, the doctors & priests –
sweep them out. Death alone
    needs them.

Or at best the stone house
on the promontory, stalked by
    bands of kings.

NO WELCOME

I'll close the door again.
No hugs or brandy-tots today,
no gossip even. Things have changed.

I mean it. Did you not see
the running men push past you
in the queued-up station?

Where are they going? – I haven't time
to spell the world in German,
or morse either. It's late.

Take your foot away, I'm sorry.
Stop that taxi passing,
here's the tip. I'm still your friend.

Forgive me if my invite's bounced.
Blame the weather. Another time
when flies are free of fever,

we can giggle, consume a crate
of beer with meat & mustard.
Today is different.

So go – don't ask me where,
I'm human. But hurry.
And whistle as you leave.

LAST SUPPER

It's time for wild cooking.
A wind skims the Atlantic
so fierce it draws the future.
Cairns & transmitters shake on hilltops.
Rain reproduces the sea.

So call the butcher on the telephone,
halve his stock. Send the child
in a thick anorak up the garden.
Set the six gas-rings on at once.
Gather the herbs and go.

Beyond the pane, slates are falling.
The mail is late. But the water
piped from the reservoir on the horizon
is flowing freely. Enough
for six pots & more.

And the guests owed for years
can arrive with wine,
abondoning cars in the yard,
hats held tight with gloves
as they ring the bell,

then enter the vacuumed corridor
to lights dimmed, candles arrayed
on tables with Christmas silver.
And the odour adrift in the air
preceding the feast.

And the sound of Brahms, say,
drowning the wind. And the topics,
between mouthfulls, kept to the past:
religion's mercy, and Mass
in those days read in Latin.

THE STATUE
after Ritsos

Woken, we dressed
and followed the noise like magi
through narrow streets to the main square
where a fire fought the darkness
& around it a crowd sang.
Sleepyeyed, we stood there,
wine was thrust in our hands
then we too were singing.

The crowd grew, the flames probed the stars
and above the din a single voice soared
like a bull. Then we saw him,
young head high & laughing
flinging his clothes behind him
clambering up the statue.
And we suddenly knew his song:
of heroes & wild bristling horsemen
and now he was one. As proof
silence claimed him
and up there on that stone horse
stonewhite in the moonlight he sat
motionless. We all watched
as the noise seeped away,
then we slunk into the dark streets
from the dying fire and the statue
of two riders on the one horse
stood for years in the square.

A ROUND HOUSE

Will somebody build me a round house
low on a headland. With thick walls
& shrunken windows, a view on all sides.
And an acre of sandy grass.

I will move there, like the birds in winter.
Unloading a trunk & domestic trophies,
then quickly a bucket of whitewash
while the dry wind lasts.

Fields away, the weather-station
will probe the sky.
Ships will cross in the distance
with goods for the city.

I will have rabbit-snares,
a boat for cod. And a high
fence for summer, its day-trippers.
I will invest in a gun.

Matthew Sweeney

GOLF

The ball is pockmarked & depressable,
meant for long parabolas over mown grass
ending in a punctured green.
Striking it is a science: studies are made
with vectors & angles, pivots, stance,
the arc of the swing. It is not a game.
Experts loom in & out of the television
in their peaked caps & bright green slacks,
crowds of women curved around them.
Watch how the ball obeys them.

Back at the local course it wanders.
Goes lost, or lies camouflaged with furze
till a search-party unearths it.
It sits like a round pebble in sand
waiting to emerge in a golden cloud.
Often counting is a sadness
best kept strictly private
but the sea is a glamorous companion,
the air is safe, there's whiskey in the clubhouse
and one's game must soon come right.

THE RETURN

When you return as if you had never left
what will they say to you will startle –
they who have grown towards walking-sticks
cut from local hillside briars, and
who have learnt rumours of your whereabouts
by heart, enough to flay the memory
of the boy once excellent at Latin
who never soiled his hands on village cattle

and who now stands there, amid boxes
carrying clothes of a future fashion,
back at the mat that once felt your tread,
as eyes find the paper in your pocket
and you know voices speak behind windows
but to you will say nothing, not ever.

LILI MARLENE

He sits at a table in artificial light
drawing circles on a page. A record
plays behind him, painting the air
the colour of old cleaned-up wars.

He thinks of the new strategies
that leave no room for blue fictions
only facts, such as radiation
& cockroaches who'll inherit the earth.

And stopped cars with their skeletons,
hotel-suites, galleries, wine-cellars,
music such as this – all for them
if they want. They possibly know.

The song begins again: words
about barracks, a corner light
and a girl who waits there at night.
He recalls a chemistry lesson –
how a tear makes a perfect meniscus.

IMAGINED ARRIVAL

White are the streets in this shabbiest-
grown of the world's great cities,
whiter than marshmallow angels.
Descending by parachute, one would be
arriving in a world long dead.
One would also be stiff with cold.

And if one, perhaps, would dangle there
in a skeletal tree, swigging brandy
from the equipment, rubbing fur ear-flaps,
one would have a view of the street
unhindered by involvement, as about one
the parachute would hang like snow.

And while getting one's wits back, groping
for a knife, a slow van would stop
leaving bottles of snow; and a man nearby
would dig the white from his steps
while a woman in a window opposite
might smile as he uncovered dirt.

By this stage pigeons would investigate
and one's toes would long be numb.
One would give up, and call for help
or if successful with the knife, drop down
leaving onlookers noticing the parachute
as one asked for soup and began to explain.

NEW YEAR PARTY

I know your ways, older brother
and as the year ends I'll reveal them.
It's a good time for knowledge
an easy time for new pictures
even one as capsized as yours.

I adjust my tie, brush my suit
& organise the layout of the food.
You are on the phone this hour:
your laughter goes longdistance,
cheers up those who'll miss your party.

Half-visible, I hover by the door.
Hundreds are expected. I hear the bell,
obey it – they rush to touch you
while I flit towards the stereo
to play your latest favoured band.

Coincidence, of course, has spoiled me
with that exclusive rear view
two years back in your cool slipstream.
And sometimes even I drew breath
in awe at your acting style.

But I stayed quiet, no-one knew –
till this last stroke of midnight.
I have facts like a nazi-hunter:
dates, letters, the odd photograph –
evidence stoked-up over years.

This night is asterisked a long time
and when I take the microphone
to list your New Year praise
I will watch your mouth collapse,
your smile freeze & fly at me.

THE DANCEHALL

Music jumps in the open window.
My feet fidget, test the boards, tap some
and I'm off out the door beyond the streetlight
to a dancehall built without my knowing.

Television has been ruining me.
I queue with strangers. Behind us
a bus with bald tyres empties.
I say: how will we all fit in?

At the door banknotes are requested.
Wrestlers in plainclothes stand & watch.
I pass and round the corner
to the first real blast of the band.

They are old & young, like a family.
A monkey in velvet by the drummer's elbow.
Floorboards have felt dreamier music.
The singer smiles & climbs his song.

And, my coat still on, I'm asked to dance
though how my feet know I can't say.
A girl with pink hair – I like her,
she grins like a puppet & speaks as much.

We whirr like windmills. The walls rock –
are we on a ship, in neutral waters?
There are all shapes of people here.
Fans like captive helicopters cool the air.

It's Christmas. But what's that din?
and shouting out of time with music?
That's punching, and those are knives
glinting in the spotlights. That's blood.

It's not yours, I say, dance on
and I do but I'm tired.
I leave with a last look around.
I am the first one home.

THE SHOPLIFTER

The shoplifter has cut his hair
and bought a house by the sea.

His books come in useful now
as each time he has shinned

with an aerial up the chimney
Viking wind has ripped it down.

Outside the door, a black
mound of mussel shells has grown

near the fronds of marijuana
& carrots that thrive in the sandy soil.

He has learned the use of coins
for milk & beef, bakes daily

and lopes through the chill of daybreak
leaving footprints for the sea.

News is an old phenomenon.
Last year a bottle landed –

green, it sits on his mantelpiece.
He thinks it is Scandanavian.

LISSADELL
for Raymond Tyner

The last thing I remember are Yeats' po
there on the floor by a four poster,
and, on the landing, a lofty yarn
about a ghost the poet encountered
who sent him banging his host awake.

The aunts, of course, were the top story
as we strolled behind our guide,
hearing anglo vowels that survived
the slow tumble of a family
to tours of portraits, relics of wealth.

She paused at a piano in the great room
where windows opened to the south,
asked if we could play. An American
proved the famed acoustics, smiled,
shook the rust from suntanned hands.

I remember, too, watching her arrive –
we were early, walked through trees,
then flowers, till the gardener called.
We turned to see his Miss Gore Booth
draw up, in a mini, at exactly eleven.

THE LAME WALTZER

Crushed by an ambulance, he survived
to grow cacti for a living
and wear out tapes of Strauss.
We grew used to the lilt in the sea air
heard through holes in the wind,
to the limping shadow on the curtain
on the half-bright August nights
before the marquee pegged in town.

Together we traced his missing years –
his mail came from Germany, and once
a truck with Munich numberplates
braked on the brae to ask me
where Herr Coyne, the cactus grower, lived.
Ah ja, I said, you want
the best lame waltzer in Europe,
and I aimed them at the tideline.

SIMULTANEOUS STORIES

There was the story of a power station
sinking into the very bog that fed it,
an inch or so a year, and still it burned
all the turf around it, so the hi-fi's,
shavers, and vibrators could drone on
as near as upstairs, as far as the city.

And at the same time there was a hill
two of us climbed, earning our sleep,
to the wide, uncanny blue of the ocean
where a glimpse of Scotland bobbed.
Coming down, we found a ruined pram
from the 1950s, and spooked a hare
to skedaddle on up the promontory.

SPLIT LEVEL

A split-level bungalow has erupted
by the ruined parental home –
its walls are prison-modern,
its aerial nets Scottish tv,
its bay window magnifies the sea.
Portholes punctuate the corridor
past the main loo, to the garage
where doors open inside and out.
The site was a fairy mound, it's said,
before bulldozers or common sense.
Now a curly, tarmacked drive
stops at a gate, at the worn road.

Last week a tricycle sat out there
all night long, without theft.
It's gossip-evenings still –
at the bar the old boys relive
wakes in the adjacent ruin
when its thatch was rain-tight
and whiskey went down within,
and one, a mason, mutters
that six weeks would right it,
that the pair in the same grave
must be dizzy with turning,
that the buldozer's due to return.

SARSAPARILLA

Caravans in the marram by the 17th green –
this is where you'll find them on nights asleep,
six miles from the border in a European Mexico.

A flag and a proclamation, some photographs,
are tacked to the walls. Cars with foreign plates
graze outside, mud on their backs and tails.

The terrain ramps to the cliff of a quarry
where night-urinators would weigh up privacy
against freefall. These men piss in headlights

and gravity leads their porter under the traffic
to an arm of the ocean, where the lights
of a Soviet fishing ship are fixed as stars.

A song to a hero might waver on, twisting
into the dark, and a shot might follow,
liberating a puny avalanche of gravel –

though their firearms are mostly quiet,
kept for urban duty, those active nights
when their crouched figures move among graffiti

and others with the same tattoos lean on the bar.
Or perhaps the same veterans, a little early,
checking their watches, sticking to sarsaparilla.

A SCRIPTWRITER'S DISCIPLINE
for Aidan Murphy

The last week in March the rains come.
I move indoors with two brown bags
of freezer fodder, a bottle of malt,
a score of beers, half a dozen clarets
and a new ribbon for my typewriter.
I use the wet to get things done.

For ten days the flat roof suffers
while underneath I fill a bucket
with olive stones, bacon rind and pages.
Deaf to the doorbell, I invent
lines for an Esperanto-learning cop
and his dumb, dope-smoking son.

There is a beauty in blank paper
as in a skilful tv silence
where the eyes' work is undistracted.
I have a cupboard full of videos
of silent movies, and Kojak
in colour with the soundtrack lost.

The studio knows not to phone me.
Curtained off, in my rocking chair,
not at home to Marconi or Baird,
I concoct fake lives, while
a forest of empties grows around me
and outside stray rivers course by.

THE NIGHT POST

All night the filaments stayed red
courtesy of the nation, and I wore
wool beneath my tunic and smoked
while Grant sucked mints the loud way.
We'd each made coffee, I remember,
and I'd waved a whiskey-smuggler through
after receiving a sample, and Grant
had turned a Morris Minor inside out,
hunting in vain for a similar cargo –
when the Mercedes hearse came along.

It was 3 a.m. or thereabouts, a moonless
sky, and the driver wore a top hat.
Was as courteous as any ambassador.
I moved my beam down the long box
trying to picture the bloodless face –
was a beard still growing there, or
did it breathe, indeed, eyes on the lid,
or were there dozens of Armalites?
I bid the man a gruff goodnight,
walked in, envying his Brando face.

ENDS

At my end of the earth the Atlantic began.
On good days trawlers were flecks far out,
at night the green waves were luminous.
Gulls were the birds that gobbled my crusts
and the air in my bedroom was salty.
For two weeks once a whale decayed
on the pale beach while no-one swam.
It was gelignite that cleared the air.

The uses of village carpenters were many.
Mine made me a pine box with a door,
tarpaulin-roofed, a front of fine-meshed wire.

It suited my friend, the albino mouse
who came from Derry and ate newspaper
and laid black grains on the floor.
When he walked his tail slithered behind.
And when I holidayed once, he starved.

CUBA STREET

Midnight on the Isle of Dogs.
Taxis gather on Cuba Street
like roaches in a kitchen.
Black stockings, foxes round the neck
and grey stilettos. . . They peer
through sodium fog at Rik's place.
Each has a passport of wine.
The throbs of a bass guitar
pass through them to the tankers
whose oil tints the water.
Purple bulbs down the stairs,
a woman's arm through the banisters
while a new friend fucks her. . .
Someone yells from the bathroom
for a corkscrew, and they
continue their hunt for Rik.
They unearth him in the bedroom
holding court by his coffin,
the black one on four legs.
He is explaining relativity
with patience to an art-
college crowd, his centre parting
impeccable as a fish skeleton,
his red line of a tie unstained.
He yawns, climbs in his coffin
onto stitched red satin
and stretches his white toes.
'Would you be a doll,' he whispers
to a girl in a tubular dress,
'And screw the lid down.
And muffle that awful band.'

THE SUBMERGED DOOR

The bridge by the chocolate shop
arcs like a rainbow whose hues
have drained to a pool of oil
motionless on the black water,
and a boy with a bicycle
dismounts here daily, climbs down
to the canal edge and kneels
peering into the water, moving
his gaze like a torch-beam
until it lights on the door,
and sometimes he reaches
through the oily wet to touch it,
sliding his fingers over panels
smooth from eels and water,
pausing at the letterbox,
and he imagines again the dawn-
crowd leaving the party,
taking the door with them,
laughing as it fell from the bridge,
floated, then slowly sank.

ENTRIES IN A DIARY

Married the astronaut's daughter. . .
Half NASA was there –
the scent of maths and frontier riders
all through the cream house.
Made a point of speaking to no-one.
The view from the wrought veranda
got better as the day boiled on.
My bride wore a ghostly green,
sang once, was fancied by many.
Her dowry was a piece of the moon.

*   *   *

Matthew Sweeney

Daddy wants me in politics.
Gets me alone on the golfcourse
at 8 a.m., sleepwaking. . .
I still hit the ball farther
and ask him about meteors,
satellites, celestial litter. . .
I tell him about my murals,
how I'm due in Mexico
(where we honeymooned)
to liven the wall of a gaol.
We hunt his ball in the rough.

*　　*　　*

The spacesuit in the wardrobe
is too big for me, too bulky.
Better a suit of armour
in these post-orbital days,
better still a mausoleum. . .
Daddy doesn't like my slang,
doesn't recognise
the plants I'm growing.
Someday we'll share a harvest.
We get on fine for in-laws.

*　　*　　*

Got home at dawn.
Mona – my wife – woke me,
brought coffee and croissants
on a teak tray,
unleashed the sunlight at me,
circled the bed,
asked me if I knew,
really knew, who Daddy was
and where I was living.
Said the newsboys were around.
Whimpered, banged the door.

*　　*　　*

I clutch that hunk of the moon
and meditate. It's 4 a.m.
Crows are asleep, the window's open
and the snowball in the sky
is caught. I'm trying
by feel, to arrive there.
Can't sleep in this museum.
I chuck the rock on the bed,
dress, make for the east lawn
and remember morning traffic.

*   *   *

It's hot in Acupulco.
Guacamole's great, booze is cheap
and I'm up on the gable
till eleven, with a sombrero on.
I like my work
till the paint dries.
Evenings are what money's for.
Mona says she's sick
of the admiration.
Sends another card to Daddy.
I add my *miss you* scrawl.

A SURREY MORNING

Gunfire in the air at Ash Vale;
an imperceptible drizzle at the station –
I hurry in my green shirt uphill
while army boys practise for Ireland,
or is it Europe; the Suffolk coast. . . ?
A diamond of jets growls overhead,
and the train tracks lead to Portmouth
and the patient, pincushion fleet.

Ten years since the Vietnam Vets
rose from Saigon to oblivion,
and now the thanksgiving shows begin.
And the three services are full.
I walk in the Surrey morning
to a college of teenagers coaxed
by careers, remembering rag week
and the day the theme was camouflage.

THE BATS

The bats live in the old television aerials.
I hear them above me at night, and sometimes
one will blunder through the broken window,
glancing off me or the bulb, his sonar gone.

Since the hot weather, the parks are clay.
It's good to be up here, on the 13th floor
as the wind dips no lower, and when it rains
the two basins I leave on the roof get filled.

I'm clean, I drink, and I've a net for birds.
The lift broke last year so I don't get down
to the street much, and I don't have strength
to fight the market crowds for State rations.

From here I see the city, and the hills beyond
where I went often when the buses ran
though I try not to think of the dead years,
dead from the day they took the telephone.

If I could vote now, I'd head the queue
but it's as likely as hearing a bat speak.
A million X's would have stopped their march
but who can loudly say he saw it coming?

I open the door to no-one, I make no sound.
Ignore them: they may leave you alone.
I still have my books that I saved to read
and the bulb still comes on from ten to twelve.

The Inherited Boundaries

Up on the roof at midday I sit in the shade
of a chimney, and I drink the breeze
while the bats hang from the aerials, immune
to the heat, to the unnatural height, to me.

I think, then, of the bats as companions.
There is one I watch more than the rest –
already I cross the roof to touch his head,
when he moves in his sleep I back away.

Down below I stay close to the window
and pluck my wrens in the afternoon
then hang them from the ex-telephone wire
while I snitch my four hours of sleep.

Sebastian Barry

CALL

Sitting in an armchair I recalled
the clothlike heat of summer;
the room with its pencils sharpened
looking out on a waving garden
with a seat of blue
where I could rest upon a colour
and wood hid, a soft secret;
the dividing hedge and rose-bush:
a wind-rolling shape or
rambler with his thorns;
green apples on a tree,
the artist's proud eccentric fruit
brought in his rosy age
in boxes to the house;
the brick house,
the hot granite ledges,
jars upon them, late of jam,
to tempt and tune the wasp;
and I could smell it all
as an ordinary man.
This was lovely childhood,
the garden of my grandfather.

SKETCH FROM THE GREAT BULL WALL

He paints the sand when a tide has gone
and an arm of pier as ever out in water
lit clean yellow by a late-going sun.
His hand runs and taps at the rim of his hat
with a long-sticked brush among his fingers.

Green time sits on the tips of stakes
stiff to a hundred tides. Lined and
lined to the lighthouse at the end
cut stone goes in sleepered shape all warm with day
even in stretching shadow where the sun at some hour lay.

He paints a thin shimmer of the backing sea,
a dull fire tracing four serpent miles
from Bull Wall to Monkstown. Bulls
thud in herds along its back in autumn,
they spring like waves from the open sea
on leafless mornings. Tonight,
a tide will slop over the smooth wall
with water from the inner bay
oiled by entered ships.

                    O sweet
is the oil in Dublin harbour,
sweet is the song of the sewerage plant,
sweet O sweeter is the fine dust of coalyards,
but sweetest of all the tall wind
ruffling buds of the heavy seaweed
near where he paints the untided sand.

THE WATER-COLOURIST

In April here he chances on this room:
but evening parts us, the awkward find
of this face muddled in his private mind.
Still, when I was a boy he knew me, my
grandfather, gone from the darkening strand
to turn the Austin on Bull Wall, careless
of the slapping tide, his laugh of pleasure
in the dusk. He painted his son there, I
have seen the picture in another house:
a boy, before me, on the blunted stones,
caught in paint's hour; a lighthouse in the sound.
And now my father rings me from the town:
he dies, he says, perhaps without much pain.
As time turns it will be like this again.

Sebastian Barry

AN ENDING

He draws a line, the oval of a head.
It still says follow till the hour you're dead
but the hour, he knows, will soon be tasted.
The time that is left him is time wasted.
Below in the garden in a tweed of sun
two wrens tip nimbly. Though the head's begun
the birds seem better – they're drawn instead.
His wife calls 'Matt!' when his lunch is ready.
The birds fly up. His hand keeps steady.

A SEASONAL AUNT

I
In summer she arrives in cotton splendour
with a hump on her back like half the moon.

On a concrete wall where the tide is full
we lie to sun and dress, undress,

till the long sky cools in its red towel
and the salt sits hard in her eyebrows.

Back we walk with dampened hair, in sandals,
flop flop up the iron bridge and flop

on the dimpled pavement. Drinking water
is drinking icy silver. We eat wet cheese

and she eats radishes plump with red.
Down the pier she sits on every seat

picking the green paint bubbles with a finger.
At the pier's end where the blocked stone

circles and circles the small lighthouse
she carries her hump like rainbow gold.

The Inherited Boundaries

2
Fact does not make her good to be with,
it is how she talks and how she looks.

She stays in a house of elder women
among lethean terraces built by a man

who left his name on a yellow pillar.
She lives alone: Agnes below

who works the frail need of autumnal ladies
dislikes her strength. She comes on a Friday

with unusual tears. Her sleeve turns wet.
We wait together till someone returns

planted in chairs and my confusion,
indelicate autumn out in the garden.

She gives me a story of persecution.
Agnes would have her nodding and foolish.

The first I see of unconjured grief
is the condition of sorrow in her face.

3
In December I am told to visit her.
I pull the bell with the bowelled tinkle

watching for the white-cheeked gesture of the servant
to unclick the latch and shuffle me upstairs.

A heater crouches inside the room
near the clustered coal of a second fire.

Winter hears the tally of the past
which winter has made difficult to retell,

disturbing her heel on the glimmering fender.
No other story told in the shadow

Sebastian Barry

is short as the reason she never married.
Her look made distant, she creates a sailor

who is put in place of denying a secret
and expounded briefly in the flowered chair.

4
The spring that sees her with a stick
is the time I bring her up Tom Sawyer

from the shop in the village for two and six.
She knows and sanctions an extravagance

that gives me more pleasure than the book gives her.
The stick has annoyed till she can not touch it:

she prefers to finish before it breaks her.
From a guarded tin I retrieve Tom Sawyer.

We give her chattels to Agnes who hurt her
and burn her papers in the plotted fire

and bring home a picture of an unknown uncle
which hangs in the room where she sat tearful

in her fled time, and in my time too.

THE VISIONS
for James Mackintosh

We drank from the bought bottle
with the snow like fluff on the visitors
and listened in the dappled courtyard
to jazz tunes trifled on the organ.

Through the window behind us
we saw the philosopher mason
breathe the dust of his decisions
among new tangles of the church.

The Inherited Boundaries

The yellow wall ran alone
by the sleeping places of the barges,
the factories, and the birded cranes,
out of the appointments of the town.

A black barge docked at the petrol platform
where the ruffle trees grew on the bank
and we asked the occupied faces
to take us home against the stream.

Nothing so good could take us home.
Savage men argued at the crossroads
in a village that barred you from relief.
The track to the Seine between the bean plots

ended in fences and stuck bamboo.
We went back along our boundary.
We always went back with the paths got rough
and the visions too real to see.

THE RETURN

At Ropley Station the foot of night
was resting on the platform.
Two lights like yellow owls
perched on the gutter.

The town was tar.
The buses stood like boxes.
My father had drunk his mistress
and clouds were thieving the moon.

I took my place among Hampshire girls.
The driver kept silent.
He let me out where white fell
like a drinker on the road.

The house was bright in all its rooms.
I saw her pacing in the kitchen.
The horses stamped in the poppy dark.
The latch was hiding.

ROPLEY DISTRICT

I walked – the summer mud was thick,
the flies were resting on the water,
and hooves had churned the three together.
A swish of black was the dog's tail.

We found the field with green and rabbit.
His snout kept low in the grass.
He raised a hare and chased with purpose.
Where nettles were, he lost it.

I stopped at the oak – the oak went up –
and watched a squirrel till I knew him.
I thought of the trouble in her love
and stood by the English boundary.

We climbed an elm-gate and burst forward.
His cheeks wired the wind of the corn.
We ran away till our heads rolled
to know sorrow was waiting.

I had a stick I'd cut and barked.
I walked with it tucked and didn't falter.
It gave me a feeling of going homeward
even though home was set behind me.

THE WALK

We walk round this acre of old garden
where breeds of one flower grow in the grass
and thin grass pressing through the driveway
has found an entrance in the door of tar,
where I see, little brother, how quick you are
to believe the guessing fact I tell you.

We came down slowly on the sunday road
to walk by the flowers of the burnt domain.
Everything now is not true or plain.
The air hangs damp in the beech and oak
and my hand grows tired from yours again.
Let's go back carefully the way we came.

TWO BROTHERS UP

Morning. Fifteen books beside a window,
palimpsest of last year's pen upon a table,
ten good fingers to take Propertius down,
ten small winds to enter by the window-glass.

Again, little brother, you appear below,
a fishing-rod flicks above your shoulder.
The hooks in your hand see brown trout leaping
and a sliding heap between trees and water.

Your arm is raised in valediction,
white and small beside the forest.
Tracks go metalled, but never a carriage.
A strand of berries across the track:

your sudden stick takes blood for morning.
Brick wall, stone wall, walks the forest.
A hundred trees, a thousand, a hundred,
come up thick from the yearless clay.

Your boots disturb and brown the river.
Leaves boat down the trouted water.
Sun falls whitely. Propertius talks:
a stream, a god, another autumn.

CASSIBUS IMPOSITIS VENOR
Propertius, Elegies IV ii 33-40

Net from my shoulder in the wet forest:
I have been hunter on many a hill of trees.
Or, in any of our spring Italian squares
with a twig in my hand,
a twig with a ridge of sprinkled lime,
I, Vertumnus, have invented snaring.
Racing by walls of timber, whereon the citizens lean,
I have leaped my weight in fear from horse to horse.
With a supple rod, spying on purple shadow,
I have surpassed the older gods in fishing,
being better than they as we stood along the bank.
On flat-country paths, pinning my cloaks after rain,
I have grown perfectly rich as a pedlar.
Or, in quieter places, where no one came to see me,
I have been shepherd, supporting my silvered crook.
Where the shoes of farmers raise June dust
I have brought roses, along the southern roads,
bringing wet blooms in little baskets,
passing some scores of labouring people by,
an old, odd man.

THE WOUNDS

The hung cloth in the square,
the slates sheened like water over leaves,
the ragged, returning sky
remembering its electric war
companioned you perhaps
in the private dust behind the columns
where the passer-by would not detect you
reaching out to the echoed lamps

with your arms at your sides,
the round fountain on a dream of grass.
That was you constructing there
was it not, my secret friend?
You told me about it over *deux crèmes,*
gifting me a singular smile
till I thought thank you, thank you
like Groucho Marx pursuing.

You led the fogged moon at Notre Dame
like a paper read by the wind,
lifting your feet in a gray blur
among the buildings closed to history.
You slipped through the river gap
where the bushes fell modestly in the dark
and wrote the chaptered walk
all the way to the empiric gardens.

Your flagged hair flew in tatters,
a brushstroke escaped into the town
out of some Renaissance room.
The field of charcoal trees,
vertical and horizontal with dirt paths,
sold you its love for five minutes
as you gathered it into your arms
to heal the impossible wounds.

THE FEBRUARY TOWN

Who owns the garden sketched by rain
with housewifed cobbles, puddled flags
and fourteenth century buildings shined like new?
It chastens the street you wander in
as you descend towards the river
peering into geometric alleys,
progressing that way to please her whim.
Two roads serve the same ground

as you sway beside her to the first café
in the perfection of the pretty tram,
the sky with child and the snow on cue.
You embrace her charter by the kiosk
with raw noses and all of time
in a green light that sinks down from the roofs.
There is a threat which you employ
to give the square the distance of a dream.

THE WINTER JACKET

Among the rout of the drugged oak
I miss the brown lull of the civil street,
the complicity we machined
following our noses up the broken town
with its wrong perspective,

the thin, eccentric sculpture
at play in the clockwork pond.
Your ordinary jacket becomes an entry
on the gapped list of memory
since it lived with your breast,

bordering the parish of your ideas,
protecting them from mine.
Even at the café you declared it
so the hedges of fingered widows
would not cross your simple possession.

As we fidgeted there
I saw in the narrow paint of light
sea-gulls like paper fragments
lift from the leather with a defining noise
through the eye of a nervous mind.

This I can keep and arrange
in a house of alloyed, imploring shadows
while God knows what flock of birds
cellos the fear of another — I
miss that fear because I survived it.

THE YOUNG

I picture a wide unshowy river
with swans playing boats
and dippers blackly fishing
and birds with startled feathers
hurrying under pale rich water
where they silver the sprat

and a new bridge avoiding the old water
carrying packages of people and trams
and a french-looking restaurant on the far bank
with lights in its trees and moons.
Over all the stillness of the moneyed scene
drugging the purpose of the traffic

and whitening the visible cheeks
of the rash of young along the front
flagging with khaki, their ground
marked by the wired duck-ponds,
the square brown politeness of a building
and the little space their fathers leave round them.

THE WRONG SHOES
for Eoghan Nolan

A map of tracks on frosted paper
pigheadedly commanding the trees
puts anxiety in my printing feet
like an icon of every struggle,
soles fearful, chipping
past the pines' colourful black,
my back at a class-room angle

to the obstacled, senile snow,
each view from the falling corners
a canvas out of its time,

a fictional place from real life
whose genius has decayed,
and little walking to be gained,
only the slipping between the trunks,

the sky a face above the chart,
a lead lid to the dreams of colour.
I diminish the measured paths,
white bands and boundaries,
empty avenues through the counted trees
crossing each other with a breath of hats,
the snow on a pillow of minutes.

CHRIST-IN-THE-WOODS
for Jack Gilbert

You never bearded more than syllables
on the gray terrace of the cleric valley
imagining perhaps I was not impressed
by you being the thinned in your estate.
I was impressed in the lost extreme
by the remote newness slumming with your geometry,

the ten-league boots for the solo journey,
and the night-station, coffee idiom
walking like my confrère the Hampshire hare
whom white eyes in my eyes made hurry.
Monsieur, Signor, O Kirios, Mister,
my five-dollar jacket accosts your puddle,

the Italian squares supplementing it
busy with idleness under their plumage of signs.
About six the calendar begins to leaf,
the sad calendar of my dead writers
in the loo by the lake in the sad domain,
a wooden bird and a scatological recreation.

The Inherited Boundaries

Most matters seem sad till I sort them so,
the dictionary becomes a kindred of cheering up
and what I name gets pretty lively under the lamp.
Ah, Jack, we are too polite to be the same.
You can't make out the well's blood drowned in dark
and I am blinded by its black litter at midday.

You say that when the bucket hardens
you sense a brief settling like a trout,
any mooned man's signal to drag up
the helpful language his face explains,
how all silent neighbours who gripped there
remember the temporary gesture in the rock.

With a burrow of guilt I know I have forgotten,
who was a neighbour reasonably open to revelation.
But I see the alphabetical dust you raised,
a fountain in a prospect without horizon,
and your syllables under the water-colours cooling
are soon divided and etymologised: Ho là.

THE ROOM OF RHETORIC
for Rolf Aggestam, the precise traveller

The sounds of the African cicada
can not be divined
from the columns of the Sunday Times—

it is very possible there is
no such insect in Africa.
The pale Indians of South America

who die in their holding camps
after the poisoned blankets
and the blue capture

are the victims of no road
that we can imagine
unless the word 'we'

happens to be metamorphosed
into the signal 'they'.
The one true metamorphosis we have

or the best one anyway
may be poetry, and poetry
by its nature always manages

if flying under the first flag
through the first white ice
to be of the present

and of Eliot's trinity of time too.
Catullus is a contemptuous
and contemporary poet,

he speaks in the same room
as Lowell and Pound
and needs only the alchemy

of translation to talk
in his particular and proper notation.
No modern poet can ever hope

to be as contemporary
as Propertius and Catullus and Horace
until they have survived

the contemporaneity
of a hundred generations
and become continuous.

Continuous poetry is what
they all aim for and their souls
are cicadas if they exist at all.

Poets have no continent
that has not recently
been created by the sea

and no forest that they can not
pledge to guard. Everything
is in their keeping because

if they do not do the best job
by making the finest cabinets
for our detritus, they make

the sturdiest ones possible
in a mansion
that contains not one machine—

the only machine is the improvisatory,
tentative, horn-fighting,
temporal bravado

of their memory and imagination,
and the machine gives up its name
and its ghost and allows itself

to be a felt idea, relinquishing
its nuts and bolts with a grace
it does not possess

until the poet flourishes it.
Contemporary poetry,
that of Catullus and hopefully

Pound and Neruda and Cafavis
flourishes a red feather to the bull,
and the bull accepts it into his hat

and becomes civilised in the place
of the popcorn and the monkey-nuts
strewn at his sorrowing hoofs.

And so the poet sings the popcorn
in the hope of imaging the bull's soul,
and in imaging it he creates it

and therefore we are all defined
and half-created by poetry.
Here is a substance

that does not require words
but employs words none the less
in the way of a patron

feeding a Fool
he thinks he does not need,
though no food of benefit

can be prepared
by a fair-minded hand.
The more common notion of poetry

is really the reduced pleasure
of advertising and pornography –
we are in love perhaps

with our better selves
but we are content to admire them
from a distance, the distance

that the present allows us,
the boundary between doing
and thinking about what we do.

Poetry is everything before everything
receives their names,
it is ourselves and our world

before it fragments, perhaps only
the second before it does,
the tiny leaf of pleasure that comes

before the vulgarity of orgasm.
Our newer poetry does the favour
song has always had to do,

preserving our canons and our cannons,
the shotless ones,
big with ideas and small in history,

but history is strange because
it is already happening in the future
and you can only prepare for history,

for the worst and the best
it will tolerate. Luckily
poetry is history's companion

and walks on the traffic side
of the pavement with history
and when the Roman carts strike

by accident to halt history
in its tracks, poetry takes the blow
and we are manumitted

to hear the next chapter,
what happens next.
It tells us what will happen next,

and there out on the bay
are the lights of what happened before
coming opportunely but perhaps

wearily into harbour
carrying, you know, your ancestors'
lives and loves among the passengers.

All your forbears fell in love,
they ran down city streets
to meet someone

and they all were undeserving,
particularly the poets. It is because
we are undeserving

that we are issued with poetry
and it is only a serious business
because laughter and wood and iron

are inside it somewhere, reposited.
It is not the only thing
but it is still everything

and does not require honour
neither from those
who honour or dishonour it

but it requites a last-ditch integrity.
If you admit the ruffian deity
who guards the river where you fish

and leave when the noise begins
beyond the bend of the stream
where it is travelling

from volume to volume
and will soon reach the green time
under the granite bridge

where all our ancestors
and we too were undeserving,
if you fold your rod and step

across the damp geometry of the grass
that stands up because it would be
illogical for it to lie flat

but no other reason supporting it,
then you are admiring poetry
in a way that it demands

and even desires, since it is no
nonsensical and blooded tyrant
and of course the enemy

but also the celebrator
of tyrants. In Ireland
we have a tradition of poetry

that is half the irony
of the split hair
and half the madness

of the march hare.
This may be true of poets
everywhere, or elsewhere,

domains and dominions
that have to sing their trouble
before they can sing

their inventories, but we
who sing our inventories,
I mean in the South of Ireland,

the North being as much
a foreign country to some of us
or at least to me

as Patagonia
or perhaps Ithaca, we make
no quarrel with anything

except ourselves, as I think Yeats
formulated for his talisman
of poetry. Whether this

will give us the white flag
of being contemporary,
whether Thomas McCarthy and Aidan Mathews

and Matthew Sweeney and the other horsemen
of the most offensive army
will be awarded the perfection

of surrender, whether the hatred
of the troops will turn to gratitude
since only through poetry

can they be untrue
under the green time
and unbuckle their idle ideology

which is the most pilgrim
and renegade narcissism
must be left in part to you

or any of you untainted by the demand
to succour history
who must always be unlikely

but also left to eyes
that in their turn will forget
that poetry created them

to forget poetry
until the moment, a small river second,
when time strikes them too

and they find they can not pass
from wound to wound
without its redundant bridges.

THE INDIAN RIVER

To ask that allotment of darkness always
to be of itself only is a tall order.
To ask that ourselves, not as we were,
be boundaried from others similar
so we in the nouns of night-time
as their farthest local etymologies
can be proper and a case in point
is begging the grass to be blades of grass
viewed from a torchy, tarry distance.

The Inherited Boundaries

You with your farms being only colour
to collect the driftwood of arms and palms
and hold them, heal them, in moleskin mist
is its own answer to such x and y,
the mark missing at the gate of the question,
till small-hour readers must think to themselves
idiom's at warm work among our phrases.
So travel us back and leave us there
since we're not there before our epitaph
whose last principle the engine carried darkly,
a parquet of lost twigs, to the ratted bank.
This science can seal this miniature,
our berry paleography above the general grass,
your tongue's rock-painting rubbed on hunting water.

THE PARDON OF ASSISI

And explaining again, still clearer
than the Seine, an inability
monetarily to be unsmiling,
that distemper of Saint Francis,
suspecting this strips me
to an object of xenophobia
in banks, with a feline notion
of mousy compassion, messes up
the lead, stews it to a scum,
gets at least our fine lines
further from use, fine lines
between a variety of kinships.
Wondering if the movement
masquerading as pigment,
the circus provided by evening light
on the canal, is every going
to be a sufficient banknote.
Holding on even, allowing
your being far off, an old hind,
a soft behind, thank god,
before the beyonds, expecting,
a nimble eejit to this eschatology

our vows suggest, still the coloured
avrio, tomorrow, tomorrow,
not as a country putting-off,
the sane wood never to arrive,
sacks with older words cured in them,
cured of what indiscretion
you might ask, not those best roads
that the sometime had to offer,
nor cicadic melodies, nor the Greek
heroic, but as a sort of half music,
a stab at the café whatever, an
inexact wording for this towny manifesto,
look, it's been stabbed, the document,
by stapler against the city wall,
the archaeologists have been sanely
occupied in my stead, and,
reasonably speaking, they breakfast
on coffee rather than blood. But
certainly the pinch being
featured in the bill again will make
provision for newer promises,
to get up this stony street,
to survive the pardon of Assisi.

Bibliography

THOMAS McCARTHY

The First Convention, Dolmen Press, 1977.
The Sorrow Garden, Anvil Press, 1981.
The Non-Aligned Storyteller, Anvil Press, 1984.

AIDAN CARL MATHEWS

Windfalls, Dolmen Press, 1977.
Minding Ruth, Gallery Press, 1983.
The Small Hours, forthcoming.

HARRY CLIFTON

The Walls of Carthage, Gallery Press, 1977.
Office of the Salt Merchant, Gallery Press, 1979.
Comparative Lives, Gallery Press, 1982.

DERMOT BOLGER

The Habit of Flesh, Raven Arts Press, 1980.
Finglas Lilies, Raven Arts Press, 1981.
No Waiting America, Raven Arts Press, 1982.
A New Primer for Irish Schools (with Michael O'Loughlin), Raven
    Arts Press, 1985.
Internal Exiles, forthcoming.

MICHAEL O'LOUGHLIN

Stalingrad: the Street Dictionary, Raven Arts Press, 1977.
Atlantic Blues, Raven Arts Press, 1982.
The Diary of a Silence, Raven Arts Press, forthcoming.

The Inherited Boundaries

MATTHEW SWEENEY

A Dream of Maps, Raven Arts Press, 1981.
A Round House, Raven Arts and Allison and Busby, 1983.
The Lame Waltzer, Raven Arts and Allison and Busby, 1985.

SEBASTIAN BARRY

The Water-colourist, Dolmen Press, 1983.
The Rhetorical Town, Dolmen Press, 1985.
The Grammatical History of Everiu, forthcoming.

NOTE

Since the sixties, when the *Dolmen Press* was more or less the only possible publisher for poetry in Ireland, other presses have appeared, and of these the work of *The Gallery Press* and *Raven Arts Press* is reflected in this anthology, as well as that of the *Dolmen Press*. This is a good, competitive condition, at least for poets, and is another result of Liam Miller's pioneering example and established publishing. Of English publishers, *Anvil Press* and *Allison and Busby* have responded to two of the poets here, and either publish or co-publish their poetry. *Colin Smythe* have recently become Raven Arts Press's co-publisher in Britain.

Taunton's

BUILD LIKE A PRO®
EXPERT ADVICE FROM START TO FINISH

Insulate and Weatherize

For Energy Efficiency at Home

Bruce Harley

The Taunton Press

Dedication

To my parents, Robert and Barbara Harley, who taught me everything that's most important

The Taunton Press, Inc., 63 South Main Street, P.O. Box 5506, Newtown, CT 06470-5506

e-mail: tp@taunton.com

EDITOR: Alex Giannini, Peter Chapman

COPY EDITOR: Seth Reichgott

INDEXER: JIM CURTIS

JACKET/COVER DESIGN: Kimberly Adis

INTERIOR DESIGN: Kimberly Adis

LAYOUT: Kimberly Shake

PHOTOGRAPHERS: Front cover: (main photo) Randy O' Rourke; (left photos) John Curtis

Back cover: (top photo and bottom left photo) Randy O' Rourke; (bottom center photo) The Energy Conservatory; (bottom right photo) Mike Guertin & Rick Arnold

ILLUSTRATOR: Ron Carboni & Mario Ferro

Build Like a Pro® is a trademark of The Taunton Press, Inc., registered in the U.S. Patent and Trademark Office.

Library of Congress Cataloging-in-Publication Data in progress

ISBN 978-1-60085-468-2

Printed in the United States of America

10 9 8 7 6 5 4 3 2 1

ACKNOWLEDGMENTS

My hope for the second edition of this book is a continuation of the first: that its success will be in providing real and lasting benefit to many people. If it helps you, please consider it a small payment "forward" in exchange for the huge gifts others have given me. Without every one, I really couldn't have done it. Please pass it on.

Many, many thanks:

To Dan Berube, Michael Blasnik, Terry Brennan, Chris Derby-Kilfoyle, Paul Eldrenkamp, Jim Fitzgerald, Martin Holladay, Dave Keefe, Mark LaLiberte, Joe Lstiburek, Bill Reed, Bill Rose, Marc Rosenbaum, Bill Rock Smith, John Straube, Stephen Strong, Alex Wilson, and many others for teaching me lessons about buildings and building science, and for modeling a thoughtful and humorous approach to teaching people about buildings and the people who live in them.

To Caitriona Cooke, Steve Cowell, Mark Dyen, Bob Eckel, Adam Gifford, Rick Giles, Adam Parker, David Weitz, and many, many others at Conservation Services Group—past and present—for helping in ways both large and small, for contributing to a fantastic work environment, and for walking the talk.

To Mieke, Kenja, Carol, Paula, Mark, Catherine, Marsha, Roland, Elise, and Alan, for being supportive in every way imaginable, and especially for laughter.

To Scott Carrino, Chungliang Al Huang, Stephen and Ondrea Levine, Meredith Monk, Andrew Weil, and especially to the Moving Men, for inspiration and open-heartedness, which have helped me to survive and even flourish— physically, spiritually, emotionally; and for helping me find my voice.

To Peter Chapman, Dan Morrison, and many others at The Taunton Press who have helped me along the way. It's a great crew, and I'm happy to make my small contribution.

To Molly Kerns at Tsubo Massage, Nancy Quevillon at Williamstown Family Chiropractic, and Nicole Methot at Williamstown Wellness, for keeping me in shape; Dan Cote, Andy Gaines, Paul Fisette, Ron Jackson, John Livermore, Maria Loring and Al Wroblewski, Blake McClenachan, Kent Mikalsen, Ken Nardone, Ken Neuhauser, Dave Roberts, Brian Starr, Buck Taylor, and Wild Oats Community Market. Special thanks to Charley Stevenson.

And to so many others, my work is truly a reflection of all those who have inspired, nurtured, mentored, and helped me along the way.

CONTENTS

INTRODUCTION

When I wrote the first edition of
Insulate and Weatherize in 2002, my hope was
to put good-quality information in the hands
of homeowners, do-it-yourselfers, builders, and
energy professionals. Forty-five thousand cop-
ies later, I've heard countless stories of people
using the book with excellent results. One
even asked me, "How could you possibly make
it any better?" It can be difficult to improve on
a good thing, and certainly the basics haven't
changed much. Huge amounts of energy are
still wasted via hidden air leaks you can stick
your arm through, poorly insulated attics and
walls, leaky ducts, inefficient heating and cool-
ing systems, and cheap water heaters that still
rely on 1950s technology. The solutions haven't
changed very much, either: Seal the leaks and
insulate your house and ducts, and buy better
equipment. Most of what you need for success
depends on attention to detail and commit-
ment to getting the job done right, and the
benefits still include lower monthly bills, better
comfort, improved air quality, and increased
control of moisture.

At the same time, this new edition reflects
some real changes that have taken place since
2002. There are some innovative new products,

like high-performance fiberglass for blowing
into wall cavities and sprayed-on sealants for
renovation work. High-efficiency, low-cost duct-
less heat pumps can heat a house for a fraction
of the cost of oil or LP gas. Heat pump water
heaters and LED lighting have made the shift
from interesting ideas to viable products. Some
techniques have matured in the marketplace, like
the use of sprayed foam insulation combined
with other materials to control cost while maxi-
mizing control of heat, air, and moisture. While
updating the book to reflect these changes, I've
expanded the chapter on renovations to reflect a
growing movement toward "deep" energy retro-
fits, green building, and the latest techniques to
maximize the benefits of any remodeling proj-
ect. The chapter on lighting and appliances has
grown to include new technologies and prod-
ucts, and I've added a whole new chapter outlin-
ing the basics of renewable energy systems.

Even with all the new material, this book
still emphasizes the dynamic house system, with
a focus on understanding the interactions of
energy, moisture, air quality, combustion safety,
and ventilation in houses. Although this book is
intended to provide a balanced, overall view, it
is impossible to anticipate all possible situations

that could lead to trouble, including structural failure, carbon monoxide poisoning, or chronic indoor air problems. If you feel that the descriptions and background information offered here do not address your specific situation, hire a professional who is skilled in building-performance evaluations to help you plan a strategy.

In the ten years that have passed since the first edition of this book, the average family's energy expense has increased from about $1,500 to $2,200 per year. That increase makes energy efficiency more cost-effective than ever. The same decade has seen a surge in interest in energy issues, fueled by increasing prices, a growing sense of urgency about climate change and pollution, and concerns about long-term instability of energy resources. Those changes bring good news: The time is better than ever to make your house energy efficient. An investment in energy savings has a far better return than the stock market: A package of improvements with a ten-year payback amounts to a 10-percent rate of return. Prices for many efficiency measures are lower than ever, partly because of significant util-ity, state, and federal government incentives, and partly due to increased production of technologies such as solar electric modules.

Saving energy at home can fix some real problems: Ice dams on roofs, freezing pipes, and mold growth from condensation in building cavities can all be helped or eliminated by paying attention to energy flows and the house system. Saving energy is also one of the best things you can do for the environment, especially if you're remodeling or updating something anyway. Buildings (including homes) represent nearly half of the energy used in this country, and nearly half the carbon emissions—they are almost equal to transportation and industry combined. Every time someone invests in updating a home and doesn't improve the energy efficiency to substantially higher levels, the opportunity to make those gains and reduce emissions is lost for decades to come. My hope is that everyone who reads this book will be able to use it to provide real, lasting benefits for themselves, their successors, and the planet.

ENERGY BASICS

There is a lot of misconception, folklore, and conflicting information about the consequences of weatherizing a house: "A house has to breathe—you don't want it too tight"; "Too much insulation will make your house rot"; "Insulate your attic because heat rises." Although some of these statements are based on fact, they tell only part of the story.

If you're considering making energy improvements to your home, it is important to look at the big picture. Houses are complex systems: Energy, moisture, air, people, structure, and mechanical systems all influence and affect each other. In this chapter, I'll give you a basic overview of the "house system" approach and outline the basics of energy and moisture movement. I'll also explain the key concepts so you'll know why it's important to view the home as a system. With this information, you can plan and prioritize your weatherization projects; maximize your comfort, health, and safety; and minimize building maintenance. ▶ ▶ ▶

Understanding Heat Transfer

You don't need to be a heating engineer to know how to install insulation. But by understanding how the mechanisms of heat transfer work and their relative importance in your home, you can better decide how to approach any weatherization project that you undertake.

Heat transfer is the movement of heat from indoors to outdoors in the winter, and from outdoors to indoors in the summer. If heat transfer didn't occur, your house would always keep you cozy and warm in the winter and cool and comfortable in the summer, without the use of a furnace or air conditioner. In a way, the function of your furnace or air conditioner is less to "make heat" or "make cold air" than it is to replace the heat that escapes in the winter and remove the heat that enters in the summer.

There are three forms of heat transfer: conduction, convection, and radiation. Of the three,

Steel studs, joists, and headers are superb conductors of heat. Without an effective thermal break, such as rigid insulation, they conduct far more heat than conventional wood framing.

conduction and convection are larger in magnitude—how *fast* the heat moves—and radiation can have a big influence on the comfort inside a house. Let's look at how each of these mechanisms operates and affects your home.

Heat flows toward cold

Conduction refers to the movement of heat through solid materials. Conductive heat loss always moves from the warm side to the cold side of a material. For example, if you have a cup of hot coffee outside on a cold day, the heat will move through the cup and out into the cold air around it (or into your hands to help keep them warm). On the other hand, if the weather is hot and you have a cup of iced tea, the heat will move from the warm air, through the cup, and into the tea, warming it.

Always seal air leaks before insulating.

Different materials allow conduction to happen at different rates. For example, a steel pan efficiently transfers heat from a stove burner to food because steel is a very good conductor of heat. For the same reason, steel framing in an exterior wall performs poorly from an energy-efficiency standpoint. *Thermal insulation* describes a class of products designed to slow conductive heat loss in walls, ceilings, and floors. Common types of insulation, such as fiberglass, cellulose, and polystyrene foam, are poor conductors of heat (for more on insulation, see "Insulating a House").

It is important to remember that heat flows through solid materials toward cold *in any direction*. A house may lose more heat down through an uninsulated floor in a sunroom than it loses up through the well-insulated ceiling of the same room. The reason attics are usually insulated to a higher degree than walls or floors is not because heat rises; it is simply because attics have more space for insulation. The old saying "heat rises" is misguided—heat actually moves in every direction. However, that saying does have some truth to it, which brings us to the next subject: convection.

These two infrared images show a house before and after a superinsulation retrofit. In the "before" image, the white areas represent the most heat loss, followed by red, orange, and yellow. After adding R-30 to the walls, replacing the windows with triple low-e, and insulating and sealing the attic, there's not much heat loss left. (The largest heat loss is one white area where the owner could only fit R-10 insulation on one section of the foundation). This successful project reduced heating consumption by almost 70 percent, bringing the house very close to net-zero carbon emissions.

Heat moves on air

To an engineer, *convection* describes heat transfer through the movement of fluid, but convection in the engineering sense is a much more complex subject than we need to understand for weatherizing homes. For our purposes, convection can be thought of as heat transfer through air movement (an engineer would actually call this "mass flow"). What causes air to move? Three main forces cause air to move through your house: the stack effect, wind, and mechanical systems. Because air flow and its causes are often misunderstood, I will go into some detail discussing them here.

The stack effect The first convective force, the stack effect, is what is meant by the saying, "Heat rises." What is really meant is, "Warm air rises when surrounded by cold air." In the winter, a house is very much like a hot-air balloon that is too heavy to lift off the ground. If you were the pilot and wanted the balloon to go up, you would turn on the burner and add more heat; this would increase the balloon's buoyancy by increasing the temperature of the air inside it. Similarly, the amount of force pushing air through your house is proportional to the temperature difference between the indoor air and the outdoor air. Because the stack effect is driven by temperature, it is a more important force in severe climates than it is in mild climates.

If you were piloting a hot-air balloon and wanted to descend, you would let some hot air escape by opening a flap at the top of the balloon. When you open the flap, warm air escapes from the top and cooler air rushes in from the bottom to replace it. Similarly, when you heat your house in the winter, warm air leaks out of holes at the top and cold air leaks in at the bottom to replace it. Another way to picture this

IN DETAIL

The largest energy use in most houses is heating and cooling (about 55 percent). Therefore, improvements to the building enclosure and mechanical systems have the most potential to save energy. Next are hot water (15 percent), refrigeration of food (10 percent), and lighting (7 percent). It's easy to notice when lights are left on or when someone stands in front of the refrigerator with the door open, but the things we don't see have the biggest impact on our home energy use.

This photo of a building under construction displays the air pressure pushing the tarp out at the top and in at the bottom. This clearly shows the pressures that move air through a building in winter.

INDETAIL

Most combustion appliances, such as furnaces, water heaters, and fireplaces, draw their combustion air from inside the house. When they're working properly, they act like exhaust fans, drawing indoor air for combustion and exhausting combustion gases up the chimney. Some appliances, known as power vent or induced draft, have blowers that push the combustion gases out. It's easy to see how these blowers (like the one shown below) act like simple exhaust fans.

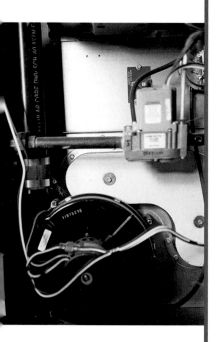

is to imagine holding a cup of air upside down in a pan of water. The air in the cup, like the warm air in your house, is lighter—more buoyant—than the water, which is heavy like the cool, outdoor air. If you poke a small hole near the top of the cup, the air will leak out slowly, and the water will come in from the bottom at the same rate to replace the air (see the drawing on p. 30 and the sidebar on the facing page).

Wind People think that wind causes most drafts, but in most houses the effect of wind is quite small. Although the pressure may be greater than the stack effect when the wind is blowing, it is a part-time occurrence; the stack effect operates 24 hours a day, 7 days a week, all year long. If your house is perched on a cliff or smack in the middle of a treeless plain, the wind may have a larger effect, but for most homes the stack effect dominates the air exchange.

One way to compare the seasonal impact of the stack effect versus the effect of wind is to ask yourself whether you would rather have me give you $10 a month or $1 a day. The $10 feels like more on the day I give it to you, but you'll be about three times richer if I give you $1 every day. So it is with the stack effect: Although it is

perhaps not as dramatic a driver of air flow as wind is, it adds up over time to be a far greater energy cost.

Mechanical systems In addition to the stack effect and wind, fans move air through houses. Exhaust fans, combustion appliances, and furnace air handlers move air in predictable and unpredictable ways. Exhaust fans push air out of a house, when they are working properly, and the air is replaced by outdoor air leaking in through openings in the building. Typical exhaust fans include kitchen and bathroom exhaust fans, dryers, and central vacuum systems (if they are vented to the outside). Combustion appliances, especially furnaces and boilers, contribute to air exchange when they are operating, which is when the weather is at its coldest.

A central vacuum system, if it vents to the outside, can also act as an exhaust appliance in the home.

The Stack Effect in Summer

One misunderstood aspect of the stack effect is that it reverses in hot weather. If the outdoor air is hotter than the indoor air, the heavier air in the house tends to sink and leak out through the bottom; it is then replaced by warmer outdoor air that comes in through leaks at the top of the house.

To use the cup analogy, a house in the summer is like a cup full of water that is held upright. If you poke a hole in the bottom of the cup, the water (which is heavier) dribbles out the bottom and the cup fills from the top with air (which is lighter) at the same rate. People who leave upstairs windows open on a hot day thinking that the hot air will escape because "heat rises" are mistaken—they are actually opening a large hole through which hot outside air can be drawn into the house.

Although it's true that the upper floor of a home tends to be much warmer on a summer afternoon, that is not because the heat is rising inside the house. It is because superheated air is being drawn from the attic and roof deck into the upper part of the house through hidden air leaks—and through open windows and skylights.

The Stack Effect Is Reversed in Hot Weather

Lighter, hot outdoor air is drawn in at the top, heating the upstairs rooms (red arrows).

Heavier, cooler air leaks out the bottom (blue arrows).

Even more significant than exhaust fans are duct systems. Furnace and air-conditioner fans are not intended to move air in and out of a house; however, if the ducts are leaky or unbalanced—and many are—your furnace fan may push a lot of air through your home. An air handler runs the most when the temperatures are extreme—cold or hot—so ducts leak the most right when it costs the most to heat or cool that air.

Whether the mechanical systems or the stack effect moves more air in a year varies from house to house, depending on the climate, the construction of the home, the size and location of leaks in the ductwork, and many other factors. In many homes, the air exchange caused by mechanical systems, though mostly unintentional, is the biggest factor in air movement. (See the chapters on sealing air leaks and ventilation systems for more information on controlling air movement in homes; see the chapters on heating systems and hot water for more on combustion equipment; see the chapters on heating systems and air-conditioning for more on sealing duct leaks.)

Furnace air handlers should move air *around* the house, not *in and out.* Normally, as air is heated or cooled, it is pushed into the house through supply ducts; house air is brought in through return ducts to begin the cycle again. However, leaky ductwork in attics, garages, or crawlspaces can push heated or cooled air directly out of the house. Pressure imbalances caused by inadequate return air can also push air out of some rooms and pull outdoor air into others. In many homes, duct leakage accounts for the majority of air moving in and out of the house when the furnace blower is running.

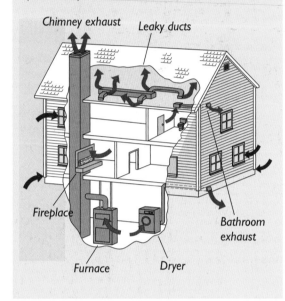

MECHANICAL SYSTEMS CONTRIBUTE TO AIR MOVEMENT

Makeup air is drawn in from the outside through cracks and gaps (blue arrows). House air is drawn into combustion equipment and exhaust fans (black arrows). Exhaust appliances, combustion equipment, and leaky ductwork all push air out of the house (red arrows).

Chimney exhaust

Leaky ducts

Fireplace

Bathroom exhaust

Furnace

Dryer

Heat moves through space

Radiation is heat transfer from one object to another through space. Like conduction and convection, radiation is driven by a temperature difference, but this time between the surfaces of objects rather than across a material. Whereas conduction moves heat through solid materials and convection depends on air movement, radiation happens only when there is a direct line of sight between two objects of differing temperatures.

Radiation plays a much smaller role than conduction or convection in the heat loss from a house in the winter. The type of window glass can influence radiative heat loss to some extent (see "Windows"). Radiation is, however, the primary factor in solar heat gain. Solar gain is a good thing in the winter (it adds some heat from the sun to your house for free), but it is often

also the largest driver of air-conditioning loads (see the chapters on windows and air-conditioning). In any season, radiation also has a large impact on comfort. A person's comfort actually depends just as much on the average temperatures of the surrounding surfaces as it does on the air temperature in the room (see the drawing on the facing page).

The biggest role radiation plays in a home's comfort is due to the surface temperatures of glass. In the winter, glass is usually the coldest surface in a house; in summer, it is the warmest. A room with lots of glass may be uncomfortable in both hot and cold weather. Uninsulated or poorly insulated walls, ceilings, and floors also create cold surface temperatures in the winter (or hot ones in the summer). Cold or hot surfaces add to the problem of conductive heat flow by making people feel uncomfortable. When people are uncomfortable, they turn up the heat (or turn down the air-conditioning) at the thermostat. This increases the temperature difference and drives the heat flow even faster, which costs them even more to stay comfortable.

Defining the Thermal Boundary

The *thermal boundary* (sometimes called the *thermal envelope*) refers to the parts of a building that separate indoor space that is served by a furnace or an air conditioner from the outdoors and from other spaces that are not heated or cooled. The spaces in your home that are heated or cooled are called the *conditioned* space, and the purpose of your furnace or air conditioner is to maintain those spaces at a comfortable temperature.

A room with lots of glass is likely to be uncomfortable in hot or cold weather, especially if it has a southwestern exposure.

PRO**TIP**

Glass is usually the coldest interior surface in winter and the warmest in summer. Rooms with a lot of glass may be uncomfortable in any season.

The thermal boundary is a key component of the *building enclosure,* the parts of a building that separate indoors from outdoors. The building enclosure typically includes the thermal- and moisture-control layers and structural support elements; finished surfaces provide weather protection and aesthetics. The enclosure has to protect the house from rain and snow and keep the building and its contents dry and comfortable. It must also resist forces that try to break it down, such as sun and wind.

In some parts of your house—such as exterior walls—a single assembly performs all these functions. In other places, like your attic, the

MEAN RADIANT TEMPERATURE

The mean radiant temperature in a room is the average temperature of all the surfaces in the room, weighted by the percentage of the room that each surface occupies.

A. Even though the room temperature may be 70°F, the person sitting in the middle experiences a mean radiant temperature of 67°F. The window, because it is both large and cold, is the surface that has the most effect on lowering the mean radiant temperature.

(NOTE: The temperatures around the edges refer to the surface temperatures of the wall, ceiling, floor, and windows.)

B. If the room has twice as much window area, the radiant temperature drops to 63°F—too cold for comfort! This happens even though the room temperature is still 70°F. To keep this room comfortable, the thermostat will need to be set higher to compensate.

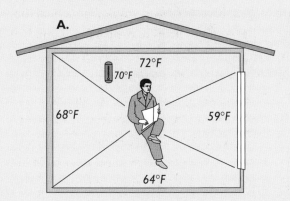

A.

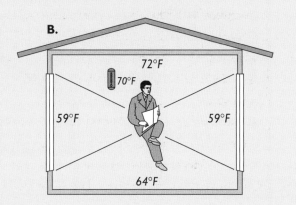

B.

functions may be divided. For example, your roof is a key enclosure component that provides weather, structural, and protection layers. But in most houses, insulation is installed on the attic floor, and the attic provides a space between the roof and the thermal boundary. A garage is another example; the exterior walls and roof of the garage form a weather shell, but the wall between the garage and the home is the thermal boundary. Together, all these elements make up the enclosure.

The thermal boundary is rarely made of a single material, and some materials may play more than one role. Walls may consist of siding, building paper, sheathing, studs, thermal insulation, and drywall or plaster. All of those materials contribute in some way to the thermal properties; some of them are also structural, and some resist weather.

For the greatest comfort and energy efficiency, it is important that the thermal boundary of the home be clearly defined. Sometimes it

The thermal boundary of a ceiling is typically made up of drywall or plaster, thermal insulation, and ceiling joists or truss members. If the attic space is vented to the outside, temperatures in the attic will be much closer to outdoor conditions, and the rafters, sheathing, and roofing materials play a minor role in the thermal boundary.

is unclear whether or not a space is part of the conditioned area. For example, a basement may be comfortably warm in the winter due to heat loss from the furnace and ducts, even though there is no insulation on the foundation wall.

THE THERMAL BOUNDARY

The boundary between the conditioned space and anything that's not conditioned is called the thermal boundary. The thermal boundary should be complete and continuous, even though the shape may be complex. Attics, garages, and crawlspaces are usually outside the thermal boundary.

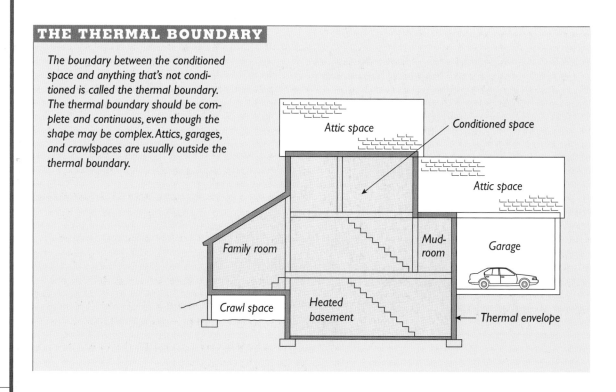

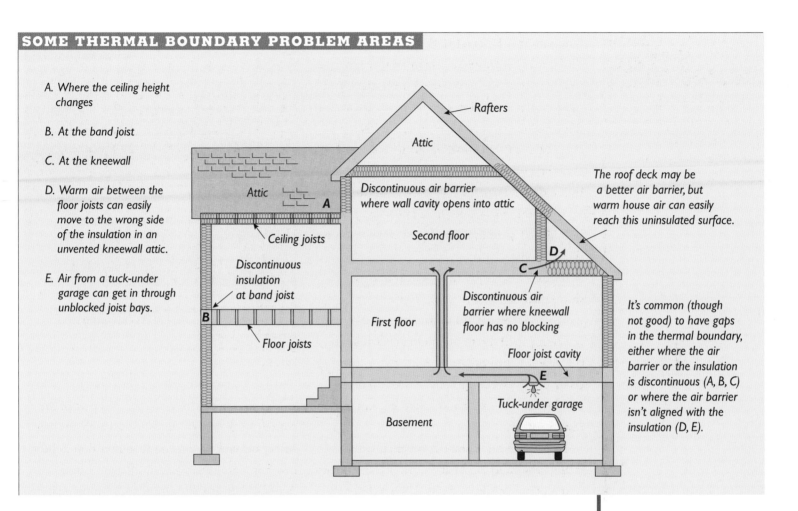

A. Where the ceiling height changes

B. At the band joist

C. At the kneewall

D. Warm air between the floor joists can easily move to the wrong side of the insulation in an unvented kneewall attic.

E. Air from a tuck-under garage can get in through unblocked joist bays.

Rafters

Attic

Discontinuous air barrier where wall cavity opens into attic

The roof deck may be a better air barrier, but warm house air can easily reach this uninsulated surface.

Attic

A

Second floor

Ceiling joists

D

C

Discontinuous insulation at band joist

Discontinuous air barrier where kneewall floor has no blocking

B

First floor

Floor joists

Floor joist cavity

It's common (though not good) to have gaps in the thermal boundary, either where the air barrier or the insulation is discontinuous (A, B, C) or where the air barrier isn't aligned with the insulation (D, E).

E

Basement

Tuck-under garage

This attic area behind a kneewall has insulation in the floor, wall, and rafters, so it's unclear whether the area is inside the conditioned space. In this example, the thermal boundary is ambiguous.

One might think that the thermal boundary is the foundation walls. What if that same basement opens into a crawlspace underneath the family room that was added on later? The crawlspace may have louvered vents (which were required by code before 2006), and it is definitely an unconditioned space. The best place for the thermal boundary is often at the foundation wall; in this case it should also separate the full basement from the crawlspace. To effectively put the thermal boundary between the basement and the house, you must insulate and seal the heating ducts as well as the floor over the basement; then the entire basement and the crawlspace would be considered effectively unconditioned, and the basement would be pretty cold in the winter.

WHAT CAN GO WRONG

The thermal boundary should always be continuous, and you should be able to draw an imaginary, uninterrupted line around your house that represents the thermal boundary. Every part of that line should represent some type of insulation—either that exists now or that you plan to install.

PRO TIP

Many common insulation materials do not stop air movement. Fiberglass batts act like an air filter, stopping only the dust.

Insulation does not stop air

Although all parts of the thermal boundary should include some type of insulation material, they must also incorporate some type of air barrier. Most insulation does not stop air. Let me repeat that: Insulation does not stop air. Although there are exceptions, the most common types of insulation materials—fiberglass and cellulose—do not stop air from moving when there is a pressure difference. Fiber-based materials such as fiberglass and cellulose do practically nothing to stop air movement under the forces of convection, except when installed at high densities using special techniques (see "Insulating a House"). People often think that if they put a lot of insulation in a house it will be airtight; this is simply not true.

When you define the thermal boundary of your home, it is critical to think about where the air barrier is located in relation to the insulation. Think of insulation as a sweater: On a cold, windy day, it doesn't keep you warm because the air moves right through it. A windbreaker has very little insulating value but, by stopping the air, it makes the sweater much more effective. Similarly, stopping air leaks makes insulation much more effective.

Air barriers and insulation

When defining the thermal boundary it is important to align the air barrier with the insulation. For example, it does not make sense to insulate the flat ceiling of a house and then create an air barrier at the roof sheathing. This often happens by accident when people insulate the attic floor but don't seal big air leaks: Warm air from the house circulates past the insulation, increasing heat loss through the roof, and often causing condensation on the roof. If you're not sure, choosing a place where it is easy to make a good air barrier can help you decide where to put insulation.

Another example is a basement, where it can be very difficult to provide a continuous air barrier between the basement and the first floor. Even if you wanted to insulate the floor over the basement and make it a cold space, if you have a solid concrete foundation wall, it may be much easier to air-seal the foundation walls and the sill area instead. This is one more reason why it often makes sense to put the thermal boundary at the foundation walls.

Energy, Moisture, and Building Durability

One key issue in the field of building science is the relationship between moisture and energy; another is the effect of moisture on building durability and indoor air quality. We've all heard horror stories about brand-new buildings that are rotting because moisture gets trapped inside them, or houses that are "built too tight" so that the air inside becomes dangerously polluted with combustion gas. These stories make good headlines and have some basis in fact, but they typically oversimplify situations and perpetuate myths about the relationships among energy, moisture, air quality, and building durability.

So, let's clear up some of the misconceptions about energy efficiency and moisture damage.

Older homes "breathed" because they were so full of leaks and lacked insulation. Although moisture didn't get trapped by the walls, neither did much heat, making these homes energy hogs.

One way to do that is to compare the moisture performance of new, energy-efficient homes to the performance of old, inefficient ones.

Energy and moisture: Myth and reality

Older homes usually had little or no insulation and were quite leaky. These houses "breathed": Heat, air, and water vapor could move easily through walls and roofs, and areas that got wet would dry easily. In fact, the heat and air flow are what dried the structure, and made these homes quite forgiving of moisture. Unfortunately, they were also uncomfortable energy hogs.

The way we construct buildings has changed dramatically since the 1950s. Exterior sheathing materials such as plywood and oriented strand board (OSB) slow air movement and act as a condensing surface for water vapor in cold weather. These materials are also more sensitive than their solid-wood predecessors. When they get wet, they swell, delaminate, lose fasteners and shear strength, and provide a nutrient source for mold growth. Unfortunately, even a moderate amount of insulation in a wall cavity lowers the sheathing temperature and slows drying. Although energy efficiency by itself does not cause moisture problems, air-sealing and insulation does change the moisture dynamics in a

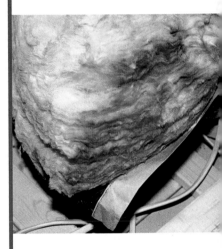

Some of the biggest air leaks are at the top of the house, but people are often unaware because there is no cold air leaking in. Those leaks actually draw warm air to that part of the house on its way out, so they are not noticed. They also cause more cold air to be drawn in from the bottom, increasing discomfort on the lower levels.

building and may make it less forgiving of moisture that is already being generated inside or leaking from outside the house.

One approach to dealing with these issues is a head-in-the-sand stance: *Let's not make this house "too efficient" in the hope that it will "breathe" and stay healthy.* A much better approach is to control moisture deliberately, to reduce risk and avoid problems.

Now that buildings are constructed with continuous sheathing materials and insulation, moisture that makes its way into a wall cavity takes much longer to dry, potentially causing structural and health problems.

Damp basements have more effect on a house than just damaging the walls; they can also be a major source of moisture that causes damage in the rest of the building. "Moisture-resistant" greenboard didn't help much here.

Water in the basement is not only annoying; it can also add a lot of moisture to the air in a house.

The importance of managing water

There are four primary strategies to reduce the risk of moisture damage. First, reduce water entry from the sky and ground: Control rainwater entry with overhangs and proper flashing techniques, and get it away from the foundation by grading and drainage. Promote drainage and drying in wall cavities with vented rain-screen siding. Separate leaking ground water from the building interior with drained foundation membranes and cavities. All these techniques are discussed in "Renovations."

Second, control the temperatures of condensing surfaces wherever you can by using spray-applied foam insulation in building cavities and on foundations, or by using continuous rigid exterior insulation for at least part of the R-value (this approach is covered in "Insulating a House"). Third, control unwanted air flows that carry moisture: Seal building enclosure air leaks (see "Sealing Air Leaks"), move ducts and air handlers inside conditioned space (or move the thermal boundary to include them; see "Insulating a House"), and tightly seal and insulate any ducts that must be outside conditioned space (see "Heating Systems").

Finally, control moisture sources and indoor pollutants with mechanical ventilation (see "Ventilation Systems"). Unless you are doing a gut renovation, it is not likely that you will tackle all these issues at the same time. But understanding these strategies and knowing the trouble spots in your house will help you prioritize these projects and approach them in a way that suits your unique situation.

These photos show the difference between water resulting from a roof leak (right) and water caused by interior water vapor that condenses on the roof sheathing in cold weather (above). Moisture from indoors often has a more damaging impact over time, partly because it's less likely to be detected until it's too late.

Where does unwanted water come from?

Unless you live in the desert, one of the largest sources of water is from outside the house: rain, snow, and groundwater. Rain can enter through roofing, siding, or flashing defects and soak into roof, ceiling, and exterior wall materials. Although roof leaks are usually pretty obvious (if not always easy to fix), water that enters sidewalls may go undetected for years (see "Renovations"). Water that enters foundations and crawlspaces may also be obvious, if you look; I've even seen water in crawlspaces in dry climates, as a result of irrigation near the house. Groundwater can also enter a house through evaporation, and it can be difficult to detect in its vapor form.

Concrete foundation walls and slabs are capable of wicking up moisture from the ground and "pumping" it into a house. Even though the floor and wall surfaces may appear dry, they can actually be the source of moderate-to-large moisture loads in a building.

Another source of water vapor is the people and activities in the house. People generate water vapor through perspiration and respiration. Everyday activities, such as showering, bathing, and cooking, also add vapor to the air. If you have a gas stove, the combustion process adds water vapor to the air as well.

In hot, humid weather, water vapor also comes from outdoors when air seeps into the house through leaks in the enclosure or is sucked in by return-air duct leaks in attics, crawlspaces, or garages.

Water vapor in itself may not be a problem, but it can wreak havoc when it condenses. Condensation can occur on any surface that is colder than the dew point temperature of the air. Common condensing surfaces in the winter include exterior wall and roof sheathing, when indoor air is allowed to reach them, and inside surfaces of inefficient windows and poorly insulated walls or ceilings. In hot weather, cold surfaces are likely to include ducts with missing or inadequate insulation or vapor jacket, interior

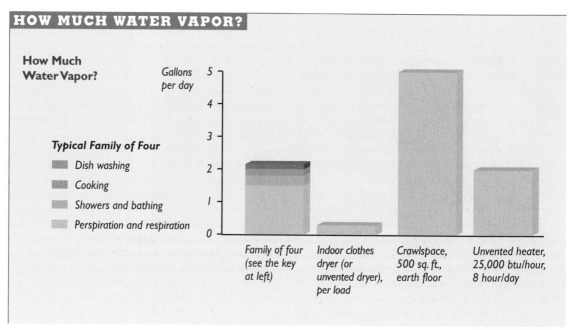

HOW MUCH WATER VAPOR?

How Much Water Vapor?

Typical Family of Four

- Dish washing
- Cooking
- Showers and bathing
- Perspiration and respiration

Gallons per day

Family of four (see the key at left) — Indoor clothes dryer (or unvented dryer), per load — Crawlspace, 500 sq. ft., earth floor — Unvented heater, 25,000 btu/hour, 8 hour/day

walls or ceilings chilled by hidden air ducts leaking cold supply air, and surfaces of foundation walls or floors that are cooled by ground contact.

Another common situation in warm, humid climates occurs when floor sheathing and framing are cooled by indoor air conditioning, and humid outdoor air in the crawlspace condenses on the underside of the floor. Finally, damaging condensation has been documented on the sheathing of flat roofs when white roofing membranes are used to reduce cooling loads. This occurs primarily in desert climates with large diurnal temperature swings, where night sky radiation dramatically cools the roof surface.

A little condensation may not hurt anything, but prolonged condensing can cause serious mold and structural damage, especially if it's out of sight. There are three basic ways to reduce condensation: Reduce the humidity, keep humid air away from cold surfaces, and insulate cold surfaces to warm them up. The following discussion outlines the strategies, and the approaches outlined in subsequent chapters reinforce these concepts.

While you are insulating and sealing your home, you will probably be crawling through the attic, basement, and/or crawlspace, which will give you the opportunity to identify existing moisture problems in the house. In all cases, be sure to identify the source of any water or vapor and plan to correct it as part of your weatherization project.

Reducing water vapor

The first step in managing water vapor in your house is to eliminate large sources that can be reduced or removed, such as unvented combustion appliances, green firewood, humidifiers, or ground water evaporating from your basement or crawlspace. Exhaust fans in kitchens and bathrooms are important in all climates to get moisture out of the house right at the point of generation. Controlled, continuous fresh-air ventilation provides effective dehumidification in cold weather; in hot, humid weather, continuous ventilation should be kept to a minimum to reduce the humidity load from outdoors.

The next step is to control vapor movement. Traditionally, water-vapor control has focused on diffusion. Water vapor is made up of individual molecules suspended in the air, and they actually move through solid materials; this movement is called *diffusion*.

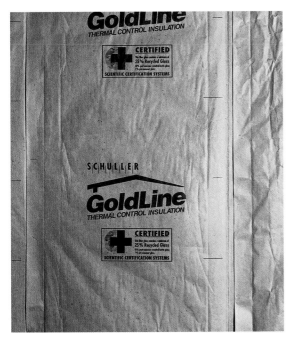

The kraft-paper facing found on some fiberglass insulation is an effective, yet forgiving, vapor barrier (Class II) and should be installed facing the inside of a house in mixed and cold climates. In hot, humid climates the vapor barrier may be omitted.

To manage water vapor, eliminate large sources that can be removed, ventilate the rest, eliminate the movement of water vapor into cold spaces, and insulate cold surfaces that vapor can reach.

Many small air leaks allow air to escape into the attic, where it can condense during cold weather and cause frost, mildew, or structural damage to rafters and sheathing.

Roof rafters

Attic

Condensation

Openings around electric fixtures

Plumbing penetrations and other openings

Insulation does not stop air leakage.

Insulated ceiling joists

Air leaks around a bathroom fan

If a fan isn't vented to the outside, even more moisture will end up in the attic whenever it runs.

Double-wall plumbing chase

Sources of water vapor inside buildings are called moisture loads. These can include exposed dirt floors in crawlspaces or basements, indoor pools or spas without proper ventilation or dehumidification, foundation drain access pipes and sump pits, unvented or improperly vented combustion appliances, firewood drying indoors, fish tanks, attached greenhouses, and even plumbing leaks.

In cold weather, vapor moves from indoors (warm and humid) to outdoors (cold and dry). In hot, humid weather, vapor moves from the outside in, especially with the use of air-conditioning.

The most common method for reducing vapor transmission is to use vapor retarders, materials that slow the rate of vapor diffusion to very low levels, generally low enough to prevent condensation. In cold climates, vapor retarders are traditionally installed on the inside of the insulated surfaces to keep water vapor from entering the cavity and reaching the cold exterior surfaces of the building.

There are two reasons this strategy is inadequate for most houses today. First, the increasing use of air-conditioning reverses the driving force in hot, humid weather; the interior vapor retarder is now on the cold side. Interior polyethylene, vinyl wallpaper, or oil-based paint can all become condensing surfaces and soak the wall in hot weather. The second reason is air leakage.

Indoor Air Quality

Building scientists have found that there are several important steps to ensure good indoor air quality, and they are generally consistent with energy conservation. These basic steps are as follows:

1. Create an effective boundary between indoor and outdoor air.

2. Minimize or eliminate pollutant sources within the house (see the sidebar on p. 24).

3. Maintain indoor humidity within a healthy range.

4. Provide adequate fresh air ventilation for people in the home.

This approach cuts heating and cooling energy losses, reduces uncomfortable drafts, permits better moisture control, and maintains an indoor environment that is healthier and more energy efficient.

Water vapor moves on air

Although the focus on controlling water vapor has traditionally been vapor retarders, a much more important effect is air leakage. This cannot be overemphasized. Although vapor retarders are important, they do no good if warm, humid air can leak into the attic or an exterior wall in the winter (see the drawing on the facing page), or reach a cold air-conditioning duct or floor deck in the summer. Building scientists have found that even relatively small air leaks actually move far more water into cold building assemblies than vapor diffusion does. This air movement is caused by the same driving forces we have already discussed, with the stack effect, duct leakage, and other mechanical systems typically being the largest factors. In fact, the lack of a vapor retarder in an insulated wall or a ceiling is secondary—in all but the most extreme climates—if air leakage into those areas can be controlled. This should come as a relief to anyone who wants to insulate an old house: It's a lot easier to seal air leaks than to add a vapor retarder.

Air Barriers and Indoor Air Quality

Perhaps the most widely misunderstood aspect of the whole-house approach is the relationship between air-leakage control and healthy indoor air. Conventional wisdom says "a house has to breathe," but what exactly does that mean? People and animals need to breathe. Houses are complex systems, but they are not living organisms, so I prefer not to use the term "breathing" for a house. There is some underlying wisdom behind that statement, however. It is vitally important to allow assemblies the opportunity to dry; this is aided by using building materials that

are permeable to water vapor. Venting of attic spaces and siding also helps, provided the vented spaces are separated from the thermal boundary by a good air barrier. To understand the dynamics of air quality, let's first look at air barriers.

What is an air barrier?

Although it may seem obvious, an air barrier stops air. We've already seen that most types of insulation don't stop air movement. Another myth that has taken root over the years is the idea that housewrap makes a house airtight. Most housewraps are good air barriers, but the biggest air leaks occur in places where housewrap is not installed, where it is installed improperly, or where it is not detailed well. The chapter on sealing air leaks explains ways to create good air barriers in existing homes, and there is more discussion of housewrap in the chapter on renovations. With this information, you should be well equipped to effectively control air leakage in your house.

Can a house be "too tight"?

Let's go back to the axiom "a house has to breathe." We certainly need fresh air in our homes, but where does that fresh air come from? In most homes, the fresh air supply enters through random air leaks in the enclosure—which may

IN DETAIL

The force that pushes water vapor through solid objects is called vapor pressure. Water molecules move from high concentrations (humidity) to low concentrations (dryness). Vapor also moves from warm areas to cold ones. One example of vapor diffusion is a loaf of bread in a paper bag. Although the bag is tightly wrapped, water molecules will escape right through the bag (from a higher concentration to a lower one) and it will dry out. A plastic bag will keep the bread fresh longer, because it is a vapor barrier.

Treat Air Like Water

We work hard to keep water out of our homes. Foundations, siding, windows, doors, roofing, and flashing represent a substantial investment in keeping out water. Then we purposefully bring water into the house through plumbing supply and drainage systems, which are another large price tag in our homes. Clean water is essential to our health, so we control it carefully. Fresh air is also essential, but in most residential buildings, we pay no attention to controlling it. If we treated air as we do water, by keeping out unwanted air and intentionally introducing fresh air, we would provide much healthier indoor environments for our families.

One example of misguided building science is the application of a vapor retarder on the inside of houses in a hot, humid climate. Although building codes have been updated to discourage this practice, it is not unusual to see vinyl wallpaper—an excellent vapor retarder—in hot, humid areas. If the exterior sheathing is vapor permeable, this can lead to big problems as outdoor moisture condenses on the back of the vinyl. In general, interior vapor retarders should be avoided in these climates, especially in Florida and the southern half of other Gulf Coast states, including southeastern Texas (zones 1A and 2A, as shown in the map on p. 74).

include gaps and holes in dirty, damp, moldy, pesticide-treated basements, crawlspaces, or attics. Most people, if given a choice, would prefer to have an *intentional* provision for fresh air in the form of a mechanical ventilation system.

Creating a tight thermal boundary that minimizes air leakage has many benefits beyond energy savings: It increases comfort, reduces the chance of moisture damage in the building structure, discourages mold growth in wall and ceiling cavities, and reduces the risk of ice dams in snow country. Most important, it allows the operation of mechanical ventilation systems to control the indoor environment for better health as weather conditions vary.

Remember that the forces that move air through a house—the stack effect, wind, and mechanical systems (especially combustion equipment and duct leakage)—move the most air when outdoor weather conditions are extreme. This is also the time when it costs the most to heat or cool that air. On the other hand, even a leaky house tends to be underventilated in mild weather, when those forces are minimal and windows and doors are closed. Ideally, a house should be tight enough to avoid overventilating when outdoor conditions are the most extreme; then the difference can be made up with mechanical ventilation.

Attic and Crawlspace Venting

Most building codes have minimum requirements for attic, cathedral-ceiling, and crawlspace venting. It is important to remember that this passive venting is different from fresh-air ventilation. Venting is designed to carry excess moisture out of those spaces so it does not damage the building structure. These venting strategies actually have nothing to do with indoor air, but they are often called "ventilation," which leads to confusion. Remember that there is (usually) an intentional thermal boundary between the conditioned spaces and the attic or crawlspace. Ideally, there should be no air exchange at all between those spaces and indoors; when air flows through the thermal boundary materials, there is much more potential for condensation and damage.

Basically, attic, roof, and crawlspace venting attempts to carry away moisture that should not be there in the first place. Good air sealing at the thermal boundary and proper water management of basements and crawlspaces (with good drainage; see "Insulating a House" and "Renovations") are more important to a building's health.

Passive roof vents are designed to transport moisture out of attics.

Crawlspace vents do little to reduce moisture in the living space, and they can introduce warm humid air into the crawlspace in the summer.

Controlling Humidity

In winter, excessive dryness can be controlled by a tight building enclosure. People often think their heating system is what dries out the air in winter, but actually it is the dry outdoor air constantly seeping in and needing to be heated that lowers the humidity indoors. Many people use humidifiers, but these devices need a lot of maintenance, and some types may create health problems of their own. Excess humidity in winter is best handled by mechanical ventilation, particularly by fans that exhaust moisture at its source: in bathrooms and kitchens.

In the summer, air leakage tends to add humidity to the indoor environment. The best way to control this is with a tight building enclosure and air-conditioning or other mechanical dehumidification. Air-conditioning dehumidifies better when it is sized properly (see the chapter on air-conditioning), and it will work better if the enclosure is tight, because excessive air leakage in humid weather brings moisture into the house. Of course, spot ventilation in bathrooms and kitchens is also important in the summer. (For more on humidity, see p. 18.)

It is important that bathroom fans work properly and exhaust air to the outside, not just into the attic.

Kitchens are another source of moisture; range hoods should always be vented directly to the outside.

Mechanical ventilation

Mechanical ventilation, as opposed to random air leaks, ensures the right amount of air exchange year round, under all conditions. When I talk about mechanical ventilation in this book, I am referring to ventilation of indoor spaces to provide fresh air and remove unwanted moisture. A mechanical ventilation system always consists of one or more fans, usually with ductwork, which bring fresh outdoor air into the living space, exhaust indoor air to the outside, or do a combination of both. It can also include filtration of incoming air. This is very different from passive (or fan-induced) venting of the roof, attic, or crawlspace, but people often assume that the purpose of those attic and crawlspace vents is to ventilate the entire building (i.e., "Let the house breathe"). See "Ventilation Systems" for a discussion of installing basic mechanical ventilation systems.

Indoor air quality

Controlling the indoor environment through tight building and a mechanical ventilation system offers health benefits as well. The best way to control indoor relative humidity is to control air exchange with a combination of an air-tight thermal boundary, air-tight ductwork,

IN DETAIL

Unlike water vapor, air can't leak through solid materials. Air leaks through cracks where different parts and materials of the building are connected together. Gaps between window and door frames and rough framing, places where exterior walls make a jog or are interrupted by a cantilever, and connections between dormer walls and roofs are areas often missed by housewrap. And the biggest leaks (as you'll see in the chapter on sealing air leaks) are often hidden in attics, basements, and crawlspaces, where housewrap is never installed.

Minimizing Pollutants in the Home

• **Source reduction** is the most important way to deal with toxins; keep them out of the house whenever possible. Learn which household products are the most toxic, get rid of any you don't use, and substitute less toxic products whenever you can. If your house was built before 1978, beware of lead paint; follow EPA guidelines for testing, remediation, and lead-safe remodeling practices, even during weatherization projects.

• **Separate toxic materials** from everyday living spaces. Don't just put dangerous chemicals in a childproof cupboard; keep them in a metal cabinet in the garage, or in a locked, outdoor storage shed.

• **Dilution of toxins** is helpful, too. Installing a mechanical ventilation system helps bring in fresh air regardless of the weather conditions; such a system helps reduce concentrations of harmful substances.

• **Combustion appliances** must be vented properly. Don't use unvented heaters of any kind, including "vent-free" fireplaces.

• **Moisture control** reduces mold growth by keeping indoor surfaces warm and maintaining relative humidity.

• **Radon testing** can detect this invisible, cancer-causing underground soil gas, which can occur anywhere. The only way to tell whether you have dangerous levels in your house is to test for it. Use an EPA-certified laboratory and follow the directions carefully for an accurate test.

Whether you have a tight or a leaky house, any natural-draft combustion appliance may produce deadly carbon monoxide. The only way to know is to have a professional test the flue gases.

and controlled mechanical ventilation. Contain the air, then you can control it.

There are, of course, many sources of indoor air pollution besides moisture and its related effects. Volatile organic compounds (VOCs) can be found in paints, stains, cleaners, solvents, wood preservatives, and carpeting. Formaldehydes are found in manufactured wood products, such as interior-grade plywood, medium-density fiberboard (MDF), carpets, and furniture. Fuel, automotive products, and hobby supplies stored in the home or garage can also be toxic, as well as many common household chemicals: cleaning products, aerosol sprays, moth repellents, pesticides, and herbicides, for example. Pesticides, herbicides, and radon gas can be drawn into the house from underground (yes, air can move underground, too). Running automobiles and improperly vented (or unvented) combustion appliances can send deadly carbon monoxide (CO) into the home. How can you deal with these pollutants? Isn't it bad to tighten a house with these substances present?

The answer is, "It depends." Of course, if you tighten a house that already has a significant source of toxic fumes, the concentration of pollutants will likely increase. Source reduction is always the first priority, and separating unavoidable toxins from the living space is critical. At the same time, unintended airflow can also contribute to indoor pollution. For example, sealing air leaks between a house and garage, and sealing leaky ducts in the garage can cut paths for auto exhaust to migrate indoors. Meanwhile, a mechanical ventilation system that introduces fresh air helps dilute any toxins that remain. There's a slogan in the building-science industry that sums up these ideas: "Build tight, and ventilate right!"

Weighing Costs and Benefits

Typically, one of the first things people ask when they are thinking about energy improvements to a house is, "What is the payback?" I find this interesting, because most of us make hundreds of other purchase choices—from buying a car or paying for a vacation, to everyday purchases like food or entertainment—without ever asking that question. One of the obvious reasons to conserve energy is to save money, so it is understandable that homeowners think about how much they will save and how long it will take to reclaim that investment. But we do make value decisions about purchases every day, and there are many important factors that people often miss: Nonenergy benefits of whole-house efficiency, alternate ways of looking at payback, the escalation rate of energy costs, and planning ahead for opportunities that may reduce improvement cost all can help tip the balance favorably toward moving forward.

Value beyond energy saved

A cost-benefit analysis can be a useful tool, but payback should not be the only criterion for decision making. As I've pointed out in this chapter, there are many nonenergy benefits

Calculating payback from the cost and energy savings is easy; however, predicting energy savings is more complex.

Financing Energy Improvements

Instead of focusing on payback, cash flow can be a more useful way to look at financing energy improvements. Shown here are the estimated savings from air-sealing and insulating a house financed with a home-equity loan. The annual cost of financing the work is less than the annual energy savings, so the annual cost for energy plus loan payments is less than the pre-improvement cost of energy alone. The monthly payment on the loan eats up most of the energy savings, leaving about $60 per month in positive cash flow to the owner for the term of the loan. Meanwhile, the house is more comfortable, has less environmental impact, and is better protected against rising energy costs.

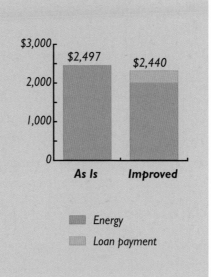

$3,000

$2,497 $2,440

2,000

1,000

0

As Is   Improved

Energy

Loan payment

Get Help with an Energy Rating or Home Performance Audit

Most areas have access to certified professionals who can provide technical assistance and financial analysis for home energy improvements. These professionals typically have insight into available incentives, rebates, preferred financing, and/or tax credits that are available; in some cases, the assessment itself may be partially covered by a local utility company or state agency. You can find information on certified Building Performance professionals and accredited Home Energy Raters at www.bpi.org and www.resnet.us.

An energy assessment can provide the following benefits:

• **A professional assessment** of your energy situation and recommendations for cost-effective upgrades.

• **Special equipment and diagnostic tools** to test your house for air leakage, duct leakage, and other energy problems.

• **Referrals to contractors.** Some states and financing programs prevent home-performance professionals from recommending themselves as contractors to work on your house, and others encourage it. Both BPI and RESNET certification programs provide quality assurance oversight and conflict-of-interest provisions so you can have confidence in their recommendations.

• **Access to financial help** that may be available.

An energy rating or home performance assessment may cost between $250 and $800.

This report shows an estimate of the energy consumption and potential savings for a house.

that may be realized simply by treating the house as a system, which means doing a thorough, thoughtful analysis. These benefits include improved health and reduced building maintenance, both of which are likely to have economic benefits for your family.

Other factors may affect your decision to invest in energy improvements. The most obvious benefit is comfort. Actually, I think that more comfortable people are likely to be happier and healthier, characteristics that probably create some economic benefits as well. Aesthetics and convenience are also important factors, for example, in the choice of whether to replace windows.

Environmental issues may also be a motivating factor. More and more people are willing to pay a premium for "green," low-carbon, and environmentally beneficial products, even if

there is no direct payback whatsoever. Energy consumption in housing is one of your family's biggest environmental impacts (transportation and food consumption are the largest), so reducing your energy budget by a significant chunk will also help the planet and reduce our dependence on nonrenewable fuels.

Cost-benefit calculations (So, what is the payback?)

The basics of cost-benefit analysis are pretty easy. If you invest $100 and it saves you $10 per year, the payback is 10 years. There are other methods for calculating cost-effectiveness that take into account the interest you could earn on that same money if you invested it as well as energy price increases. Typically referred to as a Savings to Investment Ratio (SIR) or net present value (NPV), this analysis is more guesswork than most people may think. Energy prices generally rise faster than inflation, and many experts believe that fuel prices will increase even faster over time. Cutting your energy bills—while preserving comfort and utility—is a way to "future-proof" your house.

For the average do-it-yourselfer, it's not practical to account for all these variables. Generally, the approach I advocate is to prioritize, given the information in this book and the specifics of your house, and to try to balance energy savings with a whole-house approach. For example, don't ignore fresh-air ventilation just because it doesn't result in energy savings. Also, contact your local utility companies. Electric and gas utilities often provide energy audits, and some even contribute money toward energy improvements for their customers. Many community action agencies and other aid organizations run weatherization-assistance programs for income-qualified homeowners. Find out what is offered, and take advantage of any available help when planning your home weatherization project.

Opportunity savings

One other element to consider when thinking about payback is what I call *opportunity savings.* This is sort of the opposite of what economists call *opportunity cost,* which refers to the negative impact of benefits consumers forego (for example, interest earnings on investments) when they decide to spend money. Opportunity savings is the reduction in cost of energy upgrades when you plan those upgrades to coincide with other necessary building maintenance, renovations, or equipment replacement.

For example, adding a significant amount of insulation to an insulated cathedral ceiling may be expensive, but if the roof shingles need replacing anyway, that cost may be reduced sub-

If you are already replacing a boiler or furnace, the added cost to upgrade to a high-efficiency unit is relatively small; don't miss the opportunity.

stantially. Insulating exterior walls with extra layers of rigid-foam insulation is rarely cost-effective unless you are already re-siding your home anyway. When heating or cooling equipment breaks, the added cost to replace it with high-efficiency equipment is much less than it would be otherwise, because you are already paying someone to take away the old machine and put in a new one. Remodeling provides an unparalleled opportunity for including energy upgrades. Check out the chapter on renovations, and try to take advantage of these opportunities when planning your energy retrofit projects. Aim high and do it right: Once you make an improvement in one area of the home, chances are nobody else will touch it for at least a couple of decades.

PRO TIP

Remember that an energy audit or assessment doesn't save you any energy—you only save if you act on their recommendations.

SEALING AIR LEAKS

Almost every house has a large number of hidden air leaks that rob it of heating and cooling energy. Although sealing these leaks is not the easiest job, it is one of the most cost-effective things you can do to increase your home's energy efficiency. You'll want to do this before adding any insulation, as fixing the leaks is much more difficult once extra insulation is installed. In addition to saving energy and making your home more comfortable, sealing air leaks also reduces ice dams and freezing pipes, and helps control moisture movement that can contribute to mold and structural damage.

People often think that windows and doors are the source of most air leakage in a house, but the largest leaks are almost always hidden in attics, basements, crawlspaces, and other unexpected places. This chapter will show you where to look for common air leaks and how to seal them properly. ▶ ▶ ▶

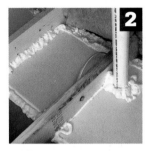

Air-Sealing Priorities

With air-sealing, as with any job, it's useful to know what your priorities are. My strategy is to identify the most important leaks first; sealing them makes the biggest difference in comfort and energy. The priorities are big leaks, and leaks at higher pressures.

Air movement and leakage areas are not always intuitively clear, but remember that air does not move through most solid objects (concrete block and masonry in general are notable exceptions). Air leaks mostly through connections and spaces between building materials.

First find the big leaks

Although it may sound obvious, the most important holes to seal are the largest ones. Not every house has every type of hole, but as you read through this chapter, you may recognize some of these big leaks—called *bypasses*—where indoor and outdoor air mix. I've seen many bypasses that are big enough to crawl through.

Sealing just one of these large bypasses may make a greater difference than replacing every leaky, rattling window in your house. Many bypasses are smaller, but still big enough for a cat to crawl through. When you head up into your attic to hunt for them, make sure your cat doesn't follow you, or he may get lost.

PROTIP

To create a comfortable environment quickly, find the big leaks first and seal them. Then look for smaller leaks.

SEALING THE ATTIC KEEPS YOU WARMER DOWN BELOW

The air barrier is most important at the attic level, where the pressure is greatest.

Warm air leaks out at the top.

Warm air pushes hardest to escape at the attic level. If you can keep the air from leaking out at the top, you will prevent cold air from seeping in at the bottom. A glass under water (see inset) demonstrates the same principle: If the lighter air is prevented from leaking out at the top, the heavier water will not be able to get in at the bottom.

The pressure is smaller in the middle of the house.

Cold air seeps in at the bottom.

The upside-down glass is a good air barrier, preventing exchange between the inside air and the outside water.

Leaks near the bottom are also important, because the pressure is greater there.

(Green dotted line = Air barrier)
(Gold arrows = Warm air)
(Gray arrows = Cold air)

(Red arrows = Air inside glass)
(Blue arrows = Water outside glass)

Ice Dams

If you live in snow country, you've seen houses with ice dams clinging to the eaves. To help prevent ice dams, thorough attic air-sealing should always be a top priority. Note that in areas of high snowfall, the snow itself acts as insulation. In very snowy, cold climates, even a superinsulated, air-tight ceiling or attic has enough heat flow to melt snow at the roof surface, and ice dams can still form. In heavy snow areas, the underside of the roof deck must be vented (regardless of how the attic is sealed and insulated) to cool the sheathing and reduce melting.

How Ice Dams Form

Air leakage is the biggest source of the heat loss that causes ice dams; poorly installed insulation comes in second. Ice dams form when snow melts and runs down the roof to the eaves, where it refreezes and seals tightly to the shingles. This leaves no escape route for further meltwater, which then backs up into the eaves or the house, causing damage.

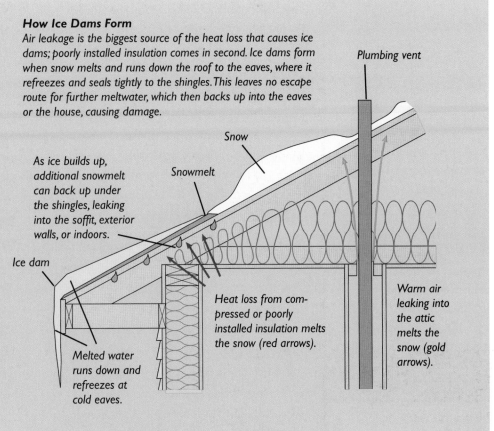

Plumbing vent

Snow

Snowmelt

As ice builds up, additional snowmelt can back up under the shingles, leaking into the soffit, exterior walls, or indoors.

Ice dam

Melted water runs down and refreezes at cold eaves.

Heat loss from compressed or poorly installed insulation melts the snow (red arrows).

Warm air leaking into the attic melts the snow (gold arrows).

Seal the high and low leaks

Remember the stack effect, which pushes out air at the top and pulls in air at the bottom during the winter? (see pp. 7–8.) The greatest pressure differences are those at the highest and lowest points in your house, and your top priority should always be the attic. Doing a complete job of sealing leaks between the house and the attic will help stop cold winter air from seeping in at the bottom of the house (see the drawing on the facing page).

When I sealed the leaks in my own attic, I was amazed at how much more comfortable my living room became. Sealing the attic also helps keep out moisture, reduce ice dams, and prevent hot air from leaking in from the attic or roof in the summer. Sealing leaks in an attic is hard

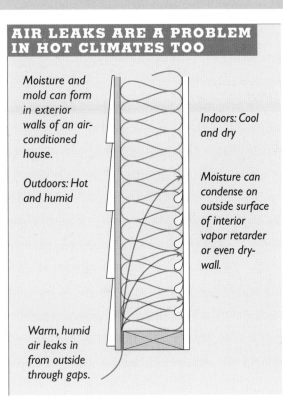

AIR LEAKS ARE A PROBLEM IN HOT CLIMATES TOO

Moisture and mold can form in exterior walls of an air-conditioned house.

Indoors: Cool and dry

Outdoors: Hot and humid

Moisture can condense on outside surface of interior vapor retarder or even drywall.

Warm, humid air leaks in from outside through gaps.

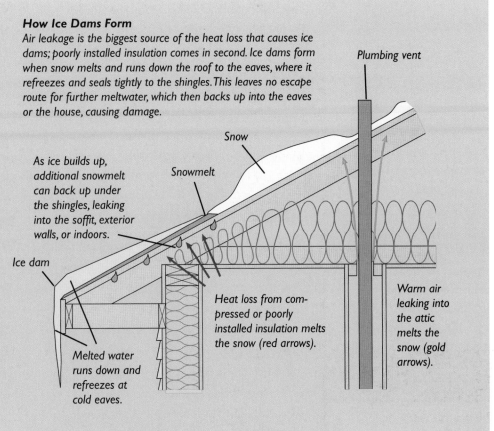

Don't depend on a fiberglass insulation batt lying across an opening to act as an air barrier. Even faced batts will not stop air movement.

TRADE SECRET

My first choice for attic air-sealing is a professional foam gun, which I use to apply low-expansion foam with precision control to a wide range of holes and gaps. Hardware-store foam cans are cheaper and smaller, but they are also awkward to use and difficult to control. Once you start a can, you must use it up quickly or throw it away. Caulking is inexpensive for small jobs, but it can't bridge gaps wider than 3/16 in., and most caulks don't stick well to dusty or dirty surfaces. Although useful in many places, caulk is not recommended for most sealing jobs in the attic.

work, but it is usually the best place to access the thermal boundary at the top of the house.

Once you have sealed the attic, the next priority is the basement, crawlspace, or slab—the home's foundation. Sealing leaks there will help prevent cold air from coming in during the winter and cool air from escaping during the summer. Then you can look for significant leaks in other parts of the house.

Attic Air-Sealing

When walking around your house, you're likely to see only the plaster or drywall. What you don't see are all the connections where building materials meet (or don't meet). The biggest leaks are hidden behind the walls, where you can't see them. The key to air-sealing an attic is to block off the large openings and seal the smaller ones as completely as possible—from one end of the attic to the other. (Note: You might skip the air-sealing if there are lots of complicated leaks as well as leaky ductwork in the attic, or if the attic

Sealing the gap between the top plates and the drywall or plaster with foam insulation is tedious, but it's a critical part of any attic air-sealing job. This is a good time to seal wiring holes as well.

is a space you plan to convert to finished space in the future. If that's the case, consider sealing and insulating the roof instead with sprayed urethane foam (see pgs. 78, 177, and 182–183).

Start by walking through the top story of your house, noticing the location of partition walls, chimneys, light fixtures, changes in ceiling height, plumbing fixtures, and other features where leaks are likely. Then put on your protective gear and head up into the attic to take a closer look.

Start with partition-wall top plates

It's best to be organized when working your way through an attic, so I usually start at one end and work my way to the other in an orderly fashion. This helps me avoid getting mixed up or missing things, particularly when I have to move existing insulation out of the way as I go. And when the attic is cramped (as it often is), it's better to limit your movements.

In most homes, it makes sense to start by first sealing the top plate along one gable end, then work your way down the center, load-bearing wall. Seal the top plate to the plaster on both sides, and seal any wiring holes with spray foam

SAFETY FIRST

Although canned foam is quite safe when fully cured, the uncured liquid has some pretty toxic components. Be careful when using foam, and read the safety notices. Especially protect your eyes and lungs from exposure, and make sure your workspace is ventilated.

ATTIC AIR-LEAKAGE DETAILS

The greatest attic air leaks typically occur where the ceiling is interrupted: at changes in ceiling height, or dropped soffits (A), and at duct and chimney chases (C). Also, check openings around the attic hatch (B); at plumbing vent pipes (D), which vary in size; wiring holes (E); light fixture boxes (F); and other electrical penetrations, which are small but fairly obvious. Less obvious is the crack that almost always occurs between the top plate and the plaster (G) when the framing lumber shrinks. You may also find walls with no top plate (especially gable-end walls) (H) or gaps of a few inches between the exterior wall's sheathing and the exterior wall's top plate (I).

When new framing lumber dries out, it shrinks, and the resulting gaps between top plates and drywall can add up to a 5-sq.-ft. hole.

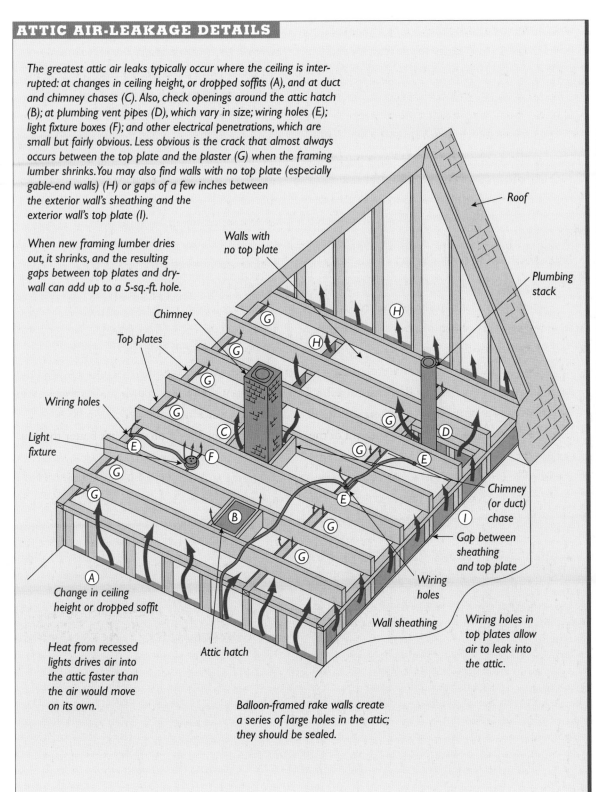

Roof

Walls with no top plate

Plumbing stack

Chimney

Top plates

Wiring holes

Light fixture

Chimney (or duct) chase

Gap between sheathing and top plate

Wiring holes

Wall sheathing

A — Change in ceiling height or dropped soffit

Heat from recessed lights drives air into the attic faster than the air would move on its own.

Attic hatch

Balloon-framed rake walls create a series of large holes in the attic; they should be sealed.

Wiring holes in top plates allow air to leak into the attic.

SAFETY FIRST

Attics can be nasty places—dusty, uncomfortable, and sometimes hazardous. At a minimum, always wear a tight-fitting paper dust mask. I prefer a good-quality respirator (one with an HEPA [High Efficiency Particulate Attenuation] filter); it works better and is more comfortable. It's also a good idea to wear coveralls or other protective clothing and gloves.

You should always wear at least a dust mask when working in an attic. Although a HEPA respirator (left) is more expensive, it is also more effective.

After cutting blocking material to fit and setting it in place, be sure to caulk or foam carefully around all four sides for an airtight, permanent seal.

or caulking (see the photo on p. 32). As the center wall meets intersecting partition walls, follow each partition toward the eaves as far as you can reach. Be sure to find all the closet and hallway walls, which can be confusing.

As you pass each room, closet, or hallway, find any light fixtures that may be in the center of the ceiling and seal the electrical boxes (be careful not to squirt any foam inside the box). Treatments for recessed lighting fixtures are covered on pp. 37–38. If your attic already has insulation in it, be sure to let the foam or caulking set before putting the insulation back in place.

Along the way, you will probably find some larger leaks, such as duct or plumbing chases, chimneys, and the like. Some of them can be sealed with foam or caulk as you go, but most will require some type of blocking. Make a note of what and where those larger leaks are, so that you can return with the right materials. Also make a note of any electrical junction boxes where wires are spliced. This will be useful later, particularly if you are going to add more insulation.

If there is enough clearance between the top plates of the eave walls and the roof sheathing, seal the top plates between the rafter tails. This may be difficult to do. It may help to use a tight-fitting vinyl tube as an extension to your foam gun. If there is a gap between the exterior sheathing and the outside edge of the top plate ("I" in the drawing on p. 33), you may have to stuff a kitchen garbage bag with fiberglass and reach over the top plate to fill this gap. This situation is more common in older plank-sheathing homes, and may be better accessed and sealed by removing the soffit or fascia if either of those needs replacement.

Through-framing into attics

Now that you are thoroughly familiar with your attic, you should have an idea of where the big holes are located. These holes typically occur wherever framing members, such as wall studs or floor joists, run from the conditioned space to the attic space. These bypasses require a little more thought to seal properly, and they are often the largest and most important leaks.

Some contemporary homes have cathedral ceilings flanking both sides of a small attic over the hallway. The studs framing the hallway walls often open into the attic. This one has a plumbing vent, too. Stuff some fiberglass into the opening before sealing it with foam.

One potentially leaky area is the gap between the housing on a bathroom ventilation fan and the ceiling drywall or plaster. Be sure to replace the fan first, if that is part of your ventilation strategy.

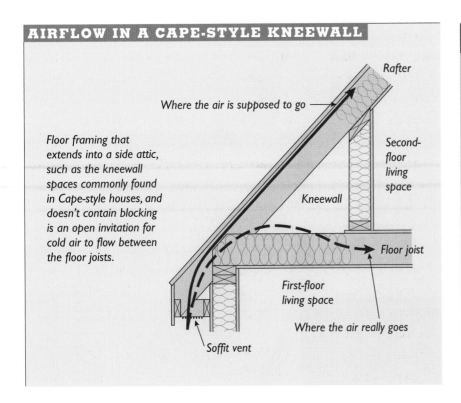

Floor framing that extends into a side attic, such as the kneewall spaces commonly found in Cape-style houses, and doesn't contain blocking is an open invitation for cold air to flow between the floor joists.

Where the air is supposed to go

Rafter

Second-floor living space

Kneewall

Floor joist

First-floor living space

Where the air really goes

Soffit vent

SAFETY FIRST

When working in an attic, make sure you support your weight on the ceiling joists. Otherwise, you may fall right through the ceiling drywall or plaster. It's a good idea to bring a 4-ft. length of 1×12 or a small piece of plywood to help support your weight. Kneepads can also help with the awkward jungle-gym moves.

The key to creating a good air barrier between the conditioned space and the attic is to make sure you bridge all the gaps and spaces between the plaster and the framing members that you can't see from the inside. Your job is to find every place where there is a gap and then patch it. Follow the plane of the plaster or drywall along the ceiling and any connecting walls. This is sort of like playing a three-dimensional "connect-the-dots" game where someone has already filled in some of the links but left out a bunch of them. Wherever the ceiling plane is interrupted or changes levels, you need to supply the connecting link.

Keep in mind that insulation batts with paper or foil facing that lie across one of these openings do *not* constitute an air barrier. Insulation does not stop air! In fact, it's best to ignore the insulation when assessing and fixing an attic's air boundary.

Be aware of some other important issues. First, don't inadvertently seal combustion air openings (see the sidebars at right and on p. 116). Second, use only noncombustible materials within 2 in. of a chimney. Third, recessed lights and some of the situations listed below require special attention.

Cape kneewalls

One of the most common through-framing leaks is found in Cape-style houses. As you can see in the drawing above, the floor joists between the first and second floors usually open into the kneewall attic area, allowing outdoor air to circulate between the floors. Even if there is no access into the kneewall space, it is worth cutting a temporary access through the wall to get in there and block off the joist bays. There are usually many joist bays; you can cut pieces of foam board to fit each one, making them slightly undersized, or cut longer pieces, notching for the joists (see the bottom right photo on p. 37). Wedge them into place and foam or caulk around all the edges. If there is a subfloor in the kneewall area, you may have to pull up some

WHAT CAN GO WRONG

If your furnace is in a closet with an attic above it, there may be combustion air openings from the closet into the attic. Don't seal those openings; if the furnace (or water heater) can't get adequate combustion air, it can generate deadly carbon monoxide gas. Codes require high and low combustion air inlets, and the low one may be fed by a stud bay that opens into the attic, so be sure to leave that unobstructed as well. These openings *can* be sealed if you replace all equipment with direct- or power-vented units.

Attic Bypasses

Although there are many variations, here are some common attic bypass situations:

1. Dropped, or soffited, ceilings are common in kitchens above cabinets, in bathrooms over showers or vanities, and sometimes over stairways (see photo B).

2. Plumbing chases (see photo B) can be much larger than the pipes that run through them.

3. Chimney chases often run all the way to the basement of a house (see photo A).

4. Tri-level homes often have open cavities that extend from the lower level into the attic, along the wall between the levels. These stud spaces are bypasses, as are the large openings that may occur near the stairs (see photo C).

5. Older homes and rowhouses with brick exteriors may have wood furring strips that extend from the attic to the basement. Walls above pocket doors may also have gaps, which open into the channel in which the door slides.

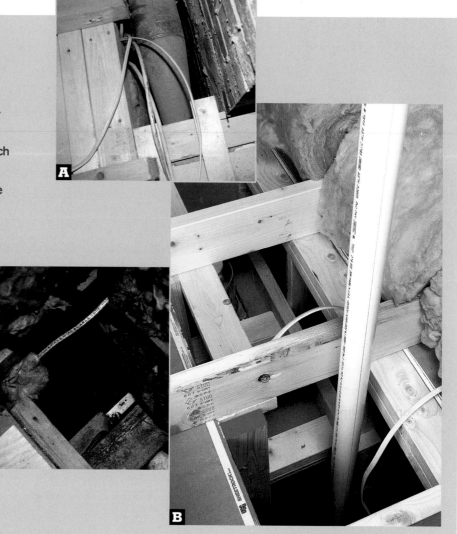

PROTIP

Search for hidden attic spaces above additions so that you don't miss areas that need sealing and insulation.

The simplest fix for most big openings is a piece of 1-in. rigid foam insulation, with canned foam around the edges to seal and hold it in place.

boards or cut away a section of plywood near the kneewall to reach that area.

This type of open floor framing occurs in other places. For example, an ell or an addition with a lower roofline, or a finished room over a garage, may be built the same way, so they need the same type of draft-stopping. Also, floor framing between the first and second floors may open into a porch roof or the attic over a single-story addition or garage. Many of these areas are not normally accessible, so you may need to cut an access through the drywall or plaster to get into them (see "Insulating a House"); because the leaks are so large, it is worth the trouble. Seal these leaks the same way you would a Cape kneewall—foam board or similar blocking material, foamed or caulked in place between the floor joists. As with a full-size attic, note that insulating and sealing at the roof line are viable options for a kneewall space, especially if there is ductwork or equipment there, or if you wish to use the space for storage (see pp. 73–75).

Recessed lights

Recessed "can" light fixtures installed in an insulated ceiling are often big air leaks. Most common styles are full of holes to vent the fixture so it doesn't get too hot. Also, an older unit can't have insulation above, or within 3 in. of any part of the fixture, so each one represents a big "hole" for both air and heat flow. If you have a lot of them, the result can be an energy disaster.

The best approach is to replace them with airtight fixtures that are rated for insulation contact, or "IC." The IC rating allows insulation to surround and cover the light fixture. Not all IC-rated fixtures are airtight (AT), but building codes in most states require airtight IC fixtures, so they are easy to find. Look for a label that says AT or ASTM™ E 283. An airtight retrofit kit or trim/lens kit may also be available for existing recessed cans. Or use an LED insert; though not rated as airtight, the integral lens and trim ring will slow leakage dramatically and save a bundle on the lighting cost as well (see the right photo on p. 208).

As an alternative to replacing your light fixtures, you can build airtight boxes over them using ½-in.-thick drywall, with a drywall or sheet metal top. The box must fit around the joists and be large enough to dissipate the heat emitted by the light. For typical 16-in. o.c. framing, for example, make a box that is about 17 in. square and 14 in. high. Set the sides of the box in place, foam around them (on the outside), and wait for the foam to cure. Then cut the top to size and seal it in place with caulking or duct mastic. Be careful not to insulate over the top;

Any draft-stopper installed within 2 in. of the chimney must be made of a material that won't burn.

The floor framing behind this kneewall is open right into the attic. Unless these gaps are blocked, outdoor air will circulate between the first and second floors.

Sealing the floor bays with foam board is the air-sealing equivalent of closing up two to four large, open windows.

Use airtight recessed lights that are certified as meeting current codes for insulated ceilings. Look for a label that says IC and AT (or insulation contact and airtight).

any insulation above a non-IC-rated light fixture is a violation of the National Electrical Code.

Other special situations

Attic air-sealing is complicated by the fact that there are so many types of houses, but there are some fairly common situations. First, don't miss hidden attic areas. Sometimes an addition, dormer, or ell may have a separate attic that you can't see, because the new roof was built right over the first roof. Cut an access in the roof sheathing once you know where the second attic area is. If you aren't sure, use a tape measure. The nail pattern may give you a hint as to where the valley rafters were nailed. Use a reciprocat-

A sheet-metal top with mastic around the edges completes the airtight box. Don't put any insulation on top of the box.

To maintain a clearance of 3 in. from every part of a non-IC-rated recessed fixture, you may need to cut the drywall to step the box up over the edges of the existing joists.

SAFETY FIRST

Recessed incandescent lights generate a lot of heat. If you build an air-sealing box around one, it is critical that the material be noncombustible, that the top be non-insulating, and that the volume of the box is large enough to dissipate heat generated by the fixture.

You can use foam to seal the box to the ceiling and joists. Be careful not to squirt any foam in under the box.

ing saw and start low. Begin with a small hole, so you can see how far up you can safely cut, and make sure you don't cut into any rafters.

Suspended ceilings can hide tremendous leakage areas, particularly if they have attic spaces above. In older houses, such ceilings are often installed to hide deteriorating plaster. There may be large holes in the ceiling or high on the walls that are hidden by the dropped ceiling. You can move the ceiling tiles as needed and patch the holes with drywall scraps. Use pieces that are large enough to cover the holes. Be sure to drive plenty of screws into the lath or ceiling joists, and caulk around the edges to obtain a good seal.

Sometimes a suspended ceiling hides open framing that is insulated with only faced fiberglass batts. This is a huge air leak: neither the insulation nor the suspended ceiling is an air

barrier. It's best to remove the suspended ceiling and install new drywall. If this is not an option, you can remove ceiling tiles and staple an air barrier to the underside of the joists. Use 6-mil poly in cold climates or nonperforated housewrap in mixed or hot climates. You must cut and fit the material around each penetration. Be sure to use good-quality tape for the seams. Also, tape the air barrier to the walls or top plates on all sides, and use a sealant (preferably foam) for all penetrations.

Another potential air-leakage disaster is a wooden tongue-and-groove ceiling. Whether the ceiling is flat or cathedral, if there is no air barrier behind the planks (which is typical), the hundreds of lineal feet of cracks in even a small room can add up to a big leak. If the aesthetic value of the wood ceiling is important, the only reliable way to add a good air barrier is to care-

PRO TIP

Suspended ceilings can hide tremendous leakage areas, particularly if they have attic spaces above them.

Sometimes, small dormer attics may be hidden behind the roof sheathing; in this case, fortunately, the attic is visible and easily accessed.

This tongue-and-groove ceiling allows lots of indoor air to reach the cold roof sheathing in winter, where it freezes; when the weather warms up, it rains indoors.

Cathedral ceilings are difficult to air-seal and add insulation to. But not all ceilings that appear to be cathedral are. If the slope of the ceiling is shallower than the slope of the roof, the roof was probably built with scissors trusses and is not a true cathedral ceiling. Although difficult, it may be possible to gain access to reach some of the larger leaks and install more insulation.

WHAT CAN GO WRONG

Acoustical-tile ceilings present a potentially large air-leakage problem. These 1-ft.-sq. tiles are basically made of compressed paper with tongue-and-groove edges, and the cracks between them leak like crazy. The only reasonable solution is to drywall right over them. If they are on sloped- or cathedral-ceiling areas where there is limited room to add insulation, this is the perfect opportunity to install some rigid-foam insulation prior to the drywall.

The plumbing wall in this house opens into the cathedral ceiling, dumping warm air into the roof cavity above and melting snow to cause this ice dam.

fully remove the planks, create an air barrier, and reinstall the wood. The air barrier can be taped drywall or, better, an inch or more of rigid foam insulation (with carefully sealed seams). The latter also adds R-value. If the wooden ceiling is not important to you, drywall can be installed over the boards. This is also a good opportunity to add rigid insulation, especially if it's a cathedral ceiling with limited room for insulation in the rafter cavity.

Before you pull apart a wooden ceiling, check to see whether there is an air barrier behind it; if there is, you may have a much smaller problem on your hands. Poke around a bit at the cracks where the wood fits together; there are almost always some places where the tongue is cracked, the wood is split, or the ends don't butt tightly. Use a small flashlight to see past the wood. If you don't see polyethylene, drywall, or some other solid material (kraft paper or foil facing doesn't count), you probably have no air barrier.

Occasionally, air leaks occur in places that are virtually impossible to reach. If your house has a lot of cathedral-ceiling areas, you may have many plumbing vents and wiring holes that lead from partition-wall cavities up into the roof. These provide a path for warm humid air to escape in winter and for hot attic air to leak into interior walls in summer. Unless you are planning to re-roof or to gut those partitions in a remodel, your most likely options involve dense-packed cellulose insulation or two-part foam. Either can be installed from indoors where the partition walls meet the roof (see the sidebar on p. 84).

Other hard-to-reach areas include gambrel and mansard roofs. Structurally, they are very similar to Cape kneewalls (see p. 35), but the kneewall area is far too narrow to access. Small eyebrow roofs, or overhangs in the middle of two-story walls, can also be a problem. It may be possible to access the area from the exterior by removing the soffit; if the space is small, you may also be able to fill it with dense-packed cellulose.

Small roofs like this one can hide big air leaks; they often hide large gaps in the wall sheathing behind them.

SAFETY FIRST

Attached garages can be a repository for deadly carbon monoxide and other toxic fumes, as well as cold air, so it is very important to seal the boundary between the house and the garage. Make sure that all joist spaces over garage walls are blocked and sealed. If drywall is in the way, try dense-pack cellulose in the garage ceiling (see the drawing on p. 87).

PROTIP

Seal leaks at the lowest level of your home to keep out radon, other toxins in the soil, and water vapor.

Basement/Crawlspace Air-Sealing

After the attic, the basement or crawlspace is the next most important area to seal for several reasons. Like the top of a home, the bottom typically has the largest air pressure pushing air in or out of the house, so sealing those leaks results in larger energy savings. Second, though often smaller than attic leaks, basement and crawlspace leaks tend to be larger than those in exterior walls. More important, in most climates, air leaks *in* from the bottom in cool or cold weather. This leaking air can carry radon gas, mold spores, gases from pesticide treatments, water vapor, and any other subsoil nasties that may become airborne. Sealing leaks at the lowest level of your home helps prevent these undesirable elements from entering your home. Finally, most pipe-freezing problems result from cold air leaking in around the sills, where the pipes are often located.

Basement walls

Generally, I consider it most effective to create a good air barrier between the basement and the outdoors by sealing the walls. This is typically true

All service penetrations in a basement should be sealed with caulking (if the gap is small) or foam (if the gap is large).

INDETAIL

Stepped foundation walls are often built on hillsides in cold climates. The vertical parts of the steps are often particularly leaky. These can be sealed from inside or out with silicone caulking. Stuff in some fiberglass as a backing, or use spray foam if the gap is large.

even if you intend to insulate the floor over the basement. There are four common leakage areas in basement walls: service penetrations, stepped-wall transitions, bulkhead doors, and the sill/band joist area. Note that if you intend to finish or renovate your basement, it might make sense to seal and insulate the walls with spray foam or flash and batt (see pp. 89–91, 177, and pp. 182–183).

Here are three grades of caulking guns. From bottom to top, they sell for about $4, $8, and $20. You get what you pay for—stay away from the $4 guns.

Service penetrations Every home has basic service penetrations, such as those for electricity, telephone, plumbing, fuel lines, and cable TV. Often, these penetrations are made in the band-joist area, also called the box sill or ribbon joist in conventionally framed houses (in older homes, this may be one large sill beam). Sometimes penetrations come through the foundation (especially plumbing drains, which are always below grade). Seal all penetrations from the inside, the outside, or both with caulking or foam. Any below-grade penetrations must be sealed from the inside. And don't assume that air can't leak in from underground; soil is often surprisingly porous to air movement.

If other joists are in the way, services that run through the band joist may be difficult to reach from the inside, so you may need to seal them from the outside. If your basement is finished, the exterior may be the only area to which you have access. Caulk or seal these openings, being careful to seal all the way around.

Bulkhead doors Another common source of basement leakage is the bulkhead door. Bulkheads are designed to keep out rain but not to stop air. If your basement is unfinished, the best way to deal with this is to install a new exterior door at the foundation wall inside the bulkhead. Use treated wood where the door contacts the foundation, and be sure to tightly seal between the framing around the door and the concrete. If your basement is fully or partially finished and already has a door inside the bulkhead, you may still have a large air leak at the top and sides. Be sure to put solid blocking in the gap between the door frame and the foundation, then caulk around all the edges.

An insulated, weatherstripped door is essential inside any bulkhead basement opening.

Although a typical steel bulkhead basement door sheds water, it barely slows cold air from leaking inside.

Be sure to seal between the door frame and the foundation wall. Remember to use only treated wood in contact with concrete.

Sills and band joists The tops of foundation walls are often far from flat. The gaps may be small, but spread around the perimeter of a home, they really add up. Even recently built homes that have a foam sill sealer between the sill and the concrete may leak a lot of cold air

there. Also, there are usually three or four framing members that are stacked on top of each other between the foundation wall and the first floor's subfloor, and each of those junctions can leak. You can seal this area from the inside or from the outside; if you have access, you may want to do both.

Sealing the band joist from the inside yields the best results, if it's not hidden behind a finished ceiling. To do this, you can cut blocks of 2-in.-thick extruded polystyrene. Cut the blocks to fit snugly in height, but leave them about ½ in. narrower than the joist spacing. Wedge them into place, as close as possible to the band joist, then foam or caulk them on all four sides. Be sure to seal the area between each block at the bottom, where the joist rests on the sill. You can do the same thing on the gable ends of the house, using long strips of foam board that are sealed on all four sides. As an alternate, you can spray a couple of inches of two-part foam from a kit to seal and insulate in one step. Whichever approach you use, be careful not to trap heating

WHAT CAN GO WRONG

When air-sealing a basement, be careful not to interfere with combustion air required by the furnace, boiler, or hot-water heater. All combustion equipment needs enough air to provide oxygen for the fire, and sealing a house can sometimes interfere with that process. If the equipment is not working properly, it can lead to the production of deadly carbon monoxide. If possible, it's best to replace equipment with direct- or power-vented, high-efficiency models.

Blower-Door Testing

Air-sealing is a job that requires much more labor than material, which often suggests a do-it-yourself approach. However, air-sealing does require attention to detail and (in many homes) a willingness to squeeze into difficult places. If these qualities don't describe you, it may be worth hiring a building-performance professional. Experienced professionals use a blower door to help find air leaks and measure the tightness of the building. The fan blows air into (or out of) the house, measuring how well the building enclosure contains pressure. This can be very handy, especially in a house with complex air-leakage paths.

It's also good to keep the big picture in mind: If you are planning on renovating or adding onto your house, you will have a unique opportunity to seal leaks while the building is opened up. It may not make sense to manually seal leaks now that you know you will deal with them more effectively at the next stage, especially leaks that are small or hard to reach. Of course, if the next stage is a few years off, it may still be well worth hitting the big leaks at a minimum. A building-performance professional can help you set priorities and make a long-term plan.

A blower door is used to measure how airtight a house is. It's also useful in helping identify where the air leaks are.

A two-part spray foam kit is a great option to seal and insulate the entire sill and joist area in one step. Be sure to wear appropriate safety gear.

Sealing the band joist (in this case, with foam-board blocks) from the inside is another effective approach.

In some cases, it's possible to seal sills from outside by caulking the space between the bottom edge of the exterior sheathing and the foundation wall. In some places, there may be gaps so large that you need to fill them with foam instead of caulk. Trim off the extra foam so you don't create any ledges that can trap water running down the siding and direct it inside.

or plumbing pipes between the insulation and the outside; they could freeze.

Sealing the floor deck

Although it is typically more difficult than sealing foundation walls, sealing the floor deck between the basement and the first floor may make sense. If you want to use the basement as living space, it's almost always better and easier to insulate and seal the exterior basement walls. But if the house sits on an unfinished basement or vented crawl-space, you may benefit from sealing the floor from below. Note that sealing the floor deck can be

very difficult if you have a finished ceiling in the basement. In this case, focus your efforts on the sill and the exterior foundation walls.

The basic idea behind floor air-sealing is the same as attic air-sealing: to create an uninterrupted air barrier between levels. Typically, this is done at the subfloor. First-floor decks have

Most floors have many service penetrations, which make them difficult to seal well.

This tub trap is a big air leak from the basement into the house. Note that the duct chase (another big air leak) in the lower right corner should also be sealed.

many holes in the subfloor for plumbing drains, supply piping, wiring, ducts, and chimney chases. Bathtubs and showers often have large cutouts underneath the drain trap. Those holes require a material that can span large spaces. The materials listed for attic bypasses will work. Also, look for openings or penetrations under kitchen and bathroom cabinets and built-in furniture.

The insulation on these crawlspace walls was carefully sealed to the vapor barrier on the floor, creating a warm, dry space.

Even better than regular poly are products such as Tu-tuf, Tenoarm, and PolyTuff®. These sheets are thinner but much stronger and more puncture resistant than regular polyethylene. (These products are available from sellers of energy-efficient building products; see Resources.)

Crawlspaces

Crawlspaces are nothing more than short basements, usually just deep enough for the footings to be below the frost line. Unlike basements, they often have exposed dirt floors. Building code requirements for vapor retarders are typically inadequate, even when they are followed properly. Crawlspaces can be pretty nasty places; they often have inadequate drainage. Building codes that require these spaces be vented to the outdoors may make matters worse.

The best treatment for a crawlspace is to include it in the conditioned space by sealing and insulating the exterior walls, just like a basement. Of course, any standing water must first be eliminated. Make sure that the crawlspace floor slopes to a low point (or create a low point by digging a trench across one side or around the perimeter) so all the water drains to that point. Install a sump pump or drain to daylight from that low point to get out any water that leaks in from outside or from a plumbing leak. And clear out any sharp rocks or other materials that

ACCORDING TO CODE

Code (and common sense) says not to use foam or other combustible materials around active chimneys or heating-equipment vent pipes. These penetrations can be sealed with high-temperature caulking; use metal flashing or cement board if you have large spaces to fill. Also, avoid using foam around heating pipes, particularly if you have steam heat.

TRADE SECRET

I often use acoustical sealant when I'm installing poly in a crawlspace, particularly to seal it to the walls. Although it is messy to work with, it sticks well to polyethylene and works even better than high-quality tape. Polyurethane caulk also works well.

Plastic button anchors (see inset: Outwater Plastics; www.outwater.com) can be pressed into ¼-in. holes drilled with a hammer drill. One button every 3 ft. can support even a heavy liner.

After the vapor retarder is hung on the walls, spread the overlapping piece on the floor. Be sure to seal it carefully at all edges and penetrations.

might damage the poly as you're installing it. Next, seal up existing crawlspace vents with a piece of 2-in.-thick polystyrene cut to fit in the vent; caulk or foam it in place from the inside.

A crawlspace should have a superbly sealed vapor retarder. The earth is such a large source of moisture that a few pieces of poly scattered on the floor can't do a good job. Use full sheets of 6-mil polyethylene or, better yet, one of the varieties of cross-laminated poly. Start by hanging a strip that covers the foundation walls; seal it to the wall a few inches above grade, using urethane caulking; hold it in place with pressure-treated nailing strips and powder-actuated nails, or drill holes and use plastic "button" anchors. Allow the bottom edge to extend at least 12 in. past the bottom of the wall onto the crawlspace floor. You'll find it easier to cut the poly to size in the driveway rather than the crawlspace. Cut it generously; it's easier to trim a bit off than to add some back.

Then, plan to cover the floor with sections that extend up the wall about 12 in. on all sides.

You can plan for two or more wide strips that run parallel to the long wall of the house so the seams are in line with rows of piers or supports as much as possible. Make the pieces wide enough to overlap 12 in. to 24 in. As you install the poly, it's best to lift up any wooden posts just enough to slip the edge of the poly underneath. This provides a capillary break and reduces the amount of sealing you'll have to do. Use a hydraulic jack (or two) supported on sections of 4×4 or 6×6 to jack up the beam resting on each support. For masonry columns or supports, lap the poly up a few inches and seal it to the column with urethane caulk. Fill in each section of floor, sealing it to the wall and the other floor sections until you've completed the job—you can tape the seams with good-quality tape such as 3M® Builders Sealing Tape or Tyvek® Sheathing Tape. If you have a sump pit, seal the poly to the edge of the sump pit liner so water will drain into the pit.

Finally, insulate the crawlspace walls with 2-in. rigid foam insulation, taping or sealing every joint; or have the walls insulated with sprayed urethane foam. Remember to seal and insulate the band joist carefully, (see pp. 43–44).

Slab-on-grade

If your home (or part of your home) has no basement or crawlspace, it is probably a concrete slab-on-grade. Those homes are somewhat simpler to seal because there are fewer connections among building materials at the foundation. Your primary job with slab-on-grade construction is to caulk or otherwise seal the exterior walls where the house framing meets the slab. Caulk any gaps between the baseboard and the floor from the inside, although with carpeting, this may be difficult. You can also caulk the exterior, where the siding or sheathing meets the slab, but that may be difficult if the slab is very close to the ground.

Also look for conduits that carry services (water pipes, etc.) from underground up into an indoor mechanical room—these may leak air, and can be sealed with spray foam or electrician's putty.

Sidewall Air-Sealing

Exterior walls are not typically the leakiest parts of a house. Leaks occur in walls where services enter the home, where the framing of the house makes transitions, around rough openings for windows, and through and around window sashes. (Windows will be covered in more detail in "Windows.")

In older wood-framed homes, the framing spaces of interior partition walls may also open into exterior wall cavities. If you have an older, uninsulated house, pay special attention to these junctions—you can treat them with dense-packed cellulose or two-part kit foam (see p. 84).

Service penetrations

Sealing cable, wiring, plumbing, and telephone service penetrations is fairly easy. Such openings are usually accessible from the exterior and are often small because some effort is made to weatherproof them during installation.

Caulk for Air-Sealing

I GENERALLY USE TWO TYPES OF CAULK: 100-percent-pure silicone and siliconized acrylic latex. My preference is pure silicone caulk. Although it's more expensive and harder to clean, pure silicone is much more adhesive, more flexible, and less prone to shrinkage as it cures. It's a must anywhere you are trying to seal wood, metal, or concrete to one another, because the differential movement of these materials will tear acrylic caulks apart. It can safely be used on gaps up to about 1/4 in. wide; wider gaps require you to stuff in some spongy material or insulation as a backing. Pure silicone is also much more durable, so it's better for exterior applications that aren't too visible;

however, it is not paintable. Acrylic can be painted easily, so I generally reserve it for interior spaces and conspicuous exterior areas. However, because it shrinks more, don't use acrylic on any gap or crack wider than 3/16 in. unless you install backing.

Stay away from clear acrylics. The cured, clear material has a shiny surface that can be quite noticeable. They also contain fewer solids than pigmented acrylic caulks do, so they shrink more. Be sure to store any type of caulking at room temperature; if it gets too cold, it can be very difficult to squeeze out, and it may not cure properly.

Pull-down attic stairs are especially difficult to insulate and seal. You can buy a prefabricated kit like this Therma-dome, which is made of 1½-in.-thick foil-faced insulation, or you can make one yourself. Make sure you have a nice, flat deck around the stairway opening on which the box can sit (the deck needs to be only 1 ft. wide), and caulk the deck to the rough opening for a good seal.

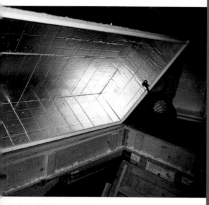

This pull-down stair kit comes with adhesive, weatherstripping, aluminum tape for the edges, and hook-and-loop tabs on each end to tie it down tightly.

This cantilever can be a source of cold-air leaks; be sure to caulk around it carefully.

I usually use caulking to seal any gaps where services enter through the siding.

Transitions in exterior wall framing

One common example of a wall transition is a cantilevered floor, typically an overhang of 1 ft. to 3 ft. that is common on raised ranches and Colonial-style homes. Often, the plywood soffit at the bottom of the overhang is not sealed tightly, and air can leak through these gaps, which are easy to caulk. If the cantilever is finished with aluminum or vinyl soffit material, the leakage is even worse. I've seen cantilevers finished with perforated vinyl and no air barrier at all. In that case, you should carefully remove the soffit and add a solid material, such as plywood. Caulk around all four edges, and replace the vinyl or aluminum soffit, if you wish.

Other places where walls make transitions can be leaky, but they often take the form of a roof or an attic interrupting a vertical wall. Most of those cases are covered under "Attic Air-Sealing" on p. 32.

Most weatherstripping is not worth the packaging it comes in. Here, from left to right, are some high-quality ones. V-seal can be used for doors and windows. Silicone rubber bulb, which stays flexible and soft at low temperatures, works well for doors with a narrow clearance. My favorite is the vinyl-covered V-section (Q-lon® is one brand). It is available without backing for stapling onto unfinished areas or for replacing worn-out magnetic weatherstripping; and with aluminum or wooden trim.

Any overhang that is finished with only a vinyl soffit material with fiberglass batts is like a 40-ft.-long door left open, with only a venetian blind pulled over it. This area needs a solid soffit material.

Weatherstripping Doors and Hatches

Most modern doors and windows have good weatherstripping built in, but older ones usually don't. In addition, many homes have at least one less-finished, or even makeshift, door or hatchway as part of the thermal boundary. This section discusses replacing or repairing weatherstripping on hinged doors, access panels, and attic hatches.

Weatherstripping a door

To seal any standard swinging exterior door, install a flexible, spongy weatherstrip on the top and both sides. First, remove old weatherstrip that may be in the way. Start with the top piece, cutting it to fit into the corners of the doorstops. Press the piece against the closed door so that the spongy side is slightly compressed, then nail or screw it in place; don't drive the nail heads in yet. Then cut the side strips to length. Install those pieces the same way, working from the top down. The trick is to compress the spongy part enough to ensure that there will be good contact, but not so much that it interferes with the door's closing and latching. Check the fit, then drive the nails home.

Door sweeps

Door sweeps cover the crack at the bottom of a door. If you plan to install weatherstripping on the sides of the door opening, be sure to do so first.

If your door has a low threshold, or if there's a thick rug or an irregular floor in front of it, a flat sweep will scrape and prevent the door from working. In that situation, use a hinged sweep, which flips down snugly when the door is closed. A few pointers: Be sure to cut the sweep ⅛ in. shorter than the doorstops, so the sweep doesn't bind. Pull out the flexible rubber strip, and use a hacksaw to cut the aluminum section to length on the end that will be at the hinge side of the door. Reinsert the strip, then cut it to length with a utility knife. Next, squeeze the ends of the aluminum track to pinch the rubber strip in place. I recommend predrilling a hole for the stop button; otherwise the doorstop is likely to split. Open and close the door a few times to make sure everything works properly.

Weatherstripping an attic or a crawlspace hatch

Attic hatches are often quite leaky. I recommend using vinyl-faced weatherstripping with an aluminum carrier strip. Usually, a kit designed for a door will do at least one access hatch, sometimes two. Cut the pieces with a pair of sharp tin snips and screw them in place. If the hatch door is too lightweight or too warped to make a good seal, replace it with ⅝-in. A/C plywood or another sturdy, flat material. Either way, you may need to add a pair of eye hooks or a barrel bolt to keep the hatch snug against the weatherstripping.

After trimming a door sweep to size, crimp the ends to hold the rubber strip in place.

This door sweep lifts out of the way when you open the door, riding clear of carpets and uneven floors.

VENTILATION SYSTEMS

Ventilation systems are important to a healthy, comfortable indoor environment. I strongly recommend sealing a house as tightly as you reasonably can and installing a simple mechanical ventilation system to provide controlled air exchange. This system should include local spot ventilation in bathrooms and kitchens, as well as some type of automatic, full-time, whole-house ventilation. The whole-house ventilation may be easily and inexpensively integrated with bathroom exhaust fans or with a heating and cooling system. More comprehensive whole-house ventilation systems offer the most control of air exchange and filtration, but they are considerably more expensive. This chapter will outline the basic options for house ventilation systems and describe how they are installed. ▶ ▶ ▶

A whole-house fan, typically installed to exhaust a large volume of air into the attic, is often effective at offsetting air-conditioning needs in the summer, but it is too large to provide a continuous background source of fresh air.

Do I Need a Ventilation System?

Why make a house tight, and then spend money to ventilate it? Doesn't it make more sense to just leave it a little bit leaky? The short answer is, "No." A leaky house experiences haphazard ventilation that is often appropriate or inadequate. A good ventilation system, on the other hand, allows you to control the introduction of fresh air into a home.

Fresh-air ventilation can help dilute pollutants in the home, manage moisture, and improve air quality. It is not something you install to compensate for a tight house. It should be installed in every house, and the house must be tight—that is, properly air-sealed—before ventilation can work properly. A tight building enclosure is an essential part of a ventilation system; without it, you don't have adequate control over the air-exchange rate.

The nameplate sticker shows a fan's airflow rating in cubic feet per minute (CFM) and its sound level in sones. The Home Ventilating Institute (HVI) maintains a directory of all listed products along with their ratings (see www.hvi.org).

Interior moisture problems, such as excessive window condensation, mildew growth, or peeling paint, may indicate that you need a fresh-air ventilation system.

"A house has to breathe..."

One of the wonderful qualities of the human respiratory system is that its level of activity adjusts to your needs. When you are active, you breathe quickly to increase the incoming oxygen flow; when you are at rest, your breathing slows. If a ventilation system acts as the "lungs" of a house, then it too needs to be capable of adjusting its airflow rate, depending on your family's ventilation needs. A good fresh-air ventilation system allows you to change the ventilation schedule, or vary the rate of airflow, so that you can add extra ventilation when the house is full of people or turn it off completely when nobody is home.

As for operating costs, in most climates a very tight home with the right amount of mechanical ventilation is less expensive to operate than a leaky house. If you leave ventilation to random air leaks, you get too much airflow when it's cold and windy outside (and heating the air costs more) and not enough when the weather is mild. With a tight house, overventilation in extreme weather is eliminated; adding controlled ventilation allows you to adjust the air-exchange rate properly for a range of outdoor conditions. But ventilation won't solve every moisture problem: Fixing or controlling moisture sources, such as an exposed earth floor in a crawlspace or improperly vented combustion equipment, is also essential.

Ventilation systems typically provide better indoor air quality, while reducing the need for building maintenance. Some of the indications that you may need ventilation include mold, mildew, attic moisture, or window condensation in winter. A stuffy-smelling house, cooking odors that linger for hours, and chronically peeling paint may also indicate poor ventilation.

Types of ventilation systems

A well-designed ventilation strategy for a house includes both whole-house and local exhaust ventilation. A whole-house ventilation system is designed to provide a minimum amount of fresh outdoor air to the living space year-round.

Several manufacturers make bathroom fans that are quiet and efficient. This Panasonic WhisperGreen® is almost silent, and uses less than 10 watts. Options include automatic low-speed controls and motion sensor.

SAFETY FIRST

Don't attempt to do the wiring for a new fan or controller unless you understand the safety and code requirements, and always turn off the appropriate circuit breakers before working on electrical circuits. This part of the job is best left to an electrician.

ACCORDING TO CODE

Code requirements for bathroom ventilation are usually satisfied by an operable window, but most people don't like to open bathroom windows in the winter. Despite the code, every bathroom should have an exhaust fan of at least 50 CFM. Range hoods are also highly recommended to reduce cooking moisture and odors. Codes generally require installed range hoods to be rated at a minimum of 100 CFM. Bathroom and kitchen fans should vent directly outdoors.

Kitchen exhaust hoods are more effective at a lower airflow than the popular downdraft exhausts are. Due to the grease and fire hazard, make sure the equipment and ductwork is rated for range applications.

PRO TIP

To improve air quality, source reduction should always precede ventilation.

A whole-house system runs either full-time at an adjustable rate or on a schedule that you set according to your needs. With the right controls, you can use a simple bathroom fan or a return-air duct in your HVAC air handler to provide whole-house ventilation. The installation for these simple, inexpensive systems is covered on pp. 55–59. Other types of whole-house ventilation systems include fully ducted central exhaust systems and heat- or energy-recovery ventila-

tion (HRV or ERV) systems, which are more complex, more expensive, and (sometimes) more effective.

Simple Ventilation Systems

The simplest type of whole-house ventilation system is an exhaust-only, or supply-only,

IN DETAIL

If you can vent an exhaust fan horizontally through a wall, a standard 4-in. or 6-in. exhaust hood with a flapper will work fine. However, to avoid long duct runs that drastically reduce airflow, it's sometimes necessary to vent it vertically through the roof. In that case, you'll need a roof jack, as shown below. Be sure to follow the installation instructions carefully and make sure that the flashing tucks under the roofing shingles to avoid leaks.

Ventilation Ductwork

Small home ventilation fans are rated for airflow assuming a standard amount of duct pressure. You may think that as long as a fan can blow air into a duct, air must come out at the other end. But if there's too much friction—caused by rough inner surfaces, too many elbows and bends, or a run that is too long—the fan will just spin in place, and little or no air will move.

What to do? First, stay away from flex duct. Flex duct is cheap, fast, and easy to use, and it fits easily in tight spaces. But there's a heavy price for convenience: All the coils and rough surfaces add resistance and slow the airflow.

Instead, use smooth, rigid-metal ducts whenever possible. Plan your ducts to keep the runs short, and keep the elbows and fittings to a minimum. For a complex, central ventilation system, I recommend hiring an HVAC contractor who knows how to design ductwork for proper airflow, using the "equivalent length" method.

Rigid-metal ducts reduce friction to give you the maximum performance from your fan.

A contorted, vinyl flex hose is fairly typical. Not only do installations like this one fail to provide the required airflow, but low spots can trap water in cold weather or even fill with ice. Flexible aluminum is not much better; use smooth, rigid metal (or PVC pipe) whenever possible.

Whole-House Ventilation Sizing

Background ventilation fans sized to meet these airflow rates will meet Standard 62.2, the ANSI/ASHRAE standard for ventilation in homes. The standard also provides an alternate calculation:
(7.5 × [number of bedrooms + 1]) + (0.01 × house square feet)

Minimum ventilation fan ratings in CFM

Floor area	# of bedrooms			
	0-1	2-3	4-5	6-7
<1,500	30	45	60	75
1,501-3,000	45	60	75	90
3,001-4,500	60	75	90	105
4,501-6,000	75	90	105	120

ventilation fan. An exhaust-only system draws outdoor air inside through small cracks and gaps that already exist, even in a tightly sealed house. I have seen it used successfully in hundreds of new homes—some of which are very tight—as well as retrofitted to solve moisture problems.

Bath-fan system

Every bathroom should have a working exhaust fan. To designate one as the whole-house system, first choose a bathroom—the one that is either most used or most centrally located—in which to set up a controlled fan. You may have an exhaust fan already, but it's unlikely that it will meet the requirements: It must be quiet, energy efficient, and rated for continuous operation at the required airflow. If you need to replace an existing fan, choose a bathroom with an accessible attic area above (or an exterior wall you can use).

Most fans are rated for noise and airflow by the Home Ventilating Institute. Noise is rated in sones—the higher the sone rating, the more noise it makes. I think that fans with sone ratings of greater than 1 are too noisy for this application; if you can, choose a fan rated at 0.5 or less.

See the chart above to get at least the minimum airflow you need to plan for your whole-house system. In most cases, a 50-CFM to 100-CFM fan will do nicely. You will then add a control to reduce it to the average ventilation you need by running the fan on low speed, or part-time, or both.

Note that exhaust airflow from a bathroom can do double duty: run continuously to provide whole-house ventilation, and also to provide the local exhaust for the bathroom. The flow has to be sized to the larger of the two CFM requirements, (not the sum.)

To do its job properly, a fan must be vented to the outside and have a duct run that is as short and direct as possible. If you can't reach an exterior wall or gable end within about 10 ft., you may be able to put in an elbow and vent it straight up to a roof jack. Always use rigid-metal duct (4-in. or 6-in. dia.); if the duct runs through an attic or other unheated space, be sure to insulate it with vinyl-covered duct wrap.

If you don't have access to add or replace a bathroom fan, another option is to install a wall-mounted fan. Several models are available for

One drawback of the simple exhaust ventilation system is that there is no control over where the make-up air comes from. Although it is generally dispersed throughout a building, make-up air may pass through leaks in basements, garages, or other places with pollutant sources. Remember: Source reduction is the first step toward improving indoor air quality.

through-wall mounting that are quiet and use very little power. It should cost between $200 and $350 for the necessary parts (including fan, ductwork, and controls).

Ventilation controls

To be considered a whole-house ventilation system, the fan must be capable of running on a regular schedule or continuously, if necessary. There are many devices available that can control fan speed, operating times, or both. When

Controls for Simple Ventilation Systems

Either of the switches shown in the left photo below is better than a regular switch, because it can run the fan for 20 or 30 minutes after you leave the bathroom and exhaust all the moisture after taking a shower.

A 24-hour timer provides flexibility and is easy to set and adjust (center, photo at right below). It controls the background air exchange—you need a separate switch to override the program, so that the fan can be turned on whenever it's needed. This system does need more wiring; I recommend locating the dial timer where you can reach it easily but do not have to look at it every day.

The Airetrak (left, photo at right below) is a good alternative when you want to

replace an existing wall switch but don't want to add new wiring box for a timer. This unit can be set at varying fan speeds and/or hourly timed settings. The button overrides the program and runs the fan for 20 minutes, then automatically goes back to the program. This unit runs the same program every hour, making it less flexible than the 24-hour timer.

An Airetrak 62.2 control by Tamarack (right side, photo below) provides continuous, low-speed operation (wired in parallel with a regular or fan-delay switch to provide full speed boost). At $30, it's probably the cheapest route of all, but once you pick the color (low-speed setting, based on your fan model and desired whole-house CFM) it's not adjustable.

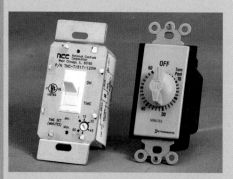

The fan delay timer switch at left turns on a bath fan when you switch it on, but when you switch it off the fan runs for a preset time that can be adjusted from 1 to 60 minutes. It can also turn a light on and off without the delay. The windup timer at right is simpler, allowing you to select the shutoff delay when you activate the fan. Both models ensure good moisture removal.

Left: The Airetrak is a special timer that includes time delay, fan speed, intermittent run times, and even an LCD clock; push buttons operate the fan alone, or the fan along with a light. Center: A 24-hour dial timer fits in a single-gang box and allows on and off times in 20-minute increments. Right: Choose one of these nifty controls to set your low-speed continuous ventilation rate.

One common type of central exhaust fan is the in-line fan, like this one made by Fantech. These fans can be sized to exhaust several bathrooms, and they may be mounted in the attic or basement for quiet operation and easy service. Note that the attic-mounted, rigid-metal ductwork and fan are fully insulated to prevent interior condensation.

you're choosing a controller for your ventilation fan, check with your supplier to make sure that the controls are compatible with the fan you are using. Regardless of the control you choose, I recommend first setting the fan to run about half the time (or half-speed), at least during the hours people are regularly home. Then you can adjust it to run more or less, as needed.

I often use controls made by Tamarack Technologies; they have several products that can replace or add to existing wall switches to control the fan speed, intermittent operation, and provide a full-speed boost for a specified time when the user presses a button. Some Panasonic WhisperGreen fans (see the left photo on p. 53) offer the ultimate in simplicity: optional controls built into the fan itself. Set the low-speed ventilation rate in CFM and the delay in minutes from 0.5 min. to 60 min.—and hook it to a regular wall switch. When you turn the switch on, it goes into high speed. When you switch it off, the

fan stays on high for the preset time delay before returning to its low-speed program.

For total flexibility in ventilation scheduling, you can use a 24-hour dial timer. I often install such a timer in a laundry area, utility room, basement stairwell, or near the electrical panel—somewhere convenient and accessible but not that visible. It's inexpensive, but it needs wiring. You will still need a standard switch or a delay timer in the bathroom as an override (see the sidebar on the facing page).

Return-air system

If you have a ducted central-air system for heating and cooling, another inexpensive (between $200 to $300 for parts) ventilation option is a supply-only system ducted through the furnace or air conditioner's air handler. This system pulls in fresh outdoor air whenever the air handler runs and distributes it throughout the house. It is a "supply-only" system because the air is coming directly from outside (there is no fan blowing air out at the same time to balance the flow).

Although a simple version of this system is common in some parts of the United States, most installations lack three important elements. First, a motorized damper is essential on the fresh-air-inlet duct—preferably where the duct enters the house. This prevents air from coming in through the duct when ventilation is not needed. Next, a timer is necessary to ensure that the air handler runs regularly, ventilating the house if there is no call for heating or cooling. This ensures a minimum ventilation rate year-round. There are a couple of products that can handle this function (see the photos on p. 58). Finally, insect screening at the inlet hood is important, and it must be kept clean. With a return-air fresh-air system, it is also important to locate the outdoor-air inlet far from potential

Don't install HRV exhaust ducts above a kitchen range. Instead, choose a separate range hood that is rated for the high temperatures and grease produced by cooking, which will help you avoid a fire hazard and a warranty problem.

WHAT CAN GO WRONG

Although some installers claim that one big HRV or ERV will solve all your ventilation needs, even a large unit may not adequately remove moisture from bathrooms if the exhaust ducts run to many locations. In my experience, it's better to use a smaller unit: Size the system between 50 CFM and 100 CFM above the whole-house requirement to have a margin of safety for flexibility. Then install separate fans for removing steam from the bathrooms.

sources of pollution, such as a dryer, a combustion-appliance vent, the garage, or the driveway.

If your house has an existing forced-air system, a return-air system may offer better overall ventilation than a bath-fan system, though it will cost more to operate. For example, a 15-watt bath fan running 100 percent of the time may cost less than $20 per year in electricity; a furnace fan running a third of the time may cost between

$50 and $150 per year. This type of system is best suited to a new HVAC installation with a high-efficiency furnace fan and a right-sized HVAC system that will run more hours at lower speeds to provide heat and cooling. This system also has two major advantages: First, fresh air is drawn from a known place and can be filtered. Second, unlike a bath-fan system, it circulates fresh air throughout the house.

Central Ventilation Systems

In addition to the simple ventilation systems mentioned previously, central-fan ventilation systems can be set up to provide fresh air to bedrooms and living areas, to exhaust stale air from bathrooms and kitchens, or both. These systems may be more effective at getting fresh air

The AirCycler® FR-V can run a central air-handler fan for ventilation, when it's not already being used for heating or cooling, at an adjustable interval each hour. It can also control a 24-volt motorized damper. Information on this and other similar products, including models that are integrated with a thermostat, is available at www.fancycler.com.

A motorized damper (right) by DuroDyne® is an essential component of any return-air ventilation system. It can be controlled by a FanCycler control (see photo at left), or by DuroDyne's AQC-1 Air Quality Control Center (above left). The DuroDyne control doesn't keep track of thermostat calls, but the 24-hour timer allows flexible ventilation schedules.

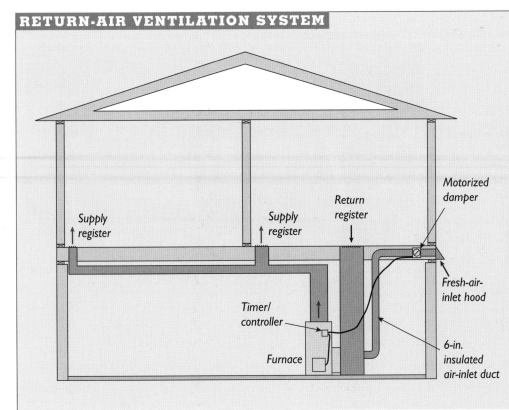

This supply-only ventilation system draws outdoor air through a screened inlet, mixes it with house air, and sends it to the furnace, where it is distributed throughout the house. The motorized damper and the fan controller are essential for managing the ventilation rate. The inlet duct should be made of sheet metal and be as short and direct as possible. It should enter the return duct as close as possible to the furnace, but not between the furnace and the furnace filter.

Supply register

Supply register

Return register

Motorized damper

Fresh-air-inlet hood

6-in. insulated air-inlet duct

Timer/ controller

Furnace

into the house than the single-point exhaust or supply-only air systems mentioned earlier, but they require quite a bit more ductwork, they are more expensive to install, and they are more difficult to retrofit in an existing home.

Central-exhaust/Supply-only systems

Central-exhaust systems are more common than central supply-only systems. They use a central fan, typically located in a basement or an attic, to exhaust air from several points in the home at the same time. These systems can be mounted in an accessible basement or attic to provide easy access for repair or replacement (see the photo on p. 50). If properly mounted, central systems can also be quieter than locally mounted exhaust fans, but that requires care to install vibration dampers on the central fan and ductwork. The

cost in materials for central exhaust systems ranges from $300 to over $600.

Ideally, the system should be sized to provide 50 CFM for each bathroom, or 50 CFM to 100 CFM more than the minimum whole-house requirement, whichever is larger (see the table on p. 55). A variable-speed control or timer sets the whole-house ventilation rate.

Central-exhaust systems typically are designed to draw air from bathrooms, the kitchen (but not from over the range), the laundry room, and other areas that have moisture or stale air. Usually, they are run at a low speed with a variable-speed control for continuous whole-house ventilation. An override switch or windup timer is usually placed in each bathroom for a temporary full-speed boost.

One disadvantage of a central-exhaust system is the greater electricity cost compared to that of a single high-efficiency bathroom fan. Also, if

PRO**TIP**

Depending on the unit, run time, climate, and fuel costs, HRV and ERV systems can save between $100 to $300 per year.

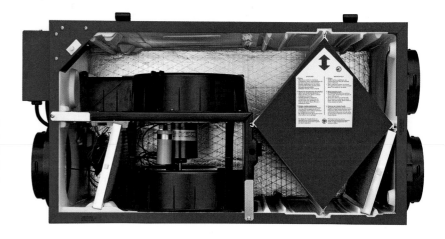

This view inside a heat-recovery system shows the diamond-shaped heat-exchanger core.

it draws air from too many locations, it may not provide effective local exhaust for bathrooms in boost mode.

Central supply-only systems use a fan and ductwork much like central-exhaust systems, but they bring fresh air from a known outdoor location and deliver it to the living space and bedrooms. This has a clear advantage, because incoming fresh air is filtered and delivered by ducts throughout the living space. However, in cold weather the fresh air can create uncomfortable drafts, so the ducts must be placed very carefully. Also, separate spot-exhaust ventilation fans are still needed, increasing the cost of the entire system.

Heat- or energy-recovery systems

If you want a top-shelf ventilation system, you should consider one of the heat-recovery systems. These systems pull exhaust air from bathrooms and kitchen and run it through a heat exchanger to pre-heat (or pre-cool) incoming fresh air. This fresh air is then delivered to living areas and bedrooms, at a temperature closer

to indoor air than outdoor air. The stale and fresh air streams don't mix, but move in parallel through a series of passages that provide a lot of surface area for heat exchange. This way, the systems can recapture 65 percent to 80 percent of the heat from the outgoing airstream, saving energy and aiding comfort.

There are two kinds of heat-recovery systems: heat-recovery ventilation and energy-recovery ventilation. HRVs are most efficient in cold weather. ERVs transfer not only heat but also humidity, using a special heat-exchanger wheel or core. This humidity exchange improves efficiency during the summer in humid climates, because it saves on the dehumidification load that outdoor air adds. This saves more energy. But be aware that ERVs do not dehumidify the air—they only help to preserve dehumidification, reducing latent cooling loads.

HRV and ERV systems are much more expensive than the simple systems outlined previously; they typically range from $1,500 to $4,000 installed (including labor). One would think that the premium price for an HRV or ERV would easily be paid for by energy sav-

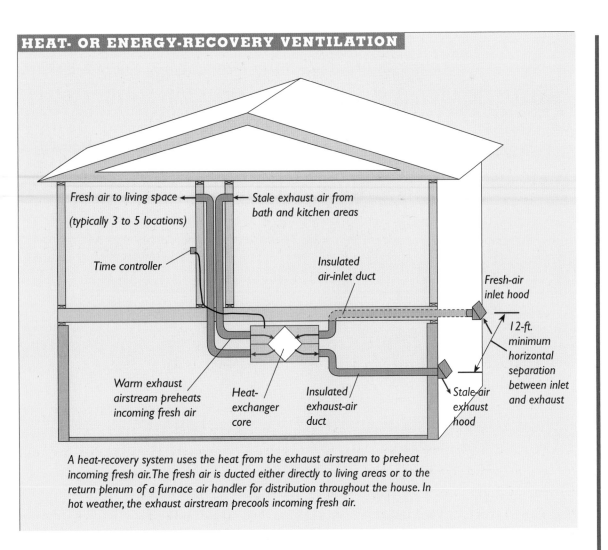

Fresh air to living space →
(typically 3 to 5 locations)

Stale exhaust air from
bath and kitchen areas

Time controller

Insulated
air-inlet duct

Fresh-air
inlet hood

12-ft.
minimum
horizontal
separation
between inlet
and exhaust

Warm exhaust
airstream preheats
incoming fresh air

Heat-
exchanger
core

Insulated
exhaust-air
duct

Stale-air
exhaust
hood

A heat-recovery system uses the heat from the exhaust airstream to preheat
incoming fresh air. The fresh air is ducted either directly to living areas or to the
return plenum of a furnace air handler for distribution throughout the house. In
hot weather, the exhaust airstream precools incoming fresh air.

ings, but the savings are usually not that large. Any unbalanced (exhaust-only or supply-only) system actually acts like a 50-percent efficient heat-recovery system, except in the very tightest of houses. This is because during severe cold or hot weather (when it costs the most to heat or cool the air), about half the make-up air for the fan is air that would have leaked into the house anyway. In fact, research has found that in a hot, humid climate, a simple, inexpensive return-air system combined with an efficient, stand-alone dehumidifier is less expensive to buy and operate, and does a better job managing humidity, than an ERV with a standard air-conditioning system.

INSULATING A HOUSE

From the attic to the basement, insulation is like a down jacket around your house that keeps you warm in the winter (and, like a thermos, cool in the summer). In many houses, it is probably easier to insulate than it is to seal air leaks, though it's a big job if you need to insulate exterior walls. Attics are relatively easy to insulate, and most houses can benefit from some added insulation.

Regardless of the age of your house, don't be fooled just because there's some insulation in the attic–even if it looks like a lot. Some homes have a thin layer that does little good; others have insulation that was installed in only the areas that were easy to reach. Even newer homes that have a lot of insulation can still have significant gaps and installation problems that are worth fixing–by someone who cares enough about the details to do it right. ▶ ▶ ▶

Attic Insulation

Attics are typically insulated first, and they usually receive the most insulation. People usually assume that attics are insulated because "heat rises," but, as I have pointed out (see pp. 6–7), *heat* doesn't actually rise at all. The reason attics tend to get more insulation is much less glamorous: The attic is simply the cheapest and easiest place to add insulation, in both old and new houses. In fact, in a moderately insulated two-story house, there may be two to four times as much conductive heat loss (not including air leakage or windows) through the exterior walls as through the attic.

True to tradition, we'll start with attic insulation because it's the easiest job. Hopefully, you have already finished air-sealing up there. If not, do it before you insulate, unless you plan to insulate with sprayed foam and complete the air sealing at the same time. Also, if you intend to vent a bath fan, install a ventilation system, change any electrical wiring, or do any other work in the attic, now is the time.

How much insulation?

Insulation is measured in R-value; the higher the R-value, the less heat loss. To some extent, there is an effect of diminishing returns in that the first 6 in. of insulation will save you more money than the next 6 in. But it doesn't pay to skimp, either. Once you're up in the attic installing insulation, you may as well do it right. Generally, the minimum recommended R-value for an attic is R-38 (see the chart on p. 179). In cold northern climates, I aim for between R-50 and R-60; in hot climates, R-30 may be adequate.

If there's no access into the attic, you can cut an opening for a roof vent. Climb in and insulate, then install the vent to cover the hole.

Estimating how many fiberglass batts to buy for a job is pretty easy, because each roll or bundle is marked for the number of square feet it covers. Blown-in materials like cellulose are a little trickier—you need to consult the tables found on the bags of material. Always go by the bag count, not the inches of thickness, to figure the amount of material and the actual R-value you're adding to your attic.

Prepping for insulation

Many building codes require attic venting. Building scientists generally agree that attic vents are less important than air sealing and indoor humidity control, but they are still an important backup. If your attic doesn't have any venting, try to put 50 percent to 80 percent of the total required vent area up high—at the ridge or

R-Values of Insulation Materials

Different materials have different R-values per inch. To find out how much R-value your insulation materials have, multiply the values in the table by the average number of inches of material. Notice that insulation performance degrades significantly with the gaps and compression found in a typical installation, especially with batts. To obtain fiberglass's high-density value, it must be installed perfectly, "by the book."

Category	Insulation Type	Description (typical)	Approximate R-value per in. thickness
Loose-Fill Insulation	Loose, chopped fiberglass or rock wool	Yellow, white, pink, or green clumps of chopped fibers	1.8
	Vermiculite (obsolete)*	Grey or brown metallic granules	2.4
	Cellulose	Grey or tan shredded newspaper, fluffy and/or "dusty"	3.3
Fiberglass Batts	Typical installation	Pink, yellow, or green "blanket," installed with gaps and compression	1.8
	Installation "by the book"	Pink, yellow, or green "blanket," installed perfectly	3.2
	High-density batts	Stiffer, denser batts installed perfectly	3.8–4.3
Rigid Foam Board	Expanded polystyrene	White "beadboard"	4
	Extruded polystyrene	Uniform blue, green, or pink "board" insulation	5
	Isocyanurate "hi-R" board	Stiff yellow or tan foam with foil facing	6
Spray-in-Place Foams	Urea-formaldehyde (obsolete)*	Yellow or gray-white, brittle, dusty foam; breaks easily	3–4
	Open-cell spray polyurethane foam (approx. ½ lb. per cu. ft. density)	Yellow, green, or white, soft foam	3.4
	Closed-cell spray polyurethane foam (approx. ½ lb. per cu. ft. density)	Yellow, green, or other color, tough foam	6

*Potential safety concerns: See Hazards of Insulation Material on p. 68 for more details.

WHAT CAN GO WRONG

Don't assume that attic insulation is optional just because you live in a warm climate. Attic and roof spaces heat up significantly in the sun and transfer heat to the living space below; insulation helps slow this heat transfer and reduce cooling loads.

PRO TIP

Powered attic fans are sometimes installed to try to keep the attic cool in summer. Usually they just amplify any air leaks between the house and attic and increase cooling loads. If you have one, shut it off and focus on insulating and sealing leaks.

gable, or using roof vents. The remainder should be down low, usually in the soffit.

In general, I avoid adding cheap aluminum ridge vents and 16-in. aluminum soffit louvers because they are ugly; continuous ridge or soffit vents that are installed during a reroofing or soffit replacement job tend to look much better. Roof vents placed near the peak on the rear of the house are inconspicuous, and they can even provide access to attics that have no other means of entry.

Whether or not you install attic venting, take some time baffling the eaves area before installing insulation. It's important to allow an air space between the insulation and the roof sheathing. The most common approach is to use standard foam or plastic ventilation chutes held in place with a wad of fiberglass. Make sure the fiberglass extends to the outside edge of the top plate so that you can get as much insulation as possible in that vulnerable area. Cardboard baffles also work well. The top of the baffle should be several inches above the height of the planned insulation, at a minimum.

In addition to the eaves-area prep, flag each electrical junction box with a piece of ribbon or caution tape stapled to a rafter above and hanging down to identify it once it's buried. Make sure that every electrical box has a proper cover on it and that the wires are properly clamped.

Estimating Cellulose

To determine how much insulation you need, measure the approximate thickness of any existing insulation, then multiply that by its R-value per inch (see the chart on p. 65). For example, if you already have 4 in. of blown-in fiberglass, you have an existing R-value of about 7. To reach R-50, you need to add R-43; 43 ÷ 3.3 = approximately 13 in. of cellulose.

Cellulose is usually packaged in 12-lb. or 25-lb. bags. After determining your target R-value, measure the square footage of the area you wish to cover. Each manufacturer provides information on the bag describing how much insulation to use for a desired R-value. In some cases, that information may be indicated by the number of square feet that a bag covers at a given R-value, in which case you just need to divide your total square feet by that number to purchase the correct number of bags.

Don't worry about cellulose losing R-value over time as it settles. For one thing, settled material is denser and has a higher R-value per inch, so settling generally does not decrease the insulation's performance. Second, most settling tends to occur in the first year or two after installation, and—unlike corn flakes in a box—once the material has reached its settled density, it cannot settle further unless it's physically compressed. The amount of air running through the hose with the material does have a big effect on its initial thickness, so pay more attention to the bag count than the depth of the installed cellulose, whether you are doing the job yourself or hiring a contractor.

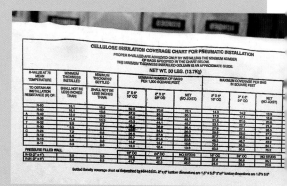

The chart printed on this cellulose bag shows how many bags of material are needed per 1,000 sq. ft. for a range of desired R-values.

Standard foam vent chutes can be held in place with fiberglass batts and pushed in tightly to cut down on wind washing.

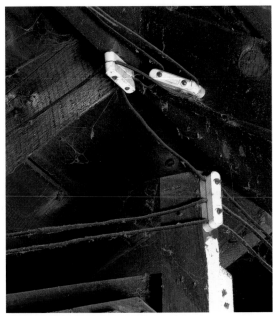

If you have an older house with knob-and-tube wiring that looks something like this, the wiring must be replaced in the attic or wall areas you intend to insulate. To make sure there's no active knob-and-tube wiring hidden in wall cavities, you may want to hire an electrician to verify that it's inactive.

You will need to find a way to keep blown insulation at least 3 in. away from chimneys (I typically use fiberglass batts; see photo p. 70 left); and don't cover combustion air intakes or recessed light fixtures that are not IC rated. Whatever you do, don't insulate over active knob-and-tube wiring. In some cases, this older type of wiring will already be deactivated; if you're not sure, you'll need to hire an electrician to check it for you.

Fiberglass attic insulation

I generally prefer to use cellulose insulation wherever possible, but if you have trouble finding a machine, or if you have only a small area to insulate, fiberglass may be the best choice. If there is little or no insulation between the ceiling joists, start by installing a batt that will come up at least to the top of the joists. Use unfaced batts in the attic and make sure you buy batts that are the same width as the spacing of the ceiling joists.

There are three important things to be aware of when installing fiberglass. First, a new bundle

WHAT CAN GO WRONG

Poorly installed fiberglass batts, like the ones shown below (and on p. 182, upper left), can lead to serious performance problems. Research and experience have shown that gaps between batts may reduce the rated R-value up to 50%, depending on the thickness of the batt, the size and number of the gaps, and the difference in temperature between indoors and out.

At some point, batts were added to the original insulation with the vapor barrier facing the wrong way. Blowing at least 14 in. of cellulose on top will add adequate insulation, ensuring that the vapor barrier stays warm enough to avoid condensation.

or roll of fiberglass is highly compressed, and it *must* be fluffed to the full thickness listed on the package. Second, it must be fit neatly between the joists and come in full contact with the ceiling, with no compression, binding, or rounding of the corners. Finally, it must be cut neatly to fit around any obstructions, such as wiring, plumbing, blocking in between the joists, or other objects. Anything that compromises the installation can have a disproportionate effect on the insulation's performance.

Choose the first layer of batts so the top of the insulation is up to—or slightly above—joist level. Then install a second layer on top, at right angles to the first layer (the second layer may be 24 in. wide if you like; it installs faster than 16-in. batts). Again, make sure each batt is fluffed to its full thickness, and lay each one snugly against the next.

Don't be satisfied with 12-in.-thick batts laid in a single layer in between the joists: The gaps that are left between the batts will really reduce

Hazards of Insulation Materials

Some older insulation materials are hazardous, but few pose significant danger if they are isolated from the living space—another argument for thorough air-sealing. Asbestos is clearly a hazardous material; even moderate levels of exposure can cause lung cancer and other diseases, and it should never be moved or disturbed except by a properly licensed asbestos-remediation contractor. Commonly found as insulation on pipes and ducts, asbestos is rare in attics. However, vermiculite insulation, sometimes added as insulation in attics and walls in the 1960s, 1970s, and 1980s, may contain traces of asbestos. When I find vermiculite, I leave it in place. Insulating over it is fine, but definitely wear a HEPA respirator, which I recommend for anyone working in any attic. (See www.epa.gov/asbestos/pubs/verm.html for more on vermiculite insulation in the home.)

Urea-formaldehyde foam insulation (UFFI) is a spray foam that was retrofitted in houses prior to 1980. This material was banned because of potentially toxic formaldehyde gas emissions, but gas emissions fade with time, so any UFFI that is still around should not be hazardous. If you find UFFI, be cautious, because it is likely to be fragile and may turn to a powdery dust if disturbed.

Modern insulation materials, including spray foams, fiberglass, and cellulose, are much safer but still involve some risk. Although fiberglass

Vermiculite insulation is grainy, not fluffy or fibrous. Although some vermiculite contains asbestos, don't try to remove it—there is more risk when disturbed than left in place.

fibers are definitely an irritant to the skin, no increased risk of cancer has been found even at occupational exposures. Cellulose is a respiratory irritant, due to the fire-retardant chemical treatments, and produces lots of dust during installation, but it is not dangerous once it has been installed. Always take precautions to protect your skin and wear a respirator when working with insulation of any kind.

the overall performance of your attic's insulation. You may need to notch the batts at the edges near the rafters, or tuck in short pieces, to bring the insulation to its full thickness as close as possible to the roof sheathing and still leave a 1-in. space between the insulation and the sheathing.

Blowing attic insulation

If your roof is made with trusses, or the attic has flooring with little or no insulation under it, it's hard to get good results with fiberglass. In those cases, your best bet is to use a loose-fill material, such as cellulose. One big advantage of blown cellulose is that it is fast and easy to install. You don't have to worry about cutting, fitting, fluffing, or most of the other details that concern fiberglass batts. You can also cover the top of existing insulation with cellulose, which will settle into all the gaps and spaces between the batts. This improves what's already there and adds R-value.

Fiberglass Batts

Fiberglass batts are typically the insulation of choice for do-it-yourselfers. The material is easy to transport and install by yourself. It's ideal for an attic where you may want to add living space later (or make other changes), because it is easy to remove and replace. But there is a price to pay for convenience. In my experience, no matter how carefully you detail fiberglass batts, they rarely work as well as the factory ratings suggest. After three winters in the house I built, I pulled out the fiberglass insulation that I had carefully installed in the attic and replaced it with cellulose; the dramatic improvement surprised even me.

Because of the annoying, itchy quality of fiberglass, several manufacturers market encapsulated batts that are surrounded by plastic. Steer clear of these products; they are more of a marketing gimmick than a worthwhile innovation. Encapsulated batts are more expensive and harder to install properly. Although the coverings may make the material more comfortable to work with, they also increase the difficulty of detailing the batts properly.

Tuck the first layer of batt insulation into each ceiling cavity as neatly as possible. These unfaced batts are being installed right over the existing 1½-in. faced insulation.

The second layer of insulation should be fluffed to its full thickness, laid across all the joists at right angles, and installed neatly and completely.

The biggest drawback with blown insulation is that you need a machine and a helper to install it. Many building-material suppliers that sell bagged cellulose will lend or rent a machine to anyone who buys the insulation from them. A local rental yard, or even a friendly local insulation contractor, may rent out a cellulose machine—but you'll have to find the helper yourself.

When installing cellulose, you must do the same prep work as for fiberglass (see pp. 65–67). In addition, get enough fiberglass batts to make a dam around each chimney and recessed light to keep the cellulose away from them. With IC-rated recessed lights, I prefer to surround and cover them with fiberglass before installing the cellulose. With non-IC-rated fixtures, all insulation must be at least 3 in. away from the sides and no insulation may cover the top (see pp. 37–38). Also, make a dam around the attic hatch so cellulose doesn't fall out when you open the door.

Set up the blowing machine in a convenient place and snake the flexible hose and control cable into the attic. You may want to run them through a second-story window or an attic window, or temporarily remove an attic gable vent. Have an assistant ready, put on protective gear, and position yourself in one corner of the attic. Turn on the switch, and the material should start to flow within a few seconds. Start in one corner, allow the material to build to the thickness you want, and then pull back the hose as you start to fill in the area.

The object is to get the insulation fairly even and avoid spraying too much into the air. You can turn off the switch occasionally to take a break, and then move yourself and the hose to another area. Use a tape measure occasionally to check the thickness of the insulation, and aim for about 2 in. more total depth than the actual depth you want to end up with (to allow for settling).

It's important to keep cellulose away from chimneys, recessed lights, and attic hatches. I like to make a dam with unfaced batts.

Keep the end of the hose low and pointed slightly down to reduce dust levels and keep the cellulose density high, especially near the eaves.

Cellulose Blowing Machines

Cellulose machines range in size from a box slightly bigger than a milk crate with a hopper to a large truck-mounted rig. All of them have an agitator to break up the material and a blower to separate the fibers, mix them with air, and send them through a hose (imagine a vacuum cleaner hose, in reverse). Most machines have a cable with an on/off switch to allow for remote control from where the work is being done. Most also allow you to control the fiber-and-air mixture, either by adjusting a gate to control the rate of material fed through the hose or by adjusting an air inlet to introduce a variable amount of air. For open-attic blowing, set it for more material and less air. The job will go faster, and the material won't settle as much after you're done.

Not all cellulose machines are created equal. The smaller machines are fine for open attics, though they are slower. But they lack the air pressure to dense-pack closed cavities. The key for doing that is to select a machine that can supply adequate air pressure, but the easiest thing to look for is a machine that requires at least two separate electrical circuits (or a single 220-volt circuit) to run. If you plan to dense-pack cellulose, stay away from a machine that can run off a single 15-amp or 20-amp, 110-volt circuit.

This medium-size cellulose blower is typical of the type of machine that you might rent or borrow from an insulation supplier.

When you are blowing near the eaves, push the end of the hose nearly all the way to the baffle, and fill the space between the rafters to the desired thickness. Pushing the hose out to the edge helps ensure that the cellulose will be packed tightly in this critical area. Slowly pull back the hose from the roof, being careful not to cover the upper end of the vent chute.

Start with five or six rafter bays at a time, then work your way across the attic toward the opposite eave, leaving space for yourself to get into the eaves area on the other side. Work your way back toward the attic hatch or access door, then start at the other end of the attic and work your way back toward the hatch. Make sure you don't "paint" yourself into a corner—it's not fun crawling through this stuff after it's installed.

Storage areas

People often use attics for storage. I prefer to eliminate attic storage, if possible. There are plenty of good reasons to get rid of stuff (both thermal and psychological). Still, many homes lack storage space, and the attic is a natural place for those boxes of holiday decorations. If you have a partially or fully floored attic, you can set aside an area near the access hatch or stairs by making a dam out of 12-in.-thick fiberglass batts. Insulate the rest of the attic, making sure there is insulation under the floorboards as well. Once the dust has settled, you should be able

IN DETAIL

If your attic is floored, you must fill the space under the flooring, unless that space has already been well insulated. With a plank floor, it's much easier to rip up a row or two of boards along the length of the attic than to blow insulation under the floor with a fill tube. A plywood floor is more difficult. You can either rip up an entire row of plywood sheets or, if that's too much trouble, use a hole saw to drill a 3-in.-dia. hole in each joist bay, then insulate with a fill tube. Once the cavities are full, apply more cellulose on top until you have the R-value you want.

Raising a floor deck above the existing framing is the best way to create storage space in the attic without compromising insulation.

to move stuff in and out without disturbing the insulation.

Even better, you can create storage above the insulation by building a raised floor deck. Run 2×6 or 2×8 joists perpendicular to the ceiling joists at 16 in. o.c. Nail a header joist across each end to hold them vertically, insulate the cavities, and cover them with planks or ½-in. plywood. You will lose some headroom, but this way you can reserve as large an area as you like for storage without compromising the insulation.

With either approach, be cautious about the amount of weight the ceiling joists are able to hold. A built-up floor adds dead load and storage adds live load to the existing framing—too much weight can create a structural problem. If you're uncertain, consult a structural engineer before proceeding.

Sloped Ceilings

Many homes have sloped ceiling areas—places where plaster or drywall is applied directly to the underside of the roof rafters. Examples include Cape-style houses, which usually have sloped ceilings between the kneewall and the flat ceiling above (see the drawing on p. 35) or rooms with partial or full cathedral ceilings. Some homes just have a narrow sloped area for a few feet near the eaves.

These enclosed cavities present more of a challenge than an open attic. Some, like the typical Cape, have fairly easy access from an attic space either above or below. Others, like a full cathedral ceiling, are more difficult. The basic techniques shown in this section for dense-packing cellulose are referred to in many other parts of the book. The biggest distinction between dense-packed and open-blown cellulose is that dense-pack is installed in an enclosed cavity. But it's not enough just to be enclosed—to dense-pack, by definition, means using enough air pressure to compress the material more densely than it could ever compress from settling.

Prepping for the job

When filling in a rafter bay with cellulose, you must prevent the insulation from pouring out of the cavity on the other end. If the rafter bay is accessible from only one end—for example, from the attic above—this may be easy enough, but you will need to plan for extra material because the eaves may become filled. If you can reach both the top and the bottom, choose the end that is more awkward to reach and stuff a piece of fiberglass into each bay; then blow in the insulation from the other (more convenient) end.

Make sure the ceiling is sound before starting. In particular, acoustical tiles pose a real potential for blowout, as well as air leakage. They should be dealt with before dense-packing. And make sure the roof is in decent shape before insulating closed cavities; any water that leaks in after insulating will make a bigger mess—and be more difficult to locate—than it would otherwise.

Roof-shingle warranties are another concern. Unvented cathedral ceilings experience hotter roof temperatures—typically by 2 percent to 4 percent—than vented roofs. Because those higher temperatures may accelerate degradation (venting is assumed to reduce roof temperatures), some roofing manufacturers won't honor warranty claims on unvented, or hot, roofs. But research has shown that shingle color actually has a much larger impact (about 10 percent) on roof temperature than venting does, and several manufacturers do provide warranty service for unvented roofs. Choose one of those, or vent the roof first if shingle-warranty service is important to you.

Reducing moisture risk

There are serious concerns relating to venting a cathedral- or flat-roof ceiling space. Good air-sealing (which dense-packing helps) and indoor humidity control via mechanical ventilation help reduce condensation and moisture buildup. But even an excellent dense-pack job can allow some air movement. In an unvented cathedral ceiling or flat roof, this can deposit moisture at the roof deck, especially in a home with high humidity. There are two basic strategies to avoid increasing the risk of condensation and potential damage to the roof deck: using foam insulation to control condensing temperatures, and ensuring an opening from the unvented cavities into a larger, vented space.

The first approach—using continuous foam insulation—is the only proven, code-approved method for an unvented roof. It can take

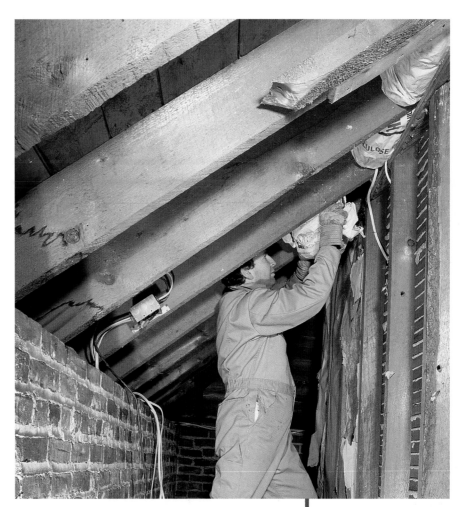

Stuff pieces of fiberglass batts into rafter bays so that cellulose won't blow through when you fill them from the other end. Stuff the batts into the empty cellulose bags, as shown here, or just stuff the fiberglass alone.

two basic forms: rigid foam insulation added above and in contact with the roof deck, or sprayed foam added directly to the underside of the roof deck. Rigid foam is typically added during a re-roof, but usually a new sheathing surface (with a furred, vented space in heavy snow areas) is needed on top of the foam. This approach is expensive, but it's a practical way to address a house with full cathedral ceilings if the roof is close to needing replacement. Consider interior sprayed foam insulation if you are planning extensive interior renovations (see

If you don't need much R-value, you can use a two-part DIY spray foam kit to provide the foam layer. Make sure to get consistent coverage; this application will need a second layer to fill the cracks.

"Renovations" for more discussion). With either foam method, once the roof deck is protected from condensation by a high enough R-value of foam, the remainder of the cavity may be insulated with blown insulation or batt (called "flash and batt"). The R-value of foam insulation depends on climate (see the table on the facing page and the map below). Both of these methods are explicitly allowed by code; both are energy efficient and low risk in any climate.

The second approach is to provide a partial venting path for the closed dense-pack area. This can be achieved in homes that have sections of sloped ceilings (such as Cape-style homes) that may be difficult or impossible to vent properly. If one end of the dense-packed area is open to a vented attic space (preferably the top); any wetting effects appear to be balanced by drying toward the vented space. This approach can also be used under low-slope roofs (for example, a row house or shed dormer), where access near the low side is impossible. Experience has shown that up to one-third of the total attic area can be dense-packed without venting, provided that the remaining attic space is vented normally. Note that this method does not conform to standard code requirements but has been accepted by many local building officials. And I would consider this approach much more risky in climate zones 6 to 8.

Of course, just as with an open attic floor, you have to be careful to avoid chimneys and non-IC-rated recessed lights. If you have a chimney in a key leak area, you may want to consider using a high-performance fiberglass (see sidebar at right). You could also open up the ceiling in that area to air-seal the chase with sheet metal (see the photos

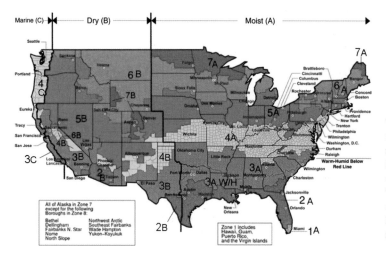

This map shows the climate zones as defined in the code: numbers 1 through 8 by increasing winter severity, and A/B/C (moist/dry/marine). These zones are used to define minimum insulation levels and moisture-control requirements.

on pgs. 37 right and 182 left) and install wood or rigid foam blocking (more than 2 in. away from the chimney) to keep the cellulose away. If you have recessed lights, you'll need to replace them with IC-rated fixtures.

If you don't have the plans or budget for sprayed foam and partial venting is not an option, you can focus on sealing the tops of walls and other air leaks where they intersect the roof. You can use this approach on all interior walls that intersect with the roof. To seal the wall tops, you'll need to drill a series of holes in each wall cavity just below the ceiling and inject two-part foam from a kit; or you can dense-pack insulation at the top of the cavity. This approach stays within code, but falls short of the continuous foam method, because it doesn't increase the roof insulation or venting. However, it can be effective in houses with air leakage–dominated problems such as ice dams or roof-cavity condensation.

On this machine, you increase the air-to-cellulose mix for dense-packing by closing a gate in the hopper, which reduces the material feed. Other machines have air-inlet ports that open to increase the air pressure; either type will adjust the air-to-material ratio.

A 1¼-in.-dia. vinyl fill tube attached to the end of a larger-diameter hose makes it easy to snake into confined spaces for dense-packing cellulose. The marker line near the end warns you that the end is near as you pull the tube out.

Minimum R-values of Foam Insulation by Climate Zone

IECC Climate Zone	Minimum Foam R-value*
2B and 3B (tile roof only)	none required
1 (all), 2 (all), 3 (all)	5
4C	10
4A, B	15
5	20
6	25
7	30
8	35

*These R-values are only the minimum of foam needed and must be supplemented by other cavity insulation to meet the total R-value required by code or design.

High Performance Fiberglass

A new breed of blown-in fiberglass materials is now on the market. High-performance fiberglass (such as Johns-Manville Spider® and Knauf Perimeter Plus™) can be dense-packed to reduce air movement as effectively as cellulose in closed cavities.

These products have slightly higher R-values than cellulose, but at much lower densities—and lower risk of plaster blow-out. The Building Performance Institute is developing a standard (Standard BPI-3202-T) to qualify other insulation products based on air-leakage control. Because these products are noncombustible, they are also safe to use in cavities adjacent to a chimney or fireplace.

I've insulated a number of unvented roofs (including my own, which is partially vented), and I know a number of contractors who regularly insulate closed roof cavities with cellulose. But there have also been cases of significant roof-sheathing moisture damage in homes that have been treated this way, usually in homes with high humidity levels, so the decision is yours. Your choice will depend on the climate, building inspector, shingle warranty, and condition of the roof, as well as your confidence in the success of mechanical ventilation and indoor humidity control.

Filling rafter bays: Dense-packing cellulose

To dense-pack cellulose, you'll first need to set up the blowing machine. Depending on the machine, this means setting it for either *less* material or *more* air. If you have a large, open ceiling cavity, use 3-in. flex hose. For cavities less than 5 in. deep, or for those that already contain some insulation, use a 2-in. hose or a smaller vinyl fill tube. Starting at one end of the house, insert the hose into the first cavity. Try to insert it so that the end is within 1 ft. of the far end of the cavity, and cover your end of the cavity with a loose piece of fiberglass to keep the cellulose from blowing back out. It helps if you keep the fill tube or hose in one corner of the open-

DENSE-PACKING CELLULOSE IN A SLOPED CEILING

Air pressure in the enclosed cavity pushes the loose fibers tightly against the sides, packing them into place. Once installed, the high-density material slows air movement through the cavity, gives the insulation a higher R-value, and prevents future settling.

Note that the proper packed density (about 3.5 lb. per cu. ft.) cannot be achieved in areas beyond about 1 ft. from the end of the hose, so don't try this unless you can reach the far end of the cavity, and don't try it in very deep cavities or open spaces.

Cellulose fibers are suspended in air; air pressure fills the cavity, pushing out in all directions.

Attic

Cellulose is packed in place by the force of air pressure.

Fiberglass-batt plug is stuffed in tightly to retain cellulose.

Keep the end of the fill tube near the packed cellulose.

Fiberglass-batt plug held in place while dense-packing this rafter bay

Rigid foam on back of kneewall

Fiberglass batts

Rafter

Kneewall

Second floor

Sealant

Floor joist

Fiberglass or cellulose

Draftstop blocking

ing. Make sure the switch is handy, turn on the machine, and let the fun begin!

The tricky part of any dense-pack operation is making sure that you pack in as much material as possible without clogging the hose or blowing out the drywall or plaster. As the material fills near the end of the tube, the flow through the hose will start to back up. When it does, pull back the tube 6 in. to 8 in. to relieve the pressure and allow more packing of the cavity. It may take a while before you have to back up the first time, but then you may have to pull back every 5 to 10 seconds until the cavity is full (depending on the size of the fill tube and the pressure of the machine). When the cavity is full, turn off the blower and let the pressure drop before pulling out the hose. You will know that you have reached the proper density based on the amount of material you use: For every square foot of area you should use about 1 lb. of cellulose in an

When insulating a closed cavity, such as this rafter bay, hold a piece of fiberglass batt across the opening. Wear a respirator and safety glasses in case the cellulose blows back at your face.

Dense-Packing

It's not difficult to notice the changes that happen just before your blowing machine starts to bog down. The sound changes, the material feed slows, and the added pressure may make the hose wiggle. If you wait too long to pull the tube back, the cellulose can back up and dense-pack the hose instead of the wall. If you pull the tube out too quickly, the density will suffer.

Clogs occur most at a reducer or other restriction. Usually, opening up the hose at the restriction will do the trick. If not, a long stick or a heavy-duty tape measure and a lot of thwacking on the side of the hose can loosen it. If you are getting a lot of clogs, try reducing the material feed or increasing the amount of air. If you have a machine with separate switches for the agitator and the blower, you can maintain the air pressure

and reduce clogging by turning off the agitator for short periods of time. This handy technique allows the air pressure to build without feeding any material; it's especially useful near the end of each cavity.

Clogs occur where hoses reduce in size. To clear the blockage, disassemble the joint.

PROTIP

If you insulate a roof with spray foam and there's a furnace in the attic, you need to pay attention to combustion air requirements. You should be okay if the furnace is a modern power-vented or condensing unit. But if it's an older atmospheric-vented unit, you may need to add some transfer grilles from the attic into the living space. Better yet, replace the furnace with a high-efficiency direct-vent unit.

If you do insulate blind roof cavities, make sure the rafters aren't already full of insulation. If so, you'll have trouble getting a fill tube—or much cellulose—into the space.

empty 2×4 cavity, 1.5 lb. in a 2×6 cavity, or 2 lb. in a 2×8 cavity. If you use much less, the density is inadequate.

If your sloped or cathedral ceilings aren't accessible from an attic space and you do choose to fill them with cellulose, you have several options for dense-packing cellulose. You can get at the rafter bays by opening up the soffit and/or fascia, or by removing the cap layer of shingles and cutting back the sheathing a few inches. Either method allows you to run a fill tube into the rafter cavity to fill it with insulation. Another option is to drill and patch cathedral ceilings from the inside, similar to filling walls from indoors. Of course, be extra careful whenever you work on a roof or on a ladder.

Cathedralized Attics

If an attic area is free of mechanical equipment and you can reach the air leaks, sealing the leaks

as shown in the chapter on "Sealing Air Leaks" and then insulating with blown cellulose is a great approach. It's inexpensive, and you can do much or all of the work yourself. But what if you have a complex space with floored areas that obscure big leaks, or lots of mechanical equipment and ductwork in the attic space? Or what if you plan to renovate and finish the attic space at some point in the future? You may not want to spend the time treating the attic floor, only to have the extra insulation in the way later on.

In these cases, consider insulating and sealing the roof and gable walls with sprayed polyurethane foam. Often referred to as a "cathedralized attic," this is not a do-it-yourself job: Spray rigs are expensive and require specialized training. But compared to the time and effort it would take to air-seal and insulate the attic floor and thoroughly seal and insulate the ducts, it may be well worth the extra investment. It may also be easier to find a competent spray-foam contractor than to get someone who is willing and able to do those other jobs right.

Spraying foam on the roof to create a complete, air-tight thermal enclosure reduces air leakage and adds an insulation layer in one step. I have created new, finished top-floor space by insulating with sprayed foam before hanging drywall; these houses have lower total energy cost, even with significantly increased living area. If a cathedralized attic is left unfinished, ductwork may be left as is; losses from the ducts are retained inside the new, enlarged thermal boundary. Although it's a good idea to connect any disconnected ducts, you won't benefit substantially from any duct insulation or sealing.

Insulating Walls

If you have little or no insulation in your walls, you will definitely benefit from installing some. Conductive heat loss through uninsulated walls represents a significant heating and cooling load, and it's usually cost-effective to add insulation.

Exterior walls are fairly difficult to insulate, unless you are remodeling, installing new drywall, or re-siding the house. Retrofitting insulation almost always means blowing in insulation; the process is very much like that for sloped-ceiling dense-pack outlined above. The type of siding has a big impact on how easy it is to get into the wall, and it may help you decide whether to tackle the job yourself or hire an insulation contractor.

What's in there now?

How do you know what's in the walls already? If you have done any remodeling on the house, you may already know. If not, there are a several ways to find out. It's important to know what is in there, because that will have a big impact on how easy—or useful—it will be to insulate the walls.

Remember that there may be different types of insulation (or none at all) in different parts of

Existing Insulation in Older Homes

Most homes built before the 1930s had no insulation at all, so if your home is from that era, you will be looking for insulation that was added later. It may be blown-in cellulose or urea-formaldehyde foam. If the walls are already insulated, it is rarely worth adding more, unless you find large areas that were never done at all, or if the walls were not insulated properly. If the installed insulation has settled and each wall bay has a large empty space at the top, it may be worth filling them in. Also look out for "back-plastering." Although unusual, back-plastered walls are built with an extra layer of lath and plaster in the middle of the stud space, to add an extra airspace and reduce heat loss through the wall. Those walls are difficult to insulate due to the narrow space, and it's probably better to leave them alone unless you do major remodeling or re-siding.

Homes that were built prior to 1960 may have minimal insulation; some have insulation that is sandwiched between layers of paper. It is possible to add cellulose insulation to walls with those thin insulation layers, but only with a fill tube. If the wall has thicker batts, it will probably be almost impossible to get the fill tube into the wall cavity without bunching the insulation; in that case, it won't be worth trying to add more.

ACCORDING TO CODE

Whenever you insulate a roof with sprayed foam, you must pay attention to fire safety codes. Codes generally require all foam insulation to be covered with ½-in. drywall (or other 15-minute thermal barrier), but many foam products have been tested for use in unoccupied spaces such as attics and crawlspaces. Ask to see the "ICC-ES" Evaluation Service report from the product manufacturer you're considering. This report will specify maximum insulation thickness, and any additional coatings needed to satisfy the code requirements, for each application. There may be separate rules for attic roof sheathing, attic gable walls, crawlspace walls, or crawlspace ceilings. Be sure the installer follows these requirements; if you have any questions, it may be best to discuss them with your local code official before signing a contract.

PRO**TIP**

Whether you drill from inside or outside to blow in cellulose, it's important to make a hole in every stud or rafter bay.

TRADE SECRET

Make a probe out of a piece of insulated wire, stripping the jacket off a piece of electric cable and pulling out one wire with the insulation still on it. You can use it to explore stud bays after drilling them, probing sideways to find the next stud. Aim for the center of the next stud bay to drill the next hole.

Vinyl siding can usually be unlocked one course at a time (two clapboards in height) with a "zip" tool, which is simply an insulation push rod with a hook at one end and a handle at the other. Unlock the top of the course where you want to drill holes, then reach in with a prybar and remove the nails holding the siding strip. Short pieces of siding may not flex enough to pull out safely; you can slide them down between the trim channels to expose the sheathing. Make sure your hands are clean, or you could permanently stain the plastic. Try to avoid cold weather when the vinyl is brittle and easily broken. Aluminum siding can also be removed with a zip tool, but watch out—it dents easily. On a windy day, the material can easily bend; once damaged, both vinyl and aluminum siding are difficult to match.

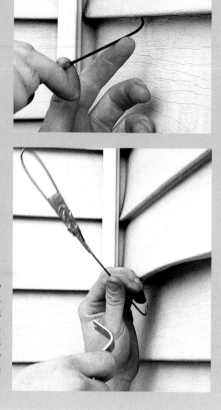

The unlocking tool for vinyl or aluminum siding is just an insulation push rod, with a bent hook at one end and a round handle at the other. Be very gentle, especially near the corners and around window trim. You can also use a prybar to help open the siding, but be careful not to mar, bend, or break the lower piece.

the house. If some rooms have been remodeled, or built at a different time, they will likely be insulated differently. Sometimes people start to insulate a house and don't finish, so look in several places to be fairly certain of what is there. If the insulation is spotty or inconsistent, it may be worth hiring someone to scan your walls with an infrared camera in order to identify all the areas that are uninsulated.

Insulating from outdoors

If you have wooden clapboard, shingles, or vinyl siding, it probably makes sense to insulate from outdoors. First, you'll need to remove a row of siding and drill a hole into each stud bay. If you

are using a fill tube (my preferred method), plan for a row of holes one-third to halfway up the wall on each story. The fill tube should be long enough to reach from the hole to the top and bottom of the wall cavity.

You'll also need to drill a hole in each stud bay below windows (and sometimes above windows), too. Make those holes about 12 in. down from the bottom of the window. Odd-shaped cavities are often formed by diagonal bracing, bridging, fire-stopping, and other blocking. The more careful you are to find and access those cavities, the better the insulation job will be.

To drill the holes, first strip off a layer of siding for each horizontal row of holes. Shingles or clap-

Estimating Wall Insulation

To figure the amount of cellulose needed to insulate walls, multiply the height and width of the walls to obtain the square footage. Subtract areas that are already insulated, as well as any large window or door areas, and aim for 100 lb. of material for every 100 sq. ft. of area. For high-performance fiberglass, plan on 60 lb. for every 100 sq. ft. This method may overestimate, but it's easier to bring back some unopened bales than to run out and buy more before you finish.

boards can be removed by cutting just at the line of the next overlapping layer. Carefully insert a small prybar from the bottom to lift out any nails (in clapboards) and help snap the wood at the cut. Set the siding pieces aside carefully—you may want to label the backs with a marking pen, using letters or numbers to match their locations. Note that after replacing any type of painted siding, you'll need to do some patching and touch-up painting. Holes will be easier to drill with a self-feed bit or a heavy-duty hole saw; aim for $2\frac{9}{16}$-in. or $2\frac{3}{4}$-in. diameter for a $1\frac{1}{4}$-in. fill tube.

PRO TIP

When preparing to insulate walls from the outside, be sure to remove pictures from walls and breakable objects from shelves.

To remove a wooden shingle or clapboard, first cut into it with a sharp utility knife, tilting the blade upward so the joint will shed water when you put it back together.

Once the top edge is scored with a knife, pry up from the bottom to snap off the shingle.

WHAT CAN GO WRONG

Beware of loose plaster or drywall, especially in older homes with plaster on wood lath, and in newer homes with poorly installed drywall. If there are any loose or spongy areas, secure them by driving drywall screws into studs before blowing cellulose; they can be patched later. And always keep an eye on the plaster and drywall while filling wall cavities. If you are working from the outside, station a helper inside to warn you of any trouble. To reduce the risk of blow-out problems, consider using high-performance fiberglass (see the sidebar on p. 75): The lower required density exerts less pressure on the wall surface.

Start filling each wall bay by pushing the fill tube up from the center of the bay. Keep the control switch close at hand, so that you can find it in a hurry when you need to shut off the flow of cellulose.

Once you have dense-packed the upper half of the wall cavity, continue by pointing the tube down to the bottom.

Before drilling holes for blown-in insulation, remove the siding so that you're only drilling through the sheathing. That makes it easier to find stud bays and patch the holes once you're done.

When working with asbestos-cement siding, rule number one is never damage the shingles. Drilling, cutting, or sanding them can release harmful asbestos fibers.

PRO TIP

If you are insulating an overhang that is covered with a vinyl or aluminum soffit material, first remove it carefully—don't try to drill through it.

Asbestos-cement siding must be treated with care—use a small cat's paw or diagonal cutters to pull the nail heads and gently ease out the shingles. If necessary, take off two courses to expose the exterior sheathing—never drill through asbestos siding!

If the house is sided with vertical tongue-and-groove or board-and-batten, or some type of plywood siding, you'll have to make a decision. One option is to remove a substantial amount of siding. Another option is to drill and blow the wall cavities from the interior. If you have brick veneer, stucco, or other masonry cladding, you really don't have much choice but to insulate from the inside, or hire a professional with demonstrated experience working with—and repairing—your siding type.

Filling walls with a tube

Once you've drilled the holes, you're ready to begin. Whether the holes are on the inside or the outside, the basic technique is the same. Start by inserting the tube up into the wall bay, pushing it in so the end is close to the top. This is a good opportunity for feedback on whether the cavity is blocked—if the end of the tube stops short of where you expect the top of the wall to be, there is likely some blocking or diagonal bracing that will require an extra hole drilled above it. Once you've determined that the tube is all the way at the top, pull it back a couple of inches to allow the material some room to flow. It's helpful to cover the hole around the tube with a small piece of fiberglass or a rag; this helps control dust and keep cellulose from blowing back out of the hole.

Be sure to plug any holes cut in the sheathing, even if the siding will cover them later. Precut tapered plugs are generally available from a cellulose supplier.

Once the hole is plugged, set the shingle or siding in place and attach with siding nails.

Start the machine, let it fill the wall cavity until the material flow starts to back up, then pull back the tube 6 in. to 8 in. (this process is described in more detail on pp. 76–77). Continue until you have filled the upper half of the cavity, then stop and push the tube down to the bottom. Fill the lower half of the cavity in the same way, working back toward the hole. The lower part will fill up quickly, as it will already have some loose material in it.

Cavities under windows are filled in the same way, except there's no upper half. When you finish each hole, make sure that it is tightly packed; it should be difficult to push a finger through the cellulose.

When you are finished, plug the holes and refinish the surface. From the outside, tap in wooden plugs and then neatly replace the siding. You will probably need to apply some touch-up primer and paint as well, depending on the finish.

Some walls in older houses open into attic areas. Before you start drilling, check for this situation—you'll save yourself a lot of drilling if you can insulate the wall cavities from above.

WHAT CAN GO WRONG

Wall cavities that open into a basement, chimney chase, built-in cabinet, pocket door, or other open area can turn into bottomless pits for insulation. Before you start blowing cellulose, check for any of these potential cavities against exterior walls. Also, check the subfloor in the basement just above the sill. If you find any openings, you must block them to avoid filling the basement with a pile of cellulose.

In some cases, walls are framed so that the bays open into the basement. Stuff the bottoms of these wall bays with fiberglass before blowing insulation.

STRATEGIC DENSE-PACKED CELLULOSE

If you have cathedral ceilings that are already insulated with fiberglass batts, or for some other reason are unable to dense-pack the roof cavities, filling the tops of partition walls with cellulose is about the only way to reduce air leakage without demolishing the interior walls or roof.

The same approach (in plan view) can work to reduce air leakage where partitions meet exterior walls. Depending on the framing, it may be difficult to get a good solid fill on the exterior wall at such intersections, so dense-packing the first bay of the partition from inside can help.

Wiring and plumbing holes, as well as cracks between the drywall and the top plates, allow warm, moist air to escape.

Fiberglass batts in the roof cavity don't stop air leakage, but they prevent effective dense-packing of the cavity.

Filling an interior partition wall with dense-packed cellulose (or two-part spray foam) will help prevent air from leaking into the roof cavity.

Electrical wiring

The partition wall is dense-packed using a fill tube.

Some loose material will fall into the lower part of the wall; this is OK.

Whether you're insulating from the interior or the exterior, a self-feed bit makes it easy to drill the large holes you'll need.

After filling each stud bay with cellulose, the holes in the wall are patched with slightly inset polystyrene plugs and one-step patching compound. (Note that this contractor is using a nozzle rather than a fill tube. Although not my preference, a trained professional can get good results with a nozzle, using two holes per cavity. The work must be checked with an infrared camera.)

SAFETY FIRST

Before working on a ladder, always make sure it's stable. Keep your body weight in the middle—don't over-reach. Ladder jacks and staging can help. They are well worth the trouble to set up, because you can strip siding and insulate a large area before moving the staging. Follow the safety instructions carefully, use common sense, and be especially careful while drilling. The torque developed by a 1½-in. or 2-in. self-feed drill bit is dramatic. If the bit binds in the wall sheathing, the handle can kick back violently, knocking you right off your perch.

Drilling and patching from indoors

If you have siding that you don't want to deal with, it may be easier to drill and insulate from indoors. Of course, this will be much more disruptive and dusty, but it may be a lot faster and easier, especially if you are refinishing parts of the interior already.

The preparation is basically the same as insulating from the outside, except there's no siding to remove. Start by making a row of holes about halfway up the wall, with one hole in each stud bay (don't forget the spaces under windows).

After you've finished blowing cellulose into the wall, you can insert premade polystyrene foam plugs (they're usually available from a cellulose supplier), slightly inset from the existing wall surface. The holes can then be conventionally patched with a good-quality patching or setting-type joint compound. If you are doing substantial refinishing, or if you want a more solid patch, you can make drywall patches instead; they are more time-consuming but less likely to crack or pop over time.

Strategic dense-packing

You can also use dense-packing to reduce air leaks between interior partition walls and cathedral-ceiling or flat-roof cavities. The technique is the same as that for filling exterior wall cavities from the interior, provided you can achieve densities of 3.5 lb. per cu. ft. Use it for plumbing walls, duct chases, and other places that are likely to have big leaks into the ceiling cavity (avoid doing this around a chimney chase). This is a messy job, but it may be the cheapest way to solve ice dams or cathedral-ceiling dripping. In that case, try to do all the top-floor interior partitions. Be extra careful when drilling into walls that contain plumbing and other services.

Insulating Floors

Some floors need insulation, and some do not. A basement with a furnace or boiler is typically warm enough that insulating the floor won't save you much, if anything. I generally prefer to seal and insulate foundation walls to help keep that heat in the house. Most people want their

Push rods are used to hold unfaced fiberglass insulation batts in place in the floor joists. It's important not to compress the fiberglass too much with the push rods.

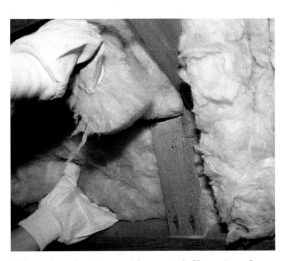

Fiberglass batts must be carefully cut and woven around any bridging, blocking, or other obstructions in the floor framing.

When insulating a cantilevered overhang, drill into the soffit at the bottom and use a nozzle or a fill tube. But be careful: Some floor cavities open into a basement or other part of the house (including recessed lights, pocket doors, etc.). If you have access, stuff each bay from inside with a big hunk of fiberglass. If there is no access, you can set the machine for more material (or less air pressure) to reduce the density and to avoid overfilling the cavities.

This overhang was hidden by a porch ceiling made of perforated vinyl soffit. The solution was to remove the soffit and insulate the overhang before installing a drywall ceiling. Note the patches below the overhang, installed after insulating the exterior house wall.

basements to be at least moderately warm, at least to reduce the risk of pipes freezing and dry things out a bit. If you don't mind having a very cold basement, you can combine floor insulation with insulating and sealing the ducts (or insulating heating pipes) to help keep the heat in the upper floors. Some floors that should be insulated are cantilevers; floors over garages, on stilts, or on piers; and slab-on-grade floors in cold climates. The open side of a conditioned walkout basement is also a slab-on-grade floor.

Insulating an open floor with batts (over a basement or crawlspace)

If your floor is open—that is, with exposed joists to which you have access from below—the easiest way to insulate it is with unfaced fiberglass batts. Be sure to buy batts that match the size of the joist spacing (usually 16 in. o.c.) and hold them in place with insulation push rods spaced every 2 ft. or so.

Don't depend on friction to hold fiberglass batts in place, or they will soon fall down. And don't use faced batts, thinking that the flanges can be stapled to the joists, because the vapor barrier will end up on the wrong side of the insulation. The batts should be in full contact with the floor and not compressed too much by the push rods. Be sure to cut and fit the batts neatly around any cross-bridging, plumbing pipes, and other obstructions in the floor system.

I recommend the following R-values for floor insulation: In mild climates, R-19 will meet or exceed energy codes, but a high-density R-21 (5.5-in.) or R-30 (8.5-in.) batt will give you more R-value for minimal extra cost. These batts are stiffer and easier to install properly. In cold climates, R-30 or R-38 will do. Plan to fill

the floor framing to its full depth. If you have only 6-in.- or 8-in.-deep joists and want more insulation, attach extruded-polystyrene (XPS) foam to the underside of the floor for a higher R-value. Use screws and 1-in.-dia. fender washers to make sure the foam stays in place. Check your local building code; foam insulation may need to be covered with ½-in. drywall or plywood for fire safety.

Insulating an enclosed-cavity floor with cellulose

Any floor that is exposed to outdoor conditions or unconditioned space and has solid sheathing on the underside can be insulated with blown-in cellulose. Examples include garage ceilings, exposed heated porches, cantilevered overhangs, and sheathed floors built on piers. The process is the same as that for filling cavities in cathedral ceilings or walls. You must drill holes in each bay, and then patch the holes when you are done.

Using a piece of fiberglass to contain the air pressure and help control dust, the cellulose is blown into a floor bay.

Protecting Foam Insulation

If you insulate a slab or foundation wall from the exterior, you must protect the insulation above grade to prevent damage from sunlight; typically, this is done with some type of stucco. Other materials that protect foam board include pressure-treated plywood, bendable vinyl coil stock, or cement tile-backer board. Several companies also make a preformed insulating panel with an exterior-duty finish already attached.

One problem with applying rigid or spray-on (shown here) foam insulation to the exterior wall of a foundation is that it is difficult to finish reliably.

You will need a heavy-duty hole saw or rotary drill bit larger than the fill tube—generally 2⁹⁄₁₆-in. or 2¾-in. diameter. Drill one hole between the joists in the middle of each floor bay. Use a stud finder to locate the first joist, or drill a hole and probe the space with an insulated wire to find the nearest joist and the direction in which it runs.

Drill a line of holes, one in each bay, across the space. The distance between the row of holes and the end of the bays should be at most 12 in. beyond the length of the fill tube (see the drawing below), because the tube cannot pack mate-

DENSE-PACKING CELLULOSE IN A FLOOR

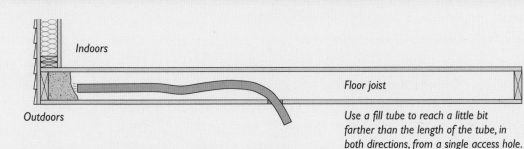

Indoors

Outdoors

Floor joist

Use a fill tube to reach a little bit farther than the length of the tube, in both directions, from a single access hole.

For floors that are enclosed on both sides with sheathing, dense-pack cellulose with a fill tube. The fill tube can reach about 12 in. beyond the length of the tube itself, but very long fill tubes are difficult to work with, so if the cavity is very long you will need a second set of holes. Watch out for blocking, cross-bridging, or other obstructions. You can use the same technique for flat ceilings and attics with subflooring (drill from above, or remove a floorboard).

PRO TIP

Avoid installing carpeting on uninsulated slab floors. Moisture may condense on the cool concrete, creating a mold problem.

WHATCAN GOWRONG

In termite-prone areas, exterior rigid foam is not recommended, because insects can hide behind the insulation on their way into the house. Some manufacturers make insect-resistant polystyrene-foam products. Typically, those products do not have insect-repelling qualities that will protect your home; they only prevent critters from nesting in the material. Check your local building code to see whether those products are acceptable for such applications in your area.

PROTIP

Most of the heat loss in a foundation occurs near the top of the wall, which is exposed to outdoor temperatures, but I recommend insulating the entire wall.

This dimple mat (Delta-FL®) provides a drainage space and vapor barrier. Seal the seams of the dimple mat carefully with high-quality acrylic tape (like 3M 8086 or Tyvek tape) before adding a layer of extruded polystyrene foam, then 1×3 sleepers at 16 in. o.c., and a plywood subfloor.

SAFETY FIRST

Insulating hides both structural and water-leakage problems in your foundation walls—at least temporarily, until the wall caves in or the space floods. Make sure the foundation is both well drained (from inside or out) and structurally sound before installing insulation.

rial farther than 1 ft. If the length of each bay is much greater than twice the length of the fill tube, drill an additional row of holes farther down, so that you can reach the entire floor. You will also need an extra row if you find solid blocking between the joists.

Blow in the insulation in the manner described for attic slopes (see pp. 76–77). Push the fill tube in as far as it will go, turn on the machine, and back the tube out slowly as the material backs up. Hold a rag or small piece of fiberglass over the hole so the dust doesn't blow in your face (always wear a dust mask and safety glasses). When the end of the tube nears the hole, turn off the machine, push the tube into the joist space in the other direction, and repeat the process. When you are done with that hole, you should have a tightly packed fill that is difficult to push a finger through.

When you are done, put a plywood plug in each hole so the surface is just shy of the drywall or sheathing material, and patch it with a one-step patching compound or nonshrinking wood filler as appropriate. Prime and paint to match.

Insulating a slab floor

An uninsulated slab floor can lose a lot of heat if the edges are close to or above grade level. It can be cold and uncomfortable in the winter,

and cool and damp in the summer. If the floor is unfinished, or you are planning to remodel anyway, a layer of extruded polyethylene, with 1×3 furring as a nail base, makes a good foundation for a plywood subfloor.

Start with a moisture barrier. This can be as simple as a layer of 6-mil polyethylene sheet, but I prefer to use a dimpled polyethylene mat if there is enough headroom, especially in a basement with any likelihood of water. The air space provides drainage to keep the subfloor dry, and helps prevent mineral efflorescence that can damage the slab from below. Attach the subfloor to the sleepers with screws, or use glued tongue-and-groove plywood and skip the sleepers. Allow the assembly to float on top of the insulation layer; don't fasten through the dimple mat. Most flooring manufacturers will accept this approach provided the subfloor is ¾-in plywood. You will lose a couple of inches of headroom, but it is worth the greater energy efficiency, comfort, and moisture control. If headroom is tight and moisture is present, the dimple mat is more important than the insulation layer.

Because most of the heat loss from a slab-on-grade floor is at the edges, you can also install rigid-foam insulation (polystyrene) vertically on the outside of the slab instead. The insulation must descend vertically at least 2 ft. from the top of the slab. The technique is typically not worth doing unless you are excavating around the perimeter of the house for some other reason, or if the soil is very loose and easy to remove.

Insulating Foundation Walls

If you have a basement or a crawlspace, chances are pretty good that the walls are not insulated. If you have heating equipment in the space, it is probably not very cold in the winter, either—the thermal boundary is ambiguous. If you use it for anything besides storage, or if you are planning to finish all or part of the basement later, I recommend insulating the foundation walls rather than the floor above. I also recommend insulating the crawlspace walls instead of the floor joists (see the bottom photo on p. 45). Remember that if you do insulate overhead, you will also need to insulate the furnace ducts or the heating pipes in the basement (see pp. 112–115 and the sidebar on p. 131).

Foam insulation with drywall

If you insulate the walls, I recommend using sprayed polyurethane foam, or rigid foam, covered by a stud wall. It's common to build a stud wall and put fiberglass in the wall cavities, but this may result in mold or moisture problems, regardless of the climate (see the drawing on p. 90).

see the bottom photo on p. 45; pp. 112–115 and the sidebar on p. 131; see the drawing on p. 90

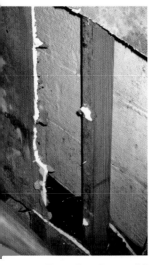

Instead, insulate behind the studs with 2-in. polystyrene insulation. The wall is then insulated with fiberglass batts, and finished with non-paper-faced drywall.

A recipe for mold and rot: wood studs and fiberglass against an uninsulated concrete foundation wall. Humid basement air can condense on the cool surfaces and damage the wall in front, or behind and out of sight.

This foundation wall was insulated with taped XPS installed above the dimple mat. Sealed at the bottom and top with canned foam, the XPS can drain under the mat.

TRADE SECRET

Slab floors that are more than a few feet below grade don't cause much heat loss, but they stay cool in the summer due to ground contact. These surfaces become magnets for condensation in humid weather. For this reason alone, a slab floor may well be worth insulating.

The surface of this uninsulated slab floor stays damp from condensation for most of the summer.

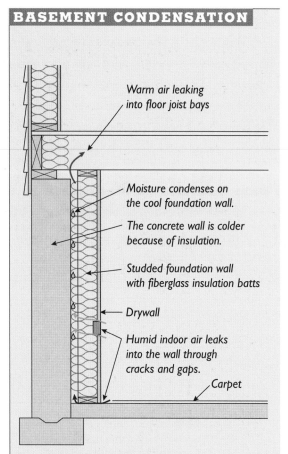

- Warm air leaking into floor joist bays
- Moisture condenses on the cool foundation wall.
- The concrete wall is colder because of insulation.
- Studded foundation wall with fiberglass insulation batts
- Drywall
- Humid indoor air leaks into the wall through cracks and gaps.
- Carpet

A common way to finish basement spaces is to build an insulated stud wall and glue carpet to the floor. This can result in a moisture and mold disaster: The finish materials keep the concrete surfaces cooler, and when humidity from the indoor air reaches these surfaces it can condense. The wood, carpet, and paper backing on the drywall all retain moisture and provide nutrient sources for mold growth.

PRO TIP

People sometime worry if insulating a foundation will increase frost in the ground and damage the wall. It's safe: Frost heave is always in the direction of heat flow, and an insulated basement is warmer than the ground.

IN DETAIL

Insulate foundation walls with rigid foam, sealed carefully to provide an air barrier and vapor control. Cover the foam with ½-in. drywall or wood studs.

Most of the heat loss in a foundation wall occurs near the top of the wall, where it's exposed to outdoor temperatures, but I recommend insulating the entire wall. The cost to insulate the entire wall is not much more than doing just the upper half. Also, if you insulate and finish the entire wall, you will have a much nicer finished space in the basement.

I recommend a minimum insulation value of R–10 (2 in. of XPS or closed-cell polyurethane foam). In cold climates with full basements, you can double the R-value with a 2×4 wall built inside the foam and insulated with batts. Either way, install the foam against the wall, then build a 2×4 stud wall just inside to hold the drywall in place. Code requires that the drywall must not depend on adhesives for its attachment to the foam insulation.

As an alternative to building an entire stud wall, you can install 1×3 vertical furring strips to hold the foam in place and provide a base for attaching the drywall. The wood furring must be mechanically attached to the foundation wall with powder-actuated nails or concrete screws. Make sure the fasteners are long enough to pass through the foam board and furring and attach reliably to the foundation wall. Then the drywall can be screwed directly to the furring strips.

Basement Finish Materials

If you are trimming finished basement walls with baseboard, consider installing molded vinyl or a fiber-cement product to help protect them against moisture and mold. Instead of paper-faced gypsum board, use a non-paper-faced board such as Georgia-Pacific DensArmor Plus® interior panel, Temple-Inland GreenGlass® interior board, or National Gypsum e2XP® Interior Extreme. Don't be fooled by "moisture resistant" paper-faced board-mold likes green paper just as well as grey paper (see the bottom left photo on p. 16).

Better Foundation Retrofits

A good insulation job can actually fix a basement moisture problem that you may not be able to solve by improving exterior drainage. Spraying 2 in. to 4 in. of closed-cell foam on the walls over a polyethylene membrane allows leaking water to drain around the perimeter; the foam controls both condensation and air flow. The wall can be finished with studs and drywall, but avoid moisture-sensitive materials: use fiberglass-faced, not paper-faced, gypsum board.

You must also drain any water that reaches the footing: It's best to add an interior perimeter drain (6 in. deep by 6 in. wide is plenty for most basements). Fill it with washed stone and drain it to daylight or a sump pump. To finish an existing slab, start with a dimpled polyethylene underlayment designed for the purpose (see photos on pp. 88–89). Lay the dimple mat down before you insulate the walls. Carefully tape any seams, and seal the wall insulation right to the edges. This will provide a complete air- and vapor-tight seal, so ground moisture stays outside the wall and floor, while the underside of the dimple mat allows drainage. Some finished flooring (such as interlocking laminates) may be installed directly over the dimple mat; check the flooring manufacturer's recommendations. I prefer to add at least 1 in. of insulation, which usually requires an additional subfloor layer on top, but this can be omitted if height is critical.

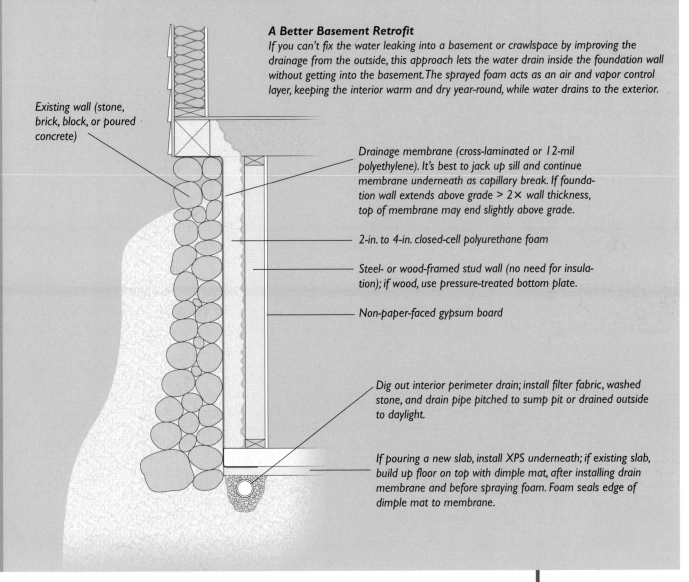

A Better Basement Retrofit

If you can't fix the water leaking into a basement or crawlspace by improving the drainage from the outside, this approach lets the water drain inside the foundation wall without getting into the basement. The sprayed foam acts as an air and vapor control layer, keeping the interior warm and dry year-round, while water drains to the exterior.

Existing wall (stone, brick, block, or poured concrete)

Drainage membrane (cross-laminated or 12-mil polyethylene). It's best to jack up sill and continue membrane underneath as capillary break. If foundation wall extends above grade > 2× wall thickness, top of membrane may end slightly above grade.

2-in. to 4-in. closed-cell polyurethane foam

Steel- or wood-framed stud wall (no need for insulation); if wood, use pressure-treated bottom plate.

Non-paper-faced gypsum board

Dig out interior perimeter drain; install filter fabric, washed stone, and drain pipe pitched to sump pit or drained outside to daylight.

If pouring a new slab, install XPS underneath; if existing slab, build up floor on top with dimple mat, after installing drain membrane and before spraying foam. Foam seals edge of dimple mat to membrane.

WINDOWS

Over the past decade, updated energy codes, rising energy prices, and improved technologies have given us much better windows at affordable prices. Aren't replacement windows always a great idea? The short answer is, not as much as most people think. Windows are expensive. Air-sealing, insulation, duct-sealing, and other thermal measures almost always save more energy for less investment.

If and when you do choose to replace your windows, don't spend your money on relatively cheap replacement windows. In this chapter, I'll show you how to select the right windows. You will see that one size does not fit all: The best window specifications vary according to climate. Finally, I'll show you how to improve the thermal performance of your existing windows, with minor upgrades or a major overhaul. ▶ ▶ ▶

Replacement windows usually don't pay for themselves in energy savings. But once a house has had air-sealing, insulation, and duct-sealing, the energy costs associated with windows make up a proportionately larger percentage of the total energy dollars. At that point, window improvements may make more economic sense.

Window and Energy Basics

Of all the systems in our homes, we probably expect the most of windows. They are constantly forced into compromise: We want them to let light in, then we add shades to keep light out. We need them to keep air and rain out, then we want to open them to let in air and add screens to keep insects out. They need to keep heat in during the winter and out during the summer. And we want them to keep intruders out, yet they need to serve as a speedy emergency egress. It's no wonder that windows end up being expensive to buy and maintain.

The lure of replacement windows

Replacement-window manufacturers and installers often sell their products with the sug-

gestion that new windows will reduce your heating and cooling bills by a large amount. In certain cases, big savings are theoretically possible, but it is rare to find a situation where that is realistic. In a typical Northern house, windows account for about 20 percent of annual energy costs. You can't save what you don't use: Even if you replaced them all with fully insulated walls, you couldn't save more than 20 percent.

I have seen people replace old single-pane and storm combination windows with cheap double-pane units, only to have their energy bills (and street noise) actually increase. Fortunately, energy codes have essentially made clear double-glass windows illegal to install in most areas. But even if you buy replacement low-e windows at a good price and install them yourself, the payback is likely to be 20 years or more. If you

WHERE YOUR ENERGY DOLLARS GO

As the chart shows, in a typical Northern house windows may account for a bit more than 20 percent of the annual heat bill. Replacing them with code-minimum double-low-e windows may save 11 percent of your heating bill, but at a cost of several thousand dollars. High-end triple-glazed low-e might save more like 15 percent. Because windows drive so much of cooling loads, you might do better in the South: Replacing single pane, metal-framed windows with high-end low-solar-gain units may save 20 percent of your total heating and cooling costs.

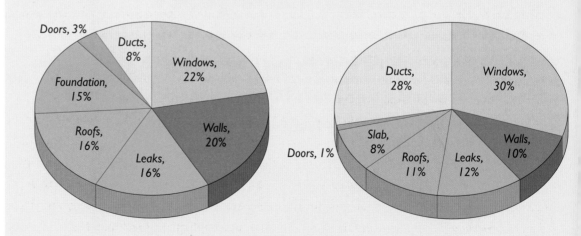

Northern house (Chicago) heating $

Southern house (Dallas) cooling $

pay someone to install replacement windows, it's more likely to be 40 years or more, far longer than the expected service life of the windows themselves. In short, the benefits of replacement windows are often overstated. If you're buying replacement windows, you need to do your homework: Windows are expensive, and buying the wrong ones can be a costly mistake.

Types of windows

Up until the 1960s, standard windows in the United States were built with a single layer of glass. In cold climates, they were often accompanied by storm windows. Since then, standard fare in cold climates has been a sealed double layer of clear glass, commonly called *insulated glass.* Today, homes with one layer of single-pane glass are relatively rare in the cold-climate areas of the United States.

The insulated glass used in most residential windows is made of two layers of glass separated by a metal spacer and sealed to keep out moisture. But not all insulated glass windows are the same: Most of the improvements in window technology over the past two decades are practically invisible, but the energy performance from window to window can vary a lot.

Most significant energy features fall into three categories: improvements in the glass, or *glazing*; improvements in the spacers at the edge of the glazing; and improvements in the sash and frame materials. Glazing improvements can be further divided into two categories: reductions in heat transfer and control of solar heat gain.

Energy-efficient features, such as low-e coatings, warm-edge spacers, and thermally improved frames, can improve window performance significantly, but they can also be confusing. The frame material matters: Aluminum frames, which are inexpensive and durable, per-

Some replacement windows can be installed without having to replace the interior or exterior trim. Although these new windows may look and perform better than the old ones, don't be lured by a promise of big energy savings.

form poorly in cold climates but are acceptable in warm climates when they include a thermal break. Wood, vinyl, and fiberglass frames conduct less heat, so they help you keep it in (or out).

Low-e coatings and gas fills

Two window technologies that are commonplace today are low-e coatings and gas fills. Low-e coatings help save energy in all climates by controlling the amount of solar energy that passes through them and decreasing the total amount of heat transfer. This virtually invisible coating is applied to one of the inner surfaces of the sealed double-glazed unit. Low-e windows also have warmer indoor surface temperatures in

PROTIP

If you are buying new windows, get the best ones that you can afford. But don't buy replacement windows just for energy savings.

WHAT CAN GO WRONG

One thing to consider when buying new windows is the quality of the edge seals. Pay attention to the manufacturer's warranty, which should give you some idea as to how long the seals will last. Well-designed and -constructed edge seals should last 20 years or more. When the seals fail, moisture and dust get in between the panes of glass, giving them a cloudy appearance.

The death knell of any sealed glazing unit is the failure of the edge seal, which allows moisture and dust to migrate into the space between the glass layers, resulting in a cloudy appearance.

LOW-E GLASS REFLECTS HEAT, SAVING HEATING AND COOLING ENERGY

A low-e coating on glass reflects heat, reducing heat transfer. Low-e coatings also reduce ultraviolet (UV) rays, which fade furnishings.

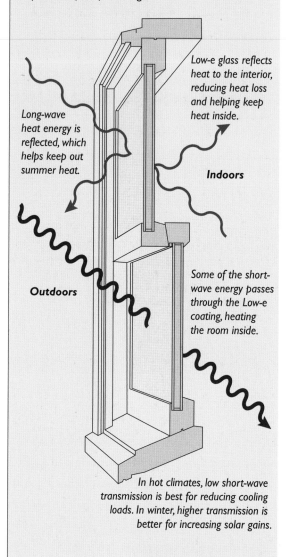

Long-wave heat energy is reflected, which helps keep out summer heat.

Low-e glass reflects heat to the interior, reducing heat loss and helping keep heat inside.

Indoors

Outdoors

Some of the short-wave energy passes through the Low-e coating, heating the room inside.

In hot climates, low short-wave transmission is best for reducing cooling loads. In winter, higher transmission is better for increasing solar gains.

Most new windows are made with sealed, double-glass units. The metal edge spacers conduct heat and are a thermal weak link in the design of a window.

winter (and cooler in summer), making indoors more comfortable year-round.

Gas fills—typically argon or krypton—replace the air that would normally be between the layers of glass. Usually added to low-e windows, these nontoxic inert gases further decrease the amount of conducted heat, primarily a heating-season benefit.

Advanced windows

A number of other window features that are relatively new to the market are gaining a foothold in the industry. Some of them, such as warm-edge

In cold or mixed climates, most homes with older single-pane windows probably have some variation of this triple-track aluminum-frame storm window.

spacers, are finding applications in a wide variety of products. Others, including multiple layers of heat mirror film and insulated fiberglass frames, previously only found in premium products, are starting to join the mainstream—though for most manufacturers they are still typically "special order" options. In general, depending upon the climate in which you live and the climate-specific features of the windows, my advice is to buy the best windows that you can afford.

Also consider the long-term view: If you can't afford super glass now, buy windows with high-quality sashes and frames and a system that allows easy replacement of the sealed glazing. Then, when the edge seal eventually fails, you (or the future owner) can replace the glass easily. There's a good chance that today's super-high-performance glass will be mainstream by then. If you are able to buy high-performance glass now, consider a third layer of glass instead of a suspended film: The jury is still out on whether films will last for decades without visible distortion or sagging.

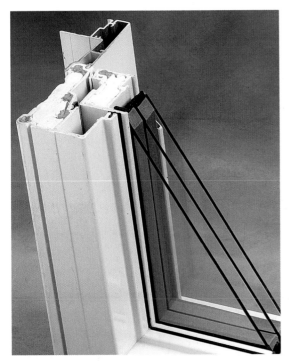

This fiberglass frame conducts much less heat than vinyl and wooden frames do, and it is more dimensionally stable, too. This Canadian-made sample has a third layer of glass, instead of plastic film.

ANATOMY OF A HIGH-EFFICIENCY WINDOW

Heat mirror glazing systems usually contain one or two layers of plastic film suspended between two layers of glass. The plastic film has an additional low-e coating embedded in it, but the film is much lighter and thinner than additional glass layers would be. These windows usually have warm-edge spacers, an alternative to the standard heat-conducting metal spacers.

Layers of heat mirror film have low-e coatings embedded in them to further enhance the unit's performance.

Low-e coating on inner surface of glass

The spaces between glass and film are filled with argon or krypton gas to improve heating performance.

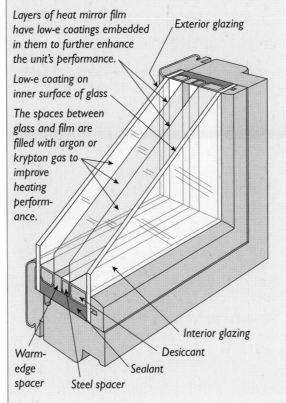

Exterior glazing

Interior glazing

Desiccant

Sealant

Warm-edge spacer

Steel spacer

ACCORDING TO CODE

Most energy codes apply not only to new construction and additions but also contain energy requirements for remodeling and replacement windows. Current codes require a maximum U-factor of 0.35 for all newly installed windows in climate zones 4–8. In hot climates, the U-factor requirements are higher but there is a maximum SHGC of 0.3. Upcoming revisions to the code are even more stringent; it's always a good idea to check with your local building official to make sure.

PRO TIP

Low-e windows can significantly reduce heat loss in winter and heat gain in summer, making your home more comfortable year-round.

Climate Matters

For a house in Orlando, Florida, with typical single-pane aluminum windows, more than half of the cooling bill may be due to the windows. Changing to clear, insulated glass (still with aluminum frames) will save less than 5 percent on annual cooling costs. On the other hand, replacing them with vinyl frames and low-e insulated glass may save 20 percent or more on the cooling bill.

If you are considering upgrading your air-conditioning system, you may first want to upgrade your windows. Window performance has a large impact on cooling loads, and thus on an air conditioner's size (see "Air-Conditioning"). If you select a new or replacement air conditioner based on regular glass and later change to low-e glazing, the air conditioner will be bigger than it needs to be. If, on the other hand, you change the glass first, you can save money later by installing a smaller air conditioner.

PRO TIP

In northern and mixed climates, south-facing windows can provide free heat gain in winter, while adding little to the cooling load in summer, when the sun's angle is high.

Replacing Windows

Window replacement rarely makes sense from purely an energy perspective. If you have already improved your insulation, performed air- and duct-sealing, and have moderately to highly efficient heating and cooling equipment—all of which are typically more cost-effective upgrades—windows are likely the last weak link in the thermal performance of your house.

Of course, there are many other reasons to replace windows. Ease of cleaning and maintenance, aesthetics, damage or rot on the existing windows, and general remodeling are all non-energy-related factors that contribute to the value of window replacement.

Choosing windows

Determining the right combination of window features and price is a complex undertaking, which is further complicated by climate differences. Broadly speaking, when you choose windows, you need to consider function (daylight, glare, egress, ventilation, and maintenance); aesthetics; energy performance (heat loss, UV transmission, condensation control, comfort, and solar gain); and warranty.

I will not say much about the non-energy qualities of windows, other than to point out that investments in maintenance features—such as cladding on wood windows, fiberglass frames, or tilt-out sashes for easy cleaning—can easily pay for themselves with saved hassle and expense. The values of aesthetics and manufacturers' warranties speak for themselves. For all those criteria, as with most products, you get what you pay for—with windows, at least as much as with other products, it is worth buying the best you can afford.

As for energy performance, consider an Energy Star® rating to be the minimum performance level for any climate in the United States. This will typically mean low-e glass and nonmetal frames for most of the country, though metal frames with a thermal break may meet the criteria in the EPA's "southern" zone.

Beyond those guidelines, the two primary characteristics to consider are a window's U-factor and solar heat gain coefficient (SHGC). In cold climates, you should generally buy the lowest U-factor you can find—that will save you the most on heating costs. In those cases, gas fills are generally desirable, and extra layers of glazing or heat mirror film are even better, if you can afford them. Try to avoid products with a U-factor above 0.30; the best products on the market are rated between 0.10 and 0.15.

In hot climates, the U-factor is secondary to SHGC—in those cases, buy the lowest SHGC available to reduce air-conditioning loads. Tinted glass or spectrally selective low-e coatings help reduce unwanted heat gain without impacting

A tilt-out sash is one useful feature found in many replacement windows.

visibility. Try to select products with SHGC ratings below 0.3; the lowest-rated products have an SHGC of about 0.2.

In a cold or mixed climate, you'll want to compromise between U-factor and SHGC. Generally, a low U-factor combined with a low SHGC is desirable. People often ask about solar gain, especially in cold climates: South-facing windows provide free heat in winter, so why would I want to reduce the SHGC? The simple answer is that as long as you get a lower U-factor, the lower SHGC is usually worth it. The reduction in solar gain is typically

NFRC Window Label

The National Fenestration Rating Council (NFRC) is a non-profit, public/private organization created by the window, door, and skylight industry. The NFRC has established a voluntary national energy-performance rating and labeling system for fenestration products, which is typically the best way to compare energy performance of windows. The label can be found on virtually all new windows, and the equivalent information is in manufacturers' catalogs. Note that the numerical values shown are for the entire window unit, including the glass, sash, and frame (this is why SHGC and visible transmittance [VT] are often lower than you would think—they represent the whole unit, and not only the glass). These standardized values make it easy to do energy calculations for any window of known frame dimensions.

The "U-factor" (U = 1/R) represents conductive heat loss—smaller is better. U-factor is especially important during the heating season.

VT is a measure of how much visible light gets through. VT includes the frame.

World's Best Window Co.	
Millennium 2000+	
Vinyl-Clad Wood Frame	
Double Glazing • Argon Fill • Low E	
Product Type: **Vertical Slider**	
ENERGY PERFORMANCE RATINGS	
U-Factor (U.S./I-P)	Solar Heat Gain Coefficient
0.35	**0.32**
ADDITIONAL PERFORMANCE RATINGS	
Visible Transmittance	Air Leakage (U.S./I-P)
0.51	**0.2**

National Fenestration Rating Council® CERTIFIED

Manufacturer stipulates that these ratings conform to applicable NFRC procedures for determining whole product performance. NFRC ratings are determined for a fixed set of environmental conditions and a specific product size. NFRC does not recommend any product and does not warrant the suitability of any product for any specific use. Consult manufacturer's literature for other product performance information. www.nfrc.org

SHGC is the amount of solar radiant heat that gets in through the window. Lower SHGC reduces summer cooling, but also decreases beneficial solar gain in winter. For mixed and hot climates, low SHGC is a plus.

Air leakage (AL) is optional on the label. It shows how much air will pass through a window per square foot. Lower AL ratings mean more energy efficiency in all seasons.

Condensation resistance (CR) is optional on the label. CR is a relative rating, from 0 (no resistance) to 100 (high resistance).

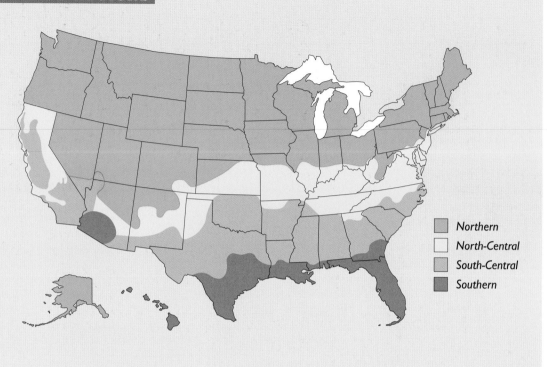

The U.S. Environmental Protection Agency rates windows for better-than-average performance in four climate areas.

The basic requirements for Energy Star windows include: U-factor of 0.3 or less (Northern); U-factor ≤ 0.32, SHGC ≤ 0.4 (North-Central); U-factor ≤ 0.35 and SHGC ≤ 0.3 (South-Central); or U-factor ≤ 0.6 and SHGC ≤ 0.27 (Southern). EPA also has criteria for doors and skylights. Remember that the Energy Star program sets a minimum standard; significantly higher efficiency levels are definitely available. Like the building code, these values are regularly updated. For more information, see www.energystar.gov/windows.

Northern
North-Central
South-Central
Southern

WHAT CAN GO WRONG

Don't try to second-guess the downsizing adjustment between the inside dimensions of an existing window frame and the frame dimensions of the replacement sash or pocket. Buy window kits from a reputable dealer who is experienced in the replacement business and let him or her do the figuring. Otherwise, you may end up with gaps that are too big to be covered by the trim, and lots of headaches.

more than offset by the reduction in heat loss during all the winter hours that the sun isn't shining. If you live in a cold climate and don't have air-conditioning, it is certainly desirable to get higher SHGC combined with the lowest U-factor you can. But if you do have air-conditioning, the higher SHGC will just come back to bite you in the summer.

If you really want to optimize your window choices, get some help calculating the benefits of different options with free window-energy software called RESFEN (available free online at windows.lbl.gov/software/resfen/resfen.html). The detailed calculations are slow, but the inputs are fairly simple. RESFEN provides results in annual heating and cooling dollars attributed to your windows, so you can compare the differences between product costs and likely annual savings and calculate your payback period. Be careful to accurately input your actual electric

and gas utility rates, which are likely to be different from the defaults supplied.

Alternatively, you can hire a certified building-performance consultant to help calculate the cost-effectiveness of various options. These professionals are more likely to understand the nuances of U-factor and SHGC (and are less likely to be biased) than the average window-replacement salesperson or website.

Replacement sashes

When you do decide to replace your windows, there are two basic approaches: replacing the entire window, including the frame, or replacing just the sash. Sash replacement is usually accomplished with a unit that includes a new frame to carry the replacement sash. The frame fits in the pocket between the old stops. This approach is less expensive and involves a lot less trim work, but most products are limited to double-hung

Many replacement windows can be set into the existing window frame, minimizing disruption to the interior and exterior trim. If you are replacing only the sash, you can use a short length of rope and snake a strip of fiberglass batt into the weight pocket.

TRADE SECRET

Some people are concerned about argon gas leaking through glass and wasting their investment, but this is largely a myth. Studies have shown that the vast majority of gas loss is due to poor design or assembly of the edge seals. In well-built units, gas loss results in just a small-percentage change in the window's performance over a 20-year lifetime. By the time the seals fail and fill the unit with moisture the window is junk; no one will care about the performance of the gas fill.

styles. If you choose that approach, keep in mind that the added frame thickness will reduce the glass area and view somewhat. Some kits include only the sash, jamb liners, and hardware, without the integral frames. They are trickier to install well, though they tend to look more like original windows.

You must accurately measure the dimensions of the existing frames, then order replacement units that will fit properly. Check both the height and the width in several places, in case the jambs are not parallel, and use the shortest distance for ordering purposes. If the existing window frames are badly out of square, replacement-sash or pocket kits will never fit properly. If the side frames are bowed inward, it may indicate that the window frame is carrying building loads from above due to inadequate header support. Either of these conditions requires replacing the entire window; in the

latter case, you may need significant structural repairs as well. Check the old frame carefully for moisture damage, and remember that a damaged sill can indicate that water has leaked into the wall beyond the window frame.

If you are replacing old double-hung windows that have rope-and-pulley sashes, be sure to remove the old steel weights and insulate the pockets before installing the new windows. One way to do this is by pulling a length of fiberglass batt into the pocket. If you are removing the old trim, seal the pockets with low-expansion foam. Be careful not to fill too much, because it may distort the frames.

As you insert the frames, carefully follow the manufacturer's instructions for shimming and supporting them, and be sure to carefully caulk any gaps between the new frame and the old before installing the trim. Don't use foam between the frames unless the new frames are

Tucking in a strip of fiberglass helps ensure a good fit, but the gap must still be caulked afterward to make an airtight seal.

Before attaching the stops, caulk the frame of a new window to the old frame to ensure a good, airtight seal.

Drafty Windows

Most people assume that their windows leak through the spaces around and between the sash. Some windows do leak pretty badly; old, rattling double-hung or aluminum horizontal sliders tend to be among the worst. (Jalousie windows are the worst: They don't even count as windows. I consider them vents, and they should never be part of the thermal boundary of a house.) Often, the space between the window and the rough opening needs to be sealed. This space is normally covered by casings on the interior and the exterior, and, depending on how tight the casings are, can leak through that area. If you aren't otherwise removing the trim, the easiest way to seal those leaks is to caulk the casings where they meet the wall and the jamb—use paintable, siliconized acrylic caulk. If you are replacing windows or removing the trim for any other reason (or if it's easy to remove), use low-expansion foam.

It is a misconception that insulation R-value is important here. Rather, the priority is to stop the air from leaking. I have seen instructions that suggest it is important to tuck little tufts of fiberglass gently into the jamb space, but they will do nothing to stop air flow. Instead, use low-expansion foam and make sure it bridges the gap completely. Be careful not to use too much foam; if the gap is large, first fill most of the space with a piece of rigid-foam insulation first.

When foaming around a new window, be sure to use a light touch (left), or you'll end up with problems. The window opening shown at right was sealed with low-expanding foam, but the space was so large that the foam distorted the window frame as it cured. This window may need some remedial work to open.

This spongy foam rope, called backer rod, can be used to fill large gaps between a window frame and the rough opening before caulking.

In old double-hung windows, the spaces in which the counterweights run tend to be drafty. If you are remodeling, the pockets can easily be sealed with spray foam.

very sturdy and well supported. If the gaps are large, tuck in backer rod to fill the spaces, and then caulk.

One detail that is especially important is the flashing of any new window frame, which keeps any wind-driven rain that gets past the siding or leaks in the window frame from seeping into the wall cavity. You may only be able to flash properly if you replace the entire window (see pp. 189–190). Also, pay attention to the instructions for trim installation and exterior caulking details. For example, the gap where a new sill sits on top of the old one is generally left unsealed to allow any water that penetrates to drain freely.

Installing new windows

Replacing the entire unit, jamb and all, offers some advantages over sash replacement. Foremost, new units often let in more light, because they don't have the extra frame thickness that's common with replacement units. Although replacing the frame requires a lot more trim work, it's also an opportunity to get a good look at the house's framing to see whether there is any damage from leaking water. It is also much easier to seal weight pockets when the interior casing has been completely removed. Of course, adding new trim is significantly less

trouble if you are also doing major renovation work on the interior or exterior.

If your existing windows are horizontal sliders, casements, or awning units, replacing the entire window will likely be your only option. However, existing double-hung windows can be replaced with a different-style unit to change the feel of the house or increase or decrease the view opening (for information on installing new and replacement windows, see *Windows and Doors,* by Scott McBride, a companion volume in the Taunton Press Build Like a Pro® series).

Improving Existing Windows

Short of replacing windows, you may be able to improve their performance significantly— and for a lot less than it would cost to replace them. The strategies for improving windows in the following section apply mostly to cold and mixed climates. For information on improving window performance in hot climates, see pgs. 107, 141–143.

On one end of the spectrum are the plastic interior storms that you can shrink-wrap onto windows with a hair dryer, as well as the reusable types with a plastic zip strip. Those "renter's

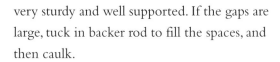

Interior plastic storm windows may save some energy, but they don't do anything for a house's value or appearance. This one is reusable.

Installing a pulley seal over the rope and pulley of old double-hung windows is one way to save a little bit of energy, and it is inexpensive and easy to do.

Adhesive vinyl v-seal weatherstripping can be applied to a window frame to reduce air leakage. Cut the weatherstripping to fit, press it in place between the sash and the frame, and peel the paper off the adhesive backing around the edge of the window.

storm windows" are cheap and are moderately effective for old, rattling single-pane windows, but they are not very practical or aesthetically pleasing. In many cases, older windows can be successfully weatherstripped, and adding storm windows can be a cost-effective improvement if your budget rules out replacement windows.

Improving old double-hung windows

The classic rope-and-pulley double-hung wood window is an elegant design that is simple, functional, and repairable. In a drafty, uninsulated house, they provide light, views, and ventilation without appreciably affecting the house's energy performance. But as the years pass, the wood sashes loosen and layers of paint disrupt their fit and operation. Once you effectively insulate and air-seal the building, they can become a large energy liability.

A Window Makeover

If you have an older house with original wood windows, consider giving them a serious overhaul instead of replacing them. Many old wood windows are made of tough, Southern yellow pine and have tremendous heritage value—especially if they are in a historic district or home.

Bi-Glass® (www.bi-glass.com) is an example of a comprehensive window-restoration system that preserves existing sashes and frames while updating to modern efficiency standards. With a system like this, you may even be able to retrofit triple or heat-mirror glazing into your existing windows at a price that's closer to a standard replacement window—and save that beautiful woodwork from the landfill.

The Bi-Glass system uses a router to make room for modern glazings in any size and shape of sash. The system includes options for complete hardware replacement, new hidden balance systems, and new high-quality weatherstripping.

An exterior storm sash (left) is still a viable option, particularly for a traditional home. The holes at the bottom are vents to let moisture escape, and they are mostly covered by an adjustable stop. Clip-on storm panels (right) with aluminum- or vinyl-edge trim can be permanently installed over fixed picture windows and casement windows.

If you aren't ready to replace them, rattling window sashes can be tightened with leaf-type or v-seal weatherstripping and pulley seals. In many cases, simply removing excess paint so that the sashes meet properly and the sash locks work can make a big difference in their performance.

Storm windows

Adding storm windows to single-pane glass will reduce the heat loss through the windows by about half, in addition to reducing interior condensation and frost, so this project is a good choice, especially if your primary windows are in very good shape. Storm windows are generally not as attractive as replacement windows, they don't add as much to the resale value of a house, and they increase the hassle of window cleaning and maintenance. But low-e storm windows can make an even bigger dent in your energy costs, and they are relatively inexpensive.

Storm windows have been around since the 19th century. Typically, they were fixed panels that were installed seasonally on the exterior of windows. That approach is still an option; a skilled do-it-yourselfer with a decent shop can probably make them for less than the cost of triple-track aluminum storm windows, and they will look better. However, they aren't as flexible. They must be installed and removed every winter and stored somewhere during the summer. If you do decide to make storm panels, try to get hard-coat low-e glass for better performance. It's a special order from a glass shop, but the better performance is worth the trouble and some extra cost.

Large picture windows and other fixed-sash glass may also be treated with permanent, fixed storm sashes. In very large openings, Plexiglas®, acrylic, or polycarbonate may be more affordable than glass, which must be tempered for safety. And the only way to add storm panels to casement or awning windows is with clip-on panels that open and close with the sash.

Today, most people who install storm windows choose triple-track aluminum combination units, with movable sashes and screens all in one package. If you do invest in those windows, go out of your way to find units with low-e glass. Regular low-e coatings used in double-glass windows are soft and can't be exposed to weather or handling, but special hard-coat low-e coatings are used for single glass such as storm windows. When installing storm windows, follow the manufacturer's instructions carefully, and don't use any glues or sealants until the frame is screwed firmly in place and you verify that all the sashes and screens operate smoothly.

It's important to allow for venting any moisture that gets between the primary window and the storm, to avoid condensation on the inside surface of the storm window in cold weather. In practice, this means that the storm window must be at least a bit leakier than the primary window. Therefore, if your primary window is very leaky, you will need to improve the weatherstripping, or the storm may cause problems. Controlling indoor relative humidity during the winter can also help, because that reduces the amount of moisture in indoor air.

Other strategies to improve cold-weather window performance

A number of other strategies can improve window performance beyond the installation of low-e storms. In cold climates, cellular shades, drapes, or movable insulation can reduce heat loss in winter, provided they are tight-fitting all around the window frame. If you are diligent, night insulation can be very effective, but few people want to move insulation panels twice a day. However, modern insulating cellular shades are easy to move and provide a significant boost to night-time R-value. A nice, top-down/bottom-up shade can be expensive (at least $250 per window) but provides multiple benefits: a very flexible combination of view, light, privacy, and efficiency. For locations where privacy is less critical, bottom-up cellular shades are more affordable.

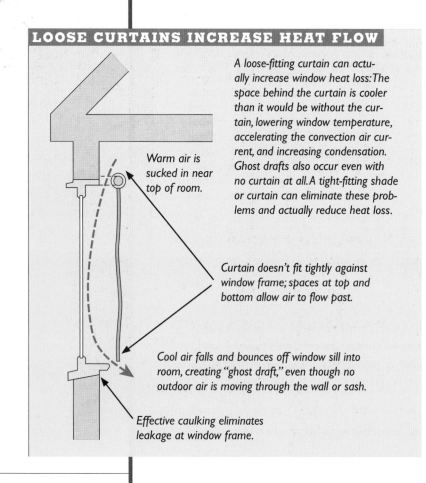

LOOSE CURTAINS INCREASE HEAT FLOW

A loose-fitting curtain can actually increase window heat loss: The space behind the curtain is cooler than it would be without the curtain, lowering window temperature, accelerating the convection air current, and increasing condensation. Ghost drafts also occur even with no curtain at all. A tight-fitting shade or curtain can eliminate these problems and actually reduce heat loss.

Warm air is sucked in near top of room.

Curtain doesn't fit tightly against window frame; spaces at top and bottom allow air to flow past.

Cool air falls and bounces off window sill into room, creating "ghost draft," even though no outdoor air is moving through the wall or sash.

Effective caulking eliminates leakage at window frame.

Also, be aware of the effect of shading on south-facing windows. The branches of deciduous trees, often touted as providing beneficial shade in summer while allowing solar gain in winter, actually diminish solar radiation by about half and should be avoided near the south side of a house. Even insect screens on the south side should be removed in winter, because they also cut solar gain significantly.

On the cooling side, even more can be done to decrease air-conditioning loads. Although shades and blinds on the inside significantly reduce solar gains, external shading is even more effective, because the sun's rays never hit the glass. Shading that is built onto the house—overhangs, awnings, or porches—or nearby, such as trellises, arbors, and other structures, can prevent or reduce solar heat gain.

Landscaping choices, such as trees and other plantings, can also shade windows. You can shade east- and west-facing windows in any climate to reduce cooling loads, without compromising solar gain in winter. The south side is a little more complicated. In a hot climate, shading south-facing windows helps cut cooling loads. In a mixed or cold climate, shading the south side reduces cooling loads slightly, but at the expense of also reducing free solar heat in winter. Moderate overhangs attached to the building right above the windows are the best choice. If they are properly sized, they will admit solar rays in winter, when the sun's angle is low in the sky, and still shade windows in summer, when the sun is higher overhead.

Whatever your approach, there are numerous types of attachments that can be used to improve window performance or to decrease negative characteristics. Unlike for windows themselves, unfortunately there are no industry-standard rating systems for performance window attach-

Be sure to caulk around the frames of new storm windows to maximize their benefit. Remember, it's important to leave the weep holes at the sill open, so any moisture that collects there can drain freely.

ments. Lots of product manufacturers provide online calculators that unsurprisingly show significant savings for their particular product. Beware: It's always good to check out the underlying assumptions, and note that the source of the information may suggest significant bias. One online resource—www.windowattachments.org —addresses the wide variety of attachments and provides unbiased guidance to help homeowners with decisions about window treatments.

HEATING SYSTEMS

People often ask me, what's the best kind of heating system? My answer: A good building enclosure. A comfortable, draft-free house with high levels of insulation is economical and easy to heat with any type of heating system. Insulate and air-seal first; you'll get the most for your heating dollars. A new or renovated home can be built with heating loads so low that a conventional heating system is too big—and thus an unnecessary expense.

While you're improving your home's thermal boundary, relatively simple mechanical upgrades, duct-sealing and insulation, and even automatic thermostats can all help save energy. New high-efficiency heating systems and controls can be very cost-effective compared to standard systems. And if you have ducts in an attic, garage, or crawlspace, sealing them can be one of the best ways to save energy. ▶ ▶ ▶

Simple Conservation

In colder parts of the United States, heating is the biggest energy expense for most homes, so heating savings can make a big difference. Aside from the building enclosure, your heating system is probably the next biggest factor in your energy use, so anything you can do to improve its operation has the potential to save a lot of energy.

There are many kinds of heating systems (which will be covered later in this chapter), but they all have three common elements: heating equipment, which converts fuel into heat; a distribution system, which delivers heat around the house; and controls, which regulate the system's operation. All three affect the efficiency of the system, and all can typically be improved to save energy.

Thermostats

The thermostat is a control that is common to virtually every heating system. A thermostat senses the room temperature and turns the heat on when the temperature drops below the set point. The simplest thing you can do to save energy is to turn down the thermostat. Depending on the climate, you can save about 10 percent if you keep the house cooler by 3°F to 5°F.

Turning down a thermostat saves energy, but only if you're consistent. If one person is always turning it down, and another is always turning it back up, the person who turns it up may set the thermostat even higher to compensate for feeling chilly—and use more energy. This "dueling manager" syndrome is particularly wasteful if you have a heat pump. Find the lowest setting that everyone in the family is consistently comfortable with, and then leave it alone (other than for regular setbacks).

I'm not advocating shivering in the dark, though that works too. However, once you have

The Nest Learning Thermostat™ is a new twist on the old thermostat. It learns from your behavior to create automatic setbacks and bring the house back to temperature when you need it. A motion sensor knows if you come home early, and a wireless network interface allows remote control from a computer or smartphone, as well as access to local weather data.

insulated and air-sealed a house, and perhaps installed high-performance windows, you may find that you are perfectly comfortable at a lower thermostat setting. For example, one of my clients built a new house just up the hill from the old Victorian farmhouse he and his wife owned. "One of the most amazing things," he enthusiastically told me, "is the change in our thermostat setting. The old house was so drafty that we had to set the thermostat at 72°F or more to stay comfortable. In this one, we get too warm if we set it above 64°F."

Another way to save energy with your thermostat is by using a regular setback. Turning down the house temperature for 6 to 8 hours while everyone is asleep, or away during the day, can save a lot—about 10 percent for an 8-hour, 10°F setback. Contrary to popular belief, it does not take more energy to bring the house back up to temperature. Remember, the heating system replaces heat that the house loses; if the indoor temperature is lower for a period of time, the house simply loses less heat during that time. But don't overcompensate by setting the thermostat higher when you return; a setting of 78°F does not warm the house up any faster than a setting of 70°F.

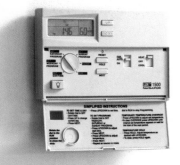

Efficiency Losses in a Heating System

Not all the energy in the fuel you buy contributes to heating your house. Your heating system's *efficiency* is the amount of useful heat you get as a percentage of purchased energy. Anything less than 100 percent represents waste, or lost efficiency. There are three kinds of heating system losses: combustion loss, cycling loss, and distribution loss.

Combustion loss is simply the heat that goes up the chimney; it varies from about 30 percent to as little as 3 percent. That leaves a *combustion efficiency* between 70 percent and 97 percent; that is, the percentage of the fuel you buy that is converted to heat in the equipment. Combustion efficiency is mostly affected by equipment design; unless the burners are badly out of tune, it can't be improved much unless you buy a new unit.

Cycling losses occur when the heating equipment starts and stops. Each time the unit shuts off, some heat remains inside; some of that heat goes up the chimney. Cycling losses are affected by the equipment design, location, and controls; some efficiency improvements can be made if the controls are set poorly to begin with.

Distribution losses occur when heat generated in the equipment gets out of the house before it reaches its destination. Distribution losses include duct air leaks and conductive losses through uninsulated ducts or pipes. Distribution losses can be significant: 5 percent to 30 percent, so in many homes a large improvement can be made.

A standing pilot flame in a furnace uses gas constantly, even during the summer; that is a waste of energy.

Comfort and energy use

Another fairly simple factor that affects heating-system performance is system balancing. Balancing refers to the temperature consistency from one room to the next. If one or more rooms are consistently too cold, people tend to set the thermostat high enough to be comfortable in those rooms. The rest of the house then overheats, using more energy.

Balancing problems can be caused by thermal defects in the building, by problems in the distribution system, or by the thermostat location. Rooms that have air leaks, drafts, or missing insulation may lose heat faster than neighboring rooms, or they may just be uncomfortable. Thermal problems should be fixed before addressing the heating system. Once the building enclosure is properly treated, the distribution system can usually be adjusted for better balance.

Furnaces or heat pumps that have a ducted distribution system should have manual balancing dampers, like this one, near the takeoffs from the main trunk duct to the branch runs. It is better to adjust the airflow here than at the supply register (shown with duct disconnected for clarity).

This is a typical hot-water radiator, or fin-tube baseboard. Like most fin-tube units, it has a hinged damper to close the slot at the top of the unit and reduce heat output.

WHAT CAN GO WRONG

One of the biggest risks in sealing leaky ducts is that you may decrease the airflow, reducing efficiency or even causing damage. If a duct system is undersized, much of the air flowing through the furnace may travel through those leaks, so sealing them has the potential to seriously choke off the air supply. Be sure to check the airflow with the temperature-rise test before and after sealing the ductwork.

Duct-Sealing

Air leaks in a duct system can have an enormous effect on your house. Duct leaks rob a furnace, heat pump, or central air system of energy—sometimes close to half. Leaks can cause comfort problems, drive moisture flows, and sometimes even lead to dangerous backdrafting of combustion equipment. Leaky basement ducts don't usually waste much energy; sealing them is pretty easy, but there's not much value to it. But ducts located in attics, garages, or vented crawl-spaces can be a big energy problem. Sealing them can be the biggest opportunity for energy savings in many homes.

Leaky ducts do more than let heat out. They also increase the air exchange in a house by 30 percent to 300 percent whenever the air handler is running. That is why furnaces have the reputation for drying out houses. Return leaks in a mechanical room or basement can backdraft a nearby water heater or even the furnace itself. Return leaks can also draw in radon gas, water vapor, subsoil pesticides, or airborne mold spores, distributing them throughout the house. Supply air leaking into an attic or enclosed

It's amazing how often I find ducts that are actually disconnected in attics, garages, or crawlspaces. Once in a while I even see sections of ductwork that were never installed.

cathedral ceiling cavity can deliver moisture at an accelerated rate to cold roof sheathing, causing condensation. If the ducts also carry central air-conditioning, return leaks can bring in outdoor humidity in the summer, reducing cooling efficiency, and leaks can draw outside air into building cavities, where moisture can lead to mold inside the house. Duct leaks are even more important than shell air leaks: Each hole and

Duct mastic is a nontoxic, latex-based compound that is used to seal holes, cracks, and seams in ductwork and fittings.

It's important to peel back the insulation and vapor jacket to seal the duct connections. The black stains are from the air leaks.

Duct-Sealing Supplies

The most important duct-sealing supplies are a good-quality latex-based mastic and a box of vinyl gloves. Fiberglass mesh tape is helpful for reinforcing large gaps and doing structural repairs. A clamp stapler is invaluable for attaching duct insulation. Sheet-metal screws are handy in many places; I prefer the ones with really sharp points, commonly called zip screws.

Although sealing ducts is a messy and dirty job, it can be done with a few inexpensive supplies and potentially save a lot of money.

crack is under pressure from the furnace fan and leaks the hot air from your furnace (or cold air from your air conditioner).

If you can reach them, sealing duct leaks is a relatively easy job. Most of the effort involves getting to the leaks; this can mean some difficult crawling in attics and crawlspaces, and peeling back duct insulation to get to them. Duct leaks can happen almost anywhere in the system. In addition to connections between duct sections, many sheet-metal fittings have built-in holes and cracks, which should be sealed with duct mastic.

Some people apply mastic with a paintbrush, or buy it in tubes that fit a caulking gun. I prefer

to put on vinyl gloves, then cheap cotton work gloves, reach into the bucket for a small handful of mastic, and smear it onto the leaky areas. The cotton gloves protect your fingers from sharp metal edges. It's pretty easy to slip the cotton gloves off when it's time to move around to avoid getting mastic on everything besides the ducts. If the duct is insulated, be sure to seal the inner lining of the duct, not the vinyl or foil facing on the outside of the insulation.

On the supply side of the system, it is usually fairly easy to follow the duct runs and identify the leakage areas. Places to focus include connections between the main trunk, the branch ducts, the end caps on trunk ducts, and the register boots. Swivel elbows and branch-duct take-offs tend to be particularly leaky. Each register boot must be sealed where the branch duct connects to it, at its corners and folds, and where the boot meets the drywall or subfloor. Sometimes it is easier to seal the boot area from inside the house—just remove the grille and reach inside to seal the leaks.

Return ducts can be a bigger challenge. Return systems are frequently patched together using a combination of plywood, sheet metal, joist or wall cavities, and a lot of wishful thinking. Many HVAC installers don't pay much attention to returns, focusing mostly on supplies that get the air to where it's supposed to go. But well-sealed returns are important for furnace efficiency, occupant health and safety, and building durability. So pay attention to the return air pathways, and get in and seal all the cracks and gaps just as you would for the supply. Pay extra attention to carefully sealing any return ducts in a garage; you don't want garage air being sucked into the house.

In some regions, platform returns are common: in this arrangement, the furnace is in

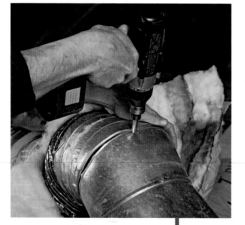

In this case, the insulation was hiding a broken elbow. It had to be repaired with sheet-metal screws before sealing.

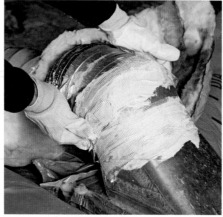

After spreading a thin layer of mastic, a length of fiberglass mesh is embedded in the mastic. This is done for any seams that are likely to be stressed, and to bridge gaps more than ¼ in. across.

After the mesh tape is applied, more mastic is spread over the surface. After it sets, the insulation and vapor jacket must be carefully replaced.

All joints in both supply- and return-duct systems should be sealed with mastic, including those in duct systems constructed in building cavities (such as this panned joist bay).

Many furnaces are located on a closet platform in the house or garage, with return grilles underneath, and lots of air leaks.

a closet or garage, mounted on a plywood base with a cutout for the return air (see the drawing on p. 116). To allow house air to return to the furnace, one or more return openings are cut through the wall; sometimes a return duct is also mounted atop a second cutout in the platform. The platforms are rarely sealed, and nearby wall or floor cavities can suck return air in from the attic, basement, crawlspace, and/or garage. It is critical to seal off these platforms from the inside so return air is pulled from only the house. Fortunately, the grilles are usually large enough to remove, allowing access to seal the area completely.

Two other places to pay close attention to are the large duct sections connected directly to the supply side and the return side of the furnace (called *plenums*). The air pressures are highest there, so any openings in the corners or connections of the supply and return plenums, at the flanges where the plenums connect to the furnace cabinet, or at the filter rack and cover panel leak the most air. Use mastic to carefully seal the supply and return plenums, especially any gaps

The solution for a platform return is to seal the entire area under the furnace with mastic to creating an actual return "duct." The only openings should be at the bottom of the furnace and the return grille(s) or duct(s). Be careful not to seal intentional airflow pathways.

An HVAC contractor or building-performance professional uses a duct tester like this one to measure duct leakage.

All ducts in unconditioned spaces should be insulated with a minimum of R-8 duct wrap. The wrap should be installed neatly and snugly, with plastic washers and screws to hold it in place. A clamp stapler is handy to close the seams.

between the filter and the air handler, where dust and dirt can be drawn in past the filter. (Don't seal the access to the filter, or the service panels to the furnace cabinet itself.) If access is limited, you may need to cut access openings in the ductwork or remove sections of ductwork in order to reach the leaky areas.

Fortunately, it's not typically necessary to seal ducts that are buried inside interior wall and floor cavities. However, you *do* want to ensure that those cavities don't leak to outside spaces; if they do, seal those leaks at the thermal boundary to keep the ducts and the indoor air inside.

Depending on how easy the access is to your duct system, you may want to hire a professional to test and seal your ducts. Building-performance professionals use a duct tester, which is like a miniature blower door (see the above right photo), to pressurize the duct system and measure leakage. If a majority of the ductwork is hidden in walls, cathedral ceilings, or restricted attic areas, hiring someone with an aerosol duct-sealing machine is another option.

See www.aeroseal.com for a list of dealers who can provide that service.

Duct insulation

Ductwork that runs through unconditioned space should be insulated, if it is not already. Typically, supply ducts are insulated but often have weak spots at register boots and other major connections. Often, return ductwork is left uninsulated.

Ducts should be insulated with vinyl-faced fiberglass wrap; R-6 is the minimum allowed by current residential codes; R-8 is required for supply ducts in attics. If possible, attic ducts should have higher R-values. Think about it: In winter, attic temperatures are nearly as cold as outdoors; in summer (for air-conditioning ducts), they are often much hotter than outdoors. If the ducts are close to the attic floor, cover them completely with loose-fill insulation. If that is not possible, try to find R-10 or higher duct wrap. Of course, seal all the duct connections tightly before insulating.

Wrong: Don't insulate ductwork with material intended for wall insulation.

Combustion Air and Platform Returns

ANY FUEL-BURNING APPLIANCE NEEDS adequate air supply for safe and efficient combustion. If you're installing a new heating unit, *sealed combustion* (see the sidebar on p. 120) is your best bet for safety and efficiency. For existing natural-draft equipment, codes generally allow two ways to provide that air. One way is to provide a minimum volume of open airspace around the appliance; it must be unobstructed by partitions, unless there is a louvered door. The other strategy is to supply outdoor air via ducts or transfer grilles. Both systems are based on the input firing rate (in Btu per hour) of the equipment. A higher input requires more volume or larger openings. However, following building codes for combustion air doesn't guarantee that equipment will

work properly. Negative pressures caused by leaky ducts, large exhaust fans, or other pressures in the house can still suck potentially deadly combustion by-products back down a chimney.

One solution is to build a tightly sealed, insulated mechanical room around the equipment and provide combustion air to just that room, preferably with a motorized damper that opens the air inlet only when the burner fires. You can also have a building-performance professional or trained HVAC contractor do a worst-case test to make sure the equipment drafts properly and produces no carbon monoxide. Finally, safety devices that can be retrofitted include gas-spillage alarms, safety switches, or power-vent kits.

Every home that has combustion equipment, a gas range, or an attached garage should have one or more carbon monoxide detectors.

PLATFORM RETURN

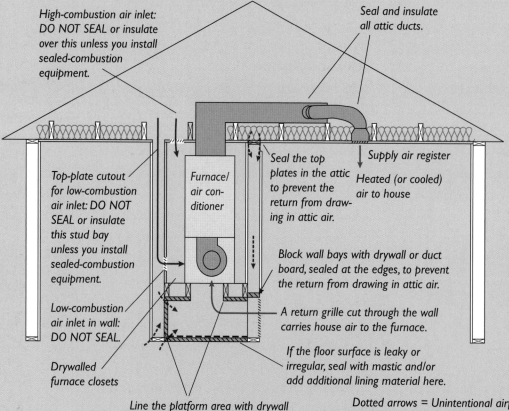

High-combustion air inlet: DO NOT SEAL or insulate over this unless you install sealed-combustion equipment.

Seal and insulate all attic ducts.

Top-plate cutout for low-combustion air inlet: DO NOT SEAL or insulate this stud bay unless you install sealed-combustion equipment.

Furnace/air conditioner

Seal the top plates in the attic to prevent the return from drawing in attic air.

Supply air register

Heated (or cooled) air to house

Low-combustion air inlet in wall: DO NOT SEAL.

Block wall bays with drywall or duct board, sealed at the edges, to prevent the return from drawing in attic air.

A return grille cut through the wall carries house air to the furnace.

Drywalled furnace closets

If the floor surface is leaky or irregular, seal with mastic and/or add additional lining material here.

Line the platform area with drywall or duct board and seal the seams to prevent the return from drawing in attic or combustion air.

A platform return can be a serious energy and safety hazard. The dotted lines show potential unintended airflows, which pull in attic, garage, or outdoor air and also cause combustion problems by allowing the return suction to interfere with the combustion air supply.

The platform should be lined with drywall or duct board and all edges sealed thoroughly with duct mastic. Be sure to identify combustion air paths and intentional return air paths, and avoid sealing those.

A furnace closet may have a louvered door instead (bringing in combustion air from inside the living space) or grilles that open into the garage or outdoors.

Dotted arrows = Unintentional airflows
Blue arrows = High and low air inlets, which supply combustion air, are required by code for a furnace in an enclosed space.
Red arrows = House air circulating through system. Ideally, the house air and combustion air should not mix.

Furnaces

The furnace is by far the most common type of heating system in the country. In fact, it's so common that many people use the word *furnace* to describe any type of heating equipment.

Furnaces create heat by burning fuel, usually natural gas. Oil and liquefied petroleum (LP, or propane) gas are also used in areas where piped gas is unavailable. By contrast, heat pumps and electric furnaces use electricity to heat the air; they also use a duct system to deliver heat, but they are not furnaces and do not have a fuel supply, chimney, or vent pipe. Boilers burn gas or oil but create hot water or steam instead of warm air. Furnace efficiency can be improved by performing regular maintenance, improving airflow, adjusting control settings, and sealing leaky ductwork.

Regular maintenance

Regular furnace maintenance is important to keep things running well, just as with any machine, but tune-ups and filter replacements

Air filters should be replaced occasionally for best furnace performance. This pleated filter is more effective than the standard cheap fiberglass filter, and it doesn't cost much more.

don't really save energy. Be sure to change the filter once or twice a year; more frequently is not much benefit because filters actually work better once some dust has built up on them. If the filter never gets dirty, however, then you may have a duct leak that is causing a loss of efficiency. Keeping registers open and free of obstructions may help your comfort, but this also won't affect your energy bills noticeably.

The next important item is regular burner maintenance. If you have a gas furnace, you should have it cleaned and tuned every two to four years. An oil burner should be tuned every year. Don't wait until cold weather hits—that's when the service companies are busy. You may get a better price if you get the tune-up in the spring.

Low airflow

Low airflow can also reduce furnace efficiency. It can be caused by clogged air-conditioning coils, low fan speed settings, loose fan drive belts, undersized ductwork, or duct obstructions. Sometimes airflow is low to one room or section of the house, causing discomfort.

Diagnosing low airflow is complex, but once identified, the fixes are usually fairly easy and inexpensive. These improvements are probably better left to a professional, but it's good to be informed, because many technicians don't bother checking airflow. If a service person is unable to explain in sensible terms what is happening in your system, you may want to get an opinion from another technician.

You can start by checking for cycling caused by the high-limit control, a safety switch that protects your furnace and house by turning off the burner if the air gets too hot (for example, if the blower motor suddenly stopped). To do that, set the thermostat high enough to run the furnace for 15 or 20 minutes. The burner

PRO TIP

Regular furnace maintenance—including filter replacements, burner tune-ups, and cleanings—is important for proper operation.

WHAT CAN GO WRONG

Once in a while, I run into a homeowner who tells me, "I never need to change the filter, because it never gets dirty." This typically happens when the filter is installed in a filter grille. If the filter isn't trapping any dirt, it's because there's no air going through it—all (or most) of the return air reaching the furnace is being pulled in through leaks in the return duct, or through some other unintentional pathway.

Filter grilles make changing the filter more convenient, but any air leaks in the duct between the grille and the furnace can pull dust and dirt into the furnace. This filter obviously works and is ready for a change.

If your return-duct system is restricting airflow, installing a grille can significantly increase airflow. But you can't install a return just anywhere; there must be a clear path for house air to reach it. If it is located in an attic, a garage, or a crawlspace, the new return will bring cold air into the unit, lowering its efficiency. You may need to add a duct (well sealed, of course) to a new grille inside the house, and of course there needs to be a filter somewhere between the return and the equipment.

GAS-FIRED HOT-AIR FURNACE

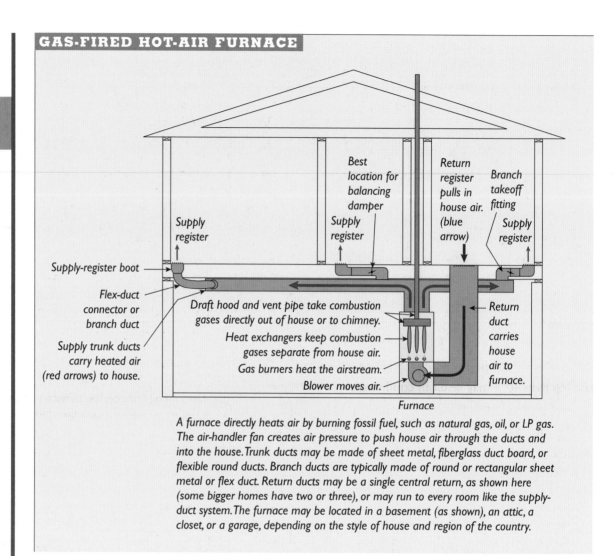

A furnace directly heats air by burning fossil fuel, such as natural gas, oil, or LP gas. The air-handler fan creates air pressure to push house air through the ducts and into the house. Trunk ducts may be made of sheet metal, fiberglass duct board, or flexible round ducts. Branch ducts are typically made of round or rectangular sheet metal or flex duct. Return ducts may be a single central return, as shown here (some bigger homes have two or three), or may run to every room like the supply-duct system. The furnace may be located in a basement (as shown), an attic, a closet, or a garage, depending on the style of house and region of the country.

should fire immediately; after a brief delay, the blower should turn on. Once the blower starts, the burner should stay on until the thermostat is satisfied (or turned back down). If the high-limit control thinks that the air is getting too hot, the burner will cycle off and on periodically while the blower runs. That could mean the control is broken or set incorrectly, or it could mean that the airflow is extremely low.

If the high limit is working properly, the next airflow test is to measure the temperature rise between the return and the supply airstreams. That can be done by using a probe thermometer (a wire thermocouple is better if available)

to measure the temperatures of the supply and return ducts. Measure the supply temperature in a main supply trunk duct close to the furnace. Drill a small hole on the supply side, close to the middle of the duct but around the first corner or bend in the main supply trunk from the furnace. Be careful not to drill into air-conditioning coils that may be located in the ductwork just above or next to the furnace.

For the return temperature, insert the thermometer into the filter slot or a small hole drilled in the middle of the return duct near the furnace. It's okay to measure the return temperature at a return grille close to the furnace, if that's your only option; insert the probe in past the grille.

Again, turn up the thermostat so the furnace will run continuously for 15 to 20 minutes. After the fan starts, let it run for at least 5 minutes before you measure the temperatures. Hold the thermometer in the return airstream, and then in the supply airstream, long enough for the temperature to stabilize, so you can get an accurate reading. The supply minus the return temperature is the temperature rise; it should be between 40°F and 75°F. Try to get a manufacturer's specifications for acceptable range of temperature rise. A temperature rise greater than 75°F indicates low airflow, which should be increased to improve efficiency. A temperature rise less than 40°F may result in condensation and rust in the heat exchanger. In that case, the airflow should be reduced or the burner tuned to increase heat output.

Furnace Tune-Up

A professional tune-up for a gas furnace includes cleaning the burner and heat exchanger, checking the adjustment of air and fuel flow, cleaning and checking the heat exchanger for leaks, and testing draft pressure and carbon monoxide levels. The air-handler fan should be cleaned and lubricated as needed, once every two or three tune-ups. In addition, internal controls may be checked and adjusted if necessary. Don't expect any real energy savings from a gas furnace tune-up; every two to four years is often enough.

Oil burners are more finicky than gas burners. Most oil furnaces benefit from annual professional service; fuel filters, burner nozzles, electrodes, combustion chamber, heat exchanger, and flue pipe all need regular cleaning and adjustment. Checking heat exchangers and testing combustion efficiency are also useful. Try to find a technician who is knowledgeable, methodical, and thorough.

If you have an oil furnace, the service technician might also recommend installing a smaller oil nozzle. This can reduce the heat output of the furnace, better matching it to the house and increasing operating efficiency slightly.

A probe thermometer can be used to check the temperature rise in a furnace. Be careful locating holes so that you don't drill into the air-conditioning coil.

Check the return temperature through a filter slot or a hole drilled in the duct near the air handler.

SAFETY FIRST

Don't attempt to change the fan speed or furnace control settings, or make other adjustments to your furnace or heat pump, unless you understand exactly what you are doing. Always turn off the main power to the unit before opening the cabinet door. And if you aren't sure, hire a professional service person.

Sealed Combustion

One common feature in today's high-efficiency gas furnaces and boilers is sealed combustion. Sealed-combustion appliances draw all their combustion air directly from the outside, usually through a PVC pipe. That makes it virtually impossible to backdraft combustion gases from the appliance (see the sidebar on p. 116). Oil-fired equipment is not usually available with true sealed combustion, but most burners accept retrofit kits that bring outdoor air through a duct directly to the burner. Both oil and gas systems are also available with induced draft, or power vent, configurations that use a small fan to send combustion products reliably outside.

Sealed-combustion appliances not only eliminate backdrafting but also reduce heating loads by eliminating the draw of outdoor air into the house to supply the combustion process.

A sealed-combustion condensing furnace or boiler is vented through a sidewall with a compact unit similar to a dryer vent. If your chimney is old, the savings from not having to improve the chimney may pay for upgrading to a sealed-combustion heating system.

see the sidebar on p. 116

PROTIP

Sealing a leaky duct system can be the single most effective way to save energy in a home.

Many furnace fans have several speed settings; often a lower speed is used for heating and a higher one for cooling. Airflow can often be increased simply by changing the heating-fan speed setting and/or adjusting the belt-drive pulleys.

Undersized or restrictive return ductwork, which can severely reduce airflow, is also common but relatively easily diagnosed. Take the cover off the blower compartment door and repeat the temperature-rise test. If there is a safety interlock switch at the cabinet door, hold it down temporarily with a piece of tape (remember to keep your fingers away from the fan). Now measure the return air temperature near the opening to the cabinet. If the temperature rise drops to an acceptable level, the low airflow is caused by a restricted return duct. If the temperature rise doesn't change much, the trouble is in the furnace fan or supply ducts.

Undersized return ducts can be relatively easy to fix; sometimes just adding a return grille can make a big difference. Often, though, you'll need to add extra ductwork with extra supply or return registers. Sometimes entire sections of ductwork will need to be replaced. Duct upgrades may range from a few hundred to a few thousand dollars, depending on the house.

Furnace control settings

The furnace controls can also have an impact on efficiency. The blower control, located above the heat exchanger, turns on the blower when it senses heat from the burner. It may be right next to the high-limit control or in the same device. The fan-on temperature should be set so the blower comes on between 90°F and 105°F; if it's set too high, the burner will fire for a long time before the fan comes on, letting excess heat go up the chimney. If it's set too low, the circulating air may feel uncomfortably cool. Attic-mounted furnaces may need higher fan-on settings so the blower doesn't turn on in the summer. As an alternative, an extra relay may be installed to turn on the fan as soon as the burner fires; that will

The blower control turns on the fan when it senses heat from the burner. The fan's on and off temperatures (the tabs at the bottom of the dial) must be set properly for maximum efficiency. This one also has a built-in adjustable peak limit (the tab on the right side of the dial).

provide maximum efficiency, if you don't mind the cooler air at the beginning of the cycle.

The fan-off temperature must be slightly lower than the fan-on temperature: between 85°F and 100°F. The lower it is set, the longer the fan will run at the end of the cycle when the thermostat turns off the burners, moving residual heat from the heat exchanger to your house. If your fan-on and fan-off temperatures are fixed (rather than adjustable) and set too high, the control can be replaced. Note that the temperature markings on adjustable controls are often poorly calibrated. Verify the actual fan-on and fan-off temperatures with a thermometer in the supply plenum.

Heat Pumps

Air-source heat pumps, popular in some parts of the country, are basically air conditioners that can work in reverse to deliver heat into the house in winter (see the drawing on p. 123). Heat pumps provide heating and cooling in one machine, with one duct system and no combustion. Heat pumps are not subject to backdrafting, combustion air requirements, or some of the off-cycle losses to which furnaces are prone.

Because they use ducts to deliver warm air to the house, heat pump ducts in attics, garages, and crawlspaces must be sealed thoroughly and insulated well. Heat pumps are more prone to airflow problems than furnaces are, and improper refrigerant charging can have a negative impact on both heating and cooling efficiency.

Operating efficiency and resistance heating

Heat pumps are rated using Heating System Performance Factor, or HSPF. An HSPF of 6.8 corresponds to an efficiency of 200 percent. Most new heat pumps vary from 7.3 to about 10 HSPF; the larger the number, the more efficient the unit. An HSPF of 10 is approximately equal to 290-percent efficient—for every kilowatt-hour (kWh) of electricity you buy, you get almost 3 kWh of heat delivered to your house. How can a heat pump generate more energy than it consumes? The difference is made up by heat energy absorbed from the outdoor air. That energy goes into the system; because it's free, it's not counted in the measurement of efficiency.

Most heat pumps, by themselves, operate at reasonable efficiencies until outside air temperatures drop to about 35°F to 40°F. As the outdoor air gets colder, less heat is available, and the heat pump output drops off, even as the house needs more heat. So cold-weather performance is

IN DETAIL

Another control setting
that affects furnace efficiency is the anticipator, which is located inside the thermostat. The anticipator does just what its name implies: It anticipates the fact that the room will heat up, and keeps the furnace from running too long and overshooting. The dial should point to the number representing the electric current (in amperes) drawn by the gas-valve circuit. A technician can check the current with an ammeter. A correct anticipator setting can improve efficiency a bit.

The anticipator is a sort of timer that prevents the furnace from firing too long as the house heats up. Setting the pointer correctly can improve the furnace's efficiency and your comfort.

In cold weather, heat pump operation is usually supplemented by an electric-resistance strip heater, like this one. It is essentially a giant toaster located in the main supply duct.

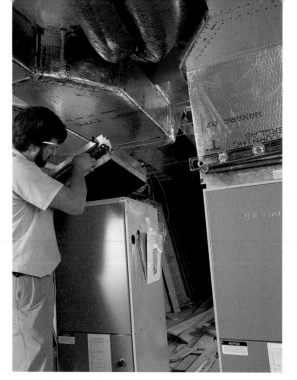

If you have a gas-fired water heater, a hydro-coil like this one can be used to replace electric-resistance backup heat.

typically supplemented with electric-resistance backup heaters.

This auxiliary heat costs about three times more per unit of heat than the compressor heating cycle. That may be fine in regions with long summers, mild winters, and relatively low electric rates, but it's not in much of the North, where electricity is expensive and winters are cold. One fairly inexpensive way to reduce the use of electric-resistance heating is to install an outdoor cutout thermostat. For about $100 to $150 installed, this device locks out the supplemental electric heat when the outdoor air temperature is above 30°F or 35°F.

One way to eliminate electric-resistance heating altogether is to replace the heat pump with a "dual-fuel" heat pump. This may be called a "hybrid" system, or described simply by its components: a heat pump combined with a gas furnace. In a dual-fuel system, when the outdoor temperature drops below a control threshold the heat pump is cut out and the gas furnace is used instead. Optimizing this "cutover tempera-

ture" depends on the relative costs of gas and electricity, and the efficiency of the heat pump. You could also remove or disable the electric coils and install a hydro-air coil, if you have a natural gas water heater. This coil is like a radiator installed in the supply plenum (about $500 to $1,000 installed). A hydro-air coil must be designed carefully to avoid significantly cutting the airflow through the heat pump, because hydro coils have higher airflow resistance than electric-resistance coils. A dual-fuel heat pump or a hydro coil is only worth considering if natural gas is available. LP gas and oil are expensive enough that it makes more sense to invest in a new, super-high-efficiency heat pump.

Airflow

Heat pumps are even more sensitive to airflow than furnaces are. Heat pumps need to move a larger volume of air, but installers who are used to working with furnaces sometimes skimp on duct sizing, leading to low-airflow problems. Unfortunately, checking the airflow of a heat pump is not as easy as checking that of a furnace. It can be done with special instruments or with a version of the temperature-rise method used with the electric-resistance backup heat. Don't attempt to take these measurements unless you understand exactly what you are doing—if you aren't sure, get a service technician to do it for you.

For best efficiency, heat pump airflow should be 375 CFM to 425 CFM per ton of heating capacity. It should never be below 300 CFM per ton. One ton equals 12,000 Btu per hour, and equipment is typically rated in increments of ½ ton, such as "24" (×1,000 Btu, or 2 tons), "30" (2½ tons), "36" (3 tons), etc.

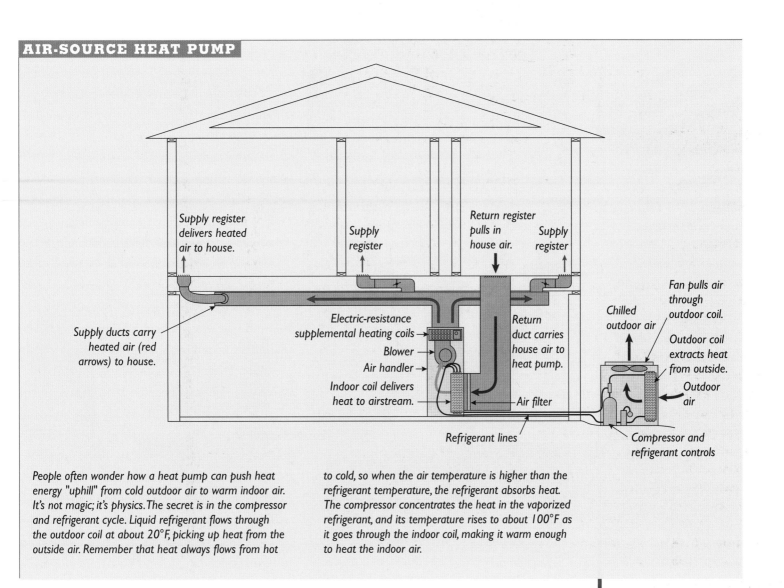

Supply register delivers heated air to house.

Supply register

Return register pulls in house air.

Supply register

Fan pulls air through outdoor coil.

Chilled outdoor air

Supply ducts carry heated air (red arrows) to house.

Electric-resistance supplemental heating coils

Blower

Air handler

Indoor coil delivers heat to airstream.

Return duct carries house air to heat pump.

Air filter

Refrigerant lines

Outdoor coil extracts heat from outside.

Outdoor air

Compressor and refrigerant controls

People often wonder how a heat pump can push heat energy "uphill" from cold outdoor air to warm indoor air. It's not magic; it's physics. The secret is in the compressor and refrigerant cycle. Liquid refrigerant flows through the outdoor coil at about 20°F, picking up heat from the outside air. Remember that heat always flows from hot to cold, so when the air temperature is higher than the refrigerant temperature, the refrigerant absorbs heat. The compressor concentrates the heat in the vaporized refrigerant, and its temperature rises to about 100°F as it goes through the indoor coil, making it warm enough to heat the indoor air.

Refrigerant charge

Older heat pumps are also finicky about refrigerant charge. Many heat pumps, even when serviced regularly, are either over- or under-charged, which has a negative impact on efficiency. Unfortunately, many service technicians don't take the time to diagnose or correct those problems; they typically get the system working and move on to the next service call. To measure charge correctly, airflow must be in the recommended range, and few technicians test airflow as a matter of course.

There are very specific ways to measure refrigerant charge during unit operation. Depending on the type of unit, the superheat or subcooling must be measured carefully, as it is for an air conditioner (see p. 148). There are also several automated systems on the market today that trained technicians can use to analyze heat pump operation. Newer high-efficiency models should also be properly charged, but they are more forgiving of varying charge conditions and their efficiency doesn't suffer as much.

PRO**TIP**

Electric-resistance auxiliary heat costs about three times as much as compressor-driven heat.

Why is the refrigerant charge so often incorrect? Frequently, the manufacturers' instructions are not followed during the initial installation, resulting in the wrong charge. Then, some technicians connect their refrigerant gauges at every service call, even when there is no evidence of refrigerant leakage. Some refrigerant escapes each time a gauge is used. To make matters worse, some service technicians add a little refrigerant each time "for good measure." The end result is an unknown quantity of refrigerant. Even if they don't do those things, many technicians do not first test for adequate indoor coil airflow or properly measure superheat or subcooling.

Always keep material and debris away from the outdoor unit of a heat pump. Proper efficiency depends on good air circulation, so never cover up or build a deck over the unit.

Ductless Heat Pumps

Ductless heat pumps, often called *mini-split* heat pumps, are available in higher heating (and cooling) efficiencies than just about any other heat pumps on the market. The most efficient ones use an *inverter-driven* compressor, and variable-speed fans that run continuously at a low speed to match the load in the house and minimize noise. One outdoor unit may be used with one or more indoor units that deliver heat and cooling to the house.

Each indoor unit connects to the outdoor unit with a small bundle of pipes and wires that carry refrigerant and electricity, so there are no duct losses.

Some models are designed for cold-climate operation and maintain a high heating capacity and decent efficiency near 0°F. A single mini-split makes a great heating and cooling system for a single-room addition or a deep energy remodel, or to offset electric resistance, oil, or LP gas heat.

The inside half of a ductless mini-split typically mounts high on a wall. Other configurations are available, such as a small hidden air handler.

The outdoor half of a ductless mini-split is also small and quiet. I was standing right next to this one and didn't even notice it was running.

Heat pump service

Like furnaces, heat pumps should be serviced regularly. Basic service can be done by anyone. Air filters should be replaced once or twice a year, as needed, and the outdoor coil should be kept free of snow and debris. Regular service calls—typically every two to three years—should include testing the controls, cleaning the blower and both the indoor and the outdoor coils as needed, and checking the insulation on the refrigerant lines.

To service your heat pump, try to find a contractor whose technicians are certified by North American Technician Excellence (NATE, see www.hvacradvice.com), or who demonstrates a commitment to attending manufacturers' programs frequently. An initial service appointment should include testing and fixing airflow problems, then carefully measuring and correcting refrigerant charge. Once that has been done, service technicians generally should *not* attach refrigerant gauges to the system unless the system performance drops off or there is other evidence that something is wrong. Refrigerant does not escape unless there is a leak.

Ground-source heat pumps

Ground-source heat pumps (or GSHPs; often called geothermal heat pumps) extract heat from the earth or from underground water, rather than from outdoor air. Because temperatures are more stable underground, GSHP systems theo-retically have much higher heating efficiencies than air-source heat pumps; rated Coefficient of Performance (COPs) range from about 3 to 5 (300 percent to 500 percent).

There are two basic types of GSHP systems. Closed-loop (ground-loop) systems are usually more efficient but can be more expensive to install. Open-loop (groundwater or water-source) systems usually cost less to install but can cost more to run, due to the power consumption of a large well pump that's often required for these systems. A third type of GSHP, called direct exchange (DX), uses a copper pipe ground loop to circulate refrigerant underground. Their long-term reliability is less clear than that of closed-loop water-based systems.

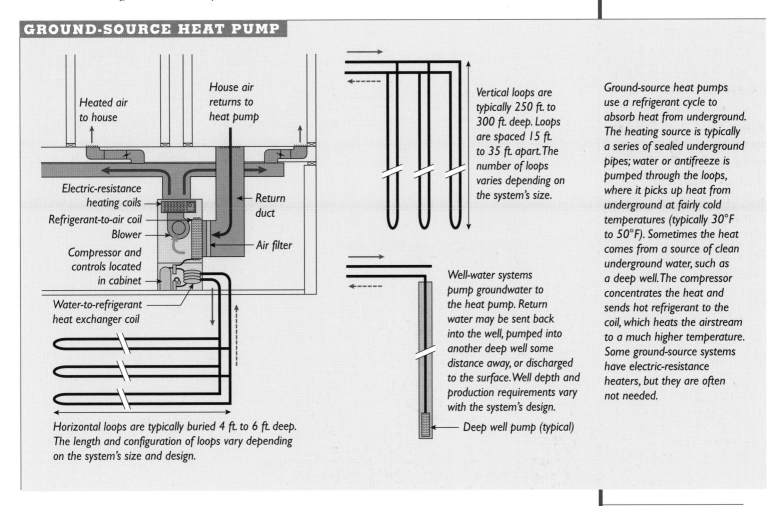

GROUND-SOURCE HEAT PUMP

Heated air to house

House air returns to heat pump

Electric-resistance heating coils

Return duct

Refrigerant-to-air coil

Blower

Compressor and controls located in cabinet

Air filter

Water-to-refrigerant heat exchanger coil

Horizontal loops are typically buried 4 ft. to 6 ft. deep. The length and configuration of loops vary depending on the system's size and design.

Vertical loops are typically 250 ft. to 300 ft. deep. Loops are spaced 15 ft. to 35 ft. apart. The number of loops varies depending on the system's size.

Well-water systems pump groundwater to the heat pump. Return water may be sent back into the well, pumped into another deep well some distance away, or discharged to the surface. Well depth and production requirements vary with the system's design.

Deep well pump (typical)

Ground-source heat pumps use a refrigerant cycle to absorb heat from underground. The heating source is typically a series of sealed underground pipes; water or antifreeze is pumped through the loops, where it picks up heat from underground at fairly cold temperatures (typically 30°F to 50°F). Sometimes the heat comes from a source of clean underground water, such as a deep well. The compressor concentrates the heat and sends hot refrigerant to the coil, which heats the airstream to a much higher temperature. Some ground-source systems have electric-resistance heaters, but they are often not needed.

Polyethylene pipe, used for most GSHP ground loops, is joined with heat-fusion techniques that are stronger than the pipe itself. Pipe failure is relatively rare and most new installations are warranted for 20 to 50 years.

Except for the ground loop, this ground-source system is entirely self-contained. Note the ground-loop circulating pumps mounted on the small white box to the right. The large, sweeping return plenum helps ensure good airflow.

Ground-Source Heat Pump Efficiency

Efficiency ratings for GSHPs come in three flavors: water loop, ground loop, and ground water. "Water loop" is used for commercial systems; "ground loop" is used for closed loops; and "ground water" for open loops. All of them rate the heating efficiency using a Coefficient of Performance, which is the ratio of heat out to electricity in: A COP of 3 represents a heating efficiency of 300 percent. There's a trick to the GSHP performance ratings: You can't achieve them in a real installation. The rating applies only to "the box" itself, and does not include most of the energy required to pump water or move air through the system. Depending on the installation, this can increase real operating costs between 20 percent and 100 percent (bringing a rated COP of 5 down to somewhere between 4 and 2.5).

Despite marketing claims that GSHPs are "renewable" and "green," they still run on electricity. Because electric generation and power lines are inefficient, a GSHP may actually be more expensive to run and generate more emissions than a high-efficiency natural gas furnace and AC system. GSHPs are, however, typically cheaper and cleaner than oil or LP gas heat. They are also quite expensive to install; my preference is to invest in a more efficient building enclosure.

Like air-source heat pumps, ground-source heat pumps can be cost-effective in regions with mild or hot climates and moderate electric rates, especially in areas where installation costs are modest. However, in regions with cold climates and high electric rates, they generally do not provide enough savings to justify the high installation cost.

Ground-source heat pumps can also have very high cooling efficiencies. The heating capacity of GSHPs is much better in cold weather than that of conventional air-source heat pumps, so there is typically little or no need for supplemental electric heat. Closed-loop systems need little or no maintenance, but open-loop systems may have water-quality issues, filters that need replacing, and well pumps with shortened life expectancies.

Electric-Resistance Heat

Most electric-resistance heating systems are simple electric baseboard heaters. There are also various types of radiant-heat systems (usually panels mounted on ceiling or walls, built into valances, or built into ceiling or wall-finish systems). Occasionally, you'll even find an electric-resistance furnace or boiler.

Cheap to install but expensive to operate, electric-resistance heat operates on the same principle as that of a toaster or hot plate. An electric current passes through a wire element, heating it. Air passes through and is heated by fins in the baseboard. Electric-resistance heat is always 100-percent efficient; every kilowatt-hour of electricity that you pay for is converted to heat.

The reason electric baseboards are expensive to operate is that electricity costs two to four times as much as natural gas. One advantage of electric heat is the ease with which rooms can be zoned (see the sidebar on p. 132). But with the high fuel cost and hidden emissions, it's dif-

Avoid "vent-free" fireplaces; despite manufacturers' claims, the devices dump combustion byproducts and water vapor into the air when they're burning.

ficult to justify except in special situations, such as isolated rooms, or extremely mild climates like southern Florida or Hawaii.

Because these systems are so simple, there is very little that can be done to improve their efficiency. Short of supplementing or completely replacing them, the best approach (as always) is to insulate and thoroughly seal the building to reduce heating loads.

An electric baseboard heater is its own distribution system and is usually precisely in the area where heat is desired, so there are no distribution losses like those found in ductwork.

Individual-room thermostats have often been a selling point for electric heat. Don't always believe your eyes, though; a poorly calibrated thermostat can fool you into thinking that you've set the room temperature lower than you really have.

Replacing or supplementing electric heating systems

Because of the high operating cost of electric-resistance heat, many people are interested in replacing or supplementing them with an alternate. This is probably the only situation in which retrofitting a new heating system can pay for itself quickly. Take, for example, a moderately sized house that uses 15,000 kilowatt-hours for heating every year. At 15¢ per kilowatt-hour, the annual heating usage costs $2,250. Let's say you get a bid to install a ductless split system for $3,500. Estimating a net savings of 30 percent to 50 percent, or about $700 to $1,100 per year (see the sidebar below), results in a simple payback of 3 to 5 years. Not bad.

Supplementing Electric Heat

A great way to reduce the cost of electric, LP or oil heat for a reasonable cost is with the installation of a variable speed ductless heat pump (see the sidebar on p. 124). The best systems are rated with an HSPF of 10 to 12, which means they use 65 percent to 70 percent less electricity per unit of delivered heat. Installing a single mini-split to heat a main living area can save 30 percent to 50 percent of a home's heating bill (leaving the existing heat for remote rooms in cold weather), at an installed cost of $3,000 to $4,000. Ductless heat pumps also provide air-conditioning much more efficiently than do window units.

Hot-Water and Steam Boilers

Boilers, an old standby in the Northeast, are becoming more popular around the country with the advent of radiant, hydro-air, and hybrid systems. Instead of heating air, a boiler heats water.

The classic boiler system uses hydronic distribution. Water is heated by the boiler and pumped through pipes to hot-water radiators or baseboard fin-tube convectors to heat the house. Some older systems use a boiler to make steam, which expands to fill steam radiators without the need for a circulator pump.

Basic maintenance

Boiler maintenance is similar to that of a gas or oil furnace (see the sidebar on p. 119), but there is no blower fan to clean. Oil boilers should be

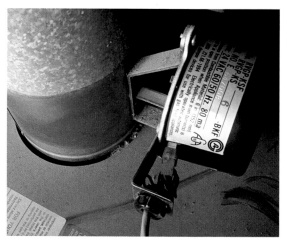

This vent damper automatically opens when the boiler fires, then closes when the burner shuts down, reducing the amount of heat lost through the chimney. Although they save energy on older gas boilers, vent dampers are not necessary on modern, high-efficiency units.

Radiant-Floor Heating

In the past decade, built-in radiant-floor hydronic systems have become quite popular. Quiet and out of sight, they employ flexible tubing embedded in a concrete slab or attached to a wood subfloor, turning the entire floor surface into a low-temperature radiator. When properly designed and installed, radiant-floor systems provide reliable, even heat. Radiant heating is commonly touted as an energy saver, because people are comfortable at a lower thermostat set point. However, research has shown no significant difference in thermostat settings between radiant-floor houses and others, suggesting that such energy savings are largely theoretical.

Staple-up radiant floor systems, such as this one, provide the benefits of a warm floor in wood-frame structures. Radiant floor systems must be insulated carefully so the heat goes only where it's wanted. Hint: Make sure the insulation is tight against the tubing and subfloor. Some installers leave an airspace, but this actually hurts performance by slowing the response to thermostat calls.

TRADE SECRET

Hydronic systems are more efficient when the circulating water is only as hot as necessary to keep the house comfortable. Most boilers are set to run at about 180°F. Because boilers—and radiators—are typically larger than necessary, the setting can often be reduced to as low as 140°F, especially if the house has been weatherized. Alternately, an *outdoor reset* control ($400 to $1,500 installed) varies the boiler temperature with the outdoor temperature. Either one of these options should be performed only by a qualified service person; water temperatures must be controlled to prevent unwanted condensation inside the boiler. Also note that any *condensing boiler* (a boiler rated at 90-percent efficiency or greater, designed to condense flue gases) works best when the circulating fluid is at the lowest possible temperature and should include an outdoor reset control.

This condensing modulating boiler is small enough to hang on the wall and has an efficiency rating of 96 percent.

serviced once a year, whereas gas boilers should be serviced every two to four years.

Any swishing or gurgling sounds that you hear in the radiators indicate air trapped in the system, which reduces heat-exchange efficiency. A service technician can bleed out the air and show you how to do it if it is needed frequently.

Occasionally, bleed valves may need to be installed or replaced. The technician should check the hydronic system pressure and expansion tank; the smallest leak anywhere in the system should be repaired immediately to prevent corrosion-causing oxygen from being brought in via makeup water connections.

Boiler controls and upgrades

A typical hot-water boiler operates throughout the winter with a water temperature determined by the low-limit setting, a thermostatic switch that senses the water temperature inside the boiler and shuts off the burner when the water is hot enough. Standard boiler controls maintain full boiler temperature throughout the year, which is inefficient but necessary if a tankless coil water heater heats the domestic hot water (see sidebar on p. 161). In the absence of a

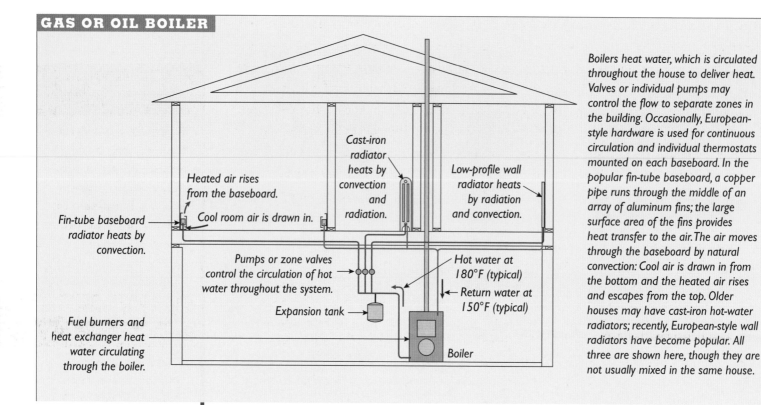

Heated air rises from the baseboard.

Cool room air is drawn in.

Cast-iron radiator heats by convection and radiation.

Low-profile wall radiator heats by radiation and convection.

Fin-tube baseboard radiator heats by convection.

Pumps or zone valves control the circulation of hot water throughout the system.

Expansion tank

Fuel burners and heat exchanger heat water circulating through the boiler.

Hot water at 180°F (typical)

Return water at 150°F (typical)

Boiler

Boilers heat water, which is circulated throughout the house to deliver heat. Valves or individual pumps may control the flow to separate zones in the building. Occasionally, European-style hardware is used for continuous circulation and individual thermostats mounted on each baseboard. In the popular fin-tube baseboard, a copper pipe runs through the middle of an array of aluminum fins; the large surface area of the fins provides heat transfer to the air. The air moves through the baseboard by natural convection: Cool air is drawn in from the bottom and the heated air rises and escapes from the top. Older houses may have cast-iron hot-water radiators; recently, European-style wall radiators have become popular. All three are shown here, though they are not usually mixed in the same house.

TRADE SECRET

If you have an oil-fired boiler or a furnace with an older, inefficient oil burner, have a technician replace the burner with a flame-retention burner. Those units, which cost about $400 to $500, do a better job of mixing the oil with the combustion air, which better controls the fire. They also reduce the amount of heat lost up the chimney, bringing the overall efficiency improvement to between 10 percent and 20 percent.

tankless coil, efficient boiler controls have a "cold start" feature that heats the boiler water only when it's needed, and a "purge" control that runs the circulating pump for a few minutes after the boiler shuts off, to extract any heat that remains inside. These controls, often standard or optional on new, high-efficiency models, can also be retrofitted to existing boilers—but you have to be careful. Cold-start boilers must be protected from condensing on start-up, which may take some extra piping and a *thermic valve* (made by Danfoss® or Termovar) to maintain adequate return-water temperature. Many newer boilers designed for cold starting have this protection built in.

Another improvement for older boilers that don't have good controls is a mechanical vent damper. This device closes off the flue pipe after the burner shuts off, stopping the flow of heat through the heat exchanger and up the chim-

ney. It costs $125 to $350 installed. Don't use a gravity-actuated vent damper that depends on the heat from the burner to stay open; they are much more likely to malfunction.

Steam boilers

Steam boilers are very different from hot water boilers. Steam systems were popular in the early 20th century, and many of them are still in service in older homes. Instead of relying on pumps to circulate hot water, steam boilers boil water to create steam. The steam naturally expands to fill all the pipes and radiators in the system, distributing heat throughout the house. Although steam-heat distribution is simple and reliable, steam boilers have a number of unique maintenance and efficiency issues.

Most residential steam systems are one-pipe systems. When the thermostat calls for heat, the boiler fires and steam begins expanding to fill the system. As the steam expands, it displaces air contained in the pipes and radiators, and that air must be allowed to escape through air vents typically located on the side of each radiator. Once the steam reaches the radiator, the air vent senses the heat and closes, keeping the steam inside. As the steam emits heat through the radiator, it condenses to water and flows back via gravity through the same pipes to the boiler.

Air-venting systems that aren't working properly can lead to uneven heating, large temperature fluctuations, and discomfort. A tune-up can increase energy efficiency and comfort dramatically. If the air vents are too small, if there are not enough of them, or if they are clogged with mineral deposits, air gets trapped in the system, and the steam cannot reach its destination. Having a professional replace malfunctioning air

PRO TIP

When air vents don't work properly on a steam-heating system, it can result in uneven heating, large temperature fluctuations, and discomfort.

Pipe Insulation

Both hydronic and steam-boiler systems can benefit from insulating distribution pipes, particularly in unconditioned basements and crawlspaces. Be sure to install insulation neatly, and miter the corners to minimize pipe exposure. Use a good-quality tape, where necessary, to hold the insulation in place and keep the seams closed. Wrap the tape several turns around the insulation; don't just run it lengthwise along the seam. And for safety's sake, don't disturb any boiler piping that appears to have asbestos insulation on it already.

Pipe insulation is inexpensive and widely available at hardware stores and home centers. Make sure the material used on heating pipes is rated to at least 180°F, because some types will melt on heating pipes.

Duct or pipe insulation that contains asbestos (the material on these steam pipes) can be dangerous if it's disturbed or falling apart. Airborne asbestos fibers can lead to lung cancer and other diseases.

High-density fiberglass pipe insulation is more expensive but necessary for the high temperatures found in steam systems. Be sure to measure the pipes carefully when ordering the insulation. Due to the large, awkward fittings, it can be difficult to cover all the elbows and tees in a steam system, but do as much as you can.

WHAT CAN GO WRONG

A common problem with steam systems is too much pressure. The boiler pressure controls should be set just high enough so that the boiler shuts down just as each radiator fills with steam. Too much steam pressure increases the boiler's cycling losses and leads to overheating. That can particularly be a problem if the building envelope's efficiency is improved dramatically and/or some radiators are removed during remodeling. Timed-cycle controllers vary the boiler cycle length to match the outdoor temperature, further improving the system's efficiency.

Zoning Distribution Systems

Dividing a house into multiple heating zones, each with separate thermostatic temperature control, is often considered an energy-saving as well as a comfort feature. The theory is that people lower the thermostat independently in parts of the house they are not using, reducing heat loss from those areas. Rooms that get significant solar gain on sunny winter days ideally should have their own zone(s), to reduce overheating. The simplest form of zoning is the installation of multiple heating systems, each serving a section of the house. In homes with electric baseboards, each room is usually a separate zone. Newer two-story homes often have a separate furnace and air conditioner to serve each floor.

Individual heating systems can be divided into separate zones with varying success. Hot-water boilers can easily be zoned with separate circulator pumps and piping. Individual thermostatic-radiator valves provide optimal room-by-room control, but they require special piping to operate. Residential steam systems are not possible to zone. Furnaces and heat pumps can be zoned with special dampers, but those installations often suffer efficiency problems.

One way around this problem is to install multispeed equipment. Many high-end furnaces, boilers, and heat pumps have two-speed, or continuously variable ("modulating") output. This allows the equipment to run more efficiently over a wide range of demand. It even improves the efficiency of a single-zone system, by matching the equipment output to the load as conditions vary. A ductless heat pump with multiple heads provides both: individual room control and variable output.

vents, add extra vents to radiators, or add special high-volume air vents to large central supply pipes can improve steam-system efficiency by quickly getting the heat where it is needed. Thermostatically controlled vents can reduce the rate of steam delivery to some rooms, reducing overheating and improving overall comfort.

Two-pipe steam systems (less common in residences) have a separate condensate-return pipe. Instead of air vents, two-pipe systems have a steam trap at each radiator. Steam-trap maintenance is critical for proper operation, and all the steam traps in a system should be replaced or rebuilt at the same time, not one by one.

In addition to the standard service that every boiler or furnace requires regularly, many steam systems need periodic adjustments to the water level, which is typically done by the homeowner. Steam boilers also need regular water maintenance; periodically, boiler water should be drained to remove sediment and rust. Chemically treating steam-boiler water reduces corrosion and improves steam distribution efficiency. Steam-boiler water maintenance should always be performed by technicians with experience in local water conditions and steam systems.

The vent on the left side of this steam radiator has an adjustment knob at the bottom to control how fast the steam fills the unit.

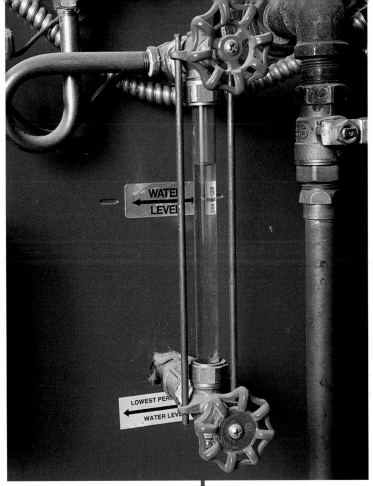

WATER LEVEL

LOWEST PER WATER LEVE

Most steam boilers require a periodic addition of water. This is done by opening a valve on the inlet water line. Like an oil dipstick in your car, this sight glass helps you monitor the water level so you can keep it just right.

Upgrading or Replacing Heating Equipment

Replacing a heating system with a newer, more efficient system is expensive, so it will typically have a long payback. However, if you have to replace a broken furnace or boiler, it is almost always cost-effective to select a high-efficiency system. However efficient (or inefficient) a house shell is, replacing a furnace from the mid-1980s or earlier with a 95-percent-efficient unit will save between 20 percent and 25 percent of the heating bill. Replacing an old boiler can save even more.

On the other hand, if you have a 15-year-old unit that's rated between 80-percent and 85-percent efficient, the savings will be much smaller. It's probably better to spend your money on other efficiency projects. Finally, if you are planning a series of efficiency improvements to the house, it can be a good idea to complete

them before upgrading equipment—you may be able to save some money by installing a smaller unit. If your existing heating system is functional but appears to be on its last legs, replacing it early can help avoid a big surprise. Deciding, rather than being forced, to replace a system reduces the panic factor and allows for a more reasoned choice. It may even reduce the cost a bit, because it won't be an emergency call.

Efficiency ratings

All new boilers and furnaces have standard-ized efficiency ratings, just like the gas-mileage ratings on automobiles. When selecting equipment, look for the highest efficiency ratings. Furnaces and boilers use Annual Fuel Utilization Efficiency (AFUE), which accounts for burner efficiency, pilot fuel, and off-cycle losses. New gas furnaces and boilers have AFUEs of 80 per-

PROTIP

When shopping for a new furnace or boiler, compare efficiency ratings and get the highest you can afford.

WHAT CAN GO WRONG

When replacing a heating system, bigger is not necessarily better. A system that is much bigger than necessary is more expensive to buy and maintain. Any heating-system-replacement bid should account for the thermal characteristics of the house, such as insulation levels, window types, and surface areas, rather than simply replacing the old unit with a new one of the same size. Many homes start out with systems that are too big; if the thermal boundary and/or ducts have been improved, the new system will be even more oversized. A notable exception to this general rule: Heat pumps in cold climates cost less to operate if they are somewhat oversized, because they will rely less on the expensive supplemental resistance heat.

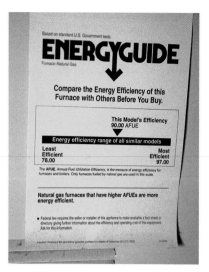

The yellow Energy Guide label indicates the efficiency rating of new equipment and provides a comparison among similar models.

If your furnace or boiler looks like this, it may be time to replace it with a more efficient one, even if it is still running.

cent to 97 percent. AFUE ratings are available from manufacturers or at www.ahridirectory.org. Air-source heat pumps are rated using HSPF (see p. 121); GSHPs are rated using COP (see p. 125).

The U.S. Environmental Protection Agency and Department of Energy (DOE) maintain a listing of high-efficiency equipment on their Energy Star website (www.energystar.gov/products); always look for the Energy Star label, which indicates that the equipment meets certain above-minimum efficiency standards set by the government. Remember that the ratings apply to only the equipment. Installation problems, improper maintenance, and distribution problems (such as duct leakage) can reduce performance dramatically. Also remember that there are many products that exceed the Energy Star minimum standards; it's still worth shopping for the highest-efficiency unit you can find.

Choosing a contractor

Replacing a heating system is not a do-it-yourself project. Because it is a big-ticket item, it's good to interview and obtain bids from at least two or three contractors. Don't be tempted by the lowest bid. Consider quality, warranty service, energy savings, and customer references. Bids should include details on the equipment, accessories, installation specs, labor, and associated costs. Try to find a contractor who is NATE certified (see pp. 124–125). If you talk to a heating contractor who gives you a definite price over the phone, or without measuring the thermal components of your house, look elsewhere.

Many high-efficiency furnaces and boilers have special installation requirements to ensure that they work reliably and don't have problems. Find out whether bidders have experience with the specific type of installation that you are discussing. Most manufacturers offer training and technical support for newer, more sophisticated equipment, so a contractor who tries to discourage you from installing high-efficiency equipment may be unwilling to read the directions or ask for help.

When replacing a heating system, it generally doesn't make sense to switch fuels or replace an existing distribution system with a different type. The most likely exception to this rule is the replacement of an electric furnace with a heat pump or fuel-fired furnace. The addition of a high-efficiency, single- or multi-zone ductless split heat pump can be a good supplement for electric-resistance heat, or to offset or replace an LP-gas or oil-fired heating system. It's less expensive than a whole new furnace or boiler and can reduce both operating costs and greenhouse gas emissions. Except for changes in the distribution system for the purpose of improving comfort or efficiency (such as duct-system changes to increase airflow), the large expense of replacing distribution equipment is rarely justified. If you are replacing a heat pump with a new, efficient unit, be aware that the indoor coil must be properly matched to the outdoor unit for proper operation and rated efficiency. If you get a proposal to replace only the outdoor unit, start asking questions.

Hydro-Air Systems

Hydro-air systems are hybrids. They deliver heat to a house by blowing warm air through ductwork, like a furnace does, but the heat source is usually a hot-water boiler. Hydro-air systems typically use only one heating appliance (such as a wall-hung condensing boiler) to produce heat and hot water for the house, improving efficiency and reducing maintenance. Hot water can be easily piped to several zones with separate air handlers in different parts of the house, without needing to match airflow to burner capacity. Hydro-air handlers can also be easily integrated with air-conditioning.

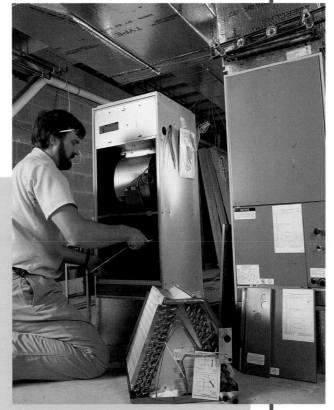

Hydro-air handlers use hot water circulating through a heat exchanger, or fan coil, to heat air pushed through by the blower. The "A" coil in the foreground is for cooling.

AIR-CONDITIONING

Air-conditioning—either centrally installed or mounted in a wall or window—can be a big electricity user in many houses, but it is possible to cut your spending and still keep cool. First, we'll explore things you can do to reduce the cooling loads in your house to cut air-conditioning costs. Next, we'll look at ways to maintain and operate any air-conditioning system properly for maximum efficiency. Simple maintenance, proper servicing, and one-time upgrades can keep your air-conditioning system in tiptop shape. Finally, we'll look at what to do when it's time for a new air conditioner, either as a replacement for an existing system or as a new home improvement.

Although you may not be able to pay for a new, efficient air conditioner in energy savings alone, when you do buy one you should buy the most efficient one you can find. This chapter will help you find a contractor who can correctly size and install a new system. ▶ ▶ ▶

Cooling Basics

Heat flows from a higher temperature to a lower one. In winter, houses lose heat; in summer, they gain it. Just as heating bills benefit by reductions in heat loss, cooling loads—and bills—benefit by reductions in heat gain. Most summer heat gain comes from three places: solar radiation, internal gains, and air leakage in the building and ducts.

Where does the heat come from?

In the winter, the largest energy loads in most homes come from conductive heat loss through walls, ceilings, and windows. Air leakage in the building enclosure and ducts are a close second. Radiation effects are minimal.

In hot weather the tables are turned. Conduction plays a minor role; the source of most air-conditioning loads is solar radiation through windows and uninsulated roofs. The same solar heat gain that provides free heat in winter is a major driver of air-conditioning in summer. And it's not just south-facing windows; in fact, east- and west-facing glass contribute more to air-conditioning per square foot than south-facing glass. Even conductive heat gains through a poorly insulated attic are largely driven by radiation, when the sun shining on the roof superheats the attic far above outdoor temperatures.

Internal gain is the name for heat that is generated inside a building by lights, appliances, and people. It is significant, and can exceed all other sources besides windows. Some things that we do indoors, such as cooking, dishwashing, showering, and bathing, are obvious sources of heat. Anything that uses electricity gives off heat: refrigerators, lighting, televisions, computer equipment, and their accessories. There are less-obvious sources too, such as standby loss from water heaters.

In addition to solar and internal heat gains, duct leakage in a central air-conditioning system

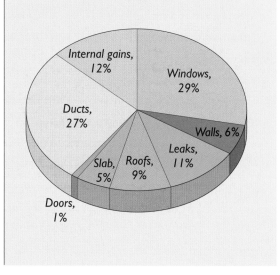

SOUTHERN HOUSE (DALLAS) COOLING DOLLARS

Here is a breakdown of the cooling loads of a typical Dallas house. The building enclosure and ducts are fairly leaky, and the ceiling and walls are moderately insulated. As the chart indicates, most of the heat comes from the windows, ducts, and the heat generated inside the house (internal gains).

Internal gains, 12%
Windows, 29%
Walls, 6%
Leaks, 11%
Roofs, 9%
Slab, 5%
Ducts, 27%
Doors, 1%

is also a large contributor to cooling energy use. Building-shell leakage is a smaller driver in hot climates, but it's still important to seal leaks in humid climates to reduce the risk of hidden condensation in wall or floor cavities.

How air conditioners work

Virtually all residential air-conditioning systems use a compressor-driven refrigerant vapor cycle to cool house air. The compressor cycle controls refrigerant temperatures in the condenser and evaporator coils, which absorb heat from indoor air at a low temperature, then reject it outdoors

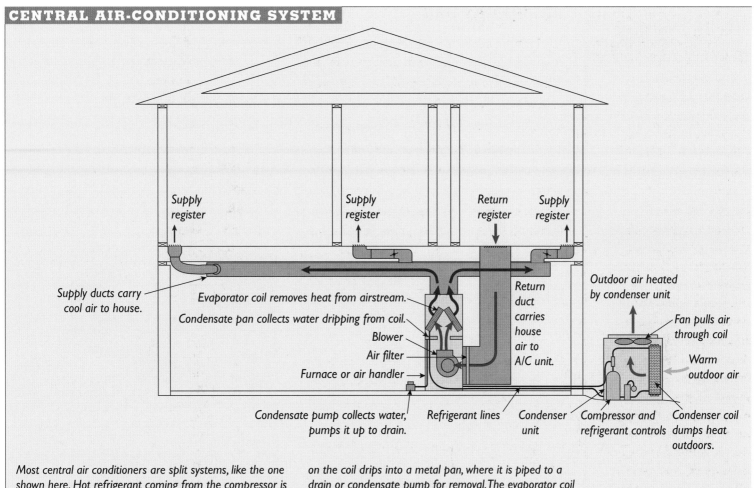

Supply register

Supply register

Return register

Supply register

Supply ducts carry cool air to house.

Evaporator coil removes heat from airstream.

Condensate pan collects water dripping from coil.

Blower

Air filter

Furnace or air handler

Condensate pump collects water, pumps it up to drain.

Refrigerant lines

Return duct carries house air to A/C unit.

Condenser unit

Outdoor air heated by condenser unit

Fan pulls air through coil

Warm outdoor air

Compressor and refrigerant controls

Condenser coil dumps heat outdoors.

Most central air conditioners are split systems, like the one shown here. Hot refrigerant coming from the compressor is cooled in the condenser coil, then piped into the air handler unit. The temperature of the liquid refrigerant drops rapidly as it expands into the evaporator coil, cooling the air by 15°F to 25°F as it passes through the coil. Water condensing

on the coil drips into a metal pan, where it is piped to a drain or condensate pump for removal. The evaporator coil may be mounted in or above a furnace or in a dedicated air handler, or it may share the air handler cabinet with a hot water hydro-air coil.

Yellow arrow = Warm outdoor air
Green arrow = Outdoor air heated by condenser coil

at a higher temperature. Air conditioners, heat pumps, and refrigerators all use the refrigerant vapor cycle to essentially push heat uphill, from a cooler place to a warmer place. An air conditioner pushes heat from the cool indoors to the hot outdoors, cooling the interior. In addition to sending indoor heat outdoors, an air conditioner must also reject the heat generated by the compressor and fan motors.

Another aspect of air conditioners is their ability to dehumidify, as well as cool, indoor air. This happens when water condenses on the cold fins of the evaporator coil as humid air passes across them. As noted in "Energy Basics" (see the sidebar on p. 23), dehumidification is an important component in maintaining healthy indoor air quality and comfort. Water that is evaporated in air contains quite a bit of heat energy, which must be accounted for in the system's design. The energy required to remove excess humidity is called *latent load,* and it comes from moisture sources within the home and, in humid climates, outdoor air leaking indoors.

PROTIP

All fans generate heat
If you run ceiling fans but don't set the thermostat at a higher temperature, this heat will actually increase your cooling energy needs.

WHAT CAN GO WRONG

All central air conditioners have a drain pan underneath the evaporator coil to collect water from the humid air that condenses on the coil. If the pan is out of level, or has a lot of junk in it, water sitting in the pan can re-evaporate during the off-cycle, undoing some of the dehumidification the system has accomplished.

If your air-conditioning unit is below the house's drain system, you should have a condensate pump to collect water and pump it up into a drain. A malfunctioning pump can be a source of moisture in the basement or crawlspace.

Reducing Loads

With cooling, just as with heating, as the loads are reduced you spend less to stay comfortable. Think of the air conditioner as removing heat that builds up, rather than "cooling down" the house. The better you are at preventing heat from building up, the less heat your air conditioner must remove and the less time it will have to run—saving you money. There are two approaches to reducing cooling loads: reducing your need for cooling, and reducing heat gains in your house.

Reduce the need for cooling

Although I always try to emphasize energy efficiency without sacrificing comfort or utility, one surefire way to cut cooling costs is to use your air conditioner less. A house with more insulation, better windows, and less air leakage is comfortable with no air-conditioning for more of the summer. Setting the thermostat higher, particularly when the house is empty, reduces the system's run time and saves energy. An automatic thermostat can do that for you, bringing the temperature to a comfortable level before you arrive home. Clock-thermostats are available to handle both heating and cooling setbacks (see p. 110).

Fans can also help raise the temperature at which you feel comfortable. By installing an efficient ceiling fan and keeping the air moving in occupied rooms, most people can comfort-

When you buy a ceiling fan, always choose an Energy Star model. Hundreds are available, with or without built-in efficient lights, for $75 to $225 each.

Whole-House Fans

A whole-house fan, unlike an indoor fan, is designed for nighttime cooling. Its purpose is to replace air rapidly, filling the house with cool, dry outdoor air. Windows or doors must be open while the fan is on; it's also important to have adequate attic venting to ensure the exhausted air gets out. Of course, it should be run only when outdoor air is more comfortable—cooler and drier—than indoor air. After running a whole-house fan for an hour or two late at night or early in the morning, close windows and doors tightly to retain the cool air as the day warms up.

Unlike most whole-house ventilation fans, this super-efficient model by Tamarack Technologies has a motorized, insulated cover with good weatherstripping.

A simple fan can keep you more comfortable in hot weather and reduce your need for air-conditioning. But turn it off when you (or your cat) aren't in the room, because fans generate heat.

ably increase the temperature setting of their thermostat by 4°F to 6°F, saving 20 percent to 35 percent on their cooling bills. Fan flow should point downward to maximize the feeling of air movement in the room. Oscillating and box fans can also provide portable comfort. When using any type of indoor fan, remember that it will keep people cool only while they are in the room. Turn off fans when you are not using them, because they generate heat.

Ceiling-mounted whole-house fans that exhaust into the attic are another popular method to reduce the need for cooling, but they must be used properly to be effective. Air leaks between the attic and house must be sealed, and the attic must be well vented to the exterior, to ensure that the fan exhaust goes outdoors rather than back into the house.

Another way to reduce air-conditioning loads (often used in commercial buildings) is with an *economizer* cycle, which uses an *enthalpy sensor* connected to a central air conditioner to determine when outdoor air is cooler and drier than indoor air. When the thermostat calls for cooling during those times, the economizer runs the air-handler fan and opens a damper to bring in outdoor air. This can serve a majority of cooling needs in relatively dry climates with large day-night temperature swings (30°F or more): that is, much of the southwest United States. DuroDyne Corporation makes a set of components for a residential economizer: the Duro-Zone® Fresh Air Intake and Economizer Control Center (www.durodyne.com/DZ_aqc. php). Advanced Energy Products makes a full-scale system: the NightBreeze®, suitable for a

Solar control screens can cut up to 80 percent of the solar heat gain while looking similar to normal insect screens. Some products can eliminate up to 95 percent of the solar energy, but with more noticeable reductions in light and view. Solar screens can be clipped onto the exterior for the season, or permanently mounted; for additional cost, interior or exterior roll-up shades are available. Exterior shades are more effective, but interior shades allow for easy adjustment. High-end products offer remote-control motorized operation from inside or out.

new installation or major renovation; see www.advancedenergyproducts.com.

Reduce heat gains

The two big sources of heat gain that create cooling loads are solar gains (through windows and the attic) and internal gains. There are several strategies to prevent solar gains from heating a house in the first place. Shade the house with trees, shades, or architectural-shading devices (see the photo at right on p. 216); reflect solar energy with light-colored roof coatings and solar-control glazing; and, of course, insulate

(see the photo at right on p. 216)

Interior shades cut down on solar gain but not as well as exterior shading does. The sun still heats the window and the air between the shade and the glass—air that slowly mixes with the house air.

SOLAR GAIN

In summer, the sun's angle is high in the sky at midday. Solar heat gain through south-facing glass is minimal.

The sun's path in spring and fall

North

The sun's path in summer

In summer, the afternoon sun shines on west-facing glass when outdoor temperatures are at their highest.

West

In summer, the sun shines on east-facing windows for much of the morning, creating unwanted heat gain.

In winter, the sun's angle is low in the sky at midday, allowing solar heat gain through south-facing windows.

South

The sun's path in winter

East

The amount of solar gain coming through a window depends heavily on the sun's angle: The closer it is to a right angle (shining straight in), the more energy that enters the house. In summer, most unwanted heat gain comes through skylights and east- and west-facing windows. In winter, most useful heat gain comes through south-facing glass.
In spring and fall, solar gains are more mixed by direction, and the best strategies to minimize energy use depend on the overall climate.

The annual route of the sun's path works to our advantage in trying to control solar gains in most of North America. Moderate shades or overhangs on the south side can virtually eliminate solar gains in summer, while still admitting plenty of free solar energy during cold months, when the sun is low. To reduce unwanted gains in summer, deep overhangs, shades, or large trees are needed to avoid punishing solar radiation from the east and west.

Large overhangs, trellises, porches, and other architectural details can significantly reduce unwanted solar gain. In mixed and cold climates, avoid large overhangs on the south side.

and seal attics, attic ducts, and exterior walls. To cut internal gains, focus on reducing the energy use of lighting and appliances.

Reduce solar gains

Shading has a large impact on cooling loads. Because of the predominance of solar gains from southeast-, east-, southwest-, and west-facing windows, the most effective strategies in any climate involve shading those windows. Internal shades can help (the lighter in color and the more opaque, the better), but they still allow some heat to come in through windows. More effective are cellular shades that fit snugly on all four sides; they provide a buffer between the house and the heated air behind the shade.

The best approaches to shading are on the exterior, preventing the sun's heat from ever reaching the glass. Solar screens can cut solar gain significantly while maintaining a low profile. Architectural details such as overhangs, awnings, light shelves, and exterior shutters all work well. Landscaping with trees or installing a trellis with thick vegetation can provide an attractive solar shield and shade the windows,

walls, and roof. In very hot climates, where wintertime solar gain is less beneficial, shading the south side of a house provides a net savings.

You can also prevent solar heat from entering windows with solar-control glazing or transparent solar-control films. Choose products with the lowest possible SHGC rating, or the highest "solar rejection" rating, for all glass on the east, southeast, southwest, and west sides. In very hot climates, you'll want the same treatment on the south as well.

Solar gain on roofs is especially important for homes where cooling ducts and equipment are located in the attic, because during peak cooling conditions the attic is typically hotter than outdoors. Research has shown that roof color has a large impact on solar gain into attics. The most reflective roofing materials do the best job, and they can reduce cooling loads by 20 percent or more when compared to dark-gray asphalt shingles (see the chart on p. 144). Although saving on cooling energy certainly won't justify replacing your roof, if you live in a hot climate, consider using reflective, light-colored sheet metal, metal tiles, or cement tiles when you do have to reroof. Don't assume that light-colored

(see the chart on p. 144)

PRO TIP

Cooking is a source of indoor heat gain. In summer, grilling outdoors and using a microwave oven can help reduce cooling loads.

asphalt shingles are highly reflective. Only the surface granules are colored, so white composition shingles are only slightly more reflective than dark-colored ones, and they won't provide much savings.

Reflective roof coatings can also save on cooling, at a much lower cost than a whole new roof. Acrylic elastomeric coatings with high reflectivity can easily be applied with a paint roller on built-up or membrane roofing materials. At $20 to $25 per gallon for high-quality products, these coatings may not be cost-effective if you consider only energy savings. However, because the roof surface will be cooler, they may also extend the life of existing roofing materials, which also saves on maintenance.

Moving into the attic, a *radiant barrier* is a retrofit that can save on cooling, but it is likely to be cost-effective only in climates with large cooling loads. Both radiant barriers and light-

A highly reflective roof can save on air-conditioning bills in hot climates.

Roofing Reflectivity

The more reflective your roofing surface, the lower your cooling bills will be. White metal, metal tiles, and elastomeric coatings have the highest reflectivity; black and gray have the lowest. White asphalt shingles also have relatively low reflectivity. Reflectivity may decline over time, but a quality product will retain at least 50 percent of its rating after several years. The Energy Star program labels roofing products (mostly coatings and commercial roofing products, as well as some clay tile and metal roofing) that meet minimum performance standards, including longevity. For a list, see www.energystar.gov/products and look for the link to "Roof Products."

Roofing Performance

Roofing Type	Typical Reflectivity	Performance
White elastomeric and acrylic coating	70%-85%	Very good*
White anodized metal	75%-80%	
White EPDM rubber	75%	
White clay tile	50%-60%	Good
White asphalt shingles	25%	Moderate
Gray asphalt	10%-20%	Poor
Black asphalt or EPDM	5%	

*Note: White roof coatings on flat or cathedralized ceilings can rot the roof—especially in desert climates. Night-sky radiation can repeatedly cool the roof below the dewpoint, causing extensive condensation. White roofs in dry climates should be insulated with closed-cell polyurethane foam sprayed onto the underside of the roof sheathing or rigid insulation above the structural deck.

Leaks in air-conditioning ducts waste a lot of money, particularly when the ducts are in an attic. Sealing connections thoroughly with mastic is vital to proper air-conditioner operation.

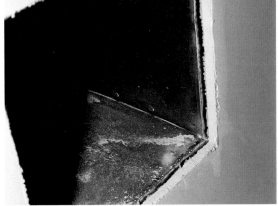

This gap between the air-conditioner return duct and the drywall sucks hot attic air into the air handler. It should be caulked or sealed with mastic.

colored roofs should take a back seat to adding attic insulation and sealing and insulating duct-work. It's easy to find misinformation and inflated marketing claims about radiant materials, so it's important to understand what they will and won't do.

Radiant barriers are not insulation, and they don't "block" heat. What they do is reduce radiative coupling, in this case between a roof and the exposed surfaces below. In a well-insulated attic with no cooling equipment or ducts, a radiant barrier provides about the same savings as 2 in. to 3 in. of additional loose-fill insulation; but insulation is generally cheaper, and it will also save heating energy. The radiant barrier may even increase winter heating costs by lowering the average attic temperature. However, if you're in a hot climate and your attic contains air-conditioning ducts and equipment, installing a radiant barrier is an inexpensive way to "move" the air-conditioning system to a cooler place, and you should see some real savings. Similarly, if you have leaky ductwork in a cathedral ceiling or an attic with no access for sealing, a white, reflective roof or coating can also mean noticeable savings.

Reduce internal gains.

As shown in the pie graph on p. 138, heat generated inside a house can add a lot to the home's cooling energy needs. Replacing lights and appliances with more energy-efficient products saves energy in two ways: by reducing the electricity required to run those products, and by reducing indoor gains. "Appliances, Electronics, and Lighting" has more detailed information on maximizing appliance and lighting efficiency;

A radiant barrier attached to the bottom of roof rafters can significantly reduce attic heat gain, but don't use it as a substitute for insulation.

Radiant Barriers

Radiant barriers are reflective surfaces—usually heavy foil or foil-coated sheet stock (mylar, kraft paper, or foam insulation)—installed between a roof deck and an insulated ceiling. The shinier the foil, the better it works. Look for products with high reflectivity (0.9 or more) and low emissivity (0.1 or less). Costs range widely ($0.10 per sq. ft. to $1.00 per sq. ft.), and the inexpensive products generally work as well as the pricey ones; stay away from fancy materials like foil-faced bubble wrap. Some radiant products have a foil facing on only

one side, which is fine, but the foil should face down toward the attic.

Many spray-on radiant paint products are also available, but they tend to have lower reflectivity. They may work better, however, in a truss attic with limited ability to apply sheet products. Don't install radiant barriers on the attic floor over existing insulation, because they won't work.

Air conditioners depend on free airflow and should never be installed (like this one) in a restricted area—even if it keeps them in the shade.

all of the steps listed there will reduce cooling energy requirements as well.

In addition to minimizing internal heat gains, it is also helpful to reduce or minimize moisture sources in the home, which add to the latent (dehumidification) loads. Use exhaust fans when cooking and bathing, and take any necessary steps to reduce large moisture loads.

Duct insulation and sealing

Air-conditioning ducts have the same leakage and insulation issues as those of heating ducts. In fact, leaks and missing insulation in attic ductwork hurt air-conditioning systems more than heating systems, because during peak cooling times attics are usually much hotter than outdoor ambient temperatures. All air-conditioning ducts in attics, crawlspaces, and garages should be thoroughly sealed and insulated (as described on pp. 112–116).

This room air-conditioner filter can easily be rinsed, dried, and replaced to keep it running as efficiently as possible.

Maintenance and Upgrades

Like most other equipment, air conditioners need regular maintenance and service. Some things you can probably do yourself, whereas others require a professional technician.

Dehumidifiers

In a humid climate, air-exchange ventilation will not reduce the relative humidity in the house in warmer months. Typically, air-conditioning controls moisture levels. But as you reduce cooling loads by cutting solar gains and installing efficient lights and appliances, air conditioners need to run for less time, reducing the dehumidification effect. You may need a stand-alone dehumidifier to control moisture levels. When combined with air-conditioning, it can actually save energy by helping you feel more comfortable at higher temperatures.

Consider using a high-efficiency dehumidifier, either integrated with your HVAC equipment or as a stand-alone unit. The high-capacity, ultra-efficient dehumidifier shown here is good for unusually heavy moisture loads, but a standard-size model will work for most houses. Always choose a unit that's Energy Star rated, and look for the most efficient one you can find.

Airflow

Like heat pumps and furnaces, air-conditioning systems depend on adequate airflow to remove heat efficiently from your house. Whether you have a central air conditioner or individual room units, check the filters regularly and clean or replace them when they are dirty—once or twice a season should be adequate. Because airflow is important, do not shut off any of the supply registers in the system—especially if the ducts are located in an attic, garage, or crawlspace.

Cleaning air coils

When filters don't work properly or air gets around them, the evaporator coil can become clogged with dirt and dust. Depending on the system, you may need a service technician to access the coil. If you can reach it yourself, lift the dirt from behind with a stiff brush. Be careful not to drive dirt further in or bend the fins.

The outdoor condenser coil should also be kept clean and free of dirt and debris. Don't spray water directly at the coil, which may drive

A filter slot without a cover allows an air conditioner to suck dust and dirt past the filter. It may also pull return air from places it shouldn't, such as the attic, garage, or crawlspace.

A good filter cover should fit tightly but not require tools to remove.

dirt deeper into the space between the fins. Instead, using a long-bristle brush with flexible bristles, carefully insert the bristles between the fins, and lift the dirt from behind.

Regular service

Regular service calls—typically every two to three years—should include testing the controls, checking and cleaning the blower, condenser, and

Dirt can build up on the surface of an evaporator coil. To remove it, carefully insert brush bristles between the fins, then lift the dirt from behind (but don't bend the fins).

Once an air-conditioner system has been emptied with a vacuum pump, the correct amount of new refrigerant can be measured with a scale (visible at right).

Other than weighing it, a proper refrigerant charge can be verified only by a superheat or subcooling test once the airflow is known to be correct.

Once the proper charge has been verified, a service technician should not attach gauges or add refrigerant to a system unless its performance declines.

IN DETAIL

In dry regions, evaporative coolers (called swamp coolers) provide very efficient cooling. Water runs through a damp pad or fiber matrix, and air is blown through the pad and into the house. As the water evaporates, it absorbs energy and cools the air in much the same way that perspiration evaporating from the skin cools our bodies. For evaporative coolers to work, the outdoor air must be dry enough to absorb a lot of moisture. Look for a unit with a high-efficiency motor. Two-stage "indirect/direct" evaporative coolers provide additional cooling capacity, though they cost more to install.

An evaporative cooler can provide indoor comfort at a much lower cost than air-conditioning, but they are effective only in a dry climate.

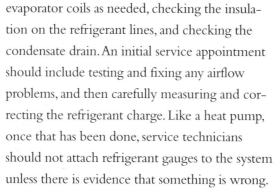

evaporator coils as needed, checking the insulation on the refrigerant lines, and checking the condensate drain. An initial service appointment should include testing and fixing any airflow problems, and then carefully measuring and correcting the refrigerant charge. Like a heat pump, once that has been done, service technicians should not attach refrigerant gauges to the system unless there is evidence that something is wrong.

Like a heat pump, an over- or undercharged air conditioner is less efficient (particularly older models), and systems are often improperly charged. Airflow must be in the recommended range of 400 CFM to 425 CFM per ton before the refrigerant charge can be measured. In practice, though, few technicians bother to test airflow.

It is difficult to test airflow in an air conditioner that has no heat source. Temperature drop (measured just like temperature rise; see p. 119) can work if you know the charge is correct. However, measuring the charge properly if you haven't checked the airflow requires purging and weighing the correct amount of refrigerant. Airflow can also be measured near the air handler by a skilled technician with a pitot tube or anemometer. A flow hood can be used at the return register(s), but it will underestimate airflow by the amount of any duct leakage.

Once airflow is correct, the superheat or subcooling must also be measured carefully (which one depends on the type of system). Technicians can also use one of several automated systems that simultaneously monitor internal temperatures and pressures and allow trained users to analyze air-conditioner operation and charge level.

New Air-Conditioning Systems

If you live in a hot climate and have central air-conditioning that is 20 years old or more, replacing your system with a new, energy-efficient model should pay for itself in a reasonable time. High-efficiency systems on the market today are more than twice as efficient as systems from the 1980s. But before running out and replacing your system, you will first need to do two other things: Finish any upgrades on the building enclosure, and become familiar with air-conditioning products and installation criteria.

Of course, if you have a fairly new system (less than 10 years old), it is probably more cost-effective to maintain it and keep it running as efficiently as possible until it wears out. As always, energy-efficient upgrades always cost the

Any air conditioner that is more than 20 years old is a good candidate for replacement with a new, more energy-efficient unit.

New air-conditioning systems are more than twice as efficient as the minimum standards of 20 years ago—the best ones have almost triple the efficiency.

least when you are fixing or replacing something anyway. If your old air conditioner is on its last legs or not operating, replace it with the most efficient unit you can find.

High-efficiency air-conditioning

New central air conditioners are rated for energy performance with a Seasonal Energy Efficiency Rating (SEER). SEER ratings are measurements under standardized test conditions of Btu per hour of cooling output, divided by input watts. The higher the SEER, the more efficient the system. New central air conditioners are required to have an SEER rating of at least 13; the most efficient units have SEER ratings from 16 to 23. Some of the best high-efficiency systems have two-speed compressors; the lower speed provides better, more efficient cooling and dehumidification under mild, part-load conditions.

When you are replacing a central air-conditioning unit with a more efficient one, it's very important to match the new outdoor unit and the indoor evaporator coil. You may be able to save some money on the installation by keeping your old coil, but be careful: you're unlikely to get the full efficiency ratings of the new unit. If you get a proposal to replace only the outdoor

unit, the contractor should be able to demonstrate that the existing indoor coil is listed for use with the new outdoor unit; don't accept "don't worry, it's fine the way it is" as an answer.

Sizing a system

Proper sizing has been emphasized as a key efficiency issue for years in the energy-efficiency world, but there's little evidence that it affects operating costs very much. Duct leakage and insulation in unconditioned spaces are far more important, especially with modern, high-efficiency equipment. Oversized air conditioners do cost more to buy and maintain and require more airflow and larger ductwork.

PRO TIP

It's better to undersize rather than oversize an air-conditioning system, because it will run more efficiently and dehumidify better.

TRADE SECRET

Ductless mini-split air conditioners are a great alternative to window units. They are more efficient and quieter, and they don't use up a window (or allow air leakage). The most efficient units on the market are also heat pumps that can save money on your heating bills, too (see p. 124). A mini-split costs about 10 times as much as a decent window unit, but may cost a third to a half as much as retrofitting central air into an existing home.

Window- or wall-mounted air conditioners have lower efficiency ratings than central systems, but there are no ducts to waste the cold air. And cooling only one or two rooms can use much less energy than cooling an entire house.

A high-velocity duct system is another option for retrofitting central air-conditioning in a house with no ducts. The narrow ducts can easily be snaked through places where conventional ductwork would never fit.

Dehumidification, which depends on air flowing through the evaporator coil for enough time to extract condensed moisture, is one important reason to carefully size an air-conditioning system in humid climates. When an oversized system runs for only a few minutes, the moisture may just start to collect on the coils before the thermostat is satisfied. Once the unit shuts down, the moisture re-evaporates into the house. An air conditioner that is too large by 50 percent to 100 percent will be unable to control humidity effectively, so people may tend to set the thermostat lower to compensate. Many new, efficient air conditioners have multiple speeds or special dehumidification modes that can effectively compensate for oversizing; if you are in a humid climate, consider one of these features, or get a stand-alone dehumidifier (see p. 146).

There are two ways that most contractors select the size of a replacement system: Match the size of the old unit, or based on the square footage of the house. These methods usually result in air conditioners that are too big; if energy improvements were made to the building, the error can be very large.

You can get a sense of how your existing system is sized by noticing the run time on a hot afternoon. For example, if your air conditioner runs 40 minutes of every hour, it is already 1.5 times too large; if it runs 30 minutes of every hour, it is twice as big as it needs to be. Of course, that assumes the machine is operating properly and does not have significant duct leaks. An air conditioner is optimally sized (and most efficient) if it runs continuously on the hottest afternoons of the year and maintains reasonable comfort.

Correct load calculations are based on your home's window size, the glass type, and the size and R-values of the walls and roof. The proper size also varies with the direction the home faces: Sometimes a 90-degree rotation can cut the cooling load in half. If a contractor gives you a price for an air conditioner on the phone, or simply offers to replace the existing unit with a new one of the same size, get a bid from someone else, especially if you have already made energy improvements in your house. The money you save by buying a smaller unit may pay for an efficiency upgrade.

When installing a new air conditioner, shop for value, not just for price. Other things to look for when assessing bids on new air-conditioning equipment include the warranties (from both the manufacturer and the installer), service contracts, longevity of the business, customer references, and technician knowledge. Try to find a contractor who is an Energy Star partner and/or NATE certified, or regularly attends manufacturer's trainings.

EER versus SEER

You can compare the efficiency of central air-conditioning systems using their Seasonal Energy Efficiency Ratings. Room air conditioners are rated using the Energy Efficiency Ratios (EER) rather than SEER. SEER and EER are both units of Btu per watt, but EER is measured under hotter outdoor conditions than SEER is, so the EER appears to be lower for an otherwise identical efficiency.

To find the SEER rating for central air-conditioning equipment, look up the model number online at www.ahridirectory.org, under "Residential Certified Products." The Energy Star labeling program covers both room and central air conditioners; any product with the Energy Star label has been tested to meet higher efficiency and performance standards. Log on to www.energystar.gov and look under "Find products—heating and cooling—air conditioners."

All new air conditioners have an Energy Guide label that shows its efficiency rating, as well as a comparison with the ratings of other units of the same type. Room units have an EER, while central systems have a SEER.

ACCORDING TO CODE

Many states have new-construction energy codes that require sizing calculations for air-conditioning equipment. Codes specify the use of statistical design temperatures, which are not the most severe temperatures ever seen in a given location. The calculation procedure allows for a generous margin of safety; other margins do not need to be built into the calculations. Unfortunately, few building inspectors pay attention to these code requirements, even where they have been adopted in their states. However, they are a critical foundation for a good system design, both in new construction and in existing homes.

HOT WATER

Hot water, like heat, is a necessity in all modern homes. In very efficient homes, water heating can be a larger load then heating, air-conditioning, or electrical appliance use. The annual cost for your hot water is driven by two factors: usage and efficiency. Reducing the amount of hot water you use can impact your utility bills as much as, or more than, improving the efficiency of your water-heating equipment, often at a lower cost.

This chapter shows you ways to cut down on hot-water consumption. It outlines basic procedures for maintaining standard water heaters for longevity and efficiency and describes some do-it-yourself projects to help improve efficiency. It also discusses how and when to replace or upgrade your water-heating equipment for the best efficiency possible. ▶ ▶ ▶

A low-flow showerhead doesn't save hot water if the faucet keeps running. This diverter needs work.

Hot-Water Conservation

One of the themes of this book is conservation without deprivation, or paying for what you need without paying for waste. Hot water is a good example of that concept: If the various jobs that use hot water can be done equally well with less water, you will save money. There are a number of ways you can reduce hot-water usage and consumption.

Low-flow showerheads

When I started working in energy efficiency in the early 1990s, low-flow showerheads had a bad reputation. If you've never had one of those little silver barrels in your house, you've probably used one in a hotel room: They produce wet air, cold feet, billowing shower curtains, and lots of steam, but nothing like a satisfying shower.

Since the 1990s, plumbing regulations for new construction have required showerheads with ratings of 2.5 gallons per minute (GPM) or less. Technology now exceeds the regulations, and today there are many great products that deliver between 1.3 GPM and 2 GPM, at retail prices from $6 to $60. Even if you already have a 2.5 GPM showerhead, consider upgrading to even lower flow along with a better shower. Shop around; if your existing showerhead dates

SHOWERHEAD SAVINGS

Because most Americans shower every day, reducing a showerhead's flow can save a lot of water and money. Depending on the flow rate at which you start—in gallons per minute—and the number of people in the household, your yearly savings can be substantial. These numbers assume a water-heater recovery efficiency of 77 percent, daily 5-minute showers for each person in the house, and a natural gas price of $1.20/therm. If you heat your water with electricity, the savings will be about double. Remember that you won't just be saving fuel costs: For every $10 in water-heating savings, you will also save about 2,000 gallons of water per year.

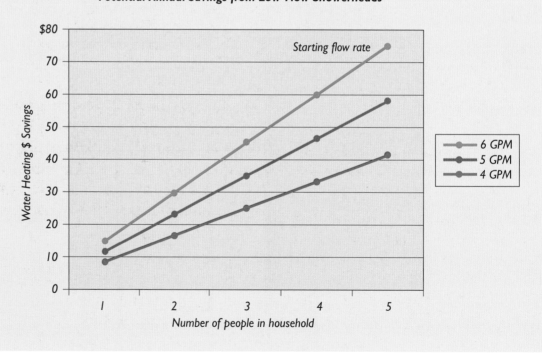

Potential Annual Savings from Low-Flow Showerheads

before 1993, almost any new one that you install will save hot water—and not at the expense of a good shower.

There are two tricks when upgrading your old showerhead: removing the old one without breaking the shower arm and installing the new one without marring it. Usually, you'll be able to unscrew the old showerhead with an adjustable wrench and screw in the new unit by hand. Be sure to support the shower arm carefully when trying to loosen the old head; too much leverage may cause an old arm to break off inside the wall. Or worse, it could create a leak in the wall that may go unnoticed.

If the old showerhead doesn't come off easily, it may be better to replace the entire arm. Use a pair of pliers to get a firm grip on the old arm and unthread it carefully from the fitting inside the wall. Before installing the new one, be sure to wrap a few turns of plumber's thread-seal (FTFE) tape around the threads.

Trying to unscrew an old showerhead without breaking off the shower arm may be more trouble than it's worth. If the shower arm is old, it is often easier to replace the entire assembly along with the showerhead.

Wrap the end of a new shower arm with several turns of plumber's tape before threading it in place. Don't forget to put the trim ring on the new arm before wrapping the threads.

Cutting Waste While You Wait

One drawback of low-flow showerheads is the longer wait for hot water to arrive at the shower. The evolve™ showerhead (at left in the photo at right) offers a unique solution: a ShowerStart valve. When hot water reaches the showerhead, the valve cuts the flow to a trickle, reducing most of the waste that occurs when people get distracted while waiting for the shower to heat up. A quick pull of the cord restores full flow until your shower is finished, and the valve resets automatically for the next time. Evolve makes a wide range of showerheads; if you already have a low-flow showerhead you like, you can get the same ShowerStart valve in the Ladybug adapter (photo at right).

I installed an evolve Ladybug adapter (at right in the photo above) on our shower at home. My six-year-old loves to pull the cord before hopping in.

Measuring Flow

If you're not sure what the flow rate of an existing showerhead is, you can measure it. Get a 1-gal. to 2-gal. bucket and make sure you know exactly how much it holds (1 gal. is 16 cups). Get a stopwatch or a clock with a second hand. Turn on the shower and start timing as you put the bucket into the stream of water. Stop timing when the bucket is full, and then calculate the flow rate in GPM. The flow equals the bucket capacity (in gallons) times 60 (seconds per minute), divided by the number of seconds it took to fill the bucket. If the flow rate of a shower is more than 2.5 or 3 GPM, it is worth replacing your showerhead.

Faucet aerators

Like showerheads, new kitchen and lavatory faucets have had maximum-flow ratings of 2.2 GPM and 1.5 GPM (respectively) since the mid-1990s. Some vintage fixtures don't have standard screw-in aerators and cannot be retro-fitted easily, but in most cases a new aerator in an existing faucet can further reduce hot-water usage.

Besides the basic aerator shown below left, some units give you more control over water flow. If you are planning to replace a kitchen faucet, an integrated faucet/retractable sprayer unit can provide flexible spray patterns and low water flow in one attractive package.

Other appliances

There are two other home appliances that use a lot of hot water: clothes washers and dishwashers. New Energy Star–rated washers save at least 37 percent of the hot water and electricity used by conventional washing machines (see p. 203). Regardless of your washing machine type, you can easily save hot water by being conscious of your usage. Use warm wash/cold rinse or cold cycles when hot is unnecessary, and set the fill level appropriately to the size of load.

Dishwashers are a little more complicated. Older units generally depend on an incoming hot-water temperature of 130°F or higher to work properly. Most new models have

Replacing an old aerator with a 2.2-GPM (or less) aerator is a simple step that can save some money. The old aerator (left) did not reduce the flow of water at all.

Two models of this kitchen aerator reduce water flow to 2.2 (or 1.5) GPM. A small lever further slows water to a trickle, which is handy when washing dishes.

Water Sense

Since 2006, WaterSense® has labeled toilets, faucets, showerheads, and weather-based irrigation controllers to demonstrate that they meet water-efficiency criteria that exceed national standards and perform well. WaterSense also labels certification programs for landscape-irrigation professionals who demonstrate proficiency in water-efficient irrigation systems. Efficient toilets and landscape irrigation won't save hot water, but they can save a lot on your water bill, and ultimately save some energy too. See www.epa.gov/WaterSense.

built-in booster heaters, which heat the wash water to at least 140°F right in the dishwasher. Not only do they use less hot water, but they also allow you to reduce the temperature setting on your water heater. Most important, remember that modern dishwashers use less hot water, energy, and water than even very careful hand dishwashing. So load up and use the dishwasher for everything that's dishwasher-safe. (For more information on dishwasher efficiency, see p. 203).

Maintenance and Efficiency Upgrades

The vast majority of homes in the United States have stand-alone water heaters. These are independent hot-water storage tanks with their own heat source, with the sole function of providing domestic hot water. A home that is heated by a boiler is likely to have a tankless coil or an indirect-fired storage tank (those systems are covered on pgs. 161 and 168–169.)

Standard gas water heaters are cheap and inefficient. They are typically expected to last only 5 to 15 years, so most people do not invest much money in them. Replacing a water heater tends

to be an emergency event, full of stress because the old water heater has suddenly failed. Proper maintenance can extend the life of a water heater, and some efficiency improvements can be made to existing tanks with minimal investment; but if you have a standard water heater made before 2005, it may make more sense to upgrade to a very high-efficiency unit and not try to make the old one last longer. If your present water heater appears to be near the end of its useful life, now is the time to do research on the right type of replacement unit. Then you will be well prepared, whether you decide to wait until the old one goes or to replace the tank at your convenience.

Two types of tanks: Gas and electric

Stand-alone water heaters come in two basic types: gas and electric. Gas water heaters, fired with piped natural or LP gas, are the most common. Gas water heaters are usually smaller than electric water heaters, because their burners produce more heat than an electric heating element. A capacity of 40 to 50 gal. is typical for most houses.

Electric water heaters in single-family homes often hold 50 to 80 gal. Electric water heaters

INDETAIL

Don't trust the temperature markings on a water-heater dial, if it even has them. To find out your water temperature, use a good-quality thermometer that reads up to at least 150°F. Choose a time when no one has used hot water for at least an hour, then run full hot water from a tap until the temperature has stabilized. Then reduce the flow to the size of a pencil, and let the water run into a small glass with the thermometer in it. When the thermometer reading has stabilized, that's your hot-water temperature.

This inexpensive probe-type digital thermometer is good for measuring hot-water temperature.

COMPONENTS OF A CONVENTIONAL GAS WATER HEATER

Flue

Draft hood

Hot-water outlet

Cold-water inlet

Insulation

Tank

Jacket

The sacrificial anode rod helps prevent tank corrosion.

Temperature and pressure relief valve

Flue baffle

Dip tube

Discharge pipe

Gas supply enters at control.

Crown

Thermostat

Drain cock

Sensing element

Thermocouple and pilot light

Combustion chamber

Drip pan

Main burner

A typical gas water heater has a sheet-steel tank with a flue in the center for venting combustion gases. The burner is mounted at the base of the tank, which is crowned to distribute the heat. As hot water is drawn off the top of the tank, cold water enters from the bottom by way of a dip tube. The cooler water is sensed by the thermostat, which then turns on the gas at the burner—provided the safety thermocouple senses the presence of a pilot flame. Gas water heaters must be properly anchored in seismically active areas (not shown).

don't require a fuel supply in the house, so they are a common choice for homes where piped natural gas is unavailable and where a heat pump provides the space heating.

Typically, gas water heaters don't have degree markings, but the recommended target temperature of 120°F is usually between "Warm" and "Medium." It may take some trial and error to find a setting that's just right.

SAFETY FIRST

The draft hood is a critical component of a standard atmospheric water heater. It provides space for surrounding air to be drawn into the flue to help carry combustion gases out the chimney. If the draft hood is blocked, removed, or otherwise restricted, the result could be carbon monoxide poisoning, or even fire. To reduce fire risk, never store items on the floor, on top of, or leaning against a water heater.

Setting the temperature

The temperature of many hot-water heaters can be lowered without any noticeable reduction in the hot-water supply. Lowering the temperature of stored hot water saves energy by reducing conductive heat loss through the tank surfaces, called *standby loss.* Standby losses depend on the location of the tank (how cold it is outside the tank), how well the tank is insulated, and where the tank is located (in a cold climate, most losses in the winter just contribute to heating the house). The better insulated the tank and

COMPONENTS OF A CONVENTIONAL ELECTRIC WATER HEATER

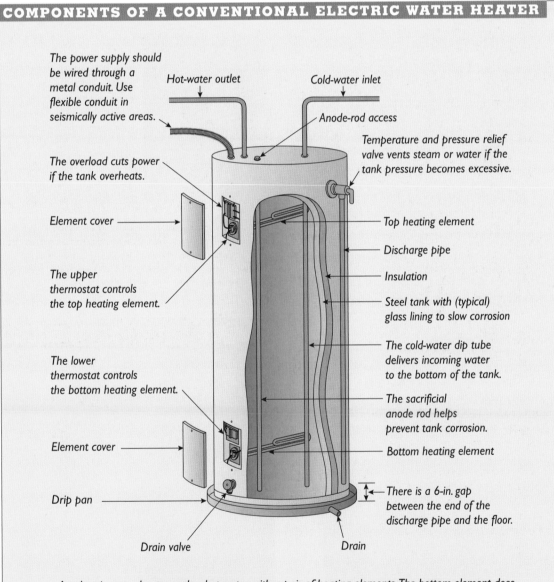

The power supply should be wired through a metal conduit. Use flexible conduit in seismically active areas.

Hot-water outlet

Cold-water inlet

Anode-rod access

Temperature and pressure relief valve vents steam or water if the tank pressure becomes excessive.

The overload cuts power if the tank overheats.

Element cover

Top heating element

Discharge pipe

Insulation

The upper thermostat controls the top heating element.

Steel tank with (typical) glass lining to slow corrosion

The cold-water dip tube delivers incoming water to the bottom of the tank.

The lower thermostat controls the bottom heating element.

The sacrificial anode rod helps prevent tank corrosion.

Element cover

Bottom heating element

There is a 6-in. gap between the end of the discharge pipe and the floor.

Drip pan

Drain valve

Drain

An electric water heater makes hot water with a pair of heating elements. The bottom element does most of the work. The top one kicks in when the hot water in the tank becomes depleted. Note the dip tube, which delivers incoming water to the bottom of the tank. This ensures that the hottest water in the tank is always available to be drawn off the top. The controls are designed to ensure that only one heating element at a time can be energized, which prevents overloading the electric circuit.

WHAT CAN GO WRONG

Hot water stored below 120°F may increase the risk of *Legionella pneumophili* bacteria, which can cause pneumonia. But Legionella infections in single-family homes are quite rare compared to the risk of scalding, which increases rapidly at tank temperatures over 120°F. The U.S. Consumer Product Safety Commission recommends all home water heaters be set at 120°F, and even at that temperature third-degree burns can occur with exposures of five minutes or more. Anti-scald mixing valves can help keep children and elders, who are at higher risk for burns, safe.

PRO TIP

The temperature and pressure relief valve is a critical safety component of any storage water heater, whether gas or electric.

the greater your hot-water use, the less savings a temperature setback will provide.

Reducing the temperature setting by 10°F may save 2 percent to 5 percent of your water heating costs. The investment is $0, and it's easy to readjust if you turn it down too much. In addition to energy savings, a lower tank temperature reduces scaling and corrosion and increases the life of the tank.

The thermostat knob on a gas water heater is usually located at the front of the gas valve. Look carefully at the markings; on many gas water heaters, counterclockwise rotation increases the temperature setting.

Electric tanks have two thermostats—one for each element—located behind metal covers near the bottom and the top of the tank. Because there is exposed wiring inside, shut off the circuit breaker before unscrewing the covers. Set both elements to about the same temperature, or set the top element just slightly cooler so the bottom element activates first.

Insulation wraps

To reduce standby losses, cover your water heater with an insulation blanket. On a cheap, poorly insulated tank, an insulation wrap may reduce water heating cost by up to 5 percent.

This tank is insulated with urethane foam. A tank with insulation rated R-10 or higher won't benefit much from an insulation wrap.

The more insulation the tank has, the less benefit there is to adding the wrap. If the tank has 1½ in. or more of foam insulation, or the label states that the R-value is 10 or more, don't bother. If the tank was manufactured since 1992, the benefit is small; if it dates from 2007 or later, don't bother.

The thermostat on an electric water heater can usually be changed with a small screwdriver. Setting the temperature requires some trial and error, because the thermostat markings are often inaccurate.

An insulation blanket can reduce by almost half the standby losses of a poorly insulated tank.

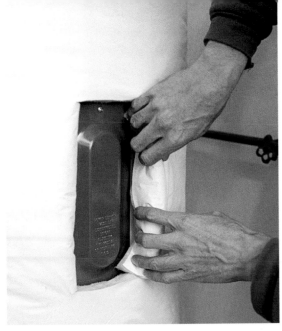

At each access panel, cut an "I" shape with a utility knife. The top and bottom of the "I" should outline the top and bottom of the panel. Then fold under the sides to expose the cover.

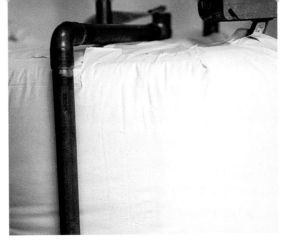

Insulation wrap should always be tucked under the temperature and pressure discharge pipe so it doesn't interfere with relief-valve operation. Or cut the wrap back at least 3 in. from the valve, which may be on the top or side.

When insulating a water heater, carefully follow the directions on the tank-wrap kit. For electric heaters, cut away the wrap over both heating-element covers to provide access; for gas heaters, wraps should not cover the gas valve or access panel. Also, don't insulate the top of a gas water heater. And take heed if you see a sticker warning against a tank wrap; adding one may void that tank's warranty.

Insulating hot-water pipes

Hot-water pipes lose energy in two ways: through conductive losses in pipe walls while hot water is running and through thermosiphon effects (see the sidebar on p. 162). Both can be reduced by insulating hot-water pipes, and thermosiphoning can be reduced or eliminated by adding heat traps to hot- and cold-water pipes.

The simplest heat trap consists of a "loop the loop" of pipe, which can be made with a flexible connector attached to the heater's hot- and cold-water connections. The trap stops thermosiphoning with basic physics: Hot water will not flow down unless it is pushed through the pipe by water pressure. The loop should have a 5-in. to 6-in. radius and be covered with pipe insulation. Alternatively, special heat-trap couplings can be installed at the tank connections. Most new high-efficiency tanks have built-in heat traps. Of course, don't attempt to modify or replace plumbing components yourself unless you know what you are doing.

Pipe insulation is readily available at most home centers and hardware stores and is easy to install. The biggest benefit from pipe insula-

How Water Pipes Lose Heat

Conductive heat loss through pipe walls robs energy from hot water, mostly when hot water flows through them. A thermosiphon is the constant circulation of hot water from the water heater into hot- and cold-water pipes when no water is being drawn. As the heat is emitted, the cooler water sinks back into the tank.

Heat loss from conduction and thermosiphoning can happen in both hot- and cold-water pipes. The effects occur for the many hours every day that no hot water is being drawn. Thermosiphoning stops when someone begins to draw hot water; so do the conductive losses on the cold side, because the pipe fills with incoming cold water. However, conductive losses on the hot side increase when the pipe you draw is filled with hot water on the way to its destination.

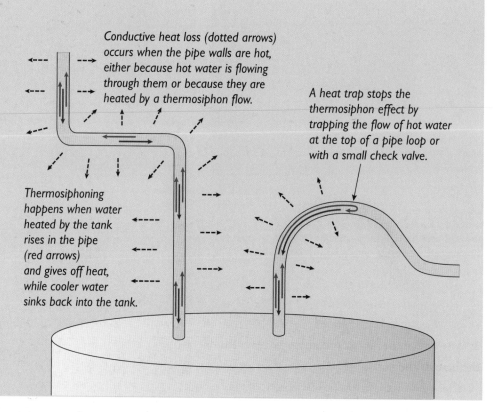

Conductive heat loss (dotted arrows) occurs when the pipe walls are hot, either because hot water is flowing through them or because they are heated by a thermosiphon flow.

A heat trap stops the thermosiphon effect by trapping the flow of hot water at the top of a pipe loop or with a small check valve.

Thermosiphoning happens when water heated by the tank rises in the pipe (red arrows) and gives off heat, while cooler water sinks back into the tank.

The hot-water line exits this water heater from the side because it has a built-in heat trap. The loop is built into the tank, so hot water can't thermosiphon up into the pipes.

tion occurs within the first 10 ft. of the tank. Be sure to use the right diameter of insulation; most homes have a mixture of ½-in. and ¾-in. pipes, so it's a good idea to measure how much of each you will need.

Maintenance

There are two basic maintenance operations that can increase a tank's lifespan. One is to regularly flush out debris and scale, which can also improve the efficiency of your tank by improving heat transfer. Annually flushing water through the drain valve at the bottom can help wash away the crud. Don't try to drain the tank; the force of the cold water pressure helps stir up the material. But you might want to shut off the heater overnight before doing this, to avoid wasting gallons of hot water.

The most common pipe insulation is made from polyethylene and is widely available at hardware stores and home centers.

Pipe insulation should be measured in place. You can miter the corners or use pre-cut fittings like this one at pipe elbows and tees.

At least once a year, flush out the sediment at the bottom of your water heater by opening the drain at the bottom. Don't turn off the water supply to the tank or empty the tank—just open the valve and let it rip (you may want to wear heavy rubber gloves to protect against scalding).

Unfortunately, most drain valves that are installed at the factory don't allow much sediment to pass through, so it's better to replace it with a full-flow ball valve. Flushing is also more effective if the tank has a dip tube with a curve at the bottom that swirls incoming water around the base of the tank.

The other thing that can be done to extend the life of a water heater is to replace the anode rod periodically. The anode rod, typically made of magnesium formed around steel wire, is designed to corrode before the steel tank does. Once the magnesium material has decomposed or is covered with scale, the anode stops working and the tank will start to deteriorate.

Anode rods are designed to last for about 5 years, depending, of course, on the water: typically just a little longer than the tank's warranty. You will probably need a heavy-duty socket wrench with a breaker bar to unthread the anode rod. Don't try to remove it until you have a new replacement rod handy. And be very careful not to damage the tank or the water fittings when removing the rod. Replacement anode rods are available at plumbing supply houses for $20 to $40. Of course, you will need to shut off the tank and the incoming water supply, and partially empty the tank before replacing an anode rod.

Minerals from water (mostly calcium and magnesium) are deposited on the tank's walls and internal flue, flaking off over time and landing on the bottom. This creates an insulating layer that slows heat transfer from the burner to the water, reducing efficiency.

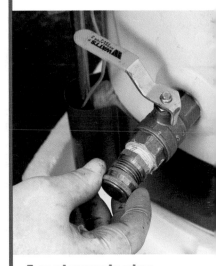

A good upgrade when installing a new water heater is a ball valve installed with a pipe nipple in place of the standard drain fitting. It is much more effective at flushing out sediment.

EF rating, is based on a standardized test that takes into account burner efficiency, pilot usage, and standby losses for "typical" hot-water usage. EF ratings for gas, oil, and electric water heaters can be found at www.ahridirectory.org under "residential water heaters." The directory also shows first-hour ratings and the burner efficiency, which is called "recovery efficiency."

Circulating Loops and Demand Controls

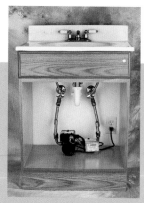

This system quickly brings hot water to all plumbing fixtures on the hot-water supply line without sending any down the drain.

Hot-water circulating loops, common in hotels, are sometimes installed in larger homes to provide fast hot water in faraway bathrooms. Hot water is pumped in a loop from the storage tank, past all the fixtures, then back again. Circulating loops can save some water from going down the drain but can use a lot of energy. If your house already has a loop, insulate it carefully to reduce heat loss. A timer that turns on the circulating pump only during high-use hours can also help.

If you have to wait a long time for hot water, or if you have an existing recirculating hot-water loop, a D'Mand® pumping system (available through Metlund and Taco) consists of a small pump and a zone valve that operate on demand. A push-button wireless remote or motion sensor starts the pump, which quickly pushes hot water into the supply pipes. A sensor shuts off the pump as soon as the water is warm enough. Demand pumping reduces water that goes down the drain while waiting for hot water. As a control for a continuous recirculation loop, it saves hot water and pump energy by pumping only when needed (see www.hvacquick.com/products/residential/Instant-Hot-Water). Parts alone range from $200 to over $500, so installation may take a few years to pay back, but the added convenience begins on day one.

The old anode rod (right) has sacrificed its life to save the tank. Replacing the rod with a new one every few years will increase the life of the tank.

Replacing Hot-Water Systems

When it is time to buy a new hot-water heater, it makes sense to install the most efficient replacement system possible. But choosing a water heater can be confusing; there are many different styles of high-efficiency units with competing claims of superiority. Which type will work best for you depends on the type of hot-water and heating systems already in your house. If you have a furnace, then you will need some type of independent, stand-alone water heater. If you have a hot-water boiler, it usually makes sense to use it for water heating, especially if the boiler is a newer, efficient model. Stand-alone, standard LP-gas, or oil-fired water heaters are the most expensive to operate; if you have one of these, or if you heat your house with electric resistance or a heat pump, you might benefit from either a super-high-efficiency condensing water heater, a heat pump water heater (HPWH; see p. 166), or a solar water-heating system (see pp. 217-220).

Water-heater efficiency

There are three basic types of replacement water heaters that work on their own (without a boiler): storage tanks, on-demand units (sometimes called tankless water heaters), and heat pump water heaters. Any of these types except the heat pump are available in either gas or electric models. Most have high-efficiency versions, and all have pros and cons. Every new water heater has an efficiency rating (called an energy factor, or EF) listed with AHRI. Today's water heaters have EFs that range from about 0.50 to 0.97 (except for heat pumps); try to get a water heater with the highest EF rating for the type of application you need.

Tank-type water heaters

Most standard gas water heaters have EF ratings in the high 50s—that means over 40 percent of the energy is wasted. Until recently, the highest-efficiency tank-type units you could buy were in the low 60s; most had efficient burners, electronic pilots, and high insulation levels. There is a new generation of high-efficiency tank-type water heaters emerging that have higher energy factors. For example, the Kenmore® Elite uses a special air intake and other features to achieve an EF of 0.7. Both the Kenmore and the Rheem® Fury (0.67 EF) use electronic vent dampers. Although not the highest efficiency available, these products provide a sizable performance boost at a modest price increase over a standard gas water heater.

The most efficient units on the market are condensing gas water heaters; they typically have EF ratings of 0.90 or higher. The best ones have stainless-steel tanks and high firing rates—typically around 90,000 to 120,000 Btu per hour, two to three times that of a typical tank.

TRADE SECRET

An electric on-demand water heater rarely makes sense for an entire house, because electricity is expensive. However, for a single bathroom or kitchen sink that's far from the nearest water heater, a small tankless electric unit can be inexpensive to install. In that application, long waits while running hot water (and the waste associated with it) can be virtually eliminated.

PROTIP

Although solar water-heating systems are expensive, they are cost-effective in many areas, particularly when compared to electric-resistance water heating.

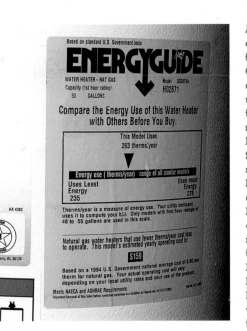

All new water heaters are required to have an Energy Guide label, which compares the energy use of this model to that of similar models. Buyers beware: "Energy Saver" is a common name found on water heaters, but it can be almost meaningless. I've seen that name on units that were near the bottom of the efficiency scale Few water heaters have their EF rating listed on the tank, but you can look it up in the AHRI directory online.

Whenever you use hot water, all the heat in the water that runs down the drain is wasted. A drain-water heat-recovery system can recover some of that heat: up to about 30 percent. A drain-water heat-recovery system needs enough vertical space to pipe it properly, which makes these systems difficult to retrofit. For an existing house, I'd look to conservation measures and more efficient water-heating equipment first.

Because of their high cost—roughly $1,500 to $2,500—condensing water heaters may be more appropriate for supplying whole-house heating as well as hot water. Their high heat output makes them well suited for supplying a hydro-air system (see the sidebar on p. 135). A hydro-air handler used in conjunction with a condensing gas water heater is probably one of the most efficient replacements for an old, inefficient gas furnace and a standard electric or gas water-heating tank, especially if you have piped natural gas and live in a cold or mixed climate. (See the photos on pgs. 168, right, and 193).

Standard electric tank-type water heaters appear to be more efficient than gas units, with EFs ranging from about 0.86 to 0.95. But the EF rating doesn't tell the whole story. Electric tanks are more efficient "at the meter" because there are no burner or chimney losses. But electricity is more expensive than natural gas per unit of energy, and electricity results in more fuel burned at the power plant and more emissions. Electric water heaters are typically installed in homes with no natural gas connection—those with electricity, LP gas, or fuel oil used for space heating. If you have an electric water heater and no natural gas available, you might want to consider a heat pump water heater (see pp. 170–171).

On-demand water heaters

At the other end of the spectrum is the on-demand water heater, also called instantaneous or tankless. The premise of an on-demand water heater is to save energy by eliminating the storage tank and its associated standby losses, using a large gas burner to heat water only when you need it. (Don't confuse this with a tankless water-heating coil that's run from a boiler; these waste far more energy by keeping the boiler hot all year; see p. 161.)

On-demand water heaters have higher EF ratings than conventional water heaters. Gas on-demand water heaters fall into two groups: those with standard gas burners and EF ratings in the low 80s, and those with condensing burners and EFs in the 90s. Savings will be lower than the EF ratings (and marketing literature) indicate, about $80 to $100 per year (assuming national average of $1.20/therm). The modest savings make it hard to recoup your investment in a reasonable time: Tankless water heaters cost between $800 and $1,500. Installation cost is also likely to be high; larger gas lines are typically needed, and in many cases new electrical service.

This "hybrid" heat pump water heater produces hot water at a savings of about 50 percent when compared to conventional electric water heaters. Alternately, some units are designed as an add-on retrofit to an existing tank.

How Much Hot Water Do You Need?

No one likes to run out of hot water. Water-heater capacity is more than the number of stored gallons; when you replace a water heater, first evaluate what you'll need. A water heater must provide enough hot water for the household, and the standard measurement of water heating capacity is called *first-hour rating*, which can be found in the AHRI directory. To determine the first-hour rating you'll need, use the chart below to estimate your family's peak-hour demand. Then look for a water heater with a first-hour rating that is at least that large.

As you draw hot water, the unit starts heating the incoming water, providing additional volume beyond the tank's storage. Therefore, the ability of a water heater to supply hot water is a tradeoff between the storage volume and the firepower. Smaller tanks can be balanced by higher Btu firing rates or vice versa. Electric tanks, for example, have relatively low heat input, so their storage volumes tend to be larger.

A jetted bathtub needs to be filled quickly, so it throws off the rules a bit. Generally, a large tub needs at least 80 percent of its capacity in storage; for example, a 60-gal. tub requires a 48-gal. tank. Water temperature also affects the balance; a higher stored temperature provides longer showers and fills bigger bathtubs, less cold water will be mixed in. But higher temperatures also waste energy by increasing standby losses.

Gallons of Hot Water Used (Approx.)

To calculate your peak-hour hot-water use, fill in the number of times someone in your home is likely to engage in each activity during the hour of maximum hot-water use (only fill in uses that will happen in the same hour). Multiply that by the number of gallons shown in the appropriate column to obtain the subtotal of hot-water consumption for each use; add those together to obtain the total. Look for the highest-efficiency model you can find with a first-hour rating at least as large as your total.

It's clear from the table that installing high-efficiency fixtures and appliances matters, so try to make these changes before you size your new water heater. For example, two showers, a hot-water laundry, and a dishwasher run in the same hour could use 87 gallons of hot water. Modestly efficient units (basically all new ones) will reduce that to 66 gal., and highly efficient units can drop the total draw down to only 28 gal.

Use	Standard Fixtures/ Appliances	Low-Flow Fixtures/ Efficient Appliances	Very Low-Flow Fixtures/ Efficient Appliances	Times Used during Peak Hour (Fill In)	Gallons Used during Peak Hour
Shower	20	15	10 to 15		
Bath	20	20	20		
Hand/face wash	4	2	1		
Dishwasher	15	15	3 to 10		
Hand dishwashing	4	4	3		
Clothes washer	32	21	5 to 15		
Food prep	5	3	3		

Sources: By permission from Chapter 49, Table 4, ASHRAE 2007 Handbook—HVAC Applications (www.ashrae.org); American Society of Heating, Refrigerating and Air-Conditioning Engineers, Inc.

If you understand sweating copper pipe joints, you may be comfortable connecting the water lines of a new tank. Only a qualified contractor, however, should do gas-line hookups. Check with your local plumbing inspector's office to see what restrictions there may be and which permits are required for any water-heater insulation. If you're going to install a water heater with a venting system that differs from the previous unit, be sure to follow the manufacturer's instructions and local codes for installation details.

This high-efficiency gas water heater has a stainsless-steel tank and an efficiency of 96 percent. It features a sealed-combustion burner.

Often referred to by their generic brand names, such as BoilerMate® or SuperStor®, indirect-fired water heaters can generate plenty of hot water and offer high efficiency and long service life.

Other advantages of on-demand water heaters are their small size and their ability to provide hot water continuously, but there are some drawbacks as well. The burner starts when a hot-water tap is opened, by sensing the drop in pressure, so some cold water always flows into the heat exchanger at first. If you use hot water intermittently, or take a shower right after another family member, you may end up with surprise "slug" of cold water each time. The total flow of hot water in GPM is also limited by the burner capacity, so sizing these units is less forgiving than water heaters with some stor-

age. Some tankless units have small storage tanks built in to reduce these troubles, or an external tank can be added. Finally, on-demand water heaters are sensitive to minerals—if you have hard water, the annual service that's needed will cut into the savings. I don't generally recommend on-demand units for most existing-tank replacements, but these heaters can make sense in a major renovation.

Electric tankless heaters are also available, but they are not typically suitable for whole-house service (see the sidebar on p. 165).

Indirect-fired tank (with boiler)

If you heat your house with a hot-water boiler, an indirect-fired water heater can generate hot water more efficiently than a tankless coil or most stand-alone units. The storage tank contains a thermostat that requests heat from the boiler, just like a separate heating zone. To get the best efficiency from an indirect storage tank, the boiler has to have the right controls: It needs to be set up for "cold start" and should also include a purge cycle (see pp. 129–130). Generally the control should also include a 30-minute hot-water priority. This ensures that you always have hot water, even on a cold morning when the boiler is needed for space heating.

Many indirect-fired tanks have a built-in heat exchanger. Boiler water is pumped through the heat exchanger, heating water in the tank without mixing boiler water with the potable water supply. Alternatively, almost any type of insulated storage tank can be combined with an external heat exchanger to produce hot water from a boiler.

An external heat exchanger requires two circulating pumps, adding a small electrical load. But when the unit is properly sized, the heat transfer is very efficient. All piping between the boiler and the storage tank must be thoroughly insulated to minimize heat loss, including any external heat exchanger (don't insulate pump bodies). Indirect tanks have AHRI efficiency ratings, but they don't have EF ratings like other water heaters. This is because any boiler can provide the heat source with a wide range of efficiencies. Indirect tanks are rated for "standby loss" in a range from 0.4 to over 1.0; try to aim for 0.8 or less. Smaller tanks tend to have higher losses per hour, but they are cheaper and take up less space. Look for the lowest standby loss available with a first-hour rating that suits your needs.

This external plate-frame heat exchanger can be used to heat domestic hot water from a boiler or to create hydronic heat from a standard water heater, without mixing the two water supplies.

PRO TIP

If you're replacing a water heater, consider your annual fuel costs as well as the initial installation cost.

Comparing Water Heater Costs

Using national average prices for fuels (2010), it's clear that a mid-high-efficiency gas-water heater is cheapest to operate, but only if it's natural gas. These results will vary with fuel prices, heater efficiency, and hot-water use. An electric heat pump with an EF of 2.3 (in a mild climate) might cost only $150 per year. On the other hand, upgrading the LP gas unit to a 0.84 EF on-demand unit will save less than $80 per year.

Installation and Operating Costs

Fuel	EF Rating	Estimated Installed Cost	Fuel Price (Rate)	Annual Water Heating Cost for a Family of Four
Electric	90%	$500	$0.12/kWh	$356
Natural Gas (mid-high efficiency)	68%	$950	$1.10/therm	$148
LP Gas	68%	$950	$2.80/gal	$413

Choosing a contractor versus doing it yourself

Replacing a water heater is a big project. Skilled do-it-yourself types can replace a conventional gas or electric stand-alone tank with a new unit of the same type (but with a higher efficiency), but you should always get a licensed professional to connect gas or other fuel pipes. If you want to change the equipment to a completely new type, or if the water heating is integrated with the space-heating system, it's a good idea to hire a professional.

When choosing a contractor, consider factors such as energy savings, quality, warranty service, and customer references, as well as price. Bids should include details on the equipment, installation specs, labor, and associated costs. Always choose a contractor who is familiar with the equipment and has a track record installing it, particularly if you want to install something out of the ordinary. And don't just think about installation cost and efficiency; fuel costs can be a major factor as well. In some areas, an LP-gas heater at 60-percent efficiency is more expensive to operate than a conventional electric water heater at 90-percent or more efficiency. Finally, tax credits or utility rebates may reduce the up-front cost for high-efficiency units, making an upgrade more cost-effective.

Heat pump water heaters

The heat pump water heater is based on a great concept: Use electricity to extract heat from the air and deliver it to the hot water at a higher temperature. The heat extracted from the air is free, and theoretically the net efficiency could be 300 percent or more. Early models had trouble with reliability, service, and price, but a new generation of HPWHs has emerged that seems to offer better efficiency and reliability at a price range of about $1,300 to $2,000.

HPWHs have EFs in the range of 2.0 to 2.5, which means that more than half the heat comes from the environment around the heater (see the description of heat pump efficiency on p. 121). There are a number of factors that affect the real installed efficiency. First, controls in most units allow for resistance heat to turn on when demand is high or surrounding air temperatures are low; this can really cut into the overall efficiency, depending on how the control is set and how you use hot water. The most efficient units have smaller electric backup heaters (less than 2,500 watts) and run the heat pump even while the resistance heat is on. Larger tanks also tend to run more efficiently than small tanks.

Also, the heat comes from the air around the tank. If you live in a cold climate, that heat may not be free: If the tank is in a conditioned space, you've already paid to heat it up. If it's in an unconditioned basement, the air may get cold and efficiency will suffer. At the same time, air that is exhausted from the heat pump is cool and dry, so running an HPWH in a basement may reduce dehumidification needs. Some units allow for a duct to divert the chilled air output outdoors in cold weather. Of course, in a warm climate a HPWH will help cool your house, saving even more on your electric bills.

The bottom line is this: If you are looking to replace an existing electric or LP-gas water heater and you don't have access to natural gas, consider getting a HPWH if you live in a mixed or hot climate. Average savings should be around $300 per year, so payback on the $1,000 to $1,500 increased cost is fairly reasonable. Savings may be higher where electric rates are higher than average, even in colder climates. Savings will tend to be largest when hot-water use is high.

IN DETAIL

Another promising idea is a combined space- and water-heating heat pump such as the Daiken Altherma® (http://www.daikinac.com). This system provides high-efficiency heating and cooling with wall cassettes (like the mini-split on p. 124) or hot water for hydronic distribution, and on-demand domestic hot water, at a high efficiency in any climate. Although expensive, a system like this should provide robust whole-house savings and environmental benefits, especially in areas with no natural-gas availability.

RENOVATIONS

The best time to invest in an energy-efficient upgrade is when you are already planning to buy a product or make improvements to your home. Because you are making a substantial investment during a renovation project, you have a rare opportunity to significantly improve the energy efficiency of your entire house. On the other hand, if the opportunity is missed, renovations carry the potential for energy, comfort, and air-quality disasters.

A renovation can mean a simple change in wall or roof cladding, or it can mean a total gut/rehabilitation project. It can involve one room, or it can involve an entire home. Additions to houses provide their own unique set of opportunities and potential pitfalls. Whatever the scope of the project, thoughtful planning and attention to detail will help you achieve the highest level of energy efficiency for your house at a reasonable cost.

▶ ▶ ▶

Consider the Big Picture

Before starting out on energy-improvement projects, take some time to think about what you have in mind for the house over time. Now is the time to look for lower-cost opportunities for bigger energy upgrades, by combining them with work you're already paying for. Second, consider the long-term economic and environmental impact of your choices. Fuel prices may rise rapidly, your kitchen remodel may look dated in a couple of decades, but the choices you make about energy performance of walls, roofs, or window frames may last 40 to 100 years.

Think of it as "future-proofing" your house; you'll save energy while you're there, and it will be more attractive to future buyers as energy prices increase.

Deep energy retrofits

Increasing awareness of carbon emissions and climate change has spurred a growing movement among homeowners, designers, and builders to pursue low-energy homes in new construction and renovations. Many of the techniques needed for very low-energy homes were pioneered in the 1970s; back then they were called "superin-

Install rigid foam over a "draining" textured housewrap for superior moisture control. The author extends the window and door sill flashings to the outside of the foam, yet water can still drain behind the foam. A hefty layer of foam (at least 1½ in., preferably 3 in to 4 in.) limits condensation in all seasons and provides a continuous thermal break; the furred space helps the whole wall dry.

Financing Energy Projects

Some states and municipalities are adopting a new system for financing energy projects, called Property Assessed Clean Energy, or PACE. PACE connects private investment with building owners to pay for energy improvements, and repayments are added to that property's tax bills until the investor is paid back. Neither a government subsidy nor a tax, PACE ensures that repayment of the loan is spread out among current and future owners, who all benefit from the work.

sulation." Fortunately, we have learned a lot since the 1970s: We better understand how to manage moisture, durability, and air quality. We also have far more efficient and reliable equipment, lighting, and appliances, so energy-savings targets between 50 percent and 90 percent (compared with standard homes) are quite achievable. Falling prices for renewable energy have made even net-zero energy homes a reality for many. With or without renewables, such an approach is typically called a "deep energy retrofit," or simply a "deep retrofit," when applied to an existing home renovation.

Turning an existing house into a very low-energy home is a challenge: It is expensive, it takes planning and attention to details, and the options may be limited by the existing structure. The possibilities are also affected by your approach. If you're planning a gut renovation, there will be many more options, at a smaller incremental cost. If you plan for a siding replacement, an exterior retrofit such as rigid insulation or a Larsen truss is a viable option; if you are going to gut and refinish one room at a time, a different approach is necessary. Be thoughtful about your plan: Try not to do work in the early stages that will increase the cost or difficulty of achieving your long-term efficiency goals. You may choose not to focus first on the items with the shortest payback. Upgrading walls and windows may be the most expensive items on the list, but once completed the entire house can be easily heated and cooled with a relatively inexpensive, very efficient ductless heat pump.

Also consider that the value of doing a deep retrofit can far exceed the energy benefits. Finding and fixing a source of air leakage and heat loss in a complex cathedral ceiling area can solve ice-dam problems and eliminate costly moisture damage. Spraying a foundation with closed-cell foam can reduce water intrusion, make the basement more comfortable, and reduce the need for costly dehumidification. Remember that choices about the energy efficiency of a building's structure (walls, roof, and foundation) tend to last the longest, and will have a bigger impact over the life of the home, than will choices of mechanical equipment, appliances, or even windows.

Retrofit options My preference for a deep retrofit is to insulate and air-seal (with rigid or sprayed foam) on the exterior of a home whenever possible. Exterior treatments typically provide the best continuity, air tightness, and moisture management, and offer the ability to increase R-values almost without limitation, while avoiding thermal bridges or intrusion into the interior living area. There are cases when an exterior treatment won't make sense: if you are gutting one room at a time; if the siding and trim are in great shape; if the geometry is complex, with many roofs/overhangs/step-backs; or if zoning setback restrictions prohibit adding any exterior thickness to the walls. Regardless of the techniques you choose or the level of efficiency you settle on, keep these things in mind:

1. Do some analysis. If you can, get some energy modeling to help assess the value of design choices.

2. Invest more in the components that will likely be around for 40 to 100 years: foundation, walls, and attic/roof assembly. Also, look for windows with low-conductivity frames (insulated fiberglass or composite extrusions) and removable glazing stops that allow easy glass replacement, for easy upgrades in future years.

Certification Programs and Performance Targets

When planning a major remodel, it can be confusing to decide just how far to go. Fortunately, there are a number of resources available to help you decide. Most are voluntary certification programs that offer additional advantages, such as the use of qualified consultants to provide analysis and on-site inspections. Whether or not you pursue certification, any of these programs can provide a framework for evaluating a design and guidance on how to achieve results.

CERTIFICATION PROGRAMS

• Energy Star (www.energystar.gov/newhomes): The Energy Star label applies to homes too; the energy target is 15 percent better than current building codes. Focused primarily on new construction, it is also suited for a gut rehab.

• Thousand Home Challenge (THC; www.thousandhomechallenge.com) is challenging, but achievable. Geared toward deep retrofits, there are two options to comply: a 75-percent reduction of energy use, or meeting an energy budget that's based on climate, house size, and heating fuel. THC is based on real-world energy use, rather than computer-modeled projections, so it recognizes both lifestyle changes and "built-in" efficiency.

• Passive House: Passive House Institute U.S. (PHIUS; www.passive-house.us) sets extremely stringent targets for heating, cooling, and total energy use, as well as air tightness and ventilation. It is impractical to reach Passive House performance in an existing home with anything short of a gut rehab.

• Green Building: Green building programs include a wide range of environmental attributes along with energy. The most notable certifications include the Leadership in Energy and Environmental Design (LEED) for Homes (www.usgbc.org/homes) and the National Green Building Standard (NGBS; www.nahbgreen.org/NGBS). Both systems include independent inspections, and have several tiers of achievement with increasing stringency. Certification under the NGBS is available for "green remodel" projects, but LEED for Homes certification is only available for a complete gut renovation or new construction.

OTHER TARGETS

• "Zero-energy" or "net-zero" energy homes: There is no single standard to define what this means, but generally zero-energy homes all depend on some amount of on-site renewable energy generation to offset energy used on site. They vary in the way they account for grid-supplied electricity, site-generated electricity, and other fuels used, but they all try to plan for a net zero energy use or net-zero cost. Zero-energy building codes have been proposed as a long-term (circa 2050) goal by many efficiency experts and U.S. policymakers.

• Rule of Thumb: For a basic guideline on low-energy renovations, aim for the R-values in the chart on p. 179. Use a ductless split heat pump, or keep all ducts inside conditioned space. In cold climates, focus on very air-tight construction with mechanical ventilation, and use a condensing gas water heater or boiler. In the south, it's critical to control solar heat gain using low-SHGC glazing and shading windows; in humid climates low air leakage and dehumidification are also key.

Whatever strategy you choose, do the best you can with the available resources. Try to invest the most in the components that will be around the longest.

3. Try to minimize the need for rework: At each step, do the job right the first time, even if it takes a bit longer to see the whole project to completion.

4. Savings follow waste. If you address the biggest users early on, the savings in energy can actually help you pay for additional work.

5. Reduce before renewables. Even with tax credits or other incentives, renewable energy systems are expensive. It almost always makes more sense to reduce the energy needs first, before you add solar electric or solar thermal equipment.

Air-Sealing

After the demolition and framing dust settles in any renovation project, the temptation is to get the space insulated quickly so that the finishing work can begin. But it's important to take a little time to seal air leaks properly. This will be your best—and only—opportunity to find and seal cracks and holes in the enclosure. It doesn't take much time or money—just awareness and attention to details.

Look for leaks

The most important place to seal leaks is between insulated surfaces and the outdoors, or unconditioned buffer spaces. The most commonly missed leaks are joist bays and wall-stud cavities that need draftstopping where they run from interior floors and walls into attics, crawlspaces, or other unconditioned areas (see "Sealing Air Leaks"). And don't forget to seal any leaks between an addition and the rest of the building.

Before you insulate a house, walk around with a foam gun and seal all wiring and plumbing penetrations between wall cavities and unconditioned spaces (attic, basement, or crawlspace). Also, seal around window and door jambs, being careful not to spray too much foam in large gaps. Pay attention to any areas that need draftstop blocking, and fill them with blocks of wood or foam board that are caulked in place. You can use the same techniques outlined in "Sealing Air Leaks," except that it will be a lot easier to reach everything before the insulation and drywall are installed.

Creating a super air-seal

In all climates, I recommend thoroughly sealing the exterior sheathing at the sill plate and at all sheathing connections. This can be done using a combination of canned foam, caulking, and high-quality tape, with a continuous layer of interior sprayed foam (flash and batt), or using a professionally sprayed sealant system like

Flash and batt:
Sealing individual air leaks with one-part foam is inexpensive but labor intensive. Instead, you can get "flash and batt": A layer of closed-cell spray foam seals air leaks and controls water vapor, and the rest of the cavity is filled with standard batts. To avoid condensation in walls, use at least 1 in. of foam in climate zones 4–5, 1½ in. in climate zone 6, and 2 in. in zones 7–8. For roofs, follow the table on p. 75. See also "In Detail," p. 187.

PRO TIP

If you live in a hot climate, don't put a vapor barrier—whether polyethylene or vinyl wallpaper—on the interior surfaces of your exterior walls.

IN DETAIL

In any building project, it's important to keep in mind the *continuity* of the thermal boundary. Your insulation and air barrier should be aligned and should surround the entire house without interruption. It's much easier to visualize this before you put up any drywall. In fact, while you are contemplating exactly where the insulation should go, think about how thorough the air barrier is. There should always be a solid air barrier in line with every insulated surface.

A specialized spray-on caulking such as EnergyComplete from Owens Corning can be used to effectively seal all the surfaces of the thermal boundary in preparation for insulating. Unlike "flash and batt," these systems only seal leaks and don't provide the R-value or vapor control of a layer of closed-cell foam.

ACCORDING TO CODE

Although any blocking or draftstops installed between a heated space and an attic area will help slow the spread of fire, some codes require that blocking be made of specific materials to qualify as firestopping. Spraying foam around wiring holes may also be forbidden; check with your local building inspector before you start sealing holes.

Owens Corning EnergyComplete™ or Knauf® EcoSeal™. *Don't* try to use polyethylene as an air barrier, especially in hot or mixed climates.

Years ago, many energy-efficiency guides promoted the use of carefully sealed and taped polyethylene as both an air barrier and interior vapor retarder. It's risky to design structures in cold climates that rely on poly as both air and vapor control. Combining water-vapor control with insulating materials reduces risk. It's best to use a layer of exterior insulating sheathing or cavity-sprayed urethane foam to control vapor movement; either approach typically provides for tighter construction and higher R-values and better condensation control.

As top plates (and end studs of partition walls) dry and shrink, the gap between the wood and the drywall will end up being anywhere from 1/32 in. to 3/16 in. along both sides of the framing.

The ceiling plane is tricky to make airtight for a few reasons. There are many penetrations, framed openings for architectural features that interrupt the ceiling plane, and light fixtures ("Sealing Air Leaks" outlines these areas). Even the top plates of walls leak, when the wood shrinks away from the drywall and leaves a gap. One approach to consider, especially if there is mechanical equipment and ductwork in the attic, is to create a "cathedralized" attic, eliminating the need to seal and insulate the attic floor or ducts (see p. 78). Alternately, you can seal plumbing and wiring penetrations with canned foam, install blocking across larger openings, and seal the top plate to drywall connections. These gaps are much easier to seal before installing drywall, but getting the drywall-to-top-plate connection is tricky. You can use a thick, continuous bead of drywall adhesive or acoustic sealant applied to the top plate before hanging the drywall to the wall studs (after the ceiling is in place). EPDM gaskets made for this purpose are more reliable and more expensive. If it's easy to get into the attic above after drywall and before insulation, it's fast and easy to use a two-part spray-foam kit.

Note that it is not important to seal partition-to-ceiling connections between a first and second floor; here, you want to focus on sealing the band joist at the exterior walls. Another area to watch out for is any change in ceiling height, from one room to another, in an insulated ceiling. Those transitions usually need blocking (see pgs. 33 and 36), which is much easier to install when the walls are open. Also, if you are installing recessed lights in any insulated ceiling areas, be sure to use airtight light fixtures (see the top right photo on p. 38).

Insulation

If you are tearing down drywall or plaster in one room or many, the temptation is to slap some fiberglass batts in the empty wall cavities and say "good enough" before refinishing. If the wall was uninsulated to begin with, that will certainly be a big improvement, but carefully choosing

Use a putty knife or a 6-in. taping knife to tuck the back corners of batts into place to help prevent the corners from rounding. When fiberglass batts are properly installed, you'll get much closer to the R-value you paid for.

and installing insulation at this point will pay big energy and comfort dividends for years to come.

Fiberglass batt insulation

Because fiberglass batts are vulnerable to installation defects, it's very important that they be installed very carefully. Batts should be fluffed up to their full rated thickness and tucked into cavities with no compression or rounding of corners. They must fill cavities completely, without gaps or spaces, so they need to be carefully cut and trimmed to the proper size and shape. They also should be cut around obstructions and split over any wiring or plumbing pipes that run through cavities.

If you have an unsheathed wall that opens into an attic space (such as a kneewall), it's also important to enclose the insulation on all sides. When a wall cavity is left open on one side, cold (or hot) air can circulate through the batt, as well as through small gaps at the framing, reducing its effectiveness. Cover the open side of the wall with 2 in. of rigid foam insulation. The rigid foam will enclose the batts, providing an air barrier, thermal break, and condensation resistance in any climate.

PRO TIP

To achieve their full R-value, fiberglass batts must be carefully installed, without gaps or compression.

TRADE SECRET

If you're planning to blow in cellulose insulation, you can leave a 4-in. space in the center of the wall between the sheets of drywall, as shown below. The gap makes it easy to insert a fill tube to insulate each wall cavity. Once insulated, fill the space with a strip of 3/8-in.-thick drywall, then mud and tape the gap as one wide seam.

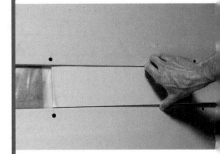

Insulation Recommendations

In general, I recommend better thermal performance for building components than current energy codes demand.

	Walls	Ceilings	Floors	Windows
Cold Climates	R-40	R-60	R-40	U-0.15–U-0.25
Mixed Climates	R-30	R-45	R-30	U-0.2–U-0.3, with SHGC of 0.2–0.4.
Hot Climates	R-20	R-30	R-20	U-0.4–U-0.5, with SHGC of 0.15–0.3

In any climate, insulate slab floors to at least R-10 (R-20 if it has embedded radiant heat) and foundation walls to R-20.

The performance of insulation suffers dramatically when there are gaps and spaces in the installation. As this chart indicates, relatively small gaps at sides or ends of cavities have a surprisingly large impact on performance, especially for higher R-values. Other typical defects include compression, rounded corners, side-stapling of faced batts, and spaces around wiring, plumbing, blocking, or other obstructions. Besides gaps, other insulation, such as loose-fill or sprayed products, suffer frequently from low densities, incomplete fill, or uneven fill. "Average" is meaningless for R-values; the minimum thickness that is found frequently across an insulated surface dominates the heat loss of that surface.

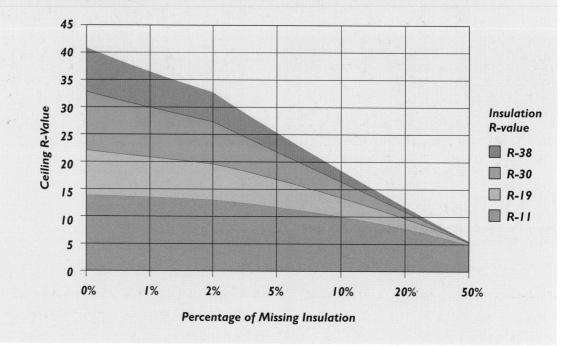

Chart — y-axis: Ceiling R-Value (0 to 45); x-axis: Percentage of Missing Insulation (0%, 1%, 2%, 5%, 10%, 20%, 50%)

Insulation R-value
- R-38
- R-30
- R-19
- R-11

Don't put all your thermal "eggs" in one basket. It doesn't make sense to superinsulate your walls and leave the single- or double-pane windows in place.

The rounded shoulders, compression, and gaps that are typical in batt installations can result in substantial loss of R-value. Batts should be cut to fit neatly around all obstructions and should fill the entire cavity.

Sprayed- or blown-in products

Sprayed- or blown-in insulation systems can perform better than batts by themselves. They have the benefit of conformity: When installed properly, they fill in gaps and avoid many of the problems that are difficult to avoid with batts.

Over the years I've seen hundreds of wall cavities insulated with cellulose, either as an open-cavity damp spray or as a dry dense-packed application. Damp-spray cellulose is not a do-it-yourself job, because it requires specialized equipment and training to do well.

Sprayed cellulose is a bit more expensive than contractor-installed fiberglass batts. At about R-3.4 per in., you get only a little more R-value

Damp-sprayed cellulose installs quickly and completely fills wall cavities.

After spraying the damp material, a worker scrubs off any excess with a special rotary brush, leaving the wall perfectly flat.

than batt insulation. In terms of performance, you'll get much more for your money with cellulose, because it is not subject to the same types of installation defects that plague fiberglass jobs.

If your remodeling project doesn't include opening the walls, or if you want to install the insulation yourself, dense-packed dry cellulose may be your best bet. This is the same process as blowing cellulose into uninsulated walls in any house (see "Insulating a House"). Even if you are gutting the walls and replastering, you can hang the drywall first, then fill the cavities with cellulose. Use a fill tube, if possible, for best results. Install the cellulose before taping and finishing the wall, so that you won't have to add another step to the finishing process. High-performance fiberglass (see p. 75 and the top photo on p. 183) can also be blown into closed cavities or behind netting and provide excellent results.

Insulating floors and ceilings

If you are insulating a flat ceiling with an open attic above, refer to the chapter on insulating; the issues are exactly the same, and the same techniques apply. Resist the temptation to install fiberglass batts only between the joist bays while the ceiling is open; instead, install loose-fill insulation after the drywall is up.

For exposed floors, my preference is either to sheathe the joists and dense-pack cellulose or to use a flash-and-batt approach. If you're going to install cellulose, be sure to note with a pencil any obstructions or blind cavities as you install rigid foam, plywood sheathing, or drywall so you will not miss them while blowing the insulation. A third option is to net the joists and blow in cellulose or fiberglass.

Cathedral ceilings and flat roofs are a bit trickier. For those that are difficult or impossible to vent properly, the only legitimate method is

WHAT CAN GO WRONG

Many folks believe that the ¼-in. or ⅜-in. layer of foam board that they install under siding is useful insulation. In reality, it's wishful thinking. Though there is some R-value, it's minimal. This "backer board" is mostly to create a nice flat surface over the existing siding. If you replace your siding, add at least a 1-in. to 2-in. layer of rigid foam, which will make a real thermal impact.

The backerboard that's installed underneath vinyl siding is mostly for the convenience of the installer.

Building codes don't allow you to use combustible materials to seal leaks around chimneys, so metal flashing is usually the preferred material. If you are gutting a building or constructing an addition, you may want to consider installing steel framing with top and bottom plate channels up against the chimney. The steel is noncombustible, and the channels provide a good draft stop at the top of the chase.

Steel studs with steel-channel top plates provide an easy way to stop air from leaking through the chimney chase. Caulk the top plates to the chimney with high-temperature silicone.

The penalty for improper batt installation is even greater in attics and cathedral ceilings than it is in walls. Whenever possible, use loose fill or sprayed types of insulation to avoid those problems.

Professional Spray Foams

There are many spray-applied foams on the market today, and most fall in one of two categories: "open-cell" (often called " ½-lb. foam," which has a density of about ½ lb. per cu. ft.) and "closed-cell" (or "2-lb. foam," based on its higher density).

At about R-3.4 per inch, open-cell foams have about the same R-value per inch as batts or cellulose and are relatively vapor-permeable, so they need a vapor retarder in cold climates. Closed-cell foams are more expensive and provide about R-6 value per inch. Both are good air barriers wherever they are sprayed continuously. Installing sprayed foam requires specialized equipment and training, so is better left to a professional.

Low-density, spray-applied foams like this ½-lb. foam are most commonly used for full-cavity sprays.

to create an unvented roof; even if it is possible to vent, if the ceiling is opened for remodeling an unvented roof may be a good option. Foam sprayed directly against the sheathing provides much of the R-value, unless you are re-roofing; in that case, you can consider rigid foam on top of the sheathing (see pp. 71–75). Batts or blown-in insulation can provide the rest of the R-value. Install foam to at least the R-value specified in the table on p. 75.

High-performance fiberglass can be blown into open walls behind netting, as shown, or used for effective dense packing in closed cavities.

Spray Foams

Sprayed foams aren't foolproof; find an installer with experience and references. Spraying at cold temperatures or onto condensation-laden sheathing can cause big bubbles, voids, and adhesion problems that are hard to spot. If the chemical components are not heated to the correct temperature and sprayed in the right proportion, foam may not cure properly and can leave lingering chemical odors. Most closed-cell foams are limited to about 2 in. per pass; the chemical reaction generates heat that can't dissipate properly in a thicker application, which can cause charring or even a fire. Fire-safety codes (or ICC Evaluation Service reports) must be followed carefully (see p. 79).

Some dealers oversell the benefits of spray foam, suggesting that foam's air-tightness somehow means that much lower R-values will suffice. Although air sealing is important, so too is R-value, so don't skimp. Don't settle for an installed "average" thickness—insist that the thickness you pay for is predominant throughout the surface you are insulating.

Once it's cured, check the thickness of foam in various places. Use an insulation push rod or stiff wire, with a piece of masking tape as a depth gauge. A ³⁄₄-in. to ¹⁄₂-in. gap between the surface of the foam and the face of the battens provides a drainage gap.

And remember, foam can't seal leaks where it's not sprayed. Cavity spray foam still needs some caulking at key areas, such as leaks between subfloor and bottom plate, between top plates, or between adjacent studs.

(see p. 79)

PRO TIP

For a given R-value, rigid foam offers more benefit than cavity insulation because it covers the thermal shortcuts of wood framing.

TRADE SECRET

If you apply drywall directly over rigid-foam board insulation that is thicker than ¹⁄₂ in., you may end up with a lot of nail (or screw) pops. It's better to cover the rigid foam with 1×3 furring strips before installing the drywall. Attached with screws at 16 in. o.c., either at right angles to or directly over the framing, the furring provides a solid nailing base that won't wreak havoc with your taping job.

When insulating walls or ceilings with thick foam board, use furring to provide a solid, stable base for the drywall.

Damp-Spray Cellulose

Damp-spray cellulose is an effective insulation material, but not a do-it-yourself project. There are a few things you should know about this type of insulation to ensure you get good results. First, moisture content is critical. If too little water is mixed with the cellulose fiber, the material will be crumbly and won't stick well. If too much water is added, it will slump away from the top plates. Pick up a handful of freshly sprayed material and squeeze it hard; no water should drip out. When checked with a moisture meter after a day or two of drying, the moisture content should be at or below 25 percent before the cavity is enclosed with drywall.

Sprayed cellulose doesn't work in walls more than 6 in. thick or in vaulted ceilings. If you have an overhead application or thicker walls, install dense-packed cellulose (see pp. 76–77) behind unfinished drywall or use netting to enclose the cavities before installing.

Drywall returns provide an attractive and inexpensive solution to window openings in thick walls. A wooden stool and apron provide a nice window shelf.

Built-Up Walls and Roofs for High R-Values

If you are insulating an older house but not remodeling or changing the surface finishes, the level of insulation you can achieve is limited by the existing structure. During moderate to substantial remodeling, however, you have more latitude in determining the level of insulation.

Using a remodeling opportunity to improve the thermal performance of your house can give you more bang for your insulation buck. With some planning and foresight, you can substantially beef up the insulation levels in walls, roofs, and floors without adding tremendously to the cost of the project.

Adding foam board

Depending on the thickness of your walls and the overall desired R-value, you can add a layer of foam insulation on the inside or the outside of walls, cathedral ceilings, or floors. There's not much point in adding it on a flat ceiling with an attic, where you can simply blow in more insulation above. Extruded polystyrene and foil-faced polyisocyanurate board are both good choices for interior or exterior applications, regardless of the climate; polystyrene is cheaper, but isocyanurate has a bit more R-value per inch of thickness.

For the same R-value, continuous insulation provides far more benefit than cavity insulation, because it covers the thermal shortcuts of wood framing. I generally discourage the use of high R-value material such as closed-cell foam to fill wood frame cavities, unless that is the only option; the compromise that the framing represents to your overall thermal performance is too large (see the chart on the facing page.) And once you install continuous insulation of at least R-5, the installation quality of the cavity insulation becomes trivial. Continuous foam suppresses the thermal weak spots to a point where they play a very minor role.

I prefer adding continuous insulation on the outside if possible. In any climate, a 2-in. layer of foam on the exterior improves moisture and condensation resistance, especially if an air space is provided under the siding. Exterior foam also keeps the structural elements warm and dry (or cool and dry in a hot-humid climate); it doesn't reduce the floor area; and most important, it's simply easier to make the foam layer continuous across interruptions like interior walls and floors.

The thickness of the foam is limited only by budget, design goals, and practical details; I've seen installations as thick as 8 in., but 2 in. to 4 in. is normally adequate to meet whole-wall R-values up to about 40. The biggest challenge is if you have don't have an adequate roof overhang at the eave or gable. In those cases, you may need to modify the roof. If the outside of the house is in very good shape, or if there are zoning restrictions that won't allow thicker walls, you may be forced to add insulation on the interior.

Rigid versus Cavity Insulation Performance

Because of the thermal "bridge" penalty of wall studs that interrupt the insulation, the overall R-value of a full cavity of closed-cell foam is lower than you'd think. This comparison between the insulation material R-value (nominal) and the whole-wall R-value (actual) shows that the penalty is even larger for a 2×6 wall than for a 2×4 wall. Your best bet to get the high R-value you paid for is 4 in. of continuous foam on a 2×4 wall.

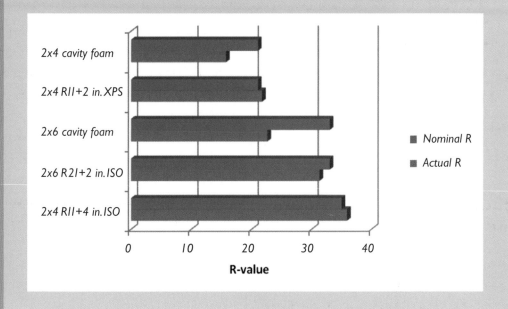

(Horizontal bar chart)

- 2x4 cavity foam
- 2x4 R11+2 in. XPS
- 2x6 cavity foam
- 2x6 R21+2 in. ISO
- 2x4 R11+4 in. ISO

Legend:
- ■ Nominal R
- ■ Actual R

X-axis: R-value (0, 10, 20, 30, 40)

One complication if you are adding insulation to the outside of an existing wall is that eave or rake overhangs may need to be extended.

One issue with built-up interior walls is that of electrical boxes, which need to be remounted to account for the new wall plane. Another complication with adding thickness to a wall, inside or out, is the need for extension jambs around window and door openings.

If the thickness is added to the exterior, you will have to either push the window and door frames out to the new exterior wall surface or build exterior extension jambs, including detailing the flashing and drainage for deeply inset frames. Of course, if you are installing new windows anyway, that will not be much of a problem. In either case, pay careful attention to proper window- and door-flashing details (see pp. 189–191).

Exterior continuous insulation can be added with rigid board foam, but it can also be sprayed to whatever thickness is desired. A ¾-in. to ½-in. gap between the surface of the foam and the face of the battens provides a drainage gap.

Wood battens, stood off from the original structure with screws or L-brackets, are fully supported by the foam.

The most important role of housewrap is as a drainage plane. All too often I see applications that are prone to trapping water. Look under the window to the left—the lower piece overlaps the upper one.

Although housewraps such as Typar® and Tyvek are marketed as air barriers, they have some inherent limitations. If you're re-siding an old house with plank sheathing, housewrap can certainly help tighten the walls, but it must be carefully detailed and taped at all seams. The places where enclosures leak the most are where housewrap is usually not detailed well or even present: at window and door openings, at cantilevers and other transitions, and where exterior walls meet attics, garages, and other unconditioned spaces. I think of housewrap primarily as a drainage membrane to prevent moisture intrusion; I seal the air leaks with other materials.

Cross-strapping walls or ceilings

Another technique for providing a thicker cavity to accommodate extra interior insulation is to nail 2×3 cross strapping, or other framing of substantial thickness, across the studs or rafters. Cross-strapping works best when you start with a 2×6 wall, because you are adding only an extra 1½ in. of insulation. Although carefully installed fiberglass batts can work with this type of wall, I prefer cellulose or blown-in fiberglass, alone or with a flash coat of closed-cell foam first. As with an exterior foam application, this system interrupts the thermal-bridge effect (except where the framing members cross, which is a small enough area to have very little impact). Electrical boxes can be mounted directly to the cross strapping.

In the past, designs for superinsulation often featured double-studded walls or deep framing members to contain a lot of insulation. However,

Adjustable Electrical Boxes

When installing interior foam board, it is often difficult to properly mount electrical boxes. The Adjust-a-Box® comes in a single- or double-gang box and has an adjustable bracket that allows for the increased thickness of interior wall sheathing.

With the turn of a screw, the bracket on this adjustable electrical box (from Carlon or Thomas & Betts) can adjust the front of the box up to 2 in. away from the face of the stud, allowing for up to 1½ in. of foam board, plus drywall.

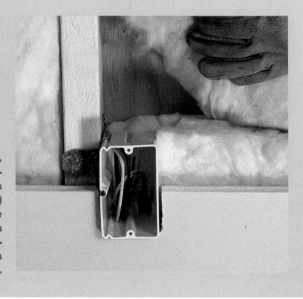

Another variation on exterior foam insulation: a continuous peel-and-stick membrane, adhered to the wall sheathing, covered by 4 in. or more of rigid foam with offset joints. As shown here, the membrane and insulation layers may be continued to cover the roof, with eave and rake details applied on top (such a system is often called *PERSIST* or *REMOTE*). This system is pricey, but highly robust in any climate: The membrane provides drainage from exterior water or summertime condensation and stays warm enough in the winter to avoid interior condensing. Siding is applied on furring attached with epoxy-coated screws.

IN DETAIL

There are guidelines for minimum R-values of exterior foam or cavity spray to avoid wintertime condensing in walls and roofs. These guidelines assume that the total insulation R-value of the foam plus any batt or blown fiber insulation added will meet code requirements, but not much more. If you are planning a much higher R-value, you'll need to increase the R-value of the foam layer to ensure protection. Aim for 40 percent of the total R-value in foam up to climate zone 5, 45 percent in zone 6, and 50 percent in zones 7 to 8. If you're not sure, it's always safe to add more foam or less fiber.

PRO TIP

Water will get past your exterior cladding, particularly around windows and doors; install sheathing wrap shingle-style to shed water.

the extra framing is expensive and usually structurally unnecessary. Instead, walls and rafters can be built to any thickness with pieces of plywood or other scrap material (which are called *gussets*). The gussets, typically installed on 2-ft. to 4-ft. centers, tie a nonstructural interior member, such as a 2×2, to the wall studs or rafters. A gusseted wall can be made as thick as you like for maximum R-value.

Lightweight trusses of any thickness, commonly called *Larsen trusses*, can also be built out of 2×2s and plywood gussets, then nailed to the building's exterior. The depth of the truss is limited by the roof overhangs, or you must build extensions to the roof edges. And keep in mind that doors and windows will need to be carefully flashed, whether they are reset to the new exterior wall plane or left in line with the original wall.

To provide a watertight seal, slip a piece of housewrap or building paper into a slit above the window or door and over the head nailing flange or flashing.

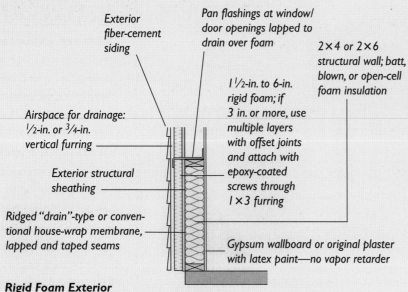

Exterior fiber-cement siding

Pan flashings at window/door openings lapped to drain over foam

2×4 or 2×6 structural wall; batt, blown, or open-cell foam insulation

Airspace for drainage: 1/2-in. or 3/4-in. vertical furring

1 1/2-in. to 6-in. rigid foam; if 3 in. or more, use multiple layers with offset joints and attach with epoxy-coated screws through 1×3 furring

Exterior structural sheathing

Ridged "drain"-type or conventional house-wrap membrane, lapped and taped seams

Gypsum wallboard or original plaster with latex paint—no vapor retarder

Sheathing, building paper or housewrap, and siding

Properly insulated floor-joist cavities

Original or new 2×4 or 2×6 exterior structural wall

Horizontal wire runs are quick and easy to install without drilling studs.

2×3s nailed flat to studs at 16 in. o.c. provide a nailing base for drywall and extra insulation space.

Rigid Foam Exterior

An effective wall for new construction or a remodel features a built-up layer of rigid foam on the exterior. The foam can double as a drainage plane if detailed carefully, but I prefer a ridged sheathing wrap under it as the primary drainage plane. The foam prevents sheathing condensation in winter and controls outside vapor in hot, humid weather.

Cross-Strapped Wall

Adding 2×3s at right angles to the wall studs or rafters provides a thicker cavity and covers most of the framing with a couple of inches of insulation to provide a thermal break. In most cases, this costs less than covering the wall surface with rigid foam but provides less moisture resistance.

Larsen Truss

A Larsen truss can be added to the exterior of a house with little disruption to the inside wall surfaces. Windows and doors can be installed at the new exterior wall surface, with extension jambs to the interior trim. As with any exterior wall, window and door flashing is critical, as is a drainage plane of house-wrap or felt paper under the exterior sheathing.

Original (or new) 2×4 exterior structural wall

Original structural sheathing

Nonstructural vertical trusses built from 2×2s with plywood gussets attached vertically at 16 in. or 24 in. o.c.

Gussets can be replaced by long epoxy-coated screws with rigid-foam blocks as standoffs (upper), or steel L-brackets (lower), on 3-ft. to 4-ft. vertical centers.

Closed-cell foam is sprayed about 3/4 in. shy of batten face to provide drainage space. Lap siding is nailed directly to battens with no need for exterior sheathing.

Exterior sheathing provides a nailing base for siding and protects insulation from wind-washing.

Drainage gap at bottom with insect screening

The preparation of a wall for exterior sprayed foam is similar, but the structure is lighter and faster because the closed-cell foam provides the shear strength to support the battens and siding. This can be installed over sheathing or original siding.

Moisture Control

Whether you're recladding a house or building an addition, don't skimp on moisture control. Good moisture control is just as important as energy improvements. When buildings were uninsulated and leaky, they dried out easily, whether the source of moisture was from indoors or out. Now that houses are built tighter and are better insulated, walls dry more slowly. Pay attention to water management to reduce the risk of serious structural damage or mold. Controlling moisture from both the interior and the exterior is important; interior moisture issues are covered in "Energy Basics" and "Ventilation Systems"; this section will focus on exterior moisture control.

Drainage planes

A large number of building failures result from poor water-management details. Flashing is often sloppy, missing, or ignores the fact that wind and capillary action can drive water uphill or through gaps in the exterior siding. Unless you live in an extremely dry climate, it's best to assume that water *will* get past the cladding, particularly in and around window and door frames.

If you accept that no siding system keeps out all water, the solution is pretty easy: Apply a drainage plane behind the siding. Often called a "weather-resistive barrier" and traditionally composed of housewrap or building paper, the drainage plane helps to keep water that gets behind the siding from soaking into the wall or pouring in at the corner of a window frame.

To be effective, the drainage layer must be waterproof (or at least water-resistant) and be overlapped to shed water running down under the force of gravity. It also must be detailed properly at intersections with roofs, overhangs, and other architectural features. While you install

it, pretend that you're not going to cover it with anything—you should create an effective weather barrier that will shed rain on its own.

The use of building paper as a drainage plane, including the installation details around window and door openings, is nothing new. But because of the marketing message that housewraps are for energy efficiency, those were largely forgotten.

In addition to window and door openings, pay close attention to where a roof connects to a taller, vertical wall. A gable roof that dies into a wall is always vulnerable to water intrusion. Applying a layer of flexible adhesive flashing membrane (ice and water shield) underneath the roofing and siding can help, but sticking it on over the housewrap is asking for trouble. To

Standard adhesive membranes are an alternative to flexible ones or metal or plastic pan flashing. Install a small patch over the corner, then adhere the main piece over it before installing the side strips.

Preparing a Window or Door Opening

Sooner or later, window and door frames leak. To make a window or door opening really waterproof, so water doesn't get into the building frame, carefully prepare each rough opening before installing the unit. Don't depend on adhesive strips stuck on picture-frame-style over nailing flanges—water will leak behind them through the sill, and adhesives fail. Attach the sill strip or pan flashing and the side strips after the housewrap or felt paper is in place, then install the window or door according to the manufacturer's instructions. You can use tape, adhesive flashing strips, silicone, or urethane caulk to seal the side nailing flanges, but leave the bottom flange open to shed water easily. Cut a slit in the housewrap or felt above the head flange and tuck in the head strip. Cover the seam with a piece of good-quality tape or an adhesive strip to hold it in place, but the water repellency won't depend on the adhesive.

This is a summary; there are many good resources available that show step-by-step procedures for flashing windows, including manufacturer's instructions. Window and flashing manufacturers may have varying instructions for specific parts of the process. If they conflict, try to follow the more conservative of the requirements.

Note: In addition to the process and steps for flashing, also verify chemical compatibility of sealant strips or flashing membranes with materials such as housewrap that you plan to adhere them to.

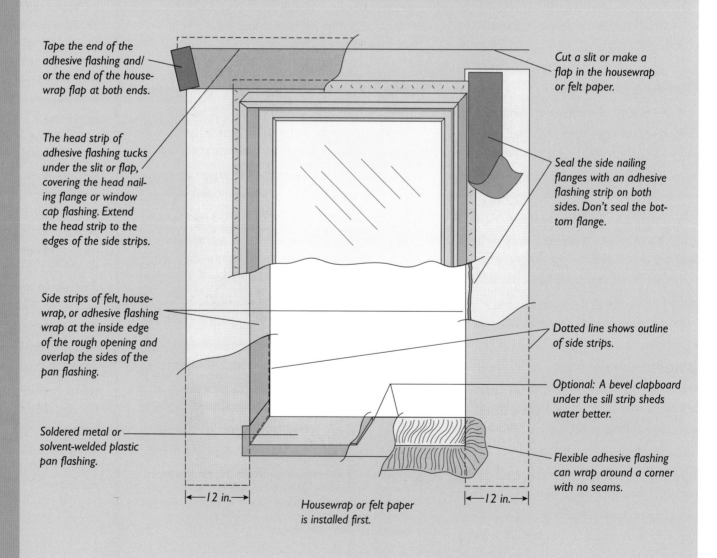

Tape the end of the adhesive flashing and/or the end of the housewrap flap at both ends.

The head strip of adhesive flashing tucks under the slit or flap, covering the head nailing flange or window cap flashing. Extend the head strip to the edges of the side strips.

Side strips of felt, housewrap, or adhesive flashing wrap at the inside edge of the rough opening and overlap the sides of the pan flashing.

Soldered metal or solvent-welded plastic pan flashing.

Cut a slit or make a flap in the housewrap or felt paper.

Seal the side nailing flanges with an adhesive flashing strip on both sides. Don't seal the bottom flange.

Dotted line shows outline of side strips.

Optional: A bevel clapboard under the sill strip sheds water better.

Flexible adhesive flashing can wrap around a corner with no seams.

|← 12 in. →| |← 12 in. →|

Housewrap or felt paper is installed first.

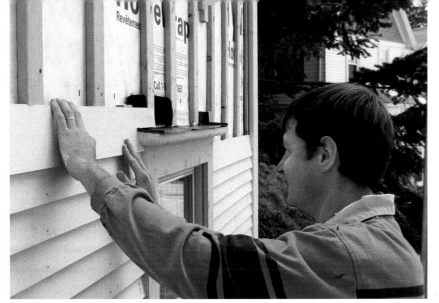

Horizontal clapboard siding can be installed on vertical furring strips mounted 16 in. o.c. Wet siding can dry into the airspace, which is screened at the bottom to keep out insects and allow drainage.

make matters worse, there can be chemical compatibility problems between adhesive membranes and various building papers, including asphalt-impregnated felt paper. The membrane may be installed under the roofing and building papers, but there it's a last line of defense. It's still important to install the other materials to shed water.

For a better solution, make sure the housewrap or building paper on the wall overlaps the adhesive membrane. Better yet, it should also overlap the roof's step flashing to keep water above the roof. If the step flashing is installed after the housewrap or building paper, simply cut a slit a few inches above the top edge of the step flashing, then tuck in a piece of counter flashing that overlaps the step flashing, just as you would above window and door openings (see the bottom photo on p. 187).

Rain screens

You can dramatically enhance the drainage plane by installing a vented drainage space behind the siding. This is called a *rain screen,* and the airspace provides multiple benefits. First, the airspace provides a place for water to drain when it leaks past the siding. Once past the siding, water tends to fall instead of being driven farther into the wall. Second, it equalizes the humidity on both sides of wood siding.

That can be a money saver, because it reduces moisture-related cupping, checking, and paint failure. Finally, when vented at the top and bottom, it helps dry the entire wall.

Rain screens can be used with horizontal siding of any type, as well as with panels and even shingles. If you install more than 1 in. of rigid foam on the exterior, you will get a rain screen automatically because you'll need to use furring attached through the foam to support the siding. Rain screens are less important with vinyl siding, which tends to drain well and does not have paint-durability issues, and they won't be of much benefit in a dry climate (less than 20 in. of rain annually). Stucco finishes should be applied over wire lath that is held off of the building paper by wood strips or special furring nails—never applied directly over plastic housewraps. Alternate approaches include a double layer of felt paper (traditional for stucco) or a felt paper/wire lath combination material that is installed over a set of thin lath strips. Be sure to provide a weep screed at the bottom and flash the drainage layer carefully at window and door openings, just as with any other cladding system.

DETAILING A RAIN-SCREEN WALL

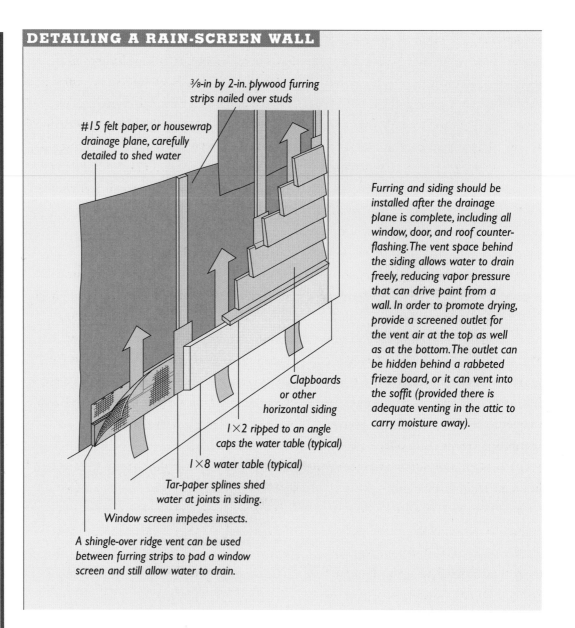

⅜-in by 2-in. plywood furring strips nailed over studs

#15 felt paper, or housewrap drainage plane, carefully detailed to shed water

Furring and siding should be installed after the drainage plane is complete, including all window, door, and roof counter-flashing. The vent space behind the siding allows water to drain freely, reducing vapor pressure that can drive paint from a wall. In order to promote drying, provide a screened outlet for the vent air at the top as well as at the bottom. The outlet can be hidden behind a rabbeted frieze board, or it can vent into the soffit (provided there is adequate venting in the attic to carry moisture away).

Clapboards or other horizontal siding

1×2 ripped to an angle caps the water table (typical)

1×8 water table (typical)

Tar-paper splines shed water at joints in siding.

Window screen impedes insects.

A shingle-over ridge vent can be used between furring strips to pad a window screen and still allow water to drain.

Mechanical Systems (Heat, Air-Conditioning, Hot Water, Ventilation)

If you are investing in remodeling and improving the energy features of your house, you might consider replacing heating and air-conditioning systems at the same time, unless they are recently purchased high-efficiency units. Once you improve the house's energy performance, the heating and cooling loads will be reduced. This is likely true even if you're building an addition and only making modest thermal improvements to the existing house, because the existing system was likely bigger than necessary to begin with. Make sure the installing contractor does a careful heating and/or cooling load calculation as part of the proposal, because right-sized equipment will cost less to install and take up less space.

Another common issue, particularly with additions, is heating and cooling distribution.

If you are improving the thermal efficiency of the rest of the house while building an addition, one option is to reconfigure some of the old distribution system to supply the new living space. The amount of distribution that you need in each room (ducts or baseboard) is directly proportional to the heating or cooling load, so significant thermal improvements can free up a substantial amount of duct capacity. Of course, any distribution system in an unconditioned space should be well insulated, and all new ductwork should be thoroughly sealed with mastic during assembly. Another option is to add a new, separate system for the addition.

Heating and cooling strategy

One thing to consider when planning the mechanical systems during a renovation is simplicity. An energy-efficient addition, or even an entire superinsulated house, can often be served by a very small system. Consider a single ductless mini-split for an addition, or a mini-split with two or three indoor units for a whole house if you are doing a major renovation. Mini-splits have no duct losses, and no ducts to route, and can heat and cool very efficiently in almost any climate (see p. 124). Alternately, a small, centrally located furnace or hydro-air handler can serve an entire highly insulated house with a few small ducts running through inside walls and floors. With a very efficient enclosure, delivering heat and cooling at the outside perimeter isn't necessary; shorter duct runs, and smaller equipment mean smaller ducts that can be fitted into the design more easily.

Another option is a high-efficiency gas water heater or compact boiler to provide heat and hot water for a well-insulated addition or an entire, remodeled home. I prefer a tank-type water heater rather than a tankless. Hot water

from the water heater or boiler can be circulated through radiators, finned-tube baseboards, or radiant floor tubing. Heat can also be distributed through ducts with a fan coil. Some models of fan coil are rated for potable water, so they don't require an extra heat exchanger. This approach also allows for air-conditioning with the same air handler, by utilizing a hydro-air coil with an added air-conditioning evaporator coil.

Planning ventilation

If you're gutting a significant part of your house or adding a lot of new space, don't forget about ventilation. This is a good opportunity to improve a home's ventilation system or add a new one to serve the whole house. It is fairly easy to retrofit a high-quality bath fan and timer or a return makeup air system (see "Ventilation Systems"), especially during a remodel.

This single, high-efficiency water heater, a Vertex™ by Smith®, has plenty of heat capacity to provide all the heat and hot water for this well-insulated remodel. The box at left is a hydro-air handler, which delivers heat from the Vertex or air-conditioning from an outdoor condenser to a small central duct system.

PRO TIP

Even if you are adding square footage to your house, you may not need a larger heating or cooling system; make sure the installer does a careful load calculation.

WHAT CAN GO WRONG

I once did an energy consultation for customers who were doubling the size of their house by adding a second floor. The plumber had already taken the hot-water boiler away, even though it was fairly new and efficient, saying that it would never be big enough to heat the expanded house. It's too bad, because my calculations showed the heat loss on the finished house to be less than 35,000 Btu per hour, *less* than the original, uninsulated house of half the size. To top it off, the new boiler was about the same as the original; if they were going to spend the money, they should have at least gotten a higher-efficiency model.

ELECTRONICS, APPLIANCES, AND LIGHTING

1 The Impact of Lights and Appliances
p. 196

2 Electronics
p. 199

3 Appliances
p. 201

4 Lighting
p. 204

Electronics, appliances, and lighting represent a significant part of the average family's energy budget: almost 45 percent of the energy dollars spent in homes across the country. Although the actual electrical consumption of most individual lights and appliances is small, most houses have a lot of them, which can add up. In addition, every house has a few major appliances that account for a large share of the total electricity consumption. Here is where thoughtful planning about how you use appliances and lights—and some inexpensive controls—can make a big difference.

Smart shopping can also help. Whenever you buy an appliance, select a product that offers performance you need but uses less power. One energy-efficient light bulb can save from $20 to over $300 over its lifetime. This chapter will discuss where and how to get the most for your energy dollar from the appliances, electronics, and lighting in your home. ▶ ▶ ▶

The Impact of Lights and Appliances

Appliances, electronics, and lights (or *plug loads*) are an important piece of the energy picture in houses. Plug loads account for 67 percent of the electricity used in homes, and 43 percent of energy dollars spent. That's more money than heating, which is the next largest category at 28 percent. The inefficiency of our electric system means that plug loads actually use more fossil fuel than any other residential energy use, and it's also the dirtiest category: 45 percent of our electricity is generated from burning coal, which generates more greenhouse gases and toxic emissions than other fossil fuels. In total, 48 percent of the source energy used in homes, which is the fossil fuel energy that is either used on site or burned at a power plant, goes to power our plug loads.

Appliance use is also rising steeply. From 1978 to 2005, the total energy used by U.S. homes stayed almost constant, but plug loads almost doubled, from a 17-percent share to 31 percent. Most households have many more plug-in devices than ever before: televisions, set-top boxes and game consoles, home office gear, chargers for cell phones and gadgets of all kinds, as well as more and larger appliances such as refrigerators and amenities like swimming pools.

So efficient appliances, and the efficient use of appliances, have a large potential for savings. Efficient plug loads not only save electricity (and money) while you use them, but they also produce less waste heat, which saves on air-conditioning expense as well. All that savings leads to even larger environmental benefit: Because it consists almost entirely of electricity use, home-appliance energy use is about on par with heating, water heating, and air-conditioning combined in contributing to climate change and air pollution.

How much am I using?

We tend to be fairly aware of a home's heating or cooling system, because we can feel when it's running. We can see when a light is turned on

NATIONAL ENERGY USE: HOUSEHOLD ANNUAL EXPENSES

Although refrigeration, lighting, and appliances represent only 31 percent of all energy used by residences nationwide, they consume 43 percent of the energy dollars of the average household (including apartments). The actual percentages may vary substantially, depending on the climate and the habits of an individual family, but these figures leave significant room for improvement. (Source: U.S. Department of Energy, Residential Energy Consumption Survey [RECS], 2005.)

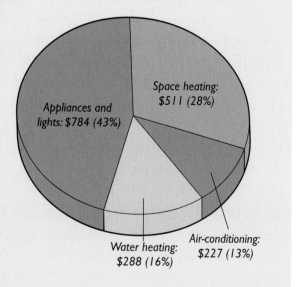

Space heating: $511 (28%)

Appliances and lights: $784 (43%)

Water heating: $288 (16%)

Air-conditioning: $227 (13%)

or when the dryer is used. But many appliances operate quietly in the background, chugging away and using electricity without really being noticed. What matters most with any electrical appliance or lighting use is the overall consumption of electricity, or *usage*.

Usage is defined by the size of a load and the amount of time it runs. The size of an electrical load is the amount of power it uses at a given moment—for example, 10 watts, 200 watts, or 1,200 watts. Large loads that run for very short periods (a few seconds or minutes at a time) may actually consume very little electricity. (Think of an SUV, or even a tractor-trailer cab, parked in your driveway. If you never drive it, it won't consume any gas at all, even though the engine power rating is high.) Small loads that run continuously can add up to a lot. The really big consumers are medium or large loads that run frequently and for long periods.

People often base their thinking about electricity usage on their perception of how much something is used. "These two small air conditioners run all the time when it's hot, and they don't keep up with the heat very well. If I got a single bigger unit that didn't have to run as much, that would surely save on my electric bill. Right?" Not exactly. It would save energy only if the bigger unit was significantly more efficient: Does it provide the same Btus per hour of cooling for fewer kilowatt-hours (kWh) of input? My new Energy Star refrigerator had a notice in the instructions that said not to be concerned that the refrigerator runs for long periods of time, because it's designed with a small motor that is meant to run for longer periods to save energy. In some cases, such as swimming-pool pumping, simply installing a smaller motor and running it longer can save a large portion of the cost for that appliance.

How Much Electricity?

The amount of electricity used by a device depends on its power in watts and on the amount of time it operates. Electricity consumption is measured in kilowatt-hours, which equals power (in thousands of watts) × hours. A hair dryer that uses 1,200 watts and runs for 15 minutes each day uses 1.2 kW × 0.25 hr = 0.3 kWh per day. At a rate of $0.15 per kWh, that adds up to about $1.40 per month (0.3 × 0.15 × 30). Compare that to a 60-watt light bulb that runs all day: 0.06 kW × 24 = 1.44 kWh per day, or $6.50 per month. You can reduce the consumption by replacing it with a more efficient bulb, by reducing the run time, or both.

How do I know how much?

The most detailed information most people get about their electricity use is a single number, once a month: your total household electric consumption, in kilowatt-hours, that you see on your bill. If you want to figure out where your electricity dollars are going every month, an electricity monitor can help you identify what users are costing you the most.

Plug-in monitor The Kill a Watt®, Conserve Insight™, or Watts Up?™ Pro (shown in the photo on p. 198) are just a few examples. Plug one into a standard wall socket and it measures the electricity used by whatever is plugged into it. You can watch the display of watts to determine both standby consumption and operating power. Most also measure kWh over time or estimate annual operating costs. Of course, plug-in monitors don't work for hard-wired light fixtures, appliances, or 220-volt devices.

The Kill a Watt (left) and the Conserve Insight (center) are both simple devices that measure the electricity use of any 120-volt device up to 15 amps. Both cost between $20 and $30. The Kill a Watt is more flexible and provides more information; the Insight is simpler to use, and the wired display saves your knees when checking on an out-of-the-way outlet. The Watts Up? Pro is shown at right.

Home-Appliance Electrical Use

The amount of energy a particular appliance uses can vary significantly with the amount and the way it's used, and with the design of the device. This chart shows typical or average usage of most common household appliances, for a house that includes one or more of each category. You can't save what you don't use; the biggest opportunities for savings are from the biggest users.

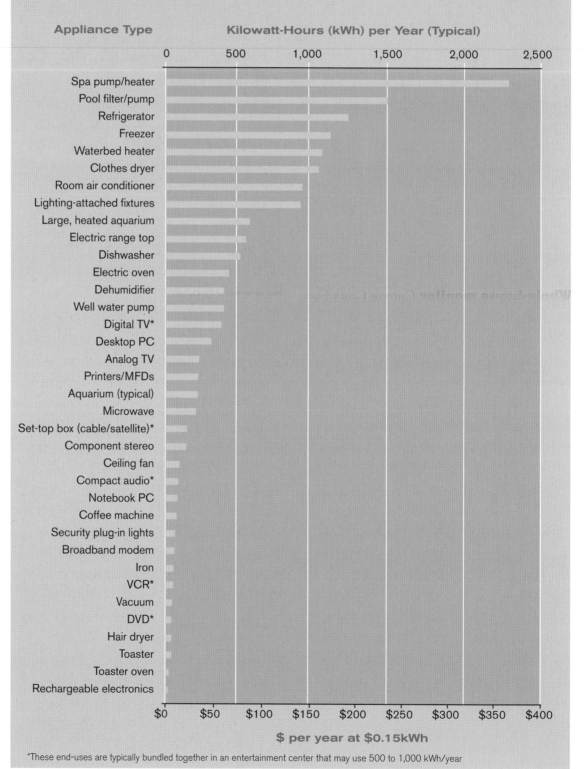

Appliance Type — **Kilowatt-Hours (kWh) per Year (Typical)**

- Spa pump/heater
- Pool filter/pump
- Refrigerator
- Freezer
- Waterbed heater
- Clothes dryer
- Room air conditioner
- Lighting-attached fixtures
- Large, heated aquarium
- Electric range top
- Dishwasher
- Electric oven
- Dehumidifier
- Well water pump
- Digital TV*
- Desktop PC
- Analog TV
- Printers/MFDs
- Aquarium (typical)
- Microwave
- Set-top box (cable/satellite)*
- Component stereo
- Ceiling fan
- Compact audio*
- Notebook PC
- Coffee machine
- Security plug-in lights
- Broadband modem
- Iron
- VCR*
- Vacuum
- DVD*
- Hair dryer
- Toaster
- Toaster oven
- Rechargeable electronics

$ per year at $0.15kWh

*These end-uses are typically bundled together in an entertainment center that may use 500 to 1,000 kWh/year

TV Power

Large-screen TVs use the most energy when they are on. The three biggest factors are technology, screen size, and brightness settings. Plasma TVs use two to three times more energy than LED and LCD screens. Size is a big driver of energy use, but brightness settings also have a large effect ("backlight," if available, and "contrast" or "picture" have the most impact on energy). Calibrating the screen to your home environment can save 20 percent to 50 percent of the electric power used and still provide a high-quality picture.

Whole-house monitor Current Cost's Envi Monitor, Blue Line's Powercost Monitor™, and The Energy Detective™ (photo at right) are some examples. Ranging from about $100 to $250, they monitor whole-house electricity use over time. A sensor connects either inside your main electric panel or outside your electric meter. Some have a Wi-Fi connection for online monitoring, and most have software that analyzes your energy usage over time. Whole-house monitors capture all appliances at once, including hard-wired (such as furnace fan, lighting, central air, or pool pump), but you have to experiment a bit to determine what is using energy at any given time. Some devices can monitor individual circuits in your breaker box simultaneously for a more detailed breakdown, but with a starting price tag of over $600, they are unlikely to pay for themselves in energy savings that you couldn't get with simpler devices.

Web-based services A growing number of Web-based info services can tell you about your home's energy use. Some (like www.MyEnergy.com) allow users to link their account information online, providing efficiency reports over time. Others, like OPower and Tendril, engage utility customers in social networks. By providing information about how you use energy relative to your neighbors, and promoting competition and collaboration for reduced energy use, these free tools can also help motivate people to find savings opportunities.

None of this information will save energy by itself. What these devices can do is help identify the big users; it's up to you to take steps to reduce consumption.

Electronics

You may think that when you turn something off at the switch that it is off. But many consumer electronics, computer equipment, and some appliances don't really turn off. They go into a standby mode, waiting for you to turn the switch back on or to click a remote. The energy used during standby is sometimes called a *phantom* or *vampire* load, creating a slow and steady drain on your electric meter. A standby mode can provide real utility (such as the clock on the coffeemaker that shows you the time and can make your coffee just before you wake up). But they can also be a waste, or in between: A set-top box or DVR needs to be on to record your favorite shows, even if you're not there.

Standby loads

Standby loads for consumer electronics have been dropping rapidly due to voluntary standards like Energy Star in combination with advances in technology. But consumers are buying more

The Energy Detective.

Smart Strips

Many gadgets are available to help manage phantom loads. They all promise to pay for themselves in a year or two, but their impact depends entirely on what's plugged in and how it's used. Any control will save the most when it shuts off larger plug loads; the best opportunities are usually found in groups of devices, like entertainment centers or home offices. Here are the main categories:

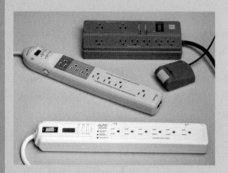

AUTOMATIC CONTROLS

The Smart Strip® (above center) is one of several brands that sense when a "primary" load (such as a computer or TV) is running. When you switch off that primary device, most of the other outlets in the strip automatically shut off power to peripherals such as monitor, printer, DVD player, or game console. Look for a load-sensing device that you can adjust to properly sense the standby or "off" power level of your primary device.

The Watt Stopper® (left, top) uses a motion sensor. When you leave the room or work area, it shuts off six of the outlets after a time delay.

The power strip by APC (left, bottom), has a built-in timer. Use timers for appliances you use during predictable hours, such as home office equipment, or to cut power to a DVR during hours you know you don't need it.

REMOTE CONTROL

Remote controls are flexible and put you in control; they also allow you keep the power cables out of sight, while allowing on/off control from anywhere nearby. The switch for the Belkin® remote power strip (above left) can mount on the wall. The remote outlets (above) from Bye Bye Standby® include six independent on/off buttons; any button can operate multiple outlets.

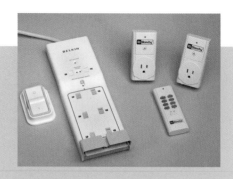

TIME-DELAY

When you click the button on top of this Belkin Conserve Socket (below), the outlet comes on; after a preset time of 30 minutes, 3 hours, or 6 hours, it shuts itself off.

and more electronics every year, so the sheer number of devices tends to offset efficiency improvements. Fortunately, there are many control devices available to help you plug up these energy leaks (see the sidebar above). If you are thoughtful about how you apply these controls, you can save energy, and in some cases even enhance convenience.

Another area of phantom energy use that you can easily control is your computer. In addition to putting peripherals and monitors on a control, you should also avoid screen savers, some of which actually increase energy use. And don't leave the computer on unless it's actually doing something. There's a lingering myth that leaving a computer running reduces wear and tear, but that advice harkens back to a time when hardware and operating systems were unreliable. All modern operating systems include standby or hibernation modes that recover quickly, and actually save wear and tear, while saving electricity. Look for settings such as Power Options or Energy Saver. Note that some standby modes require a small amount of energy, so be sure that your desktop computer is plugged into an always-on outlet so your session is preserved when everything else shuts down.

Appliances

Once you have identified your big electricity consumers, you can use three basic approaches to reduce your appliances' energy usage: Reduce the run time of appliances, improve the energy efficiency of your existing appliances, and buy new appliances that are more energy efficient.

Reducing run time

Reducing appliance run time may be as simple as turning things off when you don't need them. Some big users, such as a pool pump or dehumidifier, may run part- or full-time in the background, where you are not aware of them. In some cases, it may be possible to add a simple control to turn the appliance on only when it is needed, or adjust an existing control to cut the usage without sacrificing utility.

For example, many pool pumps are controlled by a timer to run between 8 and 12 hours per day. But proper filtration and circulation often only takes 4 to 8 hours. It's easy to cut the daily run time to 4 hours for a week or two. If the water starts to get cloudy, increase the run time a bit until it clears; if not, cut it even further until you find an equilibrium. It may need more run time in hot weather; but make sure to cut back when temperatures are more moderate. If you have a heated pool, an insulated cover can save even more—provided you close it when the pool is unoccupied.

To reduce the operating time for a dehumidifier, monitor the humidity level in the air and don't run it more than necessary. Indoor relative humidity should be kept between 30 percent and 50 percent for optimum health, so get a humidity gauge and adjust the dehumidifier to the upper end of that range.

Improving efficiency

It's also possible to improve the efficiency of some appliances. Efficiency can often be

The Modlet: A Control Device with a New Twist

The ThinkEco® Modlet® is both plug-in load monitor and control timer. It plugs into a standard duplex outlet and communicates with your computer via a wireless USB receiver. The Modlet collects information on each outlet and allows and on/off control of each. The included software graphs energy use over time and allows you to set schedules for each outlet. One receiver can control any number of Modlets around the house. The Web-based software and visuals are nice, but at $45 each it's an expensive way to monitor and control loads. One plug-in monitor can help you determine usage, and then you can buy individual controls (see the sidebar on the facing page) for a fraction of the cost. The Modlet does one thing that most other controls don't: It lets you monitor and control loads remotely with a smartphone app.

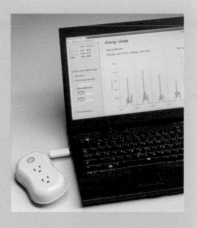

New Energy Star refrigerators use far less energy than old ones, but there is a wide range even within Energy Star models. Larger sizes, through-door services, and side-by-side designs are convenient, but they all use more energy.

increased by simple maintenance or by choosing the proper settings when using appliances.

Refrigeration The refrigerator is typically the biggest electricity user in the kitchen, and is often the largest in the house. If your refrigerator is getting old, it's probably worth replacing it with a new Energy Star model. New, efficient refrigerators use less than half the energy of standard models before 1993. If you are lucky enough to have a refrigerator that dates back to the 1970s or early 1980s and it still runs, take it to the recycle center. Even if it's the spare in the basement or garage, the energy savings will pay for a brand-new unit in just a few years. And buy the smallest, simplest fridge that will meet your needs; large Energy Star models use more electricity than smaller ones; through-door ice and water also use energy.

To keep any refrigerator running right, ensure adequate air circulation around the unit. Keep it a few inches away from the wall, and don't box it in with cabinets. It's a good idea to vacuum the grill periodically, but there is no evidence that vacuuming dust off the coils inside actually saves electricity.

Make sure the door seals are tight, keep the unit away from heat sources (don't put it next to the stove or dishwasher), and check the temperature setting. The refrigerator compartment should stay between 38°F and 42°F, and the freezer between 0°F and 5°F. If you have a power-saving switch, use it. Typically, the switch disables internal heaters that fight condensation; turn it off only if condensation occurs.

Finally, keep refrigerators and freezers reasonably full; they are less efficient when they are nearly empty. Even more important, avoid the temptation to keep the old fridge in the garage or basement for overflow (or the odd six-pack).

Buying a new, highly efficient refrigerator won't save any energy if you keep the old one running! It's a common mistake to assume that if the fridge is only keeping a few items cold it's not working very hard. A refrigerator uses most of its energy keeping the inside of the box cold—even if it's completely empty. If you can't do without it, unplug the spare until you need it to stock up for that holiday gathering. One more buying tip: A manual-defrost chest freezer uses far less energy than an upright, auto-defrost unit. Modern, airtight chest freezers rarely need defrosting, and are less likely to damage food with freezer burn.

Laundry Washing clothes uses energy in three ways: Washers and dryers have motors that move clothes and water; washers use hot water, which is heated with gas or electricity; and dryers heat

Don't use indoor dryer vents like this one. In addition to the moisture load, if you have a gas dryer you may dump carbon monoxide indoors. To reduce dryer energy, buy an efficient washer instead.

This dryer vent outlet is clogged with lint. Anything that interferes with the airflow of the dryer hose or outlet reduces its efficiency.

Horizontal-Axis Washers

Most new Energy Star–rated clothes washers are front-loading, horizontal-axis units. They save energy by using less water and by using gravity instead of brute force to agitate the clothes. They also spin out more of the water, saving dryer energy. They do a better job of cleaning while using less detergent, and they're easier on clothes, too. The top of the washer can be used to stack the dryer, or both can be set atop stands. Although it will cost more than a regular washer, the energy savings should offset the extra cost in 4 to 8 years.

Front-loading clothes washers use less water and less energy and are easier on your clothes.

clothes to dry them out. When you do a load of laundry, pay attention to the washer settings. Always use a cold-water rinse, and use a warm or cold wash for loads when you can. A warm/cold cycle uses about half as much total energy as a hot/cold cycle.

Also, pay attention to the size of the load; fill, but don't overload, the machine for best efficiency. If you do run a smaller load, set the wash level appropriately. The settings on your washer also affect drying time. Use the fastest spin setting whenever you can, to remove the most water.

For dryer efficiency, keep the lint filter clean, and check the outlet periodically for lint that may be clogging the vent. If your dryer hose is kinked, twisted, or too long, replace it with as short and direct a run as possible, preferably with a straight sheet-metal duct instead of a flexible vinyl or aluminum duct. Try to run several loads in succession to take advantage of retained heat, and fill, but don't overload, the machine. Of course, if the weather's good, you can also dry clothes outside on a line.

Dishwasher You can minimize dishwasher energy by paying attention to the settings.

Don't use the "Heavy" or "Pots and Pans" cycle unless you really need to. A fast scraping or rinsing of dishes (especially starchy stuff) does help the dishwasher do a better job, so you can use the "Light" setting. But always use cold water for pre-rinsing. Use a premium dishwasher detergent, and let the dishwasher do the job it's designed for: cutting grease. Wait until the machine is full before using it: It uses the same amount of energy whether you wash one dish or thirty. Many new dishwashers have sensors that stop the machine as particulates in the water clear (indicating that the dishes are clean). If you don't have to take the dishes out right away, you can run the machine with the "Air-Dry" setting (sometimes called "Energy Saver").

It's okay to use the dishwasher: In fact, research shows that even careful hand washing uses more hot water and soap than a modern

dishwasher. And today's very efficient dishwashers are reasonably priced—there are Energy Star–rated dishwashers at every point in the price spectrum.

Smart shopping for new appliances

Minimum efficiency regulations for new appliances have increased over the years, so even the least-efficient new models typically use much less energy than appliances that are 10 or more years old.

In most cases, it's not cost-effective to go out and buy new, energy-efficient products just to save energy. Two exceptions to this rule are older refrigerators and dehumidifiers. For other appliances, look for the most efficient products available when you do go shopping—and always choose an Energy Star–labeled appliance at a minimum. It's worth some research in advance; even within the Energy Star labeling program, there can be a wide range of efficiency. For example, to get an Energy Star label, refrigerators must save at least 20 percent over federal standards, but some models save over 50 percent. Also, minimum requirements vary with features: A side-by-side model with through-door ice can use almost 50 percent more than a top-freezer model without ice—even though both are Energy Star rated. Listings of efficiency levels by model number for most Energy Star products are available at www.energystar.gov/products.

Finally, keep your eyes open for utility rebate programs or other promotions. Local electric utilities often provide financial incentives for consumers to buy more efficient appliances. Incentives may include coupons, mail-in rebates, or point-of-sale discounts; some programs even pick up and dispose of older, inefficient refrigerators or other appliances.

Lighting

There are two basic approaches to making the lights in your home more efficient: eliminate unnecessary usage and use the most efficient products available. Many of us heard the message "turn off lights when you're not using them" while we were growing up. Of course, how much light you need is a matter of eyesight and personal taste. Turning off a light isn't always a practical solution, except when you leave the room—then there's no excuse.

One of the best ways to eliminate unnecessary light usage is with controls. Regularly used indoor lights can be put on timers or occupancy sensors so they aren't left on for hours when no one is using them. Exterior walkway and security lighting can be put on a combination of timers, motion sensors, or photocell controls to minimize their use while ensuring that they are on whenever needed.

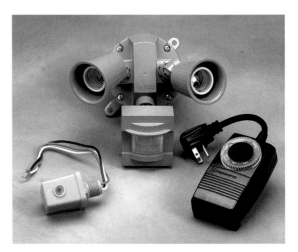

Controls such as photocells, motion sensors, and timers (left to right) can automatically turn indoor or outdoor lights on and off when needed, reducing waste. Most are available at hardware stores and home centers for hard-wired or plug-in applications.

Efficient lighting

To maximize the efficiency of your existing light fixtures, replace any high-use bulbs with efficient ones. There are two main categories of efficient lighting: compact fluorescent (CFL) lamps, and light-emitting diode (LED) lamps. Both are more expensive than incandescent bulbs, but they save two-thirds to three-quarters of the electricity for the same amount of light, and they last much longer than regular bulbs. That saves money in the long run, and it can also save a lot of hassle replacing lamps in hard-to-reach places.

Compact fluorescents

Today's CFL lamps are smaller, more reliable, and have a much better quality of light than anything that was available in the 1990s. Prices have dropped to as low as a dollar or two each, and CFLs are available in virtually any retail outlet where you can find an ordinary bulb. There are more options than ever before, including low and high light outputs, dimmable lamps, candelabra lamps, and three-way lamps. However, CFLs have some drawbacks: As they have gotten cheaper, their longevity has dropped (though they still last longer than regular bulbs). The quality of light, although much better than the CFLs of yesteryear, is typically best kept behind a lampshade or frosted-glass diffuser, or in a recessed fixture. Even the best of today's CFLs have to warm up for up to a minute to reach their full brightness, and some bulbs may not start at all in extreme cold. CFLs also contain tiny amounts of mercury, which costs extra to recycle properly, and they can be hard to clip a lampshade on. Despite these drawbacks, CFLs are affordable, efficient, and a great option for a majority of lighting needs.

The popular torchiere-type floor lamps typically come with 300-watt halogen lamps, which not only use a lot of electricity but also can be a fire hazard. Many types of CFL torchieres are available with dimmers or three-way switches; they save energy and reduce fire risk.

Compact fluorescent lamps come in many shapes and sizes and range in price from about $2 to $15. Always look for the Energy Star label.

LED Lighting

LED lighting technology is developing rapidly. In just a few years, a number of good-quality LEDs have become available (though they are still expensive). The products will keep getting better, and prices will continue to drop, over the next few years at least.

LEDs are fundamentally different than other light sources. An LED is a semiconductor—basically, a tiny computer chip—that generates light. LEDs have been around for decades in electronic equipment displays and status lights, but by nature a single LED generates a focused point-source of light in a single, saturated color such as red, yellow, or blue. Getting an LED to look like an incandescent bulb is a challenge; most manufacturers combine many LEDs of different colors to approximate warm, yellow-white light and to disperse the light in a useful pattern.

LED bulbs are still expensive. Good-quality LEDs with light output equivalent to a 40-watt to 60-watt bulb cost about $20 to $40. But their rated lifetime ranges from 25,000 to 50,000 hours (that's 8 to 16 years at 8 hours/day), three to six times longer than most CFLs. The combination of very long life and higher efficiency increases the savings compared to CFLs. The cost-effectiveness will only improve as the technology evolves and prices drop.

These are my current favorites for dimmable, screw-in LEDs (left to right): two levels of Philips® EnduraLED™ are 40W and 60W equivalents; The dimmable LSG Definity® (also 60W equivalent) "warm white"; and Sharp®'s 40W-equivalent, remote-controlled "mood light bulb".

LSG and Philips make numerous other LED styles, including dimmable globe lamps (center), flame-tip lamps (left), and others. Small reflector lamps like this 2.2W PAR20 by Maxlite® (right) are good for track fixtures to provide background light.

These bulbs from GE®, LSG, Philips, and TCP (left to right) range from 17W to 20W and replace 60W to 75W of incandescent. The GE is the brightest, and the others are all dimmable.

SWITCH is a new line of innovative LED lamps: fully dimmable, screw-in replacements for 40-Watt, 60-W, 75-W, and 100-W bulbs as well as a 3-way lamp. www.switchlighting.com

Applications of LED and CFL lamps

Because of their higher up-front cost and long life, LEDs save the most money when they replace those lights that are most used. I recommend LEDs for any lights that are used at least 3 to 4 hours every day, and also in any light fixtures that are very difficult to reach—$20 isn't much if it saves you a visit to the chiropractor (or the emergency room). Depending on your habits, hallways, circulation areas, work areas, and children's bedrooms or study areas may be good choices. Lights that are on a security timer are good candidates, too, as well as any that are regularly left on when nobody's around (whether by accident or on purpose).

Color Temperature

Many efficient lamps have a rating for "color temperature." This relates the color of the light output, ranging from warm to cool. Expressed in degrees Kelvin, most lamps dial in somewhere between 2,500 and 6,000. I consider 2,700 a good target for warm, yellow-white glow that looks like an incandescent bulb. A rating of 3,000 is a bright white (like a well-lit office), and 4,200 is cool white, like older fluorescent tubes. Daylight lamps range from 5,000 to 6,000.

Most lighting manufacturers offer interior CFL fixtures in a wide variety of styles. Always look for the Energy Star logo.

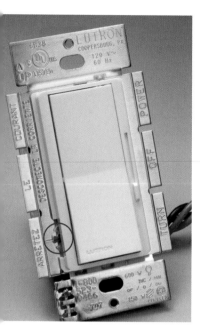

This dimmer switch in Lutron®'s C-L series uses an adjustment wheel hidden behind the cover plate (circled) to control the dimming range. This avoids problems seen with some dimmable CFLs and LEDs, such as flickering, unexpected shutoff, or trouble turning on.

This 10.5W LED insert by CREE® (roughly 50W equivalent output) is a great way to save on lighting energy and also reduce air leakage through standard 6-in. recessed cans.

Then, replace pretty much all the rest of your incandescent bulbs with CFLs. Exceptions include specialty fixtures where CFLs don't fit (note that both CFLs and LEDs are readily available with candelabra bases); bulbs that are rated for special locations, like oven lights; and halogen pendant or track lights.

Electric utility companies often promote energy-efficient lighting, so watch for rebates or promotions, or check online to find out what your local utility has to offer.

Efficient light fixtures

In addition to screw-in CFL and LED lamps, you can also purchase fixtures with built-in CFLs. CFL fixtures typically include the ballast (the electronic component that runs the fluorescent light) and a plug-in pin base for the lamp. Pin-base replacement lamps are usually less expensive than the screw-in types, because they don't include the ballast. CFL fixtures are good candidates to replace any high-use lighting fixtures in the home, particularly ones that you are planning to update anyway. They can also replace high-use fixtures for which you can't find a CFL screw-in bulb that fits properly.

CFL fixtures come in hundreds of styles and sizes, including wall sconces, ceiling-dome fixtures, pendant lights, recessed cans, exterior-wall fixtures, and floodlights. Prices are typically $20 to $30 higher than an equivalent standard light

Lumens

Lumens refers to the light output level, or brightness, of a light bulb or lamp. This chart shows the approximate lumens for common wattage levels of incandescent bulbs, as well as the wattages of typical CFLs and LEDs with equivalent light output.

Electrical Power Consumption, Watts (W)			Light Output (lumens)
Incandescent	CFL	LED	
40	9-13	8-10	450
60	13-15	12-15	800
75	18-25	17-20	1,100
100	23-30	20 +	1,600
150	30-52	*	2,600

*LED lamps with to 150W equivalent light are not commonly available as of this writing.

Many types of wall-mounted exterior fixtures are also available with built-in CFLs.

fixture, and styles range from utilitarian economy models to some pretty fancy ones. Beware of CFL fixtures that don't have the Energy Star label. Although they may save energy, some tend to be cheaply made and are unreliable.

LED light fixtures, on the other hand, are available only in certain designs. LEDs excel for some specialty applications: Fixtures such as undercabinet light strips, accent lighting, and landscape lighting are easy to find.

SAFETY FIRST

Most compact fluorescent lamps take a little longer to start in very cold conditions (below 25°F). That may be hazardous if you use them for exterior lighting—for instance, if you flick on the light just to run out on an icy sidewalk to grab the newspaper or round up the dog. If you live in an area with very cold winters, it's better to use LEDs outdoors.

RENEWABLE AND ALTERNATIVE ENERGY

With increasing concern about climate change and rising fuel prices, the production and use of renewable energy has been growing by leaps and bounds in America since the mid-1990s. Renewable energy is an important part of our energy future, but it is not a panacea: It's almost always cheaper to reduce your energy needs first. Then consider using renewables to power some, or all, of the needs that remain. This chapter is not a hands-on guide to installing renewable energy systems; that is beyond the scope of this book. Rather, it offers a look at some common alternative energy systems and how they work and guidance on what to look for and what to avoid.

Renewable energy in a home can take many forms, from simple (daylighting and passive solar heating) to complex (solar electric, wind, or small hydro systems). And renewable energy systems are not free to operate and maintain, though some come close. ▶ ▶ ▶

Photovoltaics: Solar Electricity

In the wake of the energy crises of the 1970s, solar electricity was touted as a solution to take us into the 21st century. Solar electricity, or *photovoltaics* (PV), has seen rapid growth since the mid-1990s as worldwide production of photovoltaics has grown exponentially and prices have dropped dramatically. Aided by state and federal tax credits, PV systems have seen widespread applications on homes, businesses, schools, and other buildings.

PV basics

Solar electricity is produced by silicon *solar cells,* thin wafers of semiconductor film. Each cell is several inches across, and when exposed to direct sunlight produces a DC electric current—the same type that is found in flashlight and automobile batteries.

Cells are grouped together into units called *modules,* usually rated between 50 watts and 300 watts. The cells are attached to a tempered-glass covering and frame for weather protection and mounting. Usually, several modules are mounted together in a PV *array* to provide the total desired power. Because PV modules produce DC power, an *inverter* is used to transform this output into 120-volt AC, the standard that is used in homes. (Some PV arrays are used to power DC loads directly, but that has limited use in most houses.) Along with associated wiring, circuit breakers, and safety disconnect switches, these components make up the PV system.

Most residential PV systems are connected directly to the home's electrical system and help offset electricity use. In most states, any excess electricity generated by a PV system is fed back

PV arrays can be ground-mounted if there isn't a suitable roof area on which to install them. These "tracking" ground-mounts also follow the sun each day to squeeze out some extra output, a cost-effective strategy in very sunny climates. In many cases, it's cheaper to install more panels for the same output than it is to buy a tracking mount.

Net Metering

At least 33 states have laws requiring electric utilities to purchase power generated by small residential PV installations at the same retail price the customer pays. This is called *net metering*; it means that whenever the PV array is producing more power than the house is using, the meter actually turns backward. In some states, the homeowner does not get the full retail rate for excess power generated. See www.irecusa.org/irec-programs/connecting-to-the-grid/net-metering for the latest state-by-state summary.

to the utility grid, effectively turning the electric meter in reverse. It's important to arrange for the proper hookup with the utility provider; the proper safety and metering equipment must be in place to protect utility workers. Any home-based, grid-connected power-generation equipment must either shut down or disconnect automatically in the case of a general power outage so electricity can't "back-feed" onto wires where workers don't expect it.

Photovoltaics can also be configured in a stand-alone, independent system with battery storage to provide electricity when the sun isn't shining. Although this may make sense on an isolated site where a line extension would cost big bucks, it rarely makes sense for a home that has access to utility power. The added expense and complexity of a stand-alone system is more of a liability than an advantage; the utility grid provides cheaper, safer, and more reliable short-term "storage" for electricity than batteries. And it won't get you through a power outage of more than a few hours. Although it might power a laptop and a few efficient light bulbs, a gas generator is far cheaper and better suited to run essentials like the refrigerator, stove, heating system, and well pump. Instead of buying enough batteries to power a home for a couple of days once every few years, invest in energy efficiency improvements that will save energy and money all year.

PV economics

Although the price continues to drop, PV-generated electricity still costs more than grid power. A utility-interconnected system now costs between $4 and $8 per peak watt installed, so a small system rated for 1,000 watts (1 kW) may cost $4,000 to $8,000 installed (battery back-up systems run at least double that cost).

The wiring for a PV system can be complex and needs to be done by a licensed contractor who understands the specific requirements of the National Electric Code. In addition to circuit breakers, controls, and switching hardware, the two white boxes on the lower right are the inverters that transform the DC voltage to 120-volt AC.

This system will produce 1,000 to 1,700 kilowatt-hours (kWh) per year, depending on your site, climate, and latitude, or roughly $150 to $300 worth of electricity; that's still a pretty long payback. But with a wide range of rebates and tax credits that reduce costs, falling PV prices, and rising electric rates, PV is starting to be a very attractive investment in its own right.

The National Renewable Energy Lab (NREL) has a free online calculator (www.nrel.gov/rredc/pvwatts) that can give you a good idea of how much electricity you'll get from a system in your location; for information about tax incentives and other federal, state, and utility incentives, see www.dsireusa.org. A professional site assessment is important before installing any type of PV system; an experienced consultant or contractor can help estimate projected output for your site and help to ensure that you are

IN DETAIL

A friend who designs and installs PV systems for a living says that many of his clients don't get serious about conserving electricity until after they have installed a PV system. Only *after* they see firsthand what a small contribution the new equipment really makes do they really focus on their lighting and appliance efficiency, and their habits.

Building codes regarding PV installations are still developing and regulations vary by state or municipality. The most consistently used standard for PV installations includes Article 690 of the National Electrical Code. Be sure that anyone proposing to install a PV system is a licensed contractor and that they obtain the proper permits and adhere to any relevant codes. The Interstate Renewable Energy Council (IREC) maintains a state-by-state database of licensing requirements for PV installations at: www.irecusa.org/irec-programs/workforce-development/solar-licensing-database. Of course, always check with your local building official before you start.

A SOLAR ELECTRIC SYSTEM

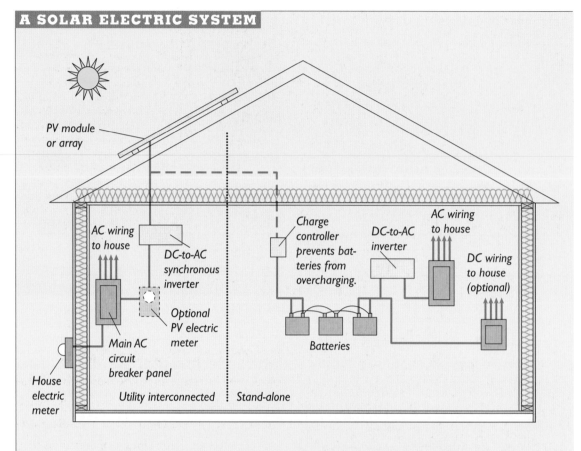

PV module or array

AC wiring to house

DC-to-AC synchronous inverter

Optional PV electric meter

Main AC circuit breaker panel

House electric meter

Utility interconnected

Charge controller prevents batteries from overcharging.

DC-to-AC inverter

Batteries

Stand-alone

AC wiring to house

DC wiring to house (optional)

A residential PV installation typically has an inverter to convert the DC voltage from the modules to the AC voltage commonly used in homes. The utility-connected system has a synchronous inverter that tracks the grid power. It shuts down during a power outage so PV-generated voltage can't endanger utility workers trying to repair the line. This type of system doesn't produce usable power unless the grid is operating and the sun is shining.

The stand-alone PV system doesn't need a synchronous inverter and can run anytime. Many off-grid systems include a mix of AC and DC wiring, so some appliances can run without the inverter.

Note: Fused disconnects and other safety components omitted for clarity. Regulations for connecting to utility power vary by state and utility company.

accessing all available incentives. Some other factors that may limit the viability of a system include shading, age or condition of your roof, and the level of efficiency of the house.

Is it a good idea to install a PV system? It depends. Because PV power is expensive, reducing your energy loads is almost always cheaper and provides greater energy savings. On the other hand, when compared to the incremen-

tal cost of some of the "deepest" building-shell retrofits, PV can be both financially and environmentally attractive. PV systems create virtually no pollution over their useful lifetime, and require little or no maintenance—there are no moving parts. Large numbers of small PV systems on rooftops help create a less centralized energy supply that is more efficient and less vulnerable to disruptions. So start by sealing,

Some PV modules are designed for direct integration with roofing systems. Configured to substitute for conventional shingles or slates, or in strips that lie flat between the seams of a standing-seam metal roof, these systems can provide PV electricity with a lower profile.

With a professional site assessment to measure solar access, the average annual production of electricity by a PV array can be predicted pretty accurately.

insulating, replacing your mechanical systems, and replacing lights and appliances with efficient models. PV is a viable option—when seen as part of an overall plan to make your home as efficient as possible.

Solar Thermal Systems

Unless you live on top of a hot spring or a natural gas well, the only "free" heat source is solar. South-facing windows provide direct solar heating whenever the sun shines, which truly is free if you consider that you need windows anyway. If you are renovating or adding on to a house, incorporating passive solar concepts in your plan is a great way to decrease your annual heating load (see "Windows").

The sun's energy can also be used to *actively* heat homes and hot water, though with more initial investment. Regardless of which solar approach you use, it always makes sense to invest in efficiency first. Any system that provides heat or hot water will be less expensive, and produce more of what you need, if you reduce the loads first.

Sunrooms and solar greenhouses

It may be tempting to buy or build a solar greenhouse or sunroom "kit," but beware of claims about comfort and energy savings. Rooms with a lot of glass look great in a photo,

Despite the high cost, the PV power industry is gaining momentum; the industry is growing at a rate of 25 percent per year worldwide. Photovoltaics are now in common use for portable power applications, provide electricity in developing countries, and are increasingly common in the United States in residential, commercial, and municipal-scale installations. Prices keep dropping, fueled by increased manufacturing capacity, lower costs for components, easier permitting, and less need for customized designs.

In addition to government incentives, many electric utilities offer subsidies for PV installations. PV reduces demand during summer air-conditioning peak hours and reduces pollution and other environmental problems related to power generation. With subsidies of $3 to $6 per installed watt, the net cost per unit of electricity to the consumer can be comparable to power bought from the utility.

WHAT CAN GO WRONG

Look out for what I call solar gimmicks: cheap, easy-to-install solar "collectors" that mount on the outside of south-facing walls and which are supposed to siphon solar heat into a room. Most of these products have no reliable controls or dampers, and can overheat the room when you don't need it. You're usually better off installing a real, energy-efficient window to capture solar gains.

Simple, added-on sunroom kits can bring light and space to a dark, dull house but may come at a price: overheating in mild sunny weather, and discomfort, condensation, and mold when it's cold.

Installer Certification

The North American Board of Certified Energy Practitioners (NABCEP) provides the most widely accepted installer certification program for solar PV systems in the United States. NABCEP also certifies PV technical salespeople, solar thermal installers, and small-wind-system installers. See www.nabcep.org.

but they can be uncomfortable as glass temperatures drop when the sun goes down. And they often overheat when temperatures are mild. Although it's important for serious plant-growing, overhead glass magnifies these problems by capturing solar gain in the summer, but little or no useful gain in the winter.

When planning a sunroom addition, try to orient it so most of the vertical glass faces south (or within 45 degrees of south), and reduce or eliminate overhead glass and skylights. Choose high-performance glass appropriate to your climate. For any addition with lots of glazing, include interior shades to reduce overheating, and use a patio door or other transition to the main house that you can close off so the sunroom isn't a liability when it's cold outdoors and the sun isn't shining.

Trombe walls—masonry walls that separate large areas of south-facing glass from living space—are another passive solar strategy that has proven difficult to design and build correctly. They simply don't work in most Northern U.S. climates; you're much better off investing in more insulation and air-sealing or better windows.

Active solar space heating

Active solar systems use pumps or fans to move heated water or air from a collector to a thermal storage area, usually a water storage tank or (in the case of an air-based system) a concrete or stone mass. Typically, air-based systems are site-built and integrated into a building during construction. Air-based systems are difficult to design and build properly. I much prefer water-based systems because water can store a lot more heat in a smaller volume and because it's easier to contain and control. I've seen many air-based systems that don't work at all—many *increase* the heating load due to flaws, and few are really effective.

This sunroom used to overheat in summer when the sun was high overhead, but the installation of mirrored light shelves cut the excess heat. The spaces in between let light through and still admit significant solar gain in winter when the sun is low.

Manufactured solar hot-water collectors are typically used to heat domestic hot water but can also be used as a supplement to or even a primary source of space heat. Systems sized for space heating need much larger collector areas and storage tanks and are unlikely to be cost-effective for most homes—especially retrofits. In fact, one way to view the tradeoff is to consider the necessary storage. To store enough energy to heat even a very efficient house for several cloudy days, you need a large collector and a big storage tank, which will cost many thousands of dollars. For a similar investment, you could install PV, effectively "bank" the solar electricity from the summer,

and heat your house with a high-efficiency ductless heat pump (see p. 124), without sacrificing a whole room for a hot-water storage tank. I generally prefer a modest-size solar thermal system to supply domestic hot water, *after* improving efficiency and reducing demand as much as you can.

The basics of solar hot water

Most solar water heating systems use either *flat plate* or *evacuated tube* collectors mounted on a roof or freestanding frame. A working fluid runs through the collector and actually brings the heat into your stored hot water; this fluid may be the home's potable water (an open-loop or *direct* system), or a separate loop of water or antifreeze (a closed-loop or *indirect* system). Open-loop systems are prone to freezing and are typically only used in the warmest climates.

The flat-plate hot-water collectors in the center of this roof will supply more than half of the hot-water needs of the two families in this duplex. Note the small PV module in the lower right corner of the collector array; this provides power to the loop pump.

PV or Solar Hot Water: Which Is a Better Value?

At first glance, a modest solar hot-water system looks like a better deal. Compared to a PV array of similar cost, solar thermal produces roughly triple the amount of "raw" annual energy. But for most homes the advantage ends there. PV offsets electricity at roughly three times the energy cost compared with natural gas. Solar electricity also has about three times the environmental impact. Solar thermal systems are more complex, and have higher maintenance costs over time; PV can't leak, freeze, or boil. Finally, solar-thermal domestic water systems need storage, unless you want to take all your showers when the sun is shining. Grid-tied PV systems effectively "store" any excess in the grid, with little efficiency penalty. Tax credits and other incentives vary, and incentives can certainly tip the scales one way or the other. If, rather than natural gas, you're directly offsetting an expensive water-heating fuel like electricity, LP gas, or oil, the solar water heater is much more likely the winner and deserves the priority for investment.

TRADE SECRET

Many "passive-solar" homes have too much south glass. If the south-facing glazed area is greater than 7 percent to 8 percent of the total heated floor area, you need thermal mass to absorb the heat when the sun shines and re-release it slowly at night. Without enough mass, indoor temperatures soar when the sun shines and plummet when it doesn't. It's best to have a slab or tile floor, without carpeting or rugs, in direct sun most of the day. A big masonry fireplace in the middle of your house won't do the job. The mass also needs to be completely insulated from the ground: A ground-coupled slab floor absorbs solar energy during the day, but re-releases more heat into the ground than into the house.

This house has a large array of evacuated-tube collectors. These collectors are more expensive than flat-plate models, but they also collect heat more efficiently. Because the working fluid is contained only in a manifold at the top of each set, there is less fluid, which is well-suited to a drainback configuration.

Local or regional zoning boards or neighborhood homeowners associations may place restrictions on solar hardware and collector placement. Be sure to check with the building inspector's office and other appropriate authorities before installing a system. Also note that at least 39 states have some sort of "solar access" laws, limiting these entities' ability to place restrictions that might effectively prohibit or increase the cost of solar equipment (see www.dsireusa.org/solar/solarpolicyguide/?id=19).

In an indirect system, the working fluid is separated from the potable water by a heat exchanger. Antifreeze such as non-toxic glycol is needed in most indirect systems. Alternately, in a *drainback* system the collector fluid returns to a small storage tank when it's not being heated. If the drainback tank is located in conditioned space where it can't freeze, plain water may be used. Because it requires the extra storage tank

A CLOSED-LOOP SOLAR WATER HEATER

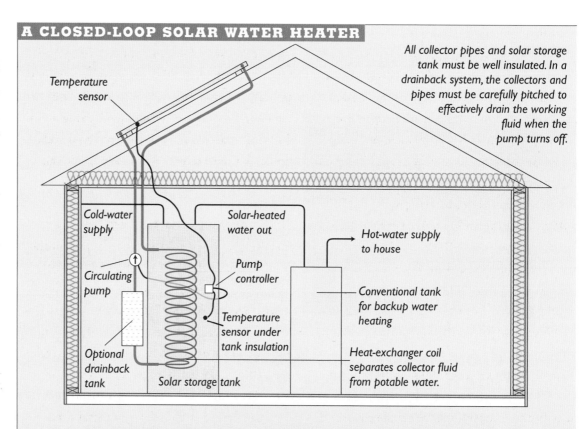

All collector pipes and solar storage tank must be well insulated. In a drainback system, the collectors and pipes must be carefully pitched to effectively drain the working fluid when the pump turns off.

Temperature sensor

Cold-water supply

Circulating pump

Optional drainback tank

Solar storage tank

Solar-heated water out

Pump controller

Temperature sensor under tank insulation

Hot-water supply to house

Conventional tank for backup water heating

Heat-exchanger coil separates collector fluid from potable water.

This is a simplified view of a typical indirect solar water heater. When the controller senses that the temperature in the collector is hotter than that in the storage tank, it turns the pump on. As the hot collector fluid circulates through the heat exchanger, the tank is heated. Alternatively, a solar electric (photovoltaic) module can directly drive a DC pump, eliminating the control system.

The conventional tank provides hot water whenever there is not enough solar heat available; some solar storage tanks contain electric elements for backup water heating, so the second tank is not necessary.

Note: Check valves, air vents, pressure and temperature relief valves, drains, and other components not shown for clarity.

Even in the winter, a deciduous tree can cast up to 40 percent shade on a south-facing façade, seriously reducing the available solar gain for passive heating, solar collectors, or PV. The roof is least likely to be shaded.

INDETAIL

The amount of solar hot water you'll get depends on the size of the collector, the amount of sunshine in your area, collector orientation and angle of tilt, and outdoor temperature (climate). In cold climates, water heating is usually a seasonal operation, but lower incoming water temperatures also boost efficiency. Short of doing a more detailed analysis, you can start by assuming that a well-sized system will produce something like half the average family's water-heating needs. Just about anywhere, a solar water-heating system will still need a backup heat source, typically an electric or gas-fired water heater.

and a larger circulating pump, drainback systems are slightly more expensive (and require a bit more electricity to operate). However, in a drainback setup the collector only contains fluid when the sun is shining and everything is working properly; this virtually eliminates the chance of costly freezing or boiling in the event of a power outage or sensor failure, reducing common maintenance headaches.

Some solar thermal systems work passively using a thermosiphon. Because this depends on the storage tank being situated above the collectors, this isn't a practical option for many homes. In mild climates, however, a relatively inexpensive system using an integrated storage tank is a viable option.

At an installed cost of about $5,000 to $12,000, a solar water heater is a large investment. Without incentives, the simple payback is likely to be in a range of 10 to 20 years if your water-heating fuel is electricity, oil, or LP gas, and longer if you have natural gas for water heating. Incentives such as tax credits can make this technology much more attractive. Note that www.dsireusa.org lists incentives for solar thermal, as well as PV and other energy-efficiency work. As always, invest in efficiency first, and then plan a solar hot-water system based on the minimum possible load.

I have found a few websites with solar hot-water calculators, but most of them are geared toward sales. Many of them low-ball system costs or make other assumptions that tend to overstate the benefits. I strongly recommend hiring a professional with solar thermal design and installation experience to help if you want to design a system.

Choose a contractor or DIY

Installing a solar hot-water system is not for the faint of heart, but if you are very capable with electrical, plumbing, and general construction skills, it is possible to pull off. Some manufacturers sell kits that include most or all of the components you'll need. But you'll need to be well prepared: *Solar Hot Water Systems* by Tom Lane is a good resource that covers the whole process.

If you decide to choose a contractor for a prospective solar water-heating project, there are several things you should look for. First, the contractor should do a thorough site assessment, interview, and analysis to determine your hot-water needs and to optimize the choice of equipment. Be wary of a "one-size-fits-all" approach, which is often focused more on selling equipment than designing a system to meet your needs. It's a good idea to get at least a couple of bids, and don't assume the lowest price is the

Permitting, zoning, installation, and siting issues are far more complex for wind than for PV. Renew Wisconsin has assembled an impressive array of factual resources called the "Small Wind Toolbox" for homeowners (and others involved in the process, from contractors to municipal authorities) to facilitate navigation of the wide array of issues surrounding the design, installation, and operation of residential wind systems (see www.renewwisconsin.org/wind/windtoolbox.htm). Although developed for Wisconsin, the toolkit is comprehensive and most of it can be applied anywhere.

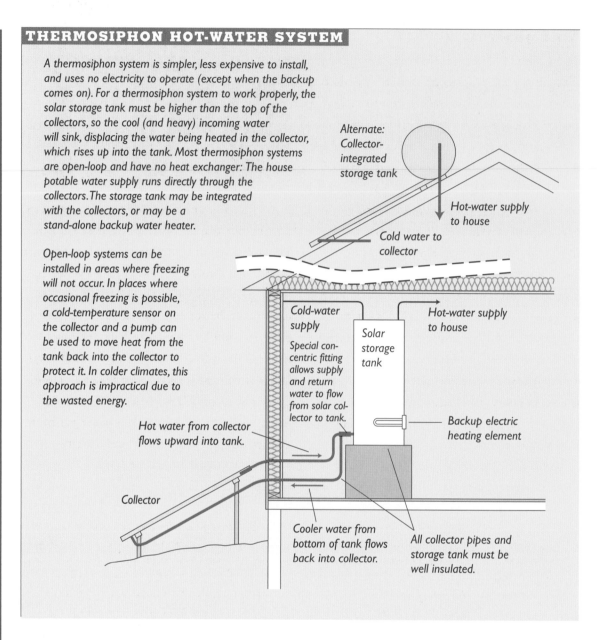

THERMOSIPHON HOT-WATER SYSTEM

A thermosiphon system is simpler, less expensive to install, and uses no electricity to operate (except when the backup comes on). For a thermosiphon system to work properly, the solar storage tank must be higher than the top of the collectors, so the cool (and heavy) incoming water will sink, displacing the water being heated in the collector, which rises up into the tank. Most thermosiphon systems are open-loop and have no heat exchanger: The house potable water supply runs directly through the collectors. The storage tank may be integrated with the collectors, or may be a stand-alone backup water heater.

Open-loop systems can be installed in areas where freezing will not occur. In places where occasional freezing is possible, a cold-temperature sensor on the collector and a pump can be used to move heat from the tank back into the collector to protect it. In colder climates, this approach is impractical due to the wasted energy.

Alternate: Collector-integrated storage tank

Hot-water supply to house

Cold water to collector

Cold-water supply

Solar storage tank

Hot-water supply to house

Special concentric fitting allows supply and return water to flow from solar collector to tank.

Backup electric heating element

Hot water from collector flows upward into tank.

Collector

Cooler water from bottom of tank flows back into collector.

All collector pipes and storage tank must be well insulated.

best value. Bids should be detailed, and the contractor should answer your questions satisfactorily; warranty, service, experience, and references are all important factors to evaluate before signing a contract. Solar hot-water systems need regular maintenance, so be suspicious if an installing contractor claims that system won't need service.

Other Technologies for Electric Generation

Two other ways to produce energy in a home without burning fossil fuels are using a residential-scale wind turbine or hydroelectric generator. Either of these is highly site-specific compared to PV or solar thermal, because they depend on an adequate supply of wind or water.

Wind generators

Small wind generators called turbines are viable for utility-connected residential service if you've got lots of wind and are able to construct a small tower. Wind installations are growing rapidly in the United States, and a new generation of simplified designs for small turbines has improved their reliability and reduced costs. Although it seems obvious, it's worth saying: A wind generator won't produce much power unless it is in a windy location. Residential wind turbines are generally installed on towers because wind speeds are much higher at 60 ft. to 100 ft. from the ground. I would steer clear of products designed for roof mounting because of concerns about noise, vibration, and wind availability. Wind generators, like PV systems, can be connected to utility lines so any excess power is fed back into the grid, subject to the rules established in each state.

A wind assessment is a critical first step before beginning a wind installation. At a site with an annual average of 10 mph to 12 mph wind speed (that's a *lot* of wind), a 2.5-kW to 3-kW turbine might produce 3,000 kWh to 5,000 kWh per year. That is between $400 and $800 worth of electricity in most areas; installed, the turbine may cost $7,500 to $20,000. (Ask yourself: How much of a tower will you need to get it up into that windy zone?) Unsubsidized, wind power still has a pretty long payback—unless you have a lot of wind or very expensive electricity.

This 10-kW wind generator produces over 6,000 kWh per year. In most locations, a tower like the 120-ft. guyed pole shown here is necessary to generate power cost effectively.

Sizing a Solar Hot-Water System

The components of a solar water-heating system must be correctly sized. Collector area is based on the hot-water demand of the particular household. One rule of thumb suggests 40 sq. ft. of collector area for the first two family members, and 8 sq. ft. to 14 sq. ft. extra for each additional person in the north; less area is needed in the "sun belt." Some installers base the collector area on the size of the storage tank, which must be adequate for the collector area. To keep collectors from overheating and damage, use at least 1.5 gal. of storage per sq. ft. of collector area, and at least 2 gal. per sq. ft. in hot, sunny climates. It's better to have too much storage than too little; not only will you reduce overheating, but you'll actually collect more heat.

With any solar water-heating system, the best heat transfer takes place when the temperature difference is largest, so a cold storage tank will accept more Btus per hour of sun than a hot one. This is why adequate storage is so important, and also why it's difficult to design a system to provide much more than half of a family's hot water. If the collectors are sized to keep up in the winter when days are short and cloudy, the tank will overheat in the summer, unless you can dump the excess into a swimming pool or other use.

Although it's difficult (and expensive) to size a solar thermal system to meet all or even most of a cold-climate space-heating load, you can increase the overall efficiency if you tie your solar thermal system into a low-temperature radiant-heating zone so that any time there is a heating load you can use all the available solar heat and wring as much as possible from the storage.

Solar Pool Heating

Solar pool heaters are relatively simple, inexpensive, and widely used. Collectors are less expensive and more efficient than domestic water-heating units. Because pool temperatures are much lower, heat-exchanger efficiency is higher. Solar pool collectors may be unglazed rubber or plastic; they heat the pool water directly using the pool's circulating pump. The pool acts like a drainback tank, so they need no freeze protection or separate storage tanks.

Solar pool heating is a mature industry; installed systems cost less than solar domestic water heaters ($2,000 to $4,000), and generate many more Btus per season. Combined with the relatively high cost of heating such a large volume of water using fossil fuels or electricity, paybacks are typically much faster than solar hot water—roughly 2 to 7 years. To maximize the benefit, it's important to cover the pool when not in use.

WHAT CAN GO WRONG

A traditional masonry fireplace should be considered for its aesthetic value, and not as a heating source. Because of the large amount of air needed to burn correctly, an open fireplace is often a net loss of heat—particularly if the damper is left open overnight (or longer), siphoning away heated air long after the fire dies down.

Small hydro

Hydroelectric or hydro power generation is less expensive to install than a PV or wind system, but because it is so site-dependent, hydro is an even smaller niche than wind in the United States. Hydroelectric power uses the energy of water moving by gravity to generate electricity. Unlike large dams and hydro plants, residential micro-hydro causes little or no habitat destruction or water-quality problems. A small hydro installation on a good site—at least 20 gal. per minute and a 75 ft. drop—can generate 1,000 to 2,000 kWh per year. For an investment of $3,000 to $4,000, this may look slightly better than PV, if you have a suitable site.

SAFETY FIRST

When installing a wood stove, carefully follow manufacturer's instructions and local codes regarding clearances to combustible floors and walls, as well as chimney connection. It's a good idea to have it inspected prior to use.

Solid Fuels

In colonial days, most homes were heated with fireplaces. Wood was plentiful, and virtually free for the taking. Wood is effectively a "renewable" energy source, but wood and other solid-fuel-burning stoves produce both outdoor and indoor air pollution.

Wood stoves

Wood burning isn't free: it costs money, time, or both to bring in a winter's supply. It's not unusual for a homeowner to install a wood stove, use it enthusiastically for a couple of years, and abandon it because of the effort and attention. Wood burning also produces both toxic and environmentally harmful emissions; according to the EPA, wood burning is a significant contributor to air pollution in some urban areas. Emissions are highest in open fireplaces and older wood stoves. Although new stoves have to adhere to federal emissions standards, they are still a source of particulate emissions.

If you're thinking of burning wood regularly to save money on your fuel bill, buy a new, EPA-certified model. To ensure it burns as cleanly as possible, follow a few simple rules: Only burn well-seasoned wood, keep the chimney and stove free of creosote (clean at least once a year, more with regular use), split the logs fairly small, and burn small, hot fires with plenty of air supply. I prefer certified stoves without catalytic converters; they are cheaper to buy and maintain, and probably have lower emissions over their lifetime, than catalytic models. Also, I'd stay away from outdoor wood boilers; they have much lower efficiency and higher emissions than modern, certified stoves.

Pellet stoves

An increasingly popular alternative is the pellet stove, which has several advantages over standard wood stoves. For one thing, they are cleaner, although delivered-heat efficiency is comparable to EPA-rated solid-wood stoves. Another advantage is that a pellet stove requires far less active involvement to operate. Most models have a hopper to feed pellets into the fire and a thermostat to manage the heat output, so they can run on "automatic" if filled a couple of times a day. Fuel pellets are made of "recycled" wood (typically mill waste) or other plant material, and are relatively clean and convenient to handle when compared with solid wood.

Pellet stoves do require an electrical supply to function; this electric power is an added operating cost. This means pellet stoves are not a good

A glass front provides a cozy view of the fire with the efficiency of a modern wood stove.

backup heat source during an extended power outage. Some models have a battery backup, but the operating time is measured in hours rather than days.

Some "Renewable" Technologies Are Not So Renewable

There is a lot of greenwashing out there, but there are also some legitimate products that tend to be oversold. One example is ground-source or "geothermal" heat pumps (see pp. 125–126), often marketed as "renewable" technology. Although the heat it extracts from the ground is free, a GSHP still needs electricity to operate, and the net environmental and operating cost is similar to that of high-efficiency natural gas heating. Any high-efficiency heat pump (including the much less expensive, inverter-drive mini-split) is cheaper to run and produces fewer emissions than fuel oil, LP gas, or electric-resistance heat, but that does not make it renewable.

Another new technology, residential-scale "micro combined heat and power," or micro CHP, is easily confused with renewable energy. Whether it uses an engine-driven generator or a fuel-cell, a micro-CHP system is not renewable; it still runs on fossil fuel. A micro-CHP is essentially an expensive heating system that also generates electricity when it runs. Although more efficient at generating electricity than the grid, the electricity still isn't free, especially when you consider the high initial cost.

For a single-family home, I'd rather spend money on increased building efficiency, PV, a supplemental mini-split heat pump, or a solar pool heater. In most cases, you'll get more savings and environmental benefits for less investment than you would from a GSHP or micro-CHP system.

PRO TIP

In order to get the most efficiency and lowest emissions from any wood stove, it's best to burn small, hot fires rather than slow, smoldering fires.

RESOURCES

This section is intended to help you access additional information about energy-efficiency ideas, designs, and products. It is a representative sample rather than an exhaustive list of all possible resources within each category; a listing here should not be considered an endorsement of products or third-party content by either the author or The Taunton Press.

BOOKS

Brower, Michael, and Warren Leon. *The Consumer's Guide to Effective Environmental Choices: Practical Advice from the Union of Concerned Scientists.* Three Rivers Press, Random House, 1999.

Goldstein, David. *Invisible Energy: Strategies to Rescue the Economy and Save the Planet.* Bay Tree Publishing, 2010.

Harley, Bruce. *Cut Your Energy Bills Now.* The Taunton Press, 2008.

Krigger, John, and Chris Dorsi. *Residential Energy: Cost Savings and Comfort for Existing Buildings.* Prentice Hall, 2009.

Lane, Tom. *Solar Hot Water Systems: Lessons Learned 1977 to Today.* Energy Conservation Services, 2004.

Lstiburek, Joseph. *Builder Guides (several climate-specific versions); Water Management Guide, Ventilation Guide, and Insulation Guide.* www.buildingsciencepress.com or www.eeba.org/bookstore.

COMPARISON-SHOPPING INFORMATION FOR EFFICIENT APPLIANCES, ELECTRONICS, OR EQUIPMENT

Air Conditioning, Heating and Refrigeration Institute

www.ahridirectory.org
A searchable database of heating, air-conditioning, and water-heating equipment efficiency ratings

Consortium for Energy Efficiency

www.cee1.org
Lists very efficient appliances that generally exceed Energy Star specifications. Click under "RESIDENTIAL" for consumer electronics, home appliances, HVAC, and lighting

DUCT-SEALING

Aeroseal automated duct-sealing system

www.aeroseal.com
Licensed contractors in more than 30 states

DUCTLESS SPLIT HEAT PUMPS

Daikin® AC

www.daikinac.com

Fujitsu®

www.fujitsugeneral.com/products

Mitsubishi®

www.mitsubishicomfort.com

Sanyo®

www.us.sanyo.com/HVAC

ELECTRIC MONITORS

Kill A Watt, Kill A Watt EZ

www.p3international.com/products/

PowerCost Monitor

www.bluelineinnovations.com

The Energy Detective

www.theenergydetective.com

Watts Up? Energy Meters

www.wattsupmeters.com/secure/products.php?pn=0

ENERGY EFFICIENCY, GREEN BUILDING, DEEP RETROFIT, TRANSITION TO LOW-CARBON ECONOMY

Affordable Comfort

www.affordablecomfort.org
Nonprofit promoting home performance and efficiency

Alliance to Save Energy

www.livingefficiently.org

American Council for an Energy-Efficient Economy

www.aceee.org/consumer
General and comparison-shopping information

Architecture 2030
www.Architecture2030.org
Promoting building efficiency

Building Green and Environmental Building News
www.buildinggreen.com

Building Science Corporation
www.buildingscience.com
Offers high-quality building science and construction information

Department of Energy Office of Energy Efficiency and Renewable Energy
www.eere.energy.gov

Energy Star
www.energystar.gov
Links for products, home improvement, and new homes

Fine Homebuilding **Magazine**
www.finehomebuilding.com

Green Building Advisor
www.greenbuildingadvisor.com

Home Energy **Magazine**
www.homeenergy.org

Oklahoma State Energy Office
www.bestofbuildingscience.com/videos.html
Building science videos

ReGreen
www.regreenprogram.org
Guidelines and educational resources applicable to remodeling projects from the U.S. Green Building Council and the American Society of Interior Designers

Rocky Mountain Institute
www.rmi.org
Resource for technology, energy policy, and advocacy

The Thousand Home Challenge (project of Affordable Comfort)
www.thousandhomechallenge.com

www.350.org
Promoting solutions to climate change

Thriving on Low Carbon (Marc Rosenbaum)
blog.energysmiths.com

Transition Towns
www.transitionnetwork.org

U.S. Department of Energy
www.energysavers.gov/your_home
Home energy information

ENERGY SELF-ASSESSMENTS

My Energy
www.myenergy.com
Track your utility use over time

U.S. Department of Energy/ Lawrence Berkeley National Laboratory
www.hes.lbl.gov
Home energy saver

U.S. Environmental Protection Agency
www.energystar.gov
Click on "Assess Your Home" under "Home Improvement"

FIND CERTIFIED PROFESSIONALS

Air Conditioning Contractors of America
www.acca.org/consumer
HVAC membership organization

Building Performance Institute
www.bpi.org
Find certified building analysts and other home-performance professionals

North American Technician Excellence
www.hvacradvice.com
Third-party certification for HVAC contractors

Residential Energy Services Network
www.resnet.us
Find certified Home Energy Raters

GENERAL "GREEN LIVING" INFORMATION

Consumer Reports®
www.greenerchoices.org
Offers comparison-shopping information in some categories

Environmental Defense Fund
www.fightglobalwarming.com

Gwendolyn Bounds
www.pureshelter.com

National Geographic®
www.thegreenguide.com

Natural Resources Defense Council
www.nrdc.org/living

U.S. Green Building Council
www.greenhomeguide.org

GREEN/RENEWABLE POWER AND CARBON OFFSET INFORMATION

Clean Air–Cool Planet
www.cleanair-coolplanet.org

Green-e
www.green-e.org
Search for renewable energy and carbon offsets by state and type

HEAT PUMP WATER HEATERS

AirTap® system
www.airgenerate.com

Nyle Systems Geyser™
www.nyle.com/water-heating

HIGH-EFFICIENCY WATER HEATERS AND SOLAR WATER-HEATING TANKS

American Water Heaters
www.americanwaterheater.com

AO Smith® Corporation
www.aosmith.com

Bradford White® Corporation
www.bradfordwhite.com

Heat Transfer Products (HTP®)
www.htproducts.com
Boilers and water heaters

Marathon®
www.marathonheaters.com
Electric-resistance water heaters

Rheem
www.rheem.com

HOT-WATER DEMAND/ RECIRCULATION SYSTEMS

Advanced Conservation Technology
www.gothotwater.com
D'MAND hot-water pumping system
(also available through Taco®,
Uponar®, and Grundfos® distributers)

Laing Thermotech, Inc.
www.lainginc.com
Autocirc® timer system

HOUSEHOLD AIR-QUALITY AND HEALTHY REMODELING RESOURCES

Business Science Corporation
www.buildingscience.com
"Read This" booklets and "Everything
you need to know about mold"

Delta-FL
www.cosella-dorken.com
Warm & Dry Floor System for
basement and on-grade slabs

National Center for Healthy Housing
www.centerforhealthyhousing.org

U.S. Environmental Protection Agency
www.epa.gov/iaq
Links for asthma, mold, lead, radon,
and other categories

HVAC EQUIPMENT

Aquatherm®
www.firstco.com
Hydro-air handlers

Duro Dyne Corporation
www.durodyne.com
High-quality duct dampers, HVAC
supplies

Spacepak
www.spacepak.com
Compact high-velocity HVAC and
ductwork
See also "Ductless Split Heat Pumps"
on p. 224

INSULATION

Dow Thermax
www.building.dow.com/na/en/
products/insulation/index.htm
Rigid foam rated for exposed service

Cellulose Installation Manufacturers Association
www.cellulose.org/members_
producer.html
Manufacturer links can provide
contractor referrals

North American Insulation Manufacturers Association
www.naima.org

Spray Polyurethane Foam Alliance
www.sprayfoam.org

LIGHTING DESIGN RESOURCES

Integrated Building and Construction Solutions
www.ibacos.com/high-performance-
lighting-guide

Rensselaer Polytechnic Institute
www.lrc.rpi.edu/researchAreas/
residential.asp
Lighting Research Center

LOW-E STORM WINDOW MANUFACTURERS

Allied Window Inc.
www.alliedwindow.com

Cityproof®
www.cityproof.com

Harvey® Industries Inc.
www.harveybp.com

Innerglass® Window Systems
www.stormwindows.com

POOL PUMP SIZING INFORMATION

Department of Energy
www.eere.energy.gov/consumer/
your_home/water_heating/index.cfm/
mytopic=13290 U.S.

Discount Pool and Spa Supplies
www.discount-pool-supplies.com/
pump-sizing-guide.php
"Notes on Pool/Spa Sizing"

Pool Plaza
www.poolplaza.com/pool-pump-
sizing-2.shtml
"Pump Sizing"

SOLAR AND ALTERNATIVE ENERGY

Alternative Energy Store
www.altenergystore.com
Information and retail sales

American Wind Energy Association
www.awea.org

Find Solar
www.findsolar.com
Solar PV and hot-water-system
estimators and links to local installers

Florida Solar Energy Center
www.fsec.ucf.edu/en/consumer/
solar_hot_water/index.htm
Information on solar thermal collectors
and pool heaters

***Home Power* Magazine**
www.homepower.com
Information for grid-connected and
remote solar, wind, and micro-hydro
systems

National Renewable Energy Laboratory
www.nrel.gov/rredc/pvwatts
Solar electric calculator

Real Goods®
www.realgoods.com
Solar and alternative energy products

Solar Rating and Certification Corporation
www.solar-rating.org
Ratings of solar water heating and pool heating collectors and systems

SOLAR-CONTROL WINDOW FILMS

CPFilms Inc.®
www.cpfilms.com/windowfilms.html

3M
www.3m.com/windowfilm

TAX CREDITS AND OTHER INCENTIVES

Database of State Incentives for Renewables & Efficiency
www.dsireusa.org
A comprehensive directory of federal, state, and utility programs by state, including loans, tax incentives, grants, rebates, and technical services. Choose your state and select "See Homeowner Incentive Summaries Only."

The Tax Incentives Assistance Project on federal tax credits
www.energytaxincentives.org/consumers
Also check the websites of your state energy office and your local electric and gas utility companies.

VENTILATION EQUIPMENT

FanCycler®
www.fancycler.com
Information on residential ventilation using air handler and controls

Fantech ventilation fans and systems
www.residential.fantech.net

Tamarack Technologies
www.tamtech.com
Whole-house fans and ventilation equipment

Venmar® ventilation equipment and controls
www.venmar.ca/en/Home.aspx

WEATHERIZATION AND VENTILATION SUPPLIES

AM Conservation Group
www.amconservationgroup.com
Water-saving and weatherization supplies

Energy Federation Incorporated
www.efi.org/store
Efficient lighting, air- and duct-sealing, weatherization supplies, ventilation equipment, energy monitors, and controls

J&R Products
www.jrproductsinc.com
Insulation machines, accessories, sealants

Positive Energy Conservation Products
www.positive-energy.com
Lighting, ventilation, air-sealing

Resource Conservation Technology
www.conservationtechnology.com
Efficient building supplies

Shelter Companies
www.sheltersupply.com
Efficient building supplies and ventilation equipment

WEATHERIZATION ASSISTANCE: FEDERAL, STATE, AND UTILITY ASSISTANCE FOR INCOME-QUALIFIED CONSUMERS

National Energy Assistance Referral service
www.liheap.ncat.org/referral.htm
866-674-6327

U.S. Department of Energy
www.eere.energy.gov/wip/project_map
Directory of weatherization agencies

WINDOW RESTORATION/ EFFICIENCY UPGRADE SYSTEM

Bi-Glass System
www.bi-glass.com

CONTRIBUTORS

Additional thanks for valuable assistance:

For written resources and inspiration, Michael Brower, John Krigger, Warren Leon, and Alex Wilson.

For giving generously of your time to help create images for this book, Rich Baldassini and Sergio Gonzales at IMC Heating and Cooling; James Clinton, Alan Connolly, Dino Cunningham, Johnny Lamarre, Ian Nadeau, Joe Sheridan, and Ray Williams at Energy Guard; Bryce Clark, Todd Dustin, Jim Godin, Joe Ricard, and Shawn Tibbetts at Quality Insulation; Jonathan Goncalvez, Paul Goncalvez, Bill Joyal, and JoBo Santos at Royal Thermal View; and Steve Bonfiglioli.

For photography, Randy O'Rourke, Art Evans, Kevin Kennefick, Sheri Riddell, and John Curtis.

For images and equipment, Betsy Petit, Joe Lstiburek, and Ken Neuhauser at Building Science Corporation; Lori Nelson at Columbia Paint and Coatings; Peter Baddeley at Convair; Gerald Best at Davis Energy Group; Larry Carlson at DEC Thermastor; Bruce Spallone at Duro Dyne; Edith Buffalohead at ECR; Andrew M. Shapiro at Energy Balance, Inc.; Gary Nelson and Frank Spevak at the Energy Conservatory; John O'Connell, Joel Orlando, Mike Pierce, and Gary Church-Smith at Energy Federation; Neil Moyer at the Florida Solar Energy Center; Bill Kennedy and Tom St. Louis at GFX; Josh Hobbs at Josh Hobbs Solar Screen Services; Patrick Hearne and Steve Cocca at Knauf Insulation; Mark Weissflog and Kevin Soucy at KW Management; John Livermore at Livermore Energy Associates; Ellie Doherty at Lutron; Larry Acker at Metlund; Jim Fitzgerald at MNCEE; Kate Brinks at Nest; David Pill at Pill-Maharam Architects; Ted Doyle at Space Pak; Mary Luisi and Linda Elmer at Switch Lighting; David Lapollo at Tamarack Technologies; and Kevin Zarzecki at Triad Marketing Group.

And thanks to Stephanie Tanner at EPA.

PHOTOS

All photos by John Curtis, except as noted below.

Introduction
p. 3: Andrew Wormer, courtesy *Fine Homebuilding* magazine, ©The Taunton Press

Energy Basics
p. 4: Randy O'Rourke
p. 6: (top) Bruce Harley ©Conservation Services Group; (bottom) Andrew Wormer, courtesy *Fine Homebuilding* magazine, ©The Taunton Press.
p. 7: ©John Livermore, Livermore Energy Associates
p. 8: (top) David Keefe ©Vermont Energy Investment Corp
p. 14: courtesy Joe Lstiburek, Building Science Corp.
p. 16: (top) Steve Culpepper, courtesy *Fine Homebuilding* magazine, ©The Taunton Press; (bottom photos) Bruce Harley ©Conservation Services Group
p. 17: (right) ©Kevin Kennefick; (left) courtesy Stephen Smulski, Wood Science Specialists, Inc.
p. 18: Steve Culpepper, courtesy *Fine Homebuilding* magazine, ©The Taunton Press
p. 19: ©Kevin Kennefick
p. 25: ©Kevin Kennefick
p. 26: ©Kevin Kennefick

Sealing Air Leaks
p. 33: ©Kevin Kennefick
p. 36: (B) ©Kevin Kennefick; (C) Dan Berube ©Conservation Services Group; (bottom) ©Kevin Kennefick
p. 37: (right) Randy O'Rourke
p. 38: Randy O'Rourke
p. 39: (right) Bruce Harley
p. 40: Bruce Harley
p. 42: (top left) ©Kevin Kennefick
p. 44: (top left) Randy O'Rourke; (top right) ©Kevin Kennefick
p. 45: (top right) ©Kevin Kennefick; (bottom) Bruce Harley ©Conservation Services Group
p. 46: Harold Shapiro
p. 48: (top right) ©Kevin Kennefick; (bottom right) Randy O'Rourke

Ventilation Systems
p. 52: (top) Susan Kahn; (bottom right) Marc Rosenbaum
p. 53: (left) courtesy Panasonic; (right) courtesy Viking
p. 54: (top right) Scott Phillips, courtesy *Fine Homebuilding* magazine, ©The Taunton Press
p. 56: (left) ©Kevin Kennefick; (right) Art Evans
p. 57: (right) ©Kevin Kennefick
p. 58: ©Kevin Kennefick
p. 60: courtesy Venmar Ventilation, Inc.

Insulating a House

p. 67: (bottom left) ©Kevin Kennefick
p. 68: (right) Tom O'Brien, courtesy *Fine Homebuilding* magazine, ©The Taunton Press
p. 69: Randy O'Rourke
p. 70: (bottom left) ©Kevin Kennefick
p. 71: (bottom right) Andy Engel, courtesy *Fine Homebuilding* magazine, ©The Taunton Press
p. 72: ©Kevin Kennefick
p. 73: Andrew Wormer, courtesy *Fine Homebuilding* magazine, ©The Taunton Press
p. 74: Justin Fink, courtesy *Fine Homebuilding* magazine, ©The Taunton Press
p. 77: (top) Bruce Harley; (bottom) Andy Engel, courtesy *Fine Homebuilding* magazine, ©The Taunton Press
p. 78: Steve Culpepper, courtesy *Fine Homebuilding* magazine, ©The Taunton Press
p. 83: (bottom left) Bruce Harley
p. 85: (right) ©Kevin Kennefick
p. 87: Bruce Harley
p. 88: Ken Neuhauser
p. 89: (left) Terry Brennan, Camroden Associates; (center top and bottom) Ken Neuhauser; (right) Bruce Harley

Windows

p. 92: Steve Culpepper, courtesy *Fine Homebuilding* magazine, ©The Taunton Press
p. 96: (bottom center) Jefferson Kolle, courtesy *Fine Homebuilding* magazine, ©The Taunton Press
p. 97: ©Kevin Kennefick
p. 99: (top left) ©Kevin Kennefick; (bottom right) ©Conservation Services Group
p. 103: (top left) ©Kevin Kennefick
p. 104: (bottom) courtesy Jim Conacher, Bi-Glass
p. 105: (top left) Steve Culpepper, courtesy *Fine Homebuilding* magazine, ©The Taunton Press; (bottom right) Bruce Harley

Heating Systems

p. 110: (left) ©Kevin Kennefick; (right) courtesy Nest Learning Thermostat
p. 112: (top) ©Bruce Harley ©Conservation Services Group; (bottom right) Randy O'Rourke
p. 114: (top left, top right, bottom left) Randy O'Rourke; (bottom right) Terry Brennan, Camroden Associates
p. 115: (top left) Neil Moyer, Florida Solar Energy Center; (top center) ©The Energy Conservatory
p. 116: courtesy Kidde
p. 122: (left) ©Kevin Kennefick; (right) ©Lin Wagner
p. 124: (top left, top right) Bruce Harley

p. 126: (top) Scott Gibson, courtesy *Fine Homebuilding* magazine, ©The Taunton Press; (bottom) Bruce Harley ©Conservation Services Group
p. 127: (top right) courtesy Buck Taylor, Connecticut Light and Power
p. 129: (bottom left) Bruce Harley; (top right) ©Lin Wagner
p. 135: ©Lin Wagner

Air-Conditioning

p. 138: ©Kevin Kennefick
p. 140: (top right) ©Steven C. Spencer; (bottom right) courtesy Tamarack Technologies.
p. 141: (left) ©Kevin Kennefick; (right) courtesy Josh Hobbs.com, Solar Screen Services
p. 143: Roe A. Osborn, courtesy *Fine Homebuilding* magazine, ©The Taunton Press
p. 144: courtesy All Weather Surfaces Hawaii, Inc.
p. 145: (top left) Bruce Harley ©Conservation Services Group
p. 146: (bottom right) courtesy Therma-Star Products
p. 148: (bottom left) courtesy Convair Cooler, Inc.
p. 150: courtesy Spacepak, a MESTEK company

Hot Water

p. 155: (bottom) Randy O'Rourke
p. 162: ©Kevin Kennefick
p. 163: (top center) Randy O'Rourke; (bottom left) ©Rex Cauldwell; (bottom right) Charles Miller, courtesy *Fine Homebuilding* magazine, ©The Taunton Press
p. 164: (top) courtesy ACT-Inc. Metlund Systems; (bottom) Charles Miller, courtesy *Fine Homebuilding* magazine, ©The Taunton Press
p. 166: (left): T. R. Strong Building Systems; (right) courtesy Rheem
p. 168: (right) Jim Kremer

Renovations

p. 172: Dan Cote, courtesy GreenBuildingAdvisor.com
p. 174: Randy O'Rourke
p. 177: Nat Rea, courtesy *Fine Homebuilding* magazine, ©The Taunton Press
p. 179: (left) Charles Bickford, courtesy *Fine Homebuilding* magazine, ©The Taunton Press; (right) ©Kevin Kennefick
p. 180: courtesy GreenBuildingAdvisor.com
p. 181: (right) ©Kevin Kennefick
p. 182: (bottom left) Bruce Harley ©Conservation Services Group; (top left) ©Kevin Kennefick; (top right) Steve Culpepper, courtesy *Fine Homebuilding* magazine, ©The Taunton Press

p. 183: (top) courtesy Knauf Insulation; (bottom left) Chris Ermides, courtesy *Fine Homebuilding* magazine, ©The Taunton Press; (bottom right) Randy O'Rourke
p. 184: ©Kevin Kennefick
p. 185: (top) John Livermore, Livermore Energy Associates; (bottom left, bottom right) Steve Baczek, courtesy GreenBuildingAdvisor.com
p. 186: (bottom right) ©Kevin Kennefick
p. 187: (top) Joe Lstiburek, Building Science Corp.; (bottom) Roe A. Osborn, courtesy *Fine Homebuilding* magazine, ©The Taunton Press
p. 189: Roe A. Osborn, courtesy *Fine Homebuilding* magazine, ©The Taunton Press
p. 191: (top) Zachary Gaulkin, courtesy *Fine Homebuilding* magazine, ©The Taunton Press; (bottom) ©Mike Guertin and Rick Arnold
p. 193: Building Science Corp.

Electronics, Appliances, and Lighting

p. 194: Chelsea Sears, courtesy *Fine Homebuilding* magazine, ©The Taunton Press
p. 198: Art Evans
p. 199: Randy O'Rourke
p. 200: Art Evans
p. 201: Art Evans
p. 202: (left) courtesy Maytag
p. 204: (left) Art Evans; (right) ©Kevin Kennefick
p. 205: (left) ©Kevin Kennefick; (right) Scott Phillips, courtesy *Fine Homebuilding* magazine, ©The Taunton Press
p. 206: (top left, top right, bottom left) Art Evans; (bottom right) courtesy Switch Lighting Company
p. 207: ©Kevin Kennefick
p. 208: Art Evans
p. 209: ©Kevin Kennefick

Renewable and Alternative Energy

p. 210: Amy Glickson--Pixl Studio, courtesy DOE/NREL
p. 212: Warren Gretz, courtesy DOE/NREL
p. 213: RB Croteau
p. 215: (top) Solar Works, courtesy DOE/NREL; (bottom) Chris Derby-Kilfoyle
p. 217: Rob Wotzak, courtesy *Fine Homebuilding* magazine, ©The Taunton Press
p. 218: Robb Aldrich, Steven Winter Associates, Inc.
p. 221: courtesy David Pill, Pill-Maharam Architects
p. 223: Charles Bickford, courtesy *Fine Homebuilding* magazine, ©The Taunton Press

INDEX